AF651856

Perspectives in Human Geography

About the Authors

Punyatoya Patra is Associate Professor in the Department of Geography, Aditi Mahavidyalaya, University of Delhi. Her research interests include Human Geography, Natural Resource Management, Remote Sensing and GIS. She is the recipient of Best Lecturer Award from Government of Delhi (2011).

Rajesh Kumar Abhay is Assistant Professor in the Department of Geography, Dyal Singh College, University of Delhi. His research interests include Resource Management, Regional Planning and Sustainability Studies. He is the recipient of Young Geographer Award of the National Association of Geographers, India (2014).

Roshani Devi is Assistant Professor in the Department of Geography, Aditi Mahavidyalaya, University of Delhi. Her research interests include Resource Management and Environmental Disasters.

Gaurav Sikka is Assistant Professor in University Department of Geography, L.N. Mithila University, Darbhanga. He holds position of Secretary and Treasurer, International Geographical Union (IGU) Task Force for Young and Early Career Geographers. His research interests include Social Geography and Gender Studies.

Sneh Gangwar is Assistant Professor in Geography at Aditi Mahavidyalaya, University of Delhi. Her research interests include Human Geography, Disaster Studies, Remote Sensing and GIS.

PERSPECTIVES IN HUMAN GEOGRAPHY

Punyatoya Patra
Rajesh Kumar Abhay
Roshani Devi
Gaurav Sikka
Sneh Gangwar

CONCEPT PUBLISHING COMPANY PVT. LTD.
NEW DELHI-110059

© Authors

All rights reserved. No part of this work may be reproduced, stored, adapted, or transmitted in any form or by any means, electronic, mechanical, photocopying, micro-filming recording or otherwise, or translated in any language, without the prior written permission of the copyright owner and the publisher. The book is sold subject to the condition that it shall not, by way of trade or otherwise, be lent, resold, hired out, or otherwise circulated without the prior publisher's written consent in any form of binding or cover other than that in which it is published.

The views and opinions expressed in this book are authors own and the facts reported by them have been verified to the extent possible, and the publishers are not in anyway liable for the same.

ISBN - 978-93-88937-82-5 (H.B.)

First Published 2021

Published and Printed by

Concept
Since 1974

Concept Publishing Company Pvt. Ltd.
A/15-16, Commercial Block, Mohan Garden,
New Delhi-110059 (India)
T: 91 11 25351460, 91 11 25351794
E : publishing@conceptpub.com, *W*: www.conceptpub.com

Cataloging in Publication Data--Courtesy: D.K. Agencies (P) Ltd. <docinfo@dkagencies.com>

Patra, Punyatoya, author.
Perspectives in human geography / Punyatoya Patra, Rajesh Kumar Abhay, Roshani Devi, Gaurav Sikka, Sneh Gangwar.
pages cm
Includes bibliographical references and index.
ISBN 9789388937825 (HB)

1. Human geography. I. Abhay, Rajesh Kumar, author. II. Roshani Devi, author. III. Sikka, Gaurav, author. IV. Gangwar, Sneh, author. V. Title.

LCC GF41.P38 2021 | DDC 304.2 23

Preface

Human Geography is one of the two major branches of Geography which deals with the nature and distribution of human activities on the earth surface. The importance of Geography in general and Human Geography in particular is becoming more widely recognized. Recently, i.e. since the beginning of this Century, many universities introduced Human Geography to its Advanced Placement Cell. The importance of Human Geographer is increasing day by day in the job market of contemporary world characterized by rapidly changing man-environment relationship, large-scale movement of people and goods, fast communication mechanism etc. Besides, use of Remote Sensing, Geographical Information System, Geographical Positioning System in all aspects of life (starting from daily life of an individual person to national and international level planning and management) have increased the demand of the Subject.

This book on Perspectives in Human Geography deals with the basic concepts of major human phenomena such as society, culture, population, settlement etc. and their spatial distribution. The book covers the curriculum of major universities of India in general and recent CBCS (Choice Based Credit System) syllabus of Delhi University in particular. The volume deals with the main topics of Human Geography that are prescribed in the syllabus of undergraduate Geography courses. It comprises five parts which include 19 chapters.

The first part introduces Human Geography as a discipline and it is divided into 3 chapters. Chapter 1 deals with concepts of Human Geography and covers meaning, definition, subject matter and themes of Human Geography. The second chapter deals with the contemporary Human Geography and covers the contemporary approaches to study Human Geography, the place of human geographer in contemporary job market and the changing nature of the subject in globalizing world which poses many questions regarding future of Human Geography. The third chapter deals with man and environment relationship around which Human Geography revolves around. The approaches to study man and environment relationship are the main focus of this chapter. The historical perspective of man and environment relationship along with environmental crisis and environmental conflicts are also discussed in this chapter.

'Space and Society' is discussed in the second part which comprises 4 chapters, i.e. chapter 4, chapter 5, chapter 6 and chapter 7. Chapter 4 deals with cultural realm and covers cultural components and world distribution of major cultural realms along with their characteristics. Chapter 5 deals with Race and covers its concept, classification and distribution. Chapter 6 deals with Religion and Tribes and covers their origin, development and distribution. Chapter 7 deals with Language and discusses major languages and different linguistic families with their distribution.

The topic of the third part is 'Population and Migration' which encompasses 5 chapters, from chapter 8 to chapter 12. Chapter 8 deals with population distribution, chapter 9 with population growth, chapter 10 with population composition, chapter 11 with migration and chapter 12 with population theories. World population distribution is discussed in regional level and in continent level along with world population density. The factors affecting population growth and world population growth since ancient time are the main focus on population growth. Discussion of population composition includes methods of its analysis, determinants and types. Determinants of migration and trends of migration from one part of the world to another part are discussed. Lastly, two population theories, Malthus theory and Demographic Transition theory are analysed.

'Settlement and Urbanisation' is discussed in fourth part which includes 4 chapters, chapter 13 to chapter 16. Chapter 13 deals with origin and development of human settlement and the difference between rural and urban settlement. Types and determinants of rural settlement along with examples are discussed in chapter 14. Classification of urban settlement on the basis of size and function is the focal theme of Chapter 15. Chapter 16 deals with trends and pattern of urbanization in developing and developed countries, since post-industrial period to contemporary period.

The relationship between population and resources is examined in part 5. It includes 3 chapters. Chapter 17 deals with concepts of population and resource relationship in terms of carrying capacity, under population, over population and optimum population. It is followed by the discussion of population-resource regions given by Ackerman in Chapter 18. The last chapter of the book deals with ecological footprint and resource curse. It is expected that the book will serve as a useful textbook for the students trying to understand the human perspectives in geographical studies.

Authors

Contents

PART 4

Settlements and Urbanization

PART 5

Population and Resources

PART 1

Perspectives in Human Geography

Chapter 1
Human Geography

1.1 Introduction: Meaning and Definition

Human Geography is one of the two main branches of Geography which studies spatial pattern of human phenomena such as population, language, religion, settlement etc. The other branch, i.e. Physical Geography studies spatial pattern of physical/natural phenomena such as landform, soil, vegetation, climate etc. Human Geography encompasses all fields of Geography that are not directly concerned with Physical environment and fields which are technical in orientation like Cartography, Remote Sensing, Geographical Information System (GIS) etc. With further explanation, Human Geography is the study of the interrelationships between man and environment, and their spatial and temporal variations within, across and between locations. On the other hand, Physical Geography is the study of environmental processes that shape the natural world and relies on the natural and physical sciences for its approaches and methods of investigation. Human Geography concentrates on the spatial pattern of processes shaping the lives and activities of people, and their interactions with places and nature. It encompasses demographic, political, cultural, social and economic aspects of the man. Though, there are distinct differences between Physical and Human Geography; it is hardly possible to discuss Human Geography without referring physical landscape on which human activities take place. Besides, Human Geography is more allied with the social sciences and humanities, such as Economics, Political Science, Sociology, Psychology etc. for it gives to those sciences the necessary spatial and system viewpoint. So, Human Geography admirably serves the objectives of a liberal education.

The study of Human Geography which revolves round people and places originated from its mother discipline—'Geography', long back. However, it becomes popular in 19th Century after the publication of Darwin's '*Origin of Species*'. Darwin's notion regarding evolution was taken up by the German and American Geographers to explain the man and environment relationship. Before that the discipline—Geography was more physical than human. Friedrich Ratzel, a strong follower of Darwin, became the founder of Human Geography. He believes Human Geography as the systematic study of relationship between human societies and earth's surface. His disciple Ellen Churchill Semple defined Human Geography as the study of changing relationship between the unresting Man and unstable Earth.

Subsequently Human Geography attained great popularity in France by the French Geographers, like Albert Demangion, Max Sorre and Vidal de la Blache. According to Demangion (1933), Human Geography is the study of human groups and societies in relationship to their physical environment. Sorre (1952) expressed his view on Human Geography in the following manner: "Human Geography is the study of man as a living organism subject to determinate conditions of existence and reacting to stimuli received from natural environment." Vidal de la Blache wrote a classic book on Principles of Human Geography in French language in the year 1922. According to him "Human Geography offers a new conception of the interrelationship between Earth and Man ..... a more synthetic knowledge of the physical laws governing our earth and the relations between the living beings which inhabit it" (Blache, 1965).

Almost during same period, Human geography became popular in America and Canada. White and Renner (1948) defined Human Geography as Human Ecology which studies human societies in the background of earth ecosystem. According to Cox (1972), "Human geography is concerned with the description and analysis of locational pattern of static and moving phenomena of human origin on the surface of the earth." Carter (1974) views Human Geography as a discipline primarily concerned with the relations between man and ways of life and places in which they live.

1.2 Subject Matter of Human Geography and Its Disciplinary Interdependence

Human Geography helps us to understand the world human beings occupy, the environment affecting human beings and affected by human beings. The spatial arrangement of a particular human phenomenon shown on map clarifies the contrast and similarities in the different parts of the earth. The study of different human phenomena explains how things are interrelated on the earth surface and gives the clear understanding of the economic, social and political systems within which we live and operate. It provides us with the broad knowledge of wider world as well as in depth study in a specific area of interest. Study of Human Geography, therefore, can help us in thinking globally and acting locally. Human Geography encompasses a vast field of study of human beings covering social, political, economic, demographic, and cultural and many developmental aspects. Accordingly, the main subfields of Human Geography are Social Geography, Population Geography, Economic Geography, Political Geography, Cultural Geography, Settlement Geography, Behavioural Geography etc.

Social Geography is one of the subfields of Human Geography, studies spatial pattern of society and its structure characterized by ethnicity, caste, language, religion etc. (Ch. 3 to Ch. 6). It also studies the origin, development, movement of different social groups and the reasons behind them. Sociology is the scientific study of society characterized by family and different types of groups/associations/institutions. It usually concerns with social rules, social changes, social behaviours and social problems. So, Social Geography overlaps Sociology.

Population Geography is also one of the subfields of Human Geography. It examines spatial distribution of population density, population growth, sex ratio, migration pattern etc. and how the physical/environmental factors affect these spatial distribution/patterns (Ch. 7 to Ch. 10). On the other hand, the discipline—'Demography' examines the study of population size, structure, distribution based on births, deaths, migration, ageing.

Demographic analysis of a society or group is carried on by criteria such as education, nationality, religion, ethnicity etc. So Population Geography overlaps Demography in many aspects.

Economic Geography, the subfield of Human Geography studies location, organization and spatial distribution of economic activities. There are many sub-branches of Economic Geography, such as Agricultural Geography, Resource Geography, Industrial Geography, and Geography of Transportation. The distribution of many economic activities are influenced by geographical conditions, viz. geology affects resource availability and resource affects industrial location; geomorphology and soil affect agricultural activities, transportation network; climate affects agricultural activities. On the other hand, the discipline 'Economics' studies production, consumption, exchange of goods and services starting from micro to macro level and theories behind them. So, there is overlapping of many aspects between 'Economics' and 'Economic Geography'.

Political Geography is a subfield of Human Geography that deals with space from the angle of political events. Study of international boundaries, space relation between countries, delimitation of political constituencies, and political behaviour of population are covered under Political Geography. Political Science, on the other hand, deals with theory and practice of politics, description and analysis of political system, public administration etc.

Cultural Geography encompasses the study and spatial attributes of various cultural elements, such as customs, food, clothing, architecture, religion, language etc. Many of these aspects are also covered by Anthropology, Archaeology and Sociology.

Settlement Geography deals with spatial variation of human habitation and their causes and effects. The human habitation includes both rural and urban settlement (Ch. 11 to Ch. 14). Town/Country Planners also study characteristics of rural and urban settlement in different socio-economic environment.

Behavioural Geography focuses on role of cognitive processes underlying human/ cultural world around us. Psychology is an academic and applied discipline which involves the study of human mind and behaviour.

From above discussion, it is clear that the subfields of Human Geography overlap many social sciences like Sociology, Psychology, Economics, Political Science etc. (Fig. 1.1). All these sciences not only focus on particular phenomena (like Sociology on Society, Political Science on Politics and Economics on Economy), but also focus on these phenomena on the perspective of time (History) and space (Geography). So, both the disciplines—History and Geography have intellectual cores defined by these perspectives along with being confined to a subject matter. Geographers also study temporal changes of space, i.e. time perspective of space. Likewise, Historians study spatial difference in different periods of time. So, not a single discipline is intra. All disciplines are interrelated.

1.3 Themes of Human Geography

Human Geography provides a spatial perspective of various human phenomena, ranging from political elections, economic activities, and social structure to folk music, birth rate, architectural style. To bring together various subfields of Human Geography and differentiate Human Geography from other allied disciplines, five themes of Geography were introduced by National Geographic Society in 1996. They are Location, Place, Region, Human-Environment Relationship and Movement.

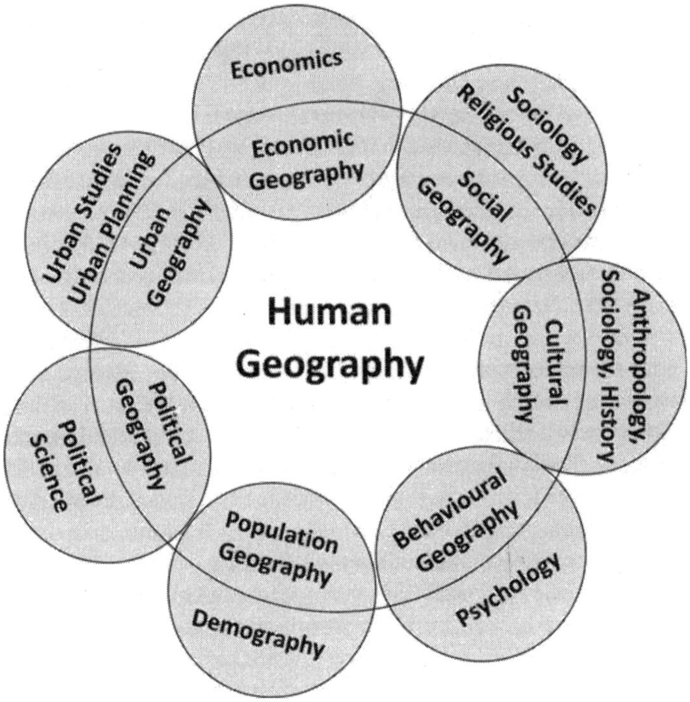

Fig. 1.1: Subfields of Human Geography

1.3.1 Location

The study of Human Geography begins with the knowledge of—"Where the objects are located or the incidents are occurred on the surface of the earth. Location can be defined as position on earth's surface. Location can be expressed in two ways—Absolute and Relative.

Absolute location refers to the identification of place by its absolute or precise location. Absolute location is unique to a particular place and is independent of any other characteristics or observation about that place. The absolute location is expressed by the co-ordinate system of earth, i.e. latitudes and longitudes. As for example, the absolute location of Chennai is 13° 5′ North latitude and 80°16′ East longitude. The absolute location can be expressed by street address. When we say the address of Art Heritage Gallery is 205, Tansen Marg, Triveni Kala Sangam, New Delhi-110001, we also refer absolute location. The individual landed property is also expressed by absolute location, e.g. in rural areas in India, it is expressed by *khasra* number in *patwari* record. It has obvious value in the legal description of places.

Relative location refers to the location of a place in relation to other place. It is very important to express relative location for two reasons—(a) to find an unfamiliar place, by comparing its location with a familiar place, e.g. Gurugram is located 28 km. south from New Delhi; (b) to understand its importance, e.g. Mumbai is the hub of sea and air transportation in India. Absolute location does not change, but relative location changes. As for example, New Mumbai was located on outskirt of Mumbai in 1990s. Now it is part of Mumbai.

The various ways to express relative location is through distance and direction. Distance refers to spatial separation between two locations. The location of a place can expressed through distance from another place, e.g. Meerut is 90 km away from Delhi. Sometimes, we express distance through time, i.e. Meerut is 3 hours away from Delhi. Though two shopping Malls are equal distance from our home, we prefer to go to the Shopping Mall where we reach early due to less traffic. Here comes the importance of expression of distance through time. Most people in fact use time distance instead of linear distance in daily life, viz. Coffee House is a 5-minute walk, and Airport is 20 minutes by bus. In some cases, money rather than time is used to express distance. The college is Rs. 100 cab ride away. This information affects the decision taking travel mode. Besides distance, we express the relative location of a place to another place through direction, e.g. Meerut is 90 km Northeast of Delhi or Palwal is 85 km south of Delhi.

Besides, absolute and relative location, we also use site and situation to describe location. Site refers to the physical characteristics or attribute of the area. It tells us about the location of the place in different ways, e.g. hill top location or sea side location. The expansion of many cities depends upon their site. Mumbai City could not expand westward due to its location towards western coast of India. Likewise, Delhi could not expand eastward as fast as compared to its expansion towards north, south and east due to the location of Yamuna River towards its east. Historically, site factor led to the development of major cities. Mumbai developed as a city as the European explorers entered into India through west coast and developed trade there due to its coastal location with natural harbour.

Situation refers to the external relations of a locale. It is an expression of relative location with particular reference to the objects or items of significance to the place in question. Situation of a place includes the accessibility, the extent of place's connections with another and how close the area is to the new materials if they are not located specifically on the site. The growth of a city depends on its situation. Mumbai has been developed as the textile city due to its situation, i.e. it is surrounded by the cotton producing areas. The Real Estate Agents many times remark "location matters"—They refer site and situation of the concerned property. When they talk about the house is sun-facing, well-ventilated and located on a higher place so that flood water cannot enter into, then they refer to the site of the house. When they talk about the housing society is well-connected with the airport, hospitals and shopping centres, then they refer to the situation.

1.3.2 Place

For a common man, place is the synonym to location. In Human Geography, place refers to the attributes and values associated with location. Every place has characteristics which give that place unique identification and also distinguish them from other places. Every place has a name which is unique. However, we come across the identical names for two places, which is very rare. Besides unique name, every place has unique physical and human characteristics. Physical characteristics include the description of landforms, climate, vegetation, soil, animals and plant life of a place. The human characteristics include the man made features of a place, such as land use, forms of livelihood, religious practices, political system, foods, architectural style, transportation etc. So places can be described with its name, physical and cultural characteristics. As for example, Kolkata is very hot and humid with flat topography, very fertile soil and tropical vegetation types. The people of Kolkata belong to Mongo-Dravidian racial family and speak Bengali language. The concept of place aid geographers to compare and contrast two places on earth.

Besides these physical and cultural characteristics, people develop behavioural characteristics of places. This behavioural characteristic is very unique to every individual. People develop a **sense of place** which is attached to their emotion. Some people feel home at certain place and some do not. In this case place refers to the attributes and values we individual associate with a location like our home town, the cities we live in different time period of our life, the schools/universities we attended, our favourite shopping places are the examples which are unique to each of us. People also develop **perception of place** where they have never been but have knowledge through books, movies, stories, pictures etc. By reading the popular book "*The Arabian Nights*", the people all over the world have different perception about Arab. The movie "Love in Paris" directed by Anne Goursaud, developed different perception among Americans about the culture of France during 1990s. Sometimes, these types of perceptions are far from reality. The sense of place and perception of place is diminished or lost or replaced by a feeling of **placelessness**. Uniformity of brand names, fast food outlets, national/international retail store chains, uniform shopping malls, metropolitan culture reduce or eliminate the uniqueness of places.

The terms 'Sense of Place', 'Perception of Place' and 'Placelessness' can be understood from the following examples. Raghav has come all the way from Tamil Nadu to study in Delhi University. He developed friendship with Rajiv in Delhi whom he tells about his life and culture in Tamil Nadu. When their Professor teaches the topic 'Geography of Tamil Nadu', Raghav develops a 'sense of place' for Tamil Nadu; Rajeev develops 'perception of place' for Tamil Nadu. When Rajiv goes Tamil Nadu and visits Patanjali stores/Nike Shoes outlets/McDonald restaurant there, he develops a feeling of 'placelessness'. There is no difference in these stores whether they are in Delhi or in Tamil Nadu or in any other places.

1.3.3 Region

Every individual on the earth surface is unique but there are some similarities in feature among a group of individuals so that we can differentiate Indians from Chinese. Likewise every place on earth surface is unique; many places have similarities in many aspects. The places having similar characteristics form a Region. In other words, a region has some sort of characteristics that unifies the areas. The concept of region is applied to bring order to immense diversities of the earth's surface. Regions are not given, they are devised. Different types of regions are devised according to the aims and objectives of the study. Regions divide the World into manageable units of Geographical studies. Regions can be formal, functional and perceptual.

A region whose boundary is formally defined is called as formal region. Within a Formal region, at least one physical/cultural characteristic is common or uniform to some degree which differentiates the region from other surrounding regions. Formal Regions can be broadly divided into Political regions, Physical regions and Cultural Regions. A Political or administrative region is unified by common political/administrative entity. Political Regions are designated by official boundaries, e.g. tehsils, districts, states, countries, continents etc. The regions distinguished by physical characteristics are called physical regions. Physical characteristics include landforms, climate, soil, vegetation etc. The Indo-Gangetic Plain of India is distinguished from Northern Mountains and Southern Plateau by its flat landform characteristics with very gentle unnoticeable slope. The Black Cotton Soil Region which is found towards western part of India is distinguished from Red Soil and Alluvial Soil Regions by its distinguished soil characteristics, such as black colour and clayey structure. Likewise Monsoon Climatic Region can be distinguished from Steppe Region, Polar Climatic Region by its distinguished climatic characteristics, such as wet summer and dry winter. These Physical regions are designated by formal boundaries, but not by official boundaries like Political Regions. The regions distinguished by cultural characteristics are called Cultural Regions. Cultural Characteristics include language, religion, ethnicity, economic activities etc.

A functional region is defined by an area in which particular set of activities or interactions occur. The functional region has shared political, social or economic purpose. This type of regions is centred on a focal point that connects other areas by various systems, such as transportation, communication, or economic activities. Cities can be considered functional regions because road ways, rail ways, subways connect the suburbs to the central areas of the city. Other examples of functional regions are television signal areas, Wi-Fi hotspots, or pizza delivery areas. Figure 1.2 shows a functional region, where major road functions with the main purpose of moving people between Bangalore (now Bangaluru) city and the outlying city region. It also functions as a method of moving people within the city.

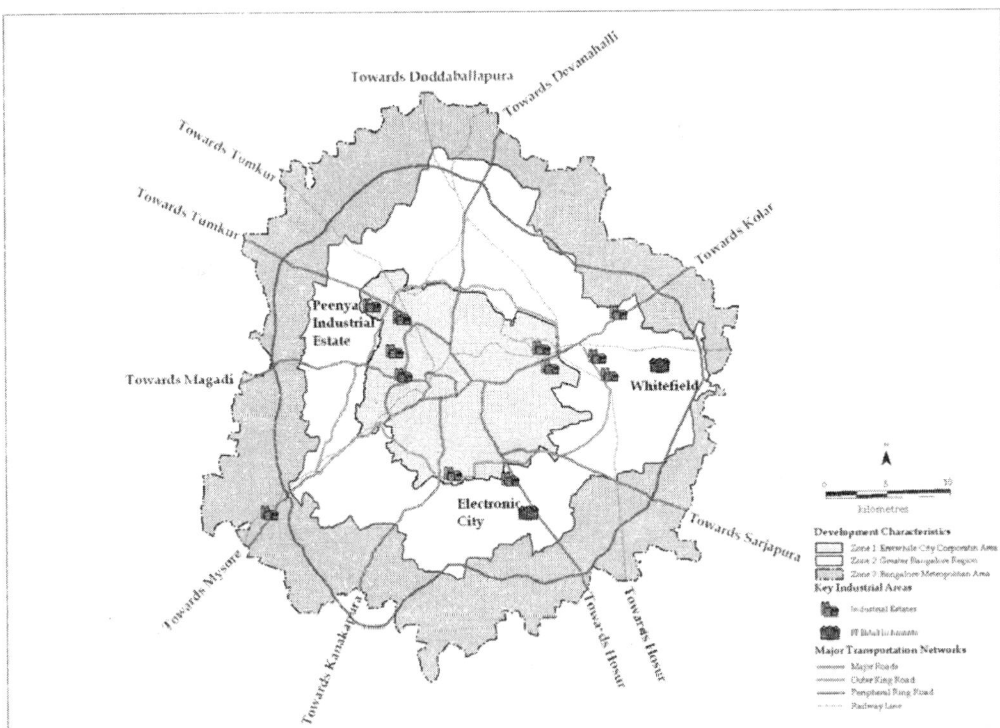

Fig. 1.2: Functional Region of Bengaluru City

Source: Sudhira *et al.* (2007).

A perceptual region is based on the shared feelings and attitudes of the people who live in the area. Perceptual regions reflect the cultural identity of the people in the region. The boundaries of perceptual regions are not always distinct, as they may be perceived differently from person to person. Perceptual regions are also called vernacular regions. The Middle-East, the Far-East are the example of the Vernacular Region.

1.3.4 Human Environment Relationship

Human Environment Relationship is the one of the main theme of Human Geography as it shapes the landscape. No landscape on the earth is purely physical in characteristics. The interrelationship between people and their environment in any place depends upon the physical and human characteristics of that place. There are three key aspects of Human Environment Relationship—dependency, adaptation and modification. For his basic needs such as food, shelter and clothing, human being depends on nature. Human beings adapt to the environment and successfully settled every corner of the world, even harsh climatic condition. For example, people who live in the extreme northern Canada, use heating units to keep their homes warm in winter. People live in the equatorial countries such as Ecuador, Congo and Indonesia use air conditioning much of the year to stay cool in the heat. People choose to adapt to their natural environment according to their economic and political conditions and their technological abilities. Human also modify his environment to fulfil his wants. He builds multi-purpose dams to irrigate in dry season; he digs deep mines to extract minerals; he constructs high rise industrial/urban complexes, multi-storied roads to maintain high standard of living.

Human Geography revolves round human-environment relationship. Since the beginning of the development of Human Geography, there have been mainly three approaches to study human-environment relationship. The first is 'deterministic' approach in which scholars believe environment controls course of human action. The variation of human behaviour in different parts of the world is the result of environmental variation. The determinists consider the way of living, culture; stages of development of a social group or nation are mainly governed by the physical environment. According to them man is the passive agent and environment is the active agent. Environmental factors constantly affect and determine man's action and behaviour. The second is the 'possibilistic' approach which explains human-environment relationship in a different way. Here, man is the active agent instead of passive agent who modifies the environment according to his needs. Natural environment provides the base, but man has many options how to act and behave in that environment. Those options/choices increase with development of science and technology. The third is 'Neo-deterministic' approach. According to this approach, man is not a free agent; his liberty is curtailed by nature. Man can choose, but only from the range given by nature. In other words, man might go to any extreme with regard to environment with the advent of science and technology, but in long run environment win the battle.

1.3.5 Movement

Movement is the fifth theme of Human Geography refers to mobility of people, goods and ideas. The dynamic earth is full of movement of human beings, their goods and their ideas from one part to another. Like blood flowing through our bodies keeps us living, movement brings life to a place. So, the theme of movement becomes an important part of geographical studies.

Movement of people is studied on space and time context: it may be local, national or international (immigration and emigration); it may be daily basis, for short duration or permanent. Movement also refers to how and why people travel from one place to another: people travel by car, bus, train, airplanes etc. depending on distance, time and money; people travel for career, job, to escape war, to meet friends and relatives.

Movement of goods from one part to another is the second aspect of 'Movement'. Trade of products and resources between places in different parts of the world has shaped human civilizations and cultures since the time immemorial. Movement of goods include types of goods (perishable/non-perishable, raw material/finished product, foods/beverages etc.); mode of transportation (tractors, trucks, ships etc.); and distance.

Movement of ideas and innovations is the third and most vital aspect of this theme. Cultural diffusion, i.e. spreading of a culture to different parts of the world from its origin comes under this type of movement. It unifies the world and promotes the growth and prosperity of human civilization. With the development of science and technology such as the phone and internet, ideas such as fashion, music and philosophical ideologies are exchanged rapidly from all areas of the globe.

1.4 Summary

Human Geography is becoming popular day by day due to its increasing demand in job market of contemporary world. The study of spatial pattern of human phenomena is the subject matter of Human Geography. Because of its highly interdisciplinary nature and its overlapping with other social sciences, it is treated as liberal discipline. Location, Place, Region, Human-Environment Relationship and Movement are the five themes of Human Geography which differentiate it from other allied disciplines.

Review Questions

1. "Human Geography serves the objective of a liberal education." Discuss.
2. Define Human Geography. What are the subfields of Human Geography?
3. Describe the themes of Human Geography.
4. Discuss 'location' as a theme of Human Geography.
5. Write notes on 'sense of place', 'perception of place' and 'placelessness'.

Analytical Questions

1. Is the liberal status of the subject matter helpful for the Human Geographers in their academic field as expertise knowledge?
2. Will social networking sites give new challenge to Human Geographers to study and analyze the virtual place/space where major human interactions take place?

Chapter 2
Contemporary Human Geography

2.1 Evolution of Geography

Like any other discipline, the study of Human Geography has always been evolving and serving the society since time immemorial. However, in critical times there have always been many questions which shake the existence of the discipline. These questions are: "Why is Human Geography still important?"; "Is the study of Human Geography still useful in modern society?"; "What the study of Human Geography research does in this present day?"; "Are there still spatial patterns to be identified and new lands and cultures to be discovered?" After going through this chapter 'Contemporary Human Geography', we will get the answers to all these questions. To understand Contemporary Human Geography, it is essential to look back and see how the discipline has changed over time. So in this chapter, first we will quickly overview how Geography has evolved in general; when and how Human Geography originated from Geography (its mother discipline) and developed over time. Then we will discuss the trends of Contemporary Human Geography.

The evolution of Human Geography cannot be discussed without the evolution of its mother discipline 'Geography'. The evolution of Geography has never been smooth and its development was also not continuous over the time. The earliest geographic knowledge traced back during Pre-classical period, i.e. around 4000 B.C., when the World's first civilization emerged in Mesopotamia. Archaeological discoveries of local maps—roughly sketched on clay tables, were perhaps used by the local communities during this time. Till the Classical period, geographical knowledge was probably similar and limited for all other civilizations, namely the Nile Valley, the Indus Valley, the Chinese etc.

During Classical period (from 1200 B.C. to 500 A.D.), the contribution of Greek geographers is worth to be mentioned. They started describing and mapping the world as they knew. As the Greeks started moving out of their country and exploring the nearby areas, the Greek geographers contributed towards geographical description, i.e. literal tradition. During 600 B.C., they also initiated mathematical tradition by contributing towards the measurement of circumference of earth and devising grid system of the maps. The parallel development was took place in Rome and also in Oriental World, i.e. in India and China.

Medieval period (from 500 A.D. to 1750 A.D.) was marked its beginning with the onset of Dark Age in Europe. The Dark Age continued till 1100 A.D. During this period, only sporadic and limited geographic work was accomplished in Europe. The Dark Age was followed by the rise of geographical knowledge in Islamic World (700 A.D. to 1400 A.D.). The significant progress was made in exploration, mapping, description and mathematical work by Muslim geographers. From 1400 A.D. to 1750 A.D., Europe expanded oversees. The period is known as Age of Discovery or Renaissance period in which geographers added significantly to our knowledge through new mapping techniques and description of the world.

With the rise of German geographers, Geography entered the Modern period of its development (1750 A.D. to 1950 A.D.). After Germany, geographers from France, America, Britain and Soviet Union contributed a lot during this period. The scholars tried to define the field, content and scope of geography, strongly influenced by the development of modern science. They discussed and elaborated on the methods of collecting, organizing and presenting the information of geographical nature.

The period after World War II is recognized as Contemporary period in the history of evolution of Geography. The geographic research experienced a new shift in methodology during this period.

2.2 Development of Human Geography

During the evolution of Geography over the time, Human Geography has also been being developed as a part and parcel of it. In the following paragraphs we will see how geographers tried to distinguish Human Geography as a separate branch of Geography and how Human Geography becoming popular day by day.

Till the Age of Discovery, Geography was not more than encyclopaedic compilations of places, which were presented and described in haphazard manner, not in orderly manner; because the knowledge of the field was not complete. By the year 1800, the German geographers tried to provide a scientific base to Geography by initially splitting the discipline into two basic branches, viz. Physical Geography and Human Geography. In the early part of 19th Century, the writings of German geographers—Alexander-von-Humboldt (1769-1859) and Carl Ritter (1779-1859), were very strong and contradictory to each other. Humboldt emphasized on natural and physical aspects in systematic manner; and Ritter emphasized on historical and human aspects in regional studies. This gives rise to two types of controversies—Systematic *verses* Regional and Physical *verses* Human. In the late 19th Century, the publication of Charles Darwin's '*Origin of Species*' strengthens the physical aspects in geographical studies. However, Darwin's ideas on adaptation to the environment and evolution stimulated Human Geographers to reappraise the old concepts.

During 19th Century, the emphasis of geographical studies kept on shifting between physical and human, with none of the field of study being prominent. However, towards the end of 19th Century, the more emphasis was given to systematic study on Physical Geography. In this field, the contribution of scholars like Davis, Gilbert, Powell, Agassiz, Peschel, Frobel, Koeppen etc. is worth to be mentioned. These scholars carried out morphological research and produced studies based on Landforms and Climate.

During the first half of 20th Century, man and environment relationship was the central theme of all geographical studies (later it became one of the five themes of Geography introduced by National Geographic Society in 1996 discussed in Ch. 1). During this period, man and environment relationship was viewed in three ways: Determinism, Possibilism and Ecological viewpoint. According to the doctrine of Determinism, the physical environment controls the non-physical world/human environment. As an antithesis to determinism, the doctrine of possibilism was developed. The supporters of the Possibilistic School favour the view that human being is an active agent and can modify his environment according to his choice. Ecological viewpoint balanced both the doctrines of determinism and possibilism. According to this viewpoint, the man and environment are equally important and are intrinsic to the particular character of the area.

During latter half of 20th Century, the discipline experienced a new shift in methodology; the main features were integration, interdependence and utilitarian approach. Each sub-discipline brought its special skills to solve the problems like poverty, environmental degradation, racial problem, over population etc. Gradually, Geography became more and more humanistic/anthropocentric. So, the contemporary geography is a spatial science increasingly focusing on the study of environmental, social and economic phenomena which revolves round human being.

2.3 Contemporary Human Geography

In the previous section we have seen the development of Human Geography as a separate branch is very recent, i.e. less than 250 years. In contemporary period, i.e. since latter half of 20th Century, Human Geography supersedes Physical Geography. Most of the geographical researches are towards solving environmental, social and economic issues. As human existence has affected every part of the world, research on pure Physical Geography is very less. In this section Contemporary Human Geography will be discussed under following three heads.

2.3.1 Approaches to Study Contemporary Human Geography

A number of approaches/doctrines have been developed time to time to handle different issues of man-environment relationship. Though the pioneers of each doctrine criticize others, the philosophies behind each doctrine is unique and may be more appropriate in handling certain situation and may be less appropriate/inappropriate in handling other situation. The important ones are discussed in following paragraphs.

Quantitative Approach

Quantitative Approach developed during 1950s was a major shift in the field of Geography. In this approach mathematical and statistical methods were introduced to establish laws and theories in Geography. Earlier Geography was more descriptive. Quantitative revolution claimed empirical or experimental nature of geography rather than its descriptive nature. The quantitative technique was first used in Physical Geography. Many geomorphologists and climatologists found immense scope in using quantitative techniques in their respective fields. The methods were later on used in Human Geography by the renowned geographers—Chorley and Haggett (1967), Gregory (1981). The revolution reached its peak in 1960 with numerous success in its use in solving many research problems. However, it was not accepted by many human geographers. The prevalent notion of unpredictability of human behaviour and freewill could not be explained by the quantification, i.e. mathematical and statistical technique. The quantitative revolution removed the human dimension from the discipline. As a result, by the end of 1970s, the quantitative revolution came under direct challenge.

Behavioural Approach

Behavioural Approach developed during the late 20th Century to understand man-environment relationship in Geography. It recognizes the complexity of human behaviour developed in different environmental conditions and the way the human beings behave and impact the environment. Human behaviour is very much unpredictable. Some human responses are mean, selfish and others are very much planned and systematic. The focus of human geographical inquiry under this approach was 'environmental perception and mental maps'. Everybody has a unique perception about his environment which creates mental map and ultimately determine his behaviour. The Behavioural Approach developed in 1970s sought to provide a greater understanding how people perceived places and surrounding environment and made locational decision. It challenged mathematical models of society developed by quantification. Julian Wolpret, Wright (1947), Kirk (1951) are the pioneers of Behavioural Geography. The behavioural approach was under criticism due to lack of sound theoretical base.

Humanistic and Marxist Approach

Geography, in the 1970s and afterwards, underwent another revolution in the form of critical revolution in the contemporary human geography. A number of humanistic and Marxists approaches constitute the part of radical geography. Radical geography emerged during the 1970s and 1980s as the inadequacies of behaviouralist and quantitative methods became clear and it was argued that these methods were not useful unless alternatives or solutions were given to human problems. The revival of humanism in geography in the 1970s owed much deep dissatisfaction with the more mechanistic models developed during the quantitative/spatial science revolution. As contrasted to behavioural geography, humanistic geography treats man as an individual ceaselessly interacting with his environment and in that process, transforming both himself and his milieu. The humanistic perspective was started in definite opposition to the dehumanizing characteristics of the methods of scientific rationality in the social sciences. The use of humanistic approach in geography more recently is an attempt to make man, the human being, the very core of geographic investigation, to make geography, people geography, about real people and for the people (Smith, 1977).

Several humanistic approaches have been advocated and canvassed for. The three most important sources of inspiration were the philosophies of idealism, phenomenology and existentialism. The Idealistic approach to humanistic geography was advocated by Harris (1971) and Guelke (1971). This approach is a system of philosophy which regards reality as residing in or constituted by the mind. All spatial expressions of human beings are the manifestations of man's thinking or thinking of a society. Idealism holds that what we refer to and perceive as the external worlds is in someway an artifice of the mind. The idealist is concerned with what the actor believes not why he believes it, since according to the idealist "all knowledge is ultimately based on an individual's objective experience of the world and comprises mental constructs and ideas." There is no real world that can be known independent of the mind. Other humanist geographers adopted a phenomenal approach which seeks to clarify the social conceptions which form an essential condition of social existence. The phenomenologist is concerned with providing a description of the life world as it is actually experienced (Buttimer, 1976). This concern avoids the abstraction involved in both positivism and idealism. Positivism also refers empiricism is actually the philosophical system of Auguste Comte, a French philosopher. The basic theme of positivism is that in scientific discipline, knowledge is based on the facts which are observed and the relationship among these facts. The science should concern itself only with empirical questions like how things are in reality. The real world is the world that can be sensed actually not mind based as in idealism. The reliable knowledge can come from basic observation of actual conditions. The phenomenological approach in human geography was introduced in 1970s by Relph. According to him, there is no objective world independent of man's existence and "all knowledge proceeds from the world of experience and cannot be independent of the world". This means that the phenomenologist describe rather than explain. Yi-Fu Tuan was an early advocate of the phenomenological approach in humanistic geography. Phenomenology has to do with beginnings with phenomena that are first lived and experienced and are only subsequently formulated as concepts. Closely associated with phenomenology is the philosophy of existentialism. (Both look at the environment from an experimental perspective.). The term existentialism was actually coined by the French philosopher Gabriel Marcel in the mid-1940. It advocates that the explanation should begin from space occupied by man or society and then the other relationships should be explored. The central concept is based on all sorts of explanations should begin from the existential space of mankind. The basic difference is that phenomenology assumes the primacy of essence—the allocation of meanings results from the existence of consciousness—the basic dictum is "being before essence" or "man makes himself". The process of defining oneself involves creating an environment. Thus environment can be read as biographies, as representations of man creating himself (Johnston, 1983) whereas existential means concerned with existence and especially human existence. In this sense existentialism may be defined as the philosophical theory emphasizing existence of the individual person as free and responsible agent determining his own development. Here the basic idea is "existence comes before essence" meaning existence comes before anything, any other reality. Since humanistic study in geography is concerned with either the study of individuals or their phenomenal environments or with the analysis of landscapes as repositories of human meanings, it cannot be easily evaluated. Unlike research in the positivist mode, humanistic work has no explicit criteria by which it can assessed, since here the purpose is not to increase explanation and predictive power but to improve understanding. For this reason research in humanistic geography is not cumulative so that the concept of progress does not apply.

One aspect of critical revolution is the revival of human ecology, the application of ecological concepts to the study of the relations between people and their physical and social environment. It was a logical extension of the system of thought and the techniques of the investigation developed in the study of man. The other distinct consequence of the revolution is development of the approach of welfare geography. It is an approach to human geography that stresses on the questions of inequality. Smith and Knox set forth the tradition of the welfare approach in geography in an organized manner. The basis of welfare approach is in "who gets what, where and how". The welfare approach in geography requires the development of social indication for the empirical identification of social inequality and injustice in territorial distribution. "Whereas welfare geography works in principle within the framework of existing economic and social system, radical geography which has been established more recently, calls for both revolutionary theory and revolutionary practice" (Holt Jenson, 1981). As a holistic, revolutionary science, Marxism provides a firm theoretical base for the radical movement in geography. Marxism offers an opportunity to develop an integrated comprehension of reality as a whole. Marxism is centrally concerned with the ways in which the production of space, place and landscape is implicated in the reproduction of specific social formations. It developed against capitalism. The system of thought developed by Marx propounds that the state, through history, has been a device for the exploitation of the masses by a dominant class and that class struggle has been the main agent of historic change. "Marx may have been able to dissect the operation of a capitalist economy, polity and society that we so often miss today. But Marx does not hold the key to every modern problem in complex pluralist societies" (Smith, 1977). Philosophical and methodological rigidity in seeking resolution of societal problem is restrictive of human initiative. Social science research must remain open to alternative perspectives which must not be condemned without giving them a try. Feminist geography is an approach to study in human geography which applies the theories, methods and critiques of feminism to the study of the human environment and society. Its principal focus of study is geographic differences in gender relations and gender equality. Gender is a particularly important facets of identity that refers to the social differences between men and women rather than their biological differences. Gender refers to socially created distinction between feminity and musculinity. It drew inspiration from the women's movements in the West as a part of radicalization of societal perspectives. In this respect feminist geography is a part of a broader post-modern approach to the subject which is not primarily concerned with the development of conceptual theory in itself but rather focuses on the real experiences of individual and groups in their own localities, upon the geographies that they live in within their own communities. Feminism aims at defining, establishing and defining equal political, economic, and social rights of women. For spatial scientist, space is a key variable in shaping the organization of human activity. Feminist geographers have focused on the ways in which space is gendered. They believe that under patriarchy, ground rules determine how men and women can use space. They examine the ways in which gender relations are expressed in space.

2.3.2 Human Geographers in Contemporary Job Market

Today human geographers concerned with the spatial aspects of human existence, the character of places and regions created by people and the relationship between humans and physical environment. Due to its interdisciplinary nature, Human Geography admirably serves the objective of a liberal education. As explained in Chapter 1, Human Geography encompasses many sub-disciplines such as Political Geography, Economic Geography, Urban Geography, Population Geography, Cultural Geography etc. Recently, more specialized fields within Human Geography have been developed to further aid in the study of cultural practices and human activities as they relate spatially to the world. These Fields are Feminist Geography, Children's Geography, Geography of Tourism, Geography of Sexuality and Space etc.

With many diverse subfields, the discipline has the capability of making the students better informed citizens, with better understanding of important issues facing our societies in local/regional/global scale and better prepared to contribute solutions. Human Geographers can also handle different issues adopting different approaches discussed in preceding section. In other words, the vast topics researched by Human Geographers with various approaches can give the students multitude of career options. The students of Human Geography can serve the society under various titles, such as location analyst, urban planner, diplomat, remote sensing analyst, geographic information scientist, area specialist, travel consultant, political analyst, intelligence officer, cartographer, educator, transportation planner, environmental consultant etc.

Table 2.1 summarizes some of the professional opportunities open to students who have specialized in one or more of the various subfields of Human Geography.

2.3.3 *Human Geography in Globalizing World/Future of Human Geography*

Globalization is the increasing interconnectedness of different parts of the world through common processes of economic, environmental, political and cultural change. It has been started in 19th Century by the emergence of international agencies and institutions, global network of communication, standardized system of global time, international law, internationally shared notion of citizenship and human rights.

In today's globalizing world, it is observed that globalization leaves Human Geography obsolete. As for example, high tech communications and global marketing of standardized products seem as if they might soon wash away the distinctiveness of people and places; they might soon diminish the importance of differences between places. However, the new mobility of money, labour, products, and ideas actually increases the significance of place in very important ways. When there is more diffusion of material culture and life styles, the regional and ethnic identities become more valuable. As for example, with the importance of branded Lee Cooper jeans, the importance of ethnic dress materials (like *phoolkari* suits of Punjab, *bandhni* suits of Rajasthan etc.) is increasing day by day. With the importance of international institutions, intergovernmental agencies; people are becoming more sensitive to local cleavages of race, ethnicity and religion. Social networking sites take people to cyber world, create new type of space, called cyber space which is not real, but seems to be real. This might cause depression among youth which would lead the need of a specific place of community which they can call their own.

In the process of globalization, global telecommunication and transport networks are replacing the importance of formal regions by that of functional regions in many parts of the world. The use/importance of time distance and money distance discussed in Chapter 1, is increasing in place of real distance. People can commute everyday more than 500 kms to reach their work place by superfast trains. The individuals of same family can stay in India as well as in France and meet each other once in a week. In this process, cultural regions are losing their identities very fast, followed by economic regions. Earlier the concept of absolute location, such as latitude and longitude, was beyond common man's understanding. Now the satellite technology (Global Positioning System) has made it possible in bringing the required device through smart phones so that every person has the knowledge of not only absolute location but also his location in relation to others. Traffic control, tracking of people and transported materials are becoming easier day by day. In this way, theft, corruption and happenings of many unsocial incidents would be

Table 2.1: Professional Opportunities of Human Geography

Field of Human Geography	*Expertise Knowledge*	*Employment Opportunities*
Economic Geography	Knowing and applying geographic information about the economy and economic processes (e.g. labour, development, industry, agriculture, transportation, trade, resources, land use, technology change)	Transportation Manager Community Resource Specialist Market Researcher Business Development Real Estate Appraiser Environmental Economist
Political Geography	Knowing and applying geogra-phic information about political systems and processes (e.g. governments, political activism, non-governmental organizations, nations, states, international relations, nationalism)	Community Organizer Policy Consultant Policy Researcher Lobbyist
Cultural Geography	Knowing and applying geographic information about culture and cultural processes (e.g. religion, language, ethnicity, diffusion, meaning of landscapes, cultural significance of place)	Area, Ethnic, and Cultural Studies Teacher Interpreter and Translator Historic Preservationist Writer/Editor
Population Geography	Knowing and applying geographic information about population, demography, and demographic processes (e.g. population density, migration, birth and death rates, fertility rates)	Market Analyst Population, Real Estate, Community Association Manager Urban and Regional Planner Demographer Public Health Officer
Urban and Regional Planning	Knowing and applying geographic information about urban system (e.g. urban settlement, business districts, urban administration)/ Possessing and applying knowledge of the physical and human geography of a specific country or world region	Urban and Regional Planner Transportation Planner Housing, Park and Recreation Planner Health Service Planner Community Developer
Environmental Studies	Knowing and applying geographic information about relationships between nature and society (e.g. pollution from industrial development, economic effects of drought)	Bio-diversity Park Developer Accredited Land Consultant Manager of Sustainability Environmental Affairs Specialist
Field Technique	Using interviews, questionnaires, observations, photography, maps, and other techniques for measuring geographic information in the field	Surveyor Water Quality Scientist Soil Scientist Field Interviewer
Studies related to Global Perspectives	Possessing and applying knowledge of how people, places, and regions are linked by global networks and processes (e.g. globalization, international trade, immigration, Internet technology, global climate system)	Logistics Manager Mapping Technician Geodetic Surveyor International Development Specialist Journalist Foreign Services Officer
Studies related to Spatial Thinking	Identifying, explaining, and ?nding meaning in spatial patterns and relationships (e.g. site conditions, how places are	Urban and Regional Planner Surveyor Geophysical Data Technician

(Contd.)

Field of Human Geography	*Expertise Knowledge*	*Employment Opportunities*
	similar and different, the influence of a land feature on its neighbours, the nature of transitions between places, how places are linked at local, regional, and/or global scales	Spatial Analysis Consultant Environmental Specialist
Studies related to International Perspectives	Drawing on and synthesizing the information, concepts, and methods of the natural and social sciences for geographic research and application	International Development Specialist Urban and Regional Planner Humanitarian Affairs Analyst International Development Specialist Programme Manager
Studies related to Diversity Perspectives	Using knowledge about population diversity (e.g. gender, ethnicity, race, sexuality, disability) to interpret social, economic, and political issues in different places	Human Resources Manager Academic Adviser Market Researcher Public Diplomacy Officer Travel Guide
Geography of Tourism	Knowing and applying geographic information about tourism industries and its related processes (e.g. tourist places, transporttation, local culture, language)	Tour Guide and Escort Tour Manager
Feminist Geography	Knowing and applying geographic information about population, demography, and demographic processes (e.g. population density, migration, birth and death rates, fertility rates)	

minimized. The reality is that globalization is variously embraced, resisted and challenged. In this process, locations, places and regions are modified and reconstructed rather than destroyed and homogenized.

Besides this, there are many issues in the globalizing world such as climate change, pollution, disease, crime, poverty, inequality etc. The Human Geographers with their specialization in various subfields and with the training of different methods/approaches discussed above are more able to solve these globalization problems. The might also increase the severity of problems for the comfort and economic gain of society.

In this world of rapid change which is observed particularly during last decade pose many questions related to future of Human Geography. As for example, What kind of problems the future bring in changing concept of location, place and region?; Will the modern man cope the environmental stresses arising due to rapid population growth and industrialization?; What new technologies are likely have the most impact in reshaping the discipline—Human Geography?

2.4 Summary

The discipline of Human Geography has been originated from its mother discipline Geography during early 19th Century and since then it is getting popular day by day. The contemporary Human Geography is different from its earlier nature in terms with its approaches to study the discipline, its varied scope in employment opportunity and fast changing nature of the subject matter in globalizing world. The future of Human Geography lies in the development of science and technology along with its changing nature of five themes.

Review Questions

1. Describe how the discipline 'Human Geography' developed from its parent discipline.
2. How quantitative approach in geography is different from behavioural geography?
3. Discuss humanistic approaches of Human Geography.
4. "The vast topics researched by Human Geographers with various approaches can give the students multitude of career options." Discuss.
5. In the globalizing world, how the nature of geography is changing?

Analytical Questions

1. Does humanistic approach of Geography practically give solution to contemporary environmental problems?
2. Changing nature of geography in globalizing world is bringing what kind of challenges to human geographers?

Chapter 3
Man-Environment Relationship and Environmental Crisis

3.1 Introduction

Man-Environment relationship is the subject matter of Geography since very beginning. In the beginning, due to no human influence of early man on surrounding natural environment (as man was part of the nature), the subject matter of Geography was purely physical/natural. Over the time from the journey of early man to modern man, with the increasing influence of human on its surrounding environment, the cultural environment/features gradually took place of physical environment/features. As a result, Human Geography was born from its mother discipline—Geography during early 19th Century and the discipline is becoming popular day by day.

Man-Environment relationship has also been being introduced as one of the five themes of Human Geography by National Geographic Society in 1996 (Ch. 1). Though it was one of the five themes of Human Geography, Man-Environment relationship is the central theme around it other four themes such as location, place, region and movement revolve. We generally talk about location of any incident or man's habitat in relation to surrounding environment. The places and regions are also characterized by its physical, cultural and behavioural characteristics; this implies the Man-Environment relationship of that place/region. Movement modifies Man-Environment relationship of places which it connects.

In this chapter Man-Environment relationship has been discussed in detail. In the first half of the chapter, the different approaches to study Man-Environment relationship have been discussed. In the second half of the chapter, historical perspective of Man-Environment relationship has been discussed with special reference to environmental crisis and environmental conflicts.

3.2 Approaches to Study Man-Environment Relationship

In the beginning man was 'physical man'—surrounded by terrain, soil, water, flora, fauna which forms man's environment. With the development of society, economy and technology, he broadens his environment for better food, shelter, access and comfort. He became 'cultural man'—surrounded by high rise buildings, industrial complexes, modern transportation networks, man-made parks etc. According to this gradual change of man from 'physical man' to 'cultural man', Man-Environment relationship is perceived and evaluated in variety of ways by different scholars from time to time. These ways/approaches are described in the following paragraphs.

3.2.1 Deterministic Approach

According to the deterministic approach, man is the product of natural environment, i.e. 'earth made man' is the basic notion behind it. All aspects of human life, starting from his health and comfort to his social, economic, political, ethical and aesthetic life, are controlled by physical environment. Deterministic thinking originated during 5th Century BC in Greece and Rome and remained dominant till the beginning of 20th Century. During this period, constant modification/change was observed in deterministic viewpoints. However, the major change was found after the publication of scientific, high profile evolutionary theory of '*Origin of Species*' in 1859 by Charles Darwin. So, the deterministic views can be discussed in two phases—Pre-Darwinian and Post-Darwinian.

1. Pre-Darwinian Phase

During ancient period, the scholars like Hippocrates, Aristotle and Strabo made attempts to explain the influence of environment on psychological and sociological temperaments of individuals taking examples of Asians, Europeans and Americans. Hippocrates discussed the easy going, relaxed and slackened life of Asians is the result of favourable physical environment; while hard and struggling life of Europeans are due to the influence of harsh climatic condition. According to Aristotle, the people of Europe and North America (cold climate) are full of spirit, but deficient in intelligence. On the other hand, the people of Asia (hot climate) are intelligent and skilful, but lack in spirit. Therefore, the Asians have been in continuous slavery and subjection. The Greeks acquire both the characters and occupies the middle position. Strabo also explained the rise and strength of Roman Empire was influenced by its location such as relief, shape and climatic condition.

The Arab scholars like Al-Battani, Al-Masudi, Ibn-Hawqal, Al-Idrisi, Ibn-Khaldun etc. attempted to study the influence of environment on life of man in medieval period. Al-Masudi states the land, where water is in abundant, there people are gay and humorous while the people of arid lands are short tempered. The nomads who live in open areas are characterized by their strength, resolution, wisdom and physical fitness. The Arab scholars also divided the habitable world into 7 *Kishwars (terrestrial zones)* on the basis of physical and cultural characteristics of nations and races.

Determinism was also strongly observed in the work of Emmanuel Kant, Humboldt and Ritter in modern period. Emmanuel Kant has given many examples in his writings. One of the examples which is different from that of the earlier scholars is—animals and men migrate to another climatic conditions are gradually affected by their environment. As for example, the brown squirrels that migrate to Siberia turn grey and the colour of white cows in winter turn grayish. Humboldt and Ritter asserted the development of Astronomical Science in Arab is due to the physical environment of that country. The open sky, desert lands of Arab gave opportunities for the solitude observation of astronomical features.

2. Post-Darwinian Phase

Charles Robert Darwin (1809-1882), a British naturalist became popular among scientific community for convincing "the occurrence of evolution of species". His theory, 'The Origin of Species' (1859) is considered as major paradigm in Biology. The origin/evolution of species is determined by environment. Darwin was mainly influenced by Population Theory of Malthus who stated that the human population when unchecked grows double in every 25 years while resources such as food cannot increase in same rate. Thus human being is in intense struggle for existence, competing for limited resources. In other words human population is controlled by limited environmental resources. Though Malthus tried to explain population theory, but a logical approach towards deterministic thinking was developed during this period. Combining the Malthus' idea of completion/struggle of man for existence with his observation, Darwin explained how evolution could occur. In struggle for existence, some species survive and others get extinct.

The survival in a particular environment is called adaptation which paves the way towards natural selection. Darwin explained it taking example of the ptarmigan (a kind of bird). Ptarmigan turns white in winter to get protection from their predators that cannot spot them in snow. Darwin implied the colour change of ptarmigan in winter is more likely to survive, reproduce and pass this adaptation to future generation. This natural selection can ultimately lead to the formation of new species if ptarmigan had to migrate to a permanently cold area and became white permanently. Sometimes, many species evolve from single ancestral species. As for example, 23 species of honeycreepers in Hawaii evolved from one ancestral species. Natural selection gives two types of evolution—divergent evolution and convergent evolution. Divergent evolution is the process of two or more related species becoming more and more dissimilar. The red fox and kit fox evolved from same ancestral species and became dissimilar by living in different climatic condition. The red fox lives in mixed farmland and forest, where its red colour helps it blend in with surrounding trees. The kit fox lives in the plain and desert, where its sandy colour helps to conceal from predators. In convergent evolution, unrelated species become more and more similar in appearance as they adapt same kind of environment. The resemblance of cactus of American desert to the euphorbia of African desert is the example of convergent evolution. The two unrelated species have adapted to desert environments developing fleshy stems armed with spines which help the plants to store water and ward off predators.

Like adaptation/evolution, extinction is also a natural process. In struggle for existence, the species who cannot adapt changing environmental condition die and finally become extinct. Extinction of many species on earth is due to destruction of habitats and climatic change which are result of developmental activities of man. The conversion of prairies of central North America into farmlands and grazing ranges caused a great decline in prairie dogs and black footed ferret. These species might get extinct in near future.

Darwin's scientific explanation triggered deterministic thinking. The adaptations, evolution, extinction of species are solely controlled by environment. The term 'environmental influence' used during Pre-Darwinian phase was replaced by 'environmental control' during Post-Darwinian Phase. The scholars of Pre-Darwinian phase were modest in their approach in comparison to the scholars of Post-Darwinian phase who were extremist in their deterministic thinking. The scholars of Post-Darwinian phase attempted to explain that man's immediate surroundings have decisive effect not only on his occupation, dwellings and materials he uses in day-to-day life but also on his personal traits, his general character and even in his religious beliefs. They found environment as superior to man and mastering man's action.

Ratzel, a follower of Darwin coined the term 'Social Darwinism'. He considered State as an Organism. He explained that like any organism, the State owes its life to the earth and strive to occupy more and more territory. He also opined similar locations of States lead to similar mode of life. As for example, the insular location of Japan and British Isles provide natural defence against invaders. He also attributed that the physical features and location of a place in relation to mountains and plains closely influence the course of history, the mode of life and people and the stage of development.

In the beginning of 20th Century deterministic thinking became very popular in United States. The leading scholars were Ellen C. Semple and Elsworth Hutington. Semple, the student of Ratzel wrote two books which were based on the philosophy of determinism. The titles of books were 'American History and Geographic Conditions' and 'influences of Geographic Environment' published in 1903 and 1911 respectively. According to Semple, there were four ways in which environment can influence man. They are: (1) Physiological Influences (on the features, stature and physical appearance of human beings; (2) Psychological Influences (on the level of thinking, beliefs, knowledge of the human beings; (3) Influences on the Economy and Society (on the occupation, culture, tradition and people); and (4) Influences on Human Mobility (on the mode of living such as sedentary and practicing transhumance).

Hutington explained determinism in terms of climate in his book, '*The Principle of Human Geography*' in 1945. His doctrine of the effects of climatic variations was based on his field studies of Central Asia. He assessed the role of climate on man in three levels, i.e. global, regional and local. The basic philosophy of Hutington was that the supreme achievements of any civilization were always bound up with particular type of climate and variation in climate led to pulsation in history of culture. He associated the climatic cycle with Golden Age in Ancient Greece, the Renaissance in Western Europe etc. Hutington divided the world into mild and harsh climatic zones. He established that the Egyptian, Mesopotamian, Chinese and Indus Valley civilization flourished in the fertile river valleys of mild climates. The great outpouring of nomadic people from Central Asia towards Turkistan, China, India could be due to dying pasture on which the nomads were dependant. According to Hutington, the religion and racial character in different parts of the world are the products of climate.

The subsequent geographers like H.J. Mackinder, Chisholm, Davies, Bowman, Robert Mill, Geddes, Herbertson, Taylor (1951) interpreted the progress of societies with deterministic approach. Many of the scholars explain the climatic influences on physical properties of soil which ultimately determines the cropping pattern, dietary habits, physique and attitudes of human societies.

Criticism

The Deterministic approach was criticized due to number of reasons. The main reasons are as follows: The approach was over simplified in nature to study Man-Environment relationship; The examples are too sweeping and lack of careful investigations; The determinists over-emphasized the role of environment in human affairs; The crude determinism was one-sided approach as there was lack of cause-effect relationship; and so on and so forth. Many geographers in the USA, France, Britain, Canada and other countries realized the above facts and the philosophy of determinism was attacked vigorously, particularly after World War II. Spate (1952) criticized the extreme approach of determinism. According to him, natural environment is only one of the factors of terrestrial differentiation which again acts through society or cultural tradition to influence the life and society of man. Hartshorne also criticized and rejected deterministic thinking purely on the ground that it separated nature and man. Therefore, it disrupted the fundamental unity of the field of Geography and contradicted the concept of Geography as integrated science.

3.2.2 *Possibilistic Approach*

As a consequence of above criticism and technological and scientific development which proved man's conquest over nature, the doctrine of Possibilism emerged in France and USA during second half of 20th Century. The essence of possibilistic thinking in Man-Environment relationship can be summed up as follows:

- Nature does not determine man's life, but it offers a number of opportunities out of which man is free to select. For the possibilists, man's action is the starting point in man-environment relationship rather than nature. However, man can never entirely get rid of environment, but within the environment he has to choose out of many choices.
- The limit set by nature varies from place to place and time to time. In marginal environment such as in hot and cold deserts, man's choices are less in comparison to more favourable areas of warm and cool temperate zones. Likewise in low stage of cultural development, man's choice was extremely restricted; while in periods when man's techniques are highly developed, man's choices became numerous.
- The debate between Determinism and Possibilism continued for more than half a century. According to the doctrine of determinism, similar environment should generate similar life styles or cultural groups. According to the doctrine of possibilism, similar environment with different cultural/technological development could generate dissimilar life styles and cultural groups.
- According to Possibilists, it is man who is the primary architect of his culture. It depends upon the choices he makes among the possibilities offered by the environment. The human choices in turn depend upon needs, tastes and capacities of human beings. Man interacts with nature with the arm of culture.

Vidal de la Blache, the founder of modern French Geography, was the strong opponent of Environmental Determinism views. He put forward the concept of possibilism through his important works, 'Geographie Universelle' and 'Regional Geography of France'. He explained that, in a given environment, in which a group of people lives, there is no necessity that the people should be influenced in a certain way, there is only possibility that they may react in a number of different ways, depending upon their cultural heritage. Jean Bruhnes, the student of Vidal de la Blache was also influenced by his teacher and strongly supported the doctrine of Possibilism.

American Geographers such as Carl Sauer and Isaiah Bowman also strongly opposed the doctrine of Determinism. Sauer argued that geographers' role is to investigate and understand the nature of the transition from the natural to cultural landscape. In this process the geographers would identify the major changes that in an area as a result of occupancy/ succession of human beings. The importance of culture is often greater in regions where it has been acclimatized than in those where it originated or domesticated. As for example, the yield of wheat is lesser in Southwest Asia, where it is first domesticated in comparison to the Western countries where it was diffused later. According to Bowman, men can never entirely rid themselves whatever they do, environment has a hold on them. Taking this into consideration, they utilize their geographical circumstances more or less completely of their geographical possibilities. The limit set by nature by man's action varies from one historical period to another. Bowman asserted "while the physical laws to which mankind responds are available in their application and degree of effect, yet this is also true that all men everywhere are affected to some degree by physical condition."

Criticism

The doctrine of Possibilism was also criticized by many contemporary thinkers. Therefore, like Determinism, Possibilism also did not hold for many years. Griffith Taylor was main critique of doctrine of Possibilism. According to him, the task of geography is to study natural environment and its effect on man, but not all problems connected to man or the 'cultural landscape'. Moreover, possibilism promotes over anthropocentrism in geography and does not encourage study of geographical environment. Geographical determinism oblige the geographer to turn attention to nature; and if the question is asked as to who is setting out to destroy geography, then the blame should be placed above all at the possibilists' door.

3.2.3 Neo-Deterministic Approach

As a result of the criticism of the doctrine of crude Determinism, it faded away in the second quarter of 20th Century. It did not die out completely. After few decades, due to criticism of the doctrine of Possibilism, it revived in a new form known as Neo-Determinism. Keeping in mind the criticism of crude Determinism, the followers of Neo-Determinism were more careful to seek records of cause and effect attributes while studying Man-Environment relationship with the help of modern techniques.

Griffith Taylor, leading Australian geographer, was the father of the doctrine of Neo-Determinism. In 1951, he used the term 'Stop and Go Determinism' for 'Neo-Determinism'. He maintained that though in well endowed part of the world, nature gives lots of opportunities for man's living; but in resource scarcity areas like cold/dry/rugged areas nature have lots of limitations. The settlers who fail to regard this nature given limitation must face disaster. According to him nature is not very rigid or crude; it can be modified, but not be ignored. It is like the flow of traffic in a busy road. The traffic policeman regulates the flow of traffic by 'stop and go' method. Likewise, the flow of nature can be regulated by human agency according to need and through the use of technology. As for example, human being cut forest according to his requirement, stop cutting forest and also grow forest to preserve environment.

3.2.4 Ecological Approach

In Man-Environment studies, the ecological approach is the latest approach cutting through the themes both Determinism and Possibilism. This approach became popular among Human geographers mainly because of two reasons: (1) Neither the Determinism nor the Possibilism is sufficient to explain the Man-Environment relationship satisfactorily. Possibilism gives importance to nature and Possibilism gives importance to man; ecological approach does not allow anyone to be supreme power over other to exert its influence. It describes the cause and effect relationship between man and nature. Man and nature are acting and reacting together. Man is modifying nature by cutting forest, constructing buildings, roads, dams etc. Likewise nature is modifying man, as for example in mountain areas by giving many hardships to him and making him bold to face them. (2) Neither of the two concepts whether it is Determinism or Possibilism can provide the discipline an analytical tool for scientific insights. The Ecological approach provides the research method that Geography so badly lacked (Eyre, 1964; Stoddart, 1972a, 1972b).

The concept 'Ecosystem', coined by the Tansley (1946), the plant ecologist in 1935, lies at the base of the philosophy of Ecological Approach. An Ecosystem can be defined as 'a set of objects together with the relationships between the objects and between their attributes', and can operate at any scale, from atoms in a molecule to the universe itself. The relationship between man and environment can be viewed as an ecosystem. The task of geographers is to identify the various elements in the system, understand how they work, discover how they are related to each other and then study their interaction as a functioning whole. This is an attractive idea because form and process can be studied in a single and ordered framework and the various elements of the system can be measured to provide an explanation of man-environment relationship. The concept of ecosystem is also useful in planning, since once the system is understood, the consequences of change in any part of it can be predicted and any necessary action be taken. This would enable management of the ecosystem to take place to lessen the consequences of pollution and make the planning and conservation of resources possible.

3.3 Historical Perspective of Man-Environment Relationship

Man's interaction with environment has been changing since the emergence of homosapiens on the earth surface. Since then man has been playing important roles with environment in different capacities, such as 'biological or physical man', 'social man', 'economic man' and 'technological man' etc. All the functions of man, such as birth, growth and death are affected by natural environment and at the same time he is capable of making substantial changes in natural environment to make it suitable for his own living.

If we look at the history, the purely natural relationship between 'physical primitive man' and natural environment during prehistoric period has been changed to hostile relationship between technological man and environment at present time. This substantial change in Man-Environment relationship has given birth to numerous environmental problems of serious consequences. The study of changing relationship between man and environment in historical perspective may help in demonstrating the gradually increasing adverse impacts of human activities on the environment. The changing relationship of man with natural environment from prehistoric to modern period can be divided into four stages: (1) Period of hunting and food gathering; (2) Period of animal domestication and pastoralism; (3) Period of plant domestication and agriculture; and (4) Period of science, technology and industrialization.

3.3.1 Period of Hunting and Food Gathering

During this period, the primitive man was a biological man or physical man because his basic requirements were limited to food only which he could collect from his surroundings by gathering fruits, nuts etc. and by hunting animals. The discovery of fire made a significant change in the attitude of man as he learned cooking animal flesh and burning forest to drive away dangerous animals. However, there was least interference of human being with the environment in terms of its destruction during this period, as man used to depend on environment for his basic needs. It may be pointed out here that fire is the first major ecological tool used by human being to change the environment for his own benefit. Indeed fire has been used around the world by early people to clear the land for improved travel, hunting and farming. During this period, early man changed the environment, (i) gathering fruits, nuts and hunting animals for his food; (ii) by decreasing abundance of some animals by hunting; (iii) by increasing the abundance of other animals when they altered the habitats of animals and made them more favourable to those species; and (iv) by burning forest to drive away dangerous animals.

3.3.2 Period of Animal Domestication and Pastoralism

With the passage of time, early man learned to domesticate animals. Gradually the number of domesticated animals increased which necessitated creating ranches (temporary) fenced with branches of trees and thorny bushes. Thus, early man used to burn forest to create temporary home for the domesticated animals and to exploit forest resources to gather fodder for his animals. With the advance of time he has gathered larger herds of domesticated animals. He still stuck to nomadic way of life as they had to move from one place to another in search of fodder for their animals and food for them. In this way he exploited natural environment but could not change natural state of environment because both human population and domesticated animals population was under manageable size. During this period, the pastoralists changed the environment, (i) by domesticating animals; (ii) by burning forest for making his movement easy with domesticated animals; and (iii) by creating temporary habitats for him along with domesticated animals.

3.3.3 Period of Plant Domestication and Agriculture

Domestication of plants is a hallmark in development of human skill in taming biotic components of natural environment. Primitive type of agriculture and sedentary settled life of people was initiated by domestication of plants. Practice of agriculture resulted into formation of social groups and organizations which gave birth to early human civilization known as 'river valley civilization' due to availability of water and fertile land in river valleys. Improvement in farming practices resulted into increase of both human population and population of domesticated animals and thus, more and more forests were cleared with the help of advanced tools and weapons. People also moved from areas of greater concentration to the areas in search of new fertile land. Man developed his new cultural environment by building houses and thus creating villages, towns and cities; and also by constructing roads, railways, canals, dams etc. So the 'natural man' gradually became 'social man', 'cultural man' and 'economic man'. Though man had changed the natural environment significantly by this time, but he had not damaged the environment. During this period he changed the natural environment, (i) by practicing agriculture, (ii) by changing erosion rates by agricultural and other land clearing practices and thus altering soil as well as vegetation; (iii) by creating settlements; and (iv) by developing transportation system and irrigation system.

3.3.4 Period of Science Technology and Industrialization

Industrial revolution in 19th Century initiated hostile relationship between man and natural environment. With the development of science and sophisticated technology, man became 'technological man' and led to reckless and indiscriminate rapacious exploitation of natural resources for industrial growth and urban expansion. The impacts of modern technological man on natural environment are varied and highly complex as the transformation or modification of one natural process leads to a series of undesirable changes in biotic and abiotic components of ecosystem. Most of the time, man could not be aware of adverse effects of environment at the initial stage due to the resilience capacity of nature. When undesirable gradual changes exceed the resilience limit of nature disastrous situations occur. During this period man is changing natural environment, (i) by the process of industrialization and urbanization; (ii) by emitting unwanted gases and pollutants to atmosphere which led to serious problems like green house effect, ozone layer depletion; (iii) by exploiting mineral and energy resources which led to resource depletion; (iv) by changing land use pattern; and (v) by polluting land and water resources etc.

3.4 Evironmental Crisis and Environmental Conficts

Environmental crisis is defined as a crucial stage of environment that has been reached in the gradual development of Man-Environment relationship over the time. This stage or situation is a very difficult or dangerous stage of human history that a real solution is needed. The environmental crisis in recent time is resulted—when the accelerating changes occurring in global scale due to improvements in environmental protection with advancement of science and technology are 'cancelled out' by the magnitude of pace of human population growth and economic development. Consequently, a wide range of environmental problems has occurred. Awareness of environmental crisis has increased since 1970s with incidents like Sahelian droughts, Chemobyl nuclear accidents etc. The main features of environmental crisis or main issues related to environmental crisis are manifolds. The important ones encompass the followings:

- **Climate change**: Modern man has changed the climatic phenomena by burning fossil fuels for industrial and urban development. The combustion of fossil fuel has increased the concentration of carbon dioxide in atmosphere which leads to global warming. Likewise release of chlorofluorocarbon from refrigerators and air conditioners to atmosphere is capable of depletion of ozone layer. The increase in atmospheric temperature, ozone depletion has resulted change in rainfall pattern, created urban smog, modified coastal ecosystem (rise in level change) and mountain ecosystem (melting of glaciers) etc.

- **Degraded air quality and water quality**: Air pollution is very significant at local and regional scales. In industrial towns carbon monoxide, oxides of sulphur, oxides of nitrogen, lead, various aromatic compounds are released to atmosphere which cause respiratory/cardiovascular diseases among people and cause damage to vegetation. All these in turn produce a range of ecological effects. The emissions from forest fire affect tropical countries like Indonesia, Malaysia in regional scale. Similarly, water quality is degraded by contamination with pollutants, giving rise to a range of ecological effects. The main sources of water pollutants are chemicals used in agricultural fields, sewage from industrial, mining and urban areas.
- **Scarcity of fresh water**: Besides the pollution of freshwater sources, scarcity of fresh water for drinking purposes in many parts of the world is a major issue. There exist vast differences in water security at the global scale, reflecting both demand for fresh water and the scale of public and private investment in water supplies, treatment and distribution. The over-extraction of ground water for irrigation purpose results in water shortages and problems of salt accumulation on agricultural land.
- **Deforestation**: Deforestation is the result of a number of causes like manmade forest fire for agriculture and pastoralism (in tropical areas); clearance of forest for industrial and urban expansion, and mining activities; destruction of trees for charcoal production and selective logging of forests for timber. It has been estimated that around half of the world's mature forests have been cleared by humans. Deforestation leads to many related problems like soil erosion, flood, droughts, global warming etc.
- **Soil erosion, land degradation and land contamination**: These problems not only affect agricultural and pastoral productivity, but also affect functioning of natural ecosystem. Reckless cutting of natural forest is main cause of soil erosion, land degradation and desertification. Land contamination occurs due to use of chemical fertilisers in agricultural fields, radioactive pollution especially by long-lived/ persistent chemical species that enter the soil.
- **Biodiversity loss**: Deforestation, alteration of drainage system, destruction of wetlands and mangrove forests are the main causes of biodiversity loss. Besides destruction of their habitats, many plant and animal species are threatened with extinction, due to the spread of disease and direct exploitation. Not only terrestrial ecosystem is threatened; serious concerns have been raised about the future of marine and coastal wildlife species as a result of the pollution, over-exploitation and acidification of ocean and seas.

In the foregoing paragraphs, we have seen a number of emerging issues related to environmental crisis. Though all these problems have physical manifestations, their causes and their potential solutions are closely related to human attitudes, beliefs, values, needs, desires, expectations and behaviours. The man-environment conflicts arise due to this. A range of social, economic, political, technological issues are the causes of environmental crisis. These are population growth, urbanization, industrialization, poverty, food/energy security, disease etc. The occurrence of natural disasters such as earthquakes, landslides, floods, tsunamis, wildfires has been increased manifolds due to large scale human interference with nature. Solution to these problems also depends upon what human being thinks about it. So, it is the human being who has to decide—the limit of economic development and environmental protection.

The environmental conflicts are not only between man and environment; it is also between different groups of people who use common environmental resources. The conflicts emerge when two or more groups of people have differences in interests, values, power, perceptions, goals etc. (Catro and Nielson, 2003; Yasmi *et al.*, 2006). Scarcity of resources whether it is actual or perceived is the main reason behind environmental conflicts. Conflicts arise for both renewable and non-renewable resources. Conflicts related to land, water, bio-diversity etc. are very common not at local level, but also at international and global level. Conflicts over water resources appear to be a major source of direct international conflict. Indirect international conflict is commonly caused by resource depletion issues—deforestation, soil erosion, desertification, flooding and pollution. The international level conflicts can be solved by the effort of international institutions, like the national level conflicts by governmental and non-governmental bodies; and local level conflicts by communities at national and local level.

Besides these, the global level conflict related to the global warming and ozone depletion may also be mentioned here. The developing countries blame developed countries and *vice versa*. According to the developing countries; global climatic change is the result of large scale development in developed countries; according to the developed countries, it is due to poverty, ignorance and unscientific use of resources in developing countries.

3.5 Summary

The study of Human Geography revolves round Man-Environment relationship. There are different approaches to study Man-Environment relationship such as deterministic, possibilistic, neo-deterministic and environmental approach. In different approaches the Man-Environment relationship is perceived or evaluated in different ways. Since pre-historic time, the Man-Environmental relationship is getting changed according to the action of man, i.e. from 'physical man' to 'social man' to 'economic man' to 'technical man'. Gradual dominance of cultural elements in Man-Environment relationship has created complex situation which would adversely affect the existence of man in future. The problems like environmental crisis and environmental conflicts are the result of unprecedented economic and social development. Balance of Man-Environment relationship is one of the keys to future peace.

Review Questions

1. Analyse the concept of determinism during pre-Darwinian and post-Darwinian phase.
2. How neo-deterministic approach is different from crude-deterministic approach in studying Man-Environment relationship.
3. Describe the concept of possibilism in detail.
4. Discuss the journey of man from 'physical man' to 'social man' to 'economic man'

to 'technological man' in relationship with his environment.

5. Write short notes on 'environmental crisis' and 'environmental conflicts'.

Analytical Questions

1. Analyze the reflection of environmental determinism taking examples of traditional habitats from different parts of rural India?
2. Analyze any type of resource conflict among different stakeholders taking example from your region.

PART 2

Space and Society

Chapter 4
Cultural Realms

4.1 Cultural Realms: Meaning and Definitions

The concept of culture lies at the heart of Human Geography. The essence of culture can be gauged by the fact that the cultural attributes influence the spatial decisions, patterns and landscapes. The origin of the term 'culture' gives few clues to its present meaning. In Latin, it meant *cultivation.* This meaning persists in usages as in agriculture or apiculture (bee culture) or pisciculture (fish farming). In English, the term culture denotes social refinement. It was only in the nineteenth century that the concept of culture was understood as set of attributes of human society that conditions behaviour. An English anthropologist E.B. Taylor was the first one to define the concept of culture. According Taylor (1874), "culture...is that complex whole which included knowledge, belief, art, law, morals, customs and any other capabilities and habits acquired by man as a member of society" (Stoddard *et al.*, 1986).

Culture cannot be understood only as arts (literature, painting, dress) of a society but is the specialized behavioural patterns, understandings, adaptations, and social systems that summarize a group of people's learned way of life (Fellmann *et al.*, 2005). The culture encompasses tangible and intangible features of human's way of life: prevailing styles of dressing, daily living habits, culinary styles, language, the architecture of houses and buildings, the layout pattern of fields and farms, and systems of education, governance, and political organization. Besides, the people's beliefs, traditions and values form the part of the invisible component of culture. These cultural elements are part of the spatial diversity that the human geographers study. There is a gradual change of culture over time which ultimately results in a contrasting characteristic between the hunter and gatherer of Stone Age and professional corporate in modern urban India.

Hoebel (1972) defined culture "as integrated system of learned behaviour patterns which are characteristics of the members of a society and which are not the result of biological inheritance... culture is not genetically predetermined; it is non-instinctive... culture is wholly the result of social invention and is transmitted and maintained solely through communication and learning." In short, Hoebel states that the culture is learned, not biologically inherited. Culture is transmitted within a society to successive generations through imitation, observation and learning. Furthermore, culture is a continuum, a form of social heredity persisting and changing gradually over time. One is born into a cultural context of beliefs, traditions and customs, just as one is born into a physical habitat of climate, vegetation, soil and topography. But, it is much easier to leave the physical habitat through migration than to reject our cultural inheritance.

4.2 Components of Culture

Human geographers analyse not only study different patterns and landscapes associated with different cultural groups, but also the ways in which cultural understandings affect both the creation and significance of those patterns and landscapes. To understand culture more meaningfully in geographical context one should be familiar with the terms like culture trait, cultural complex, cultural system, cultural region and cultural hearth which are the major components of culture (Figure 4.1).

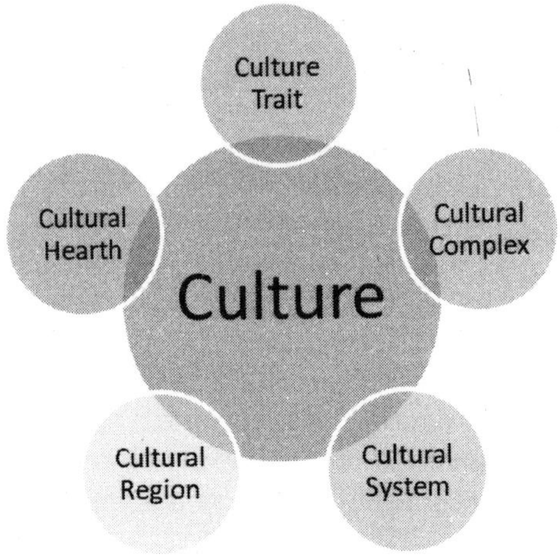

Fig. 4.1: Components of Culture

4.2.1 Culture Trait

Culture trait is a single smallest attribute of a culture. Cultural traits are units of learned behaviour ranging from language spoken to the tools used and carrying religious symbols. For example, the wearing of a turban can be a culture trait of Sikh community.

4.2.2 Cultural Complex

Culture traits are not necessarily confined to a single culture. More than one culture may exhibit a particular culture trait, but each culture will consist of a distinct combination of traits. Such a combination is referred to as a cultural complex, *e.g.* cultural complex of Sikh community. The Sikh community has such discrete combination of traits in the form of five 'K' or articles of faith that depicted the Sikh 'way of life' as commanded by *Guru Gobind Singh*. These are *Kesh*: uncut hair and beard, as given by God; and a turban: the crown of spirituality; *Kangha*: a wooden comb to groom the hair as a symbol of cleanliness; *Katchcha*: specially made cotton underwear as a commitment to purity; *Kara:* a steel circle, worn on the wrist, signifying bondage to truth and freedom from every other entanglement; and last is *Kirpan*: the sword, with which the Khalsa righteously defend the truth. The notion of cultural complexes is universal in nature. In the USA, a cultural complex exists around the automobiles (a cultural trait). Americans buy car of those models that reflect their income and status in society. Cinema and television have automobiles at their heart; movie like American Graffitti and series of Fast and Furious are some examples of this.

4.2.3 Cultural System

Culture traits and complexes may be shared by distinctive group of people, but they must be spatially associated. When enough commonalities exist, a cultural system could be recognized as a larger spatial reality. For instance, the citizens of India who are diverse in terms of religion, language, food habits and so on would identify themselves as Indians, together constituting a 'melting pot' and signify a unique cultural system in world.

4.2.4 Cultural Region

Cultural traits, complexes and systems have areal expanse. When plotted on maps, the regional character of the components of culture is revealed. Human geographers are concerned with cultural region, a portion of the earth's surface occupied by populations sharing recognizable and distinctive cultural characteristics. Identification and mapping cultural region is a significant task because they show us where particular cultural communities live with distinctive cultural traits/cultural complexes/cultural system. For example, the cultural landscape of Hinduism is found in India—its main cultural region. As one travels through India, the Hindu faith is a visual as well as an emotional experience. Temples and shrines, holy animals by the tens of millions, distinctively garbed holy men, and the sights and sounds of long processions and rituals all contribute to a unique atmosphere (Fouberg *et al.*, 2009). However, it is not logical to infer that only Hindus live there. This region is also home to millions of Muslims, Buddhists, Christians, and other non-Hindu communities. Cultural regions exhibit a certain level of diversity. Every cultural region will exist to have some or the other form of diversity.

Some cultural regions are similar to the notion of historical periods. For example, in history, the time segments are divided and labelled as the Stone Age, the Iron Age, the Industrial Age, and so forth. The purpose of these divisions is to make world history more comprehensible by dividing it into those periods that have some common culture. In a particular time period of history, the world can be divided into a number of cultural regions on the basis of different cultural characteristics. Cultural regions display considerable variety. Any number of characteristics such as religion, language etc. can be used to define cultural regions. Figure 4.2 shows cultural regions delineated by Heatwole (2006) on the basis of religions. These cultural regions are based on a single cultural component which is religion.

In contrast, if one plots maps of cultural regions of India with respect to religion, language, caste, cuisine, folk culture, dress etc, the list goes long. For having a comparative idea, one might then compare these maps with that of some other country. Furthermore, cultural regions differ greatly in size. Some are proportionately large, like the Islamic culture region that encompasses of North Africa and Southwest Asia, *vis-à-vis*, some are very small,

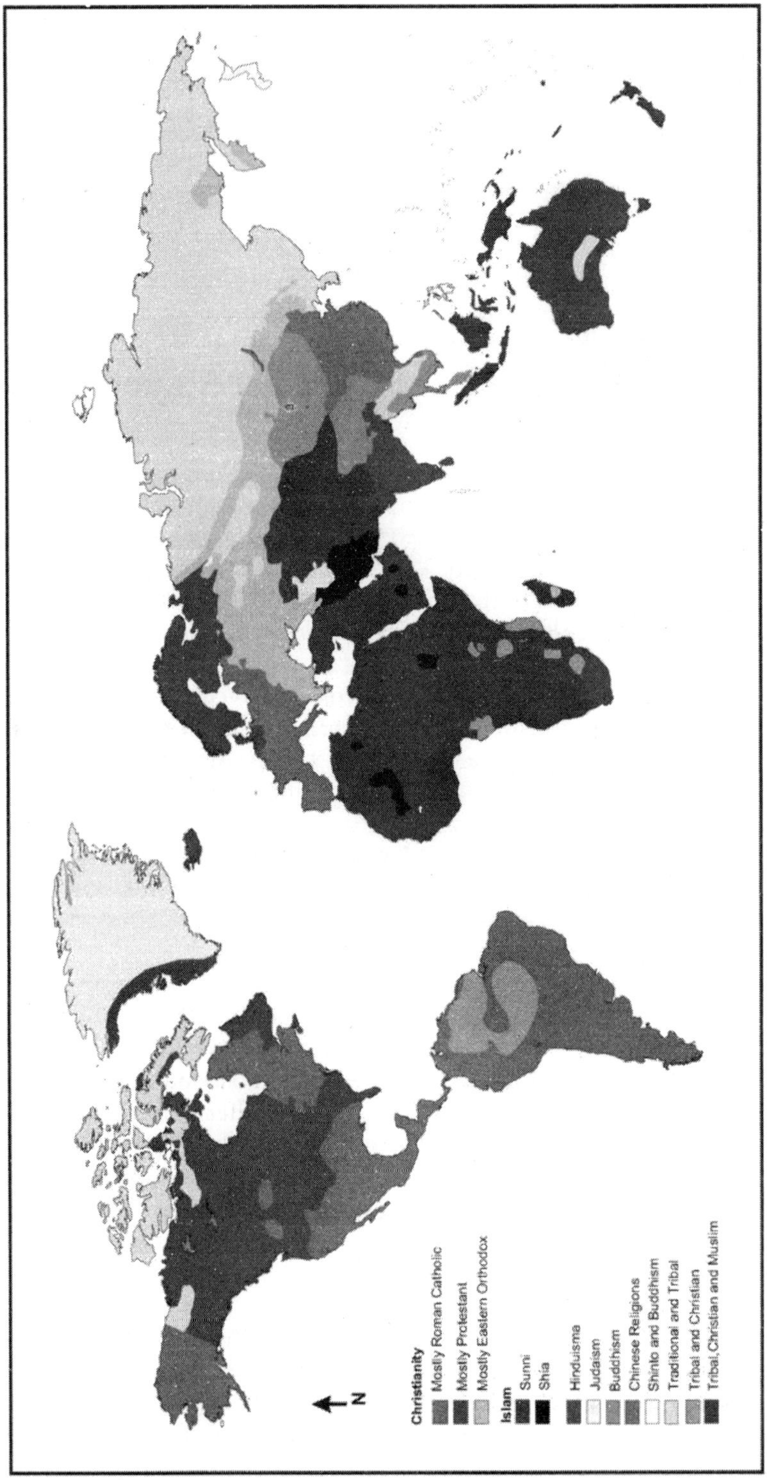

Fig. 4.2: Various Cultural Realms of the World

Source: http://www2.johnabbott.qc.ca/~geoscience/intro/worldculturalRealms.htm

like East Harlem, which is a small neighbourhood of Manhattan, New York.

4.2.5 Cultural Hearth

A cultural hearth is an area where cultural traits evolve and from where the cultural traits diffuse to other regions. For example the cultural trait of religion, the religion of Islam, can be traced to a single place and time. Prophet Muhammad founded Islam in the 7th Century in and around the cities of Mecca and Medina on the Arabian Peninsula (BBC, UK, 2014). In a same way, many cultural hearths can be traced in the world.

4.3 Characteristics of Cultural Realms

A cultural realm is a geographical region where the population has distinctive and homogenous cultural traits. Sauer's (1925) concept of cultural landscape encouraged geographers for cultural regionalization. Scholars have considered study of cultural realms as an important part of Human Geography. Cultural traits and complexes have a spatial extent and cultural regions are used to show the spatial extent of these cultural areas. In fact, a cultural realm shows similar complexes and landscape grouped together to form a larger area. In other words, the cultural region is smaller in spatial scale when compared to the cultural realm.

The characteristics of cultural realms are broadly of two categories: *first*, a unique combination of cultural features should generally pervade the area to be organized as a cultural entity. *Second*, the cultural features must be strongly different from the neighbouring area for recognition and demarcation of the boundary. The term cultural realm implies an area of relative cultural uniformity rather than the presence of absolute uniformity. There exists broad transitional zones as boundaries between the cultural realms. Moreover, cultural realms are used as a technique for manifesting the influence of culture upon the spatial organization of landscapes. James defined cultural realm as "a unique segment of the earth's surface, within which there is a unique assortment of resources and habitat conditions, a unique pattern of political organization and an arrangement of people and production that is peculiar to the area." Figure 4.2 shows various cultural realms of the world.

4.4 Major Cultural Realms in the World

Brock and Webb (1968) emphasized the integration of a cultural system and the role of language and religion in sustaining cultural traits as they have been diffused from Europe and Asia. Both tried to establish the dominance of a particular phenomenon over the evolution of cultural landscape. They observed that the impact of religion is tremendous over the entire cultural system. Across the world, human beliefs, everyday activities and even dress patterns, food habits and social values are influenced by religious practices. To many geographers, these religious practices are also influenced by the regional geography. The religion and culture of a region are interrelated and it is evident from a cultural religious investigation which revealed that the culture of a particular region becomes ineffective once the religious impact is withdrawn. Keep this phenomenon in background, Brock and Webb (1968) divided the world into four major and two minor cultural realms (Figure 4.3).

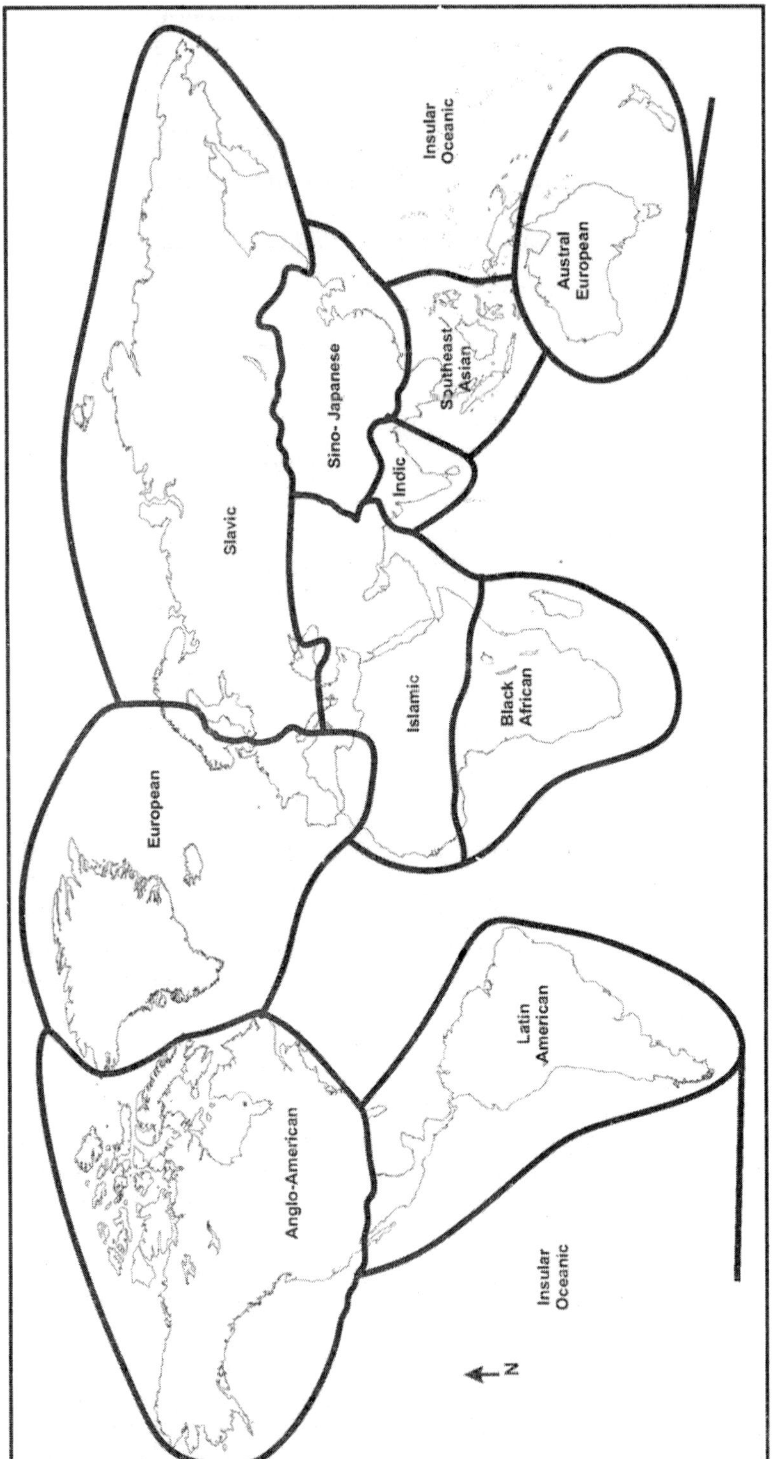

Fig. 4.2: Various Cultural Realms of World

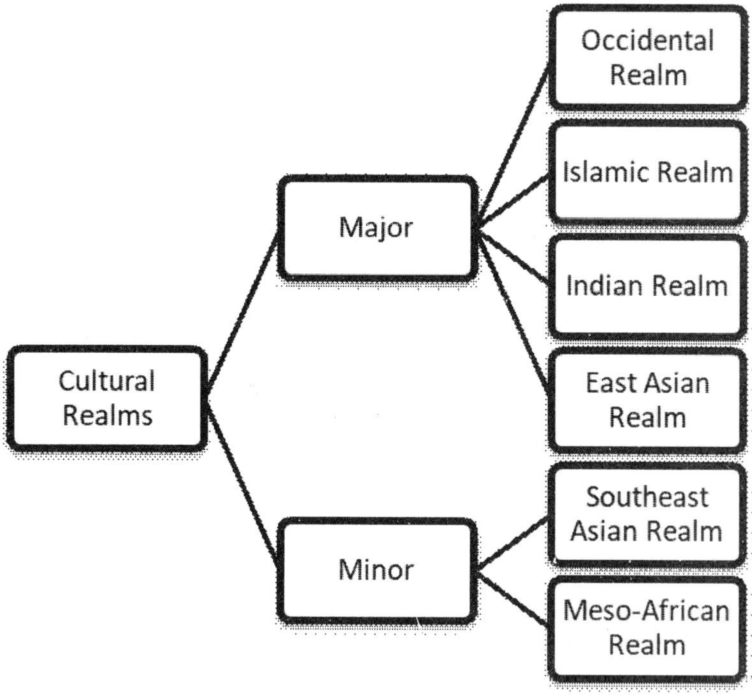

Fig. 4.3: Classification of Cultural Realms based on Brock and Webb (1968)

4.4.1 Major Cultural Realms

(a) Occidental Realm

Occidental culture is the culture of the Christianity influenced European society. This cultural realm covers entire Europe and extends across North America, Latin America, Australia and Northern Asia covering Russia. Occidental realm has regional modifications on the basis of varying levels of industrialization, polity and economic structure, colonization, commercialization, urbanization, transport system and development of social, political and economic institutions. It is observed that in many parts of the occidental culture, the impact of non-religious factors like the effect of modernization is so great that it has sidelined the influence of religious practices. Post-industrial Europe has rapidly emerged as a society where traditional values are nearly abandoned. Geographically, the occidental cultural realm is divided into six sub-regions considering the impact of regional environment.

(i) West European region comprises countries like United Kingdom, Germany, France etc. It is the most industrialized and urbanized culture.
(ii) Continental European culture, which is influenced by a variety of political and economic thoughts with Christianity as an important religion. Countries of Eastern Europe, like Poland, Hungary, Romania, Ukraine, Belarus etc. lie in this region.
(iii) Mediterranean Europe is the region of dominance of Christianity and includes

countries which are south of the Alps mountains. It is observed that the deep-rooted traditional social system is the major cause of limited economic development in countries of this sub-region comprising Spain, Portugal and southern Italy. However, when compared, the countries of northern and western Europe have adopted changes in their social structures and are ahead in economic development.

(iv) Anglo-America is an outcome of the west European culture as it is inhabited by west European migrants. United States of America (USA) and Canada forms part of Anglo-America. British Empire had great influence on this region.

(v) Australian cultural realm which is an offspring of west European culture, and has large number of migrants from west Europe.

(vi) Latin American culture is analogous to the Mediterranean culture. Mexico, Brazil, Argentina, Chile, Colombia, Panama etc. form part of Latin America. It is the only region of occidental culture which is situated in the tropics. This sub-part is underdeveloped when compared to the rest of the occidental realm. In fact, it became a part of the occidental culture as a result of the conversion of the tribes into Christianity. Moreover, the colonial languages, Spanish and Portuguese, have been granted the status of state languages by all the Latin American nations. For instance, Brazil is the only Portuguese speaking nation in South America. Also, regional architecture has impacts of the Spanish and Portuguese styles.

(b) Islamic Cultural Realm

Islamic values influence the culture of this realm to a great extent. Geographically it extends from Morocco in the west to Pakistan in the east. The British called it the Middle-East and the Germans referred it a region of oriental culture. This cultural realm lies between the traditional Indian culture in the east and the modernized European culture in the west. The realm has sparse population due to inhospitable and extreme environmental condition. The coasts and desert oasis have been the cradles of civilization in this realm. It is important to mention that Islamic culture is based on traditional beliefs and highly orthodox, the impact of which is reflected in the low female literacy rate in this region. Interestingly, the countries of this realm have high per capita income, but they have low level of modernization.

(c) Indian Cultural Realm

Indian culture realm is the culture of the Indian subcontinent. Baker called it a subcontinental culture, while Stamp used the term paddy culture (Singh, 2009). This cultural realm is well-defined and lies between Himalayas in the north, Indian Ocean in the south and Hindukush Mountains in the west. Joint family system, predominant village community, caste, semi-feudal land relations, subsistence agriculture, paddy farming and common agricultural season of the region are the characteristics of this cultural realm. Though the region is inhabited by various communities, the social system has the impacts of Vedic cultural values of Sanatana Dharma.

(d) East Asian Cultural Realm

Basically, East Asian cultural realm is a Buddhist culture with regional modifications. A true form of Buddhist culture can be observed in South Korea and Japan. However, even these two countries have felt the impacts of industrialization, urbanization and modernization upon their culture. Also, the culture of China's mainland has modified the Buddhist system and modified culture was adopted after the Second World War.

4.4.2 *Minor Cultural Realms*

(a) Southeast Asian Cultural Realm

Southeast Asian cultural realm is a transitional culture where intermingling of different cultures have occurred. This region has such peculiarities that the dominance of Buddhism can be seen in Myanmar, Thailand and Vietnam, influence of Christianity can be seen in the Philippines, Indian culture over Islands of Indonesia, and Islamic influence over Malaysia and Indonesian islands.

The existence of Hindu temples and iconography as well as inscriptions in Sanskrit, depicts a strong influence of Hinduism on Southeast Asia from the beginning of the Christian era. In fact, it is impossible to say that one ethnic group or civilization has dominated cultural values of the region. Hinduism has been a force in developing a blend of distinct religions together for thousands of years in Southeast Asia to the point that often Buddhism, Islam, Hinduism and Taoism simply fuse so that one resembles the other despite their vastly divergent roots (Asia Sentinel, 2011). The following practices are evident of this: Buddhism is practiced in Hindu temples of Cambodia, Muslim wedding rituals and wedding dress in Malaysia are based on Hindu rites. The Garuda is the name of Indonesia's airline (Garuda is a large mythical bird considered as mount of Hindu Lord, Vishnu). The Naga, the sacred Hindu serpent, is prevalent in both Buddhist and Hindu cultures. Stories from the *Ramayana* and the *Mahabharata* became widely known in Southeast Asia and are still popular in local versions (Asia Sentinel, 2011).

The spread of Buddhism has been dependent upon the missionaries. King Ashoka (Mauryan Dynasty) of India sent ambassadors, missionaries and monks to spread the teachings of Buddha in Southeast Asia. Buddhism began with the instruction of Buddhist teachings to the Mon people in Burma (Myanmar), which were the earliest ethnic group in Southeast Asia and gradually, the new inhabitants to Burma adopted the Mon people's culture, script, and religion. As a result, entire region came under the influence of Buddhism.

From tenth century onwards, Islam made presence in this region as Muslims started trading in Southeast Asia, and a few individuals from Southeast Asia travelled to the Middle-East for study. The major factor contributing Islamic influence on Southeast Asia is the trade route passing from Yemen and the Swahili coast across to the Malabar Coast and then the Bay of Bengal. The another factor was the adoption of Islam by a ruler or chief—sometimes because of "a desire to attract traders, or to be associated with powerful Muslim kingdoms like Mamluk Egypt, Ottoman Turkey and Mughal India, or because of the attraction of Muslim teaching" (Andaya and Andaya, 2015). Mystical Islam also known as Sufism, which aimed at direct contact with Allah with the help of a teacher using techniques such as meditation and trance, was very enchanting. A major development was the decision of the ruler of Melaka, on the west coast of the Malay Peninsula, to adopt Islam around 1430. Melaka was a key trading centre, and the Malay language, spoken in the Malay Peninsula and east Sumatra, was used as a lingua franca in trading ports throughout the

Malay-Indonesian archipelago. Malay is not a difficult language to learn, and it was already understood by many people along the trade routes that linked the island world including many Muslim preachers (Andaya and Andaya, 2015). A modified Arabic script displaced the previous Malay script by incorporating Arabic words into Malay, particularly in regard to spiritual beliefs, social practices, and political life. As a result of its multiple origins, the Islam that reached Southeast Asia was very varied. The diverse and varied culture is the peculiarity of this realm.

(b) Meso-African Cultural Realm

Meso-African cultural realm is also known as the Negro culture. This cultural realm includes tropical Africa and similar cultural systems of Red Indians of North America, Latin American tribes, Australian aboriginals and several tribes of Asia-Pacific region. Historians have referred these traditional culture units as 'marginalized culture'. Some geographers have even included Eskimos under this cultural realm. Therefore, it is a widely scattered cultural realm characterized by marginalized and relatively isolated communities.

In a final analysis, a cultural realm exists not because scholars designate them, but because the inhabitants share a feeling of common identity with a place, as well as each other. Such a sense of geographic distinctiveness is called *regional consciousness* (Stoddard *et al.*, 1986). In different parts of the world, where cultural groups have occupied the same area for many centuries, regional consciousness is felt very strong and *vice-versa* is true as well.

4.5 Summary

It has been stated that culture is so complex which includes knowledge, belief, art, law, morals, customs and any other capabilities and habits acquired by man as a member of society (Taylor, 1874). It is also understood that the culture is learned, not biologically inherited. Culture is transmitted within a society to successive generations through imitation, observation and learning. Cultural traits, cultural complex, cultural system, cultural region and cultural hearth are important components of culture. Cultural realms are used as a technique for classifying the impact of culture upon the spatial organization of landscapes.

Review Questions

1. Write a description of your own culture based on the components identified.
2. What is a cultural realm?
3. Explain the major cultural realms of world in detail.
4. Elaborate the minor cultural realms of world.
5. Indian cultural realm is the culture of the Indian subcontinent. Explain.

Analytical Questions

1. Write a description of your own culture based on the identified components.
2. Indian cultural realm is the culture of the Indian subcontinent. Explain.

Chapter 5
Race

5.1 Race: Meaning and Definitions

The concept of race originates from historical classification of people according to phenotypes, categories of physical difference like colour of skin, hairstyle etc., that are linked to different genetic makeup or blood. Oxford Dictionary defines race as "each of the major divisions of humankind, having distinct physical characteristics." This understanding has negative implications in form of racial discrimination like the discrimination against blacks by whites in South Africa till last century, genocide of Jews by Nazi army in 1940s etc. (Panelli, 2004).

Race is a constructed identity. It is an example of how identities are built geographically. Biologically, all people are part of the same race—the human race. The various 'races' to which people refer are not biologically based. It is interesting to know that from where did our society get the idea that humans fall into different categories of race? Fouberg *et al.* (2009) answer that throughout history, societies in different parts of the world have drawn distinctions among peoples based on their physical characteristics, but many of societies' modern assumptions about race grew out of the period of European exploration and colonialism. Anderson (1991) argues that differences in socio-economic classes fuelled the concept of superiority attached to race or racism. Racism refers to the practice of enforcing difference and relies on the power relations that inhere in relations between different groups understood as belonging to different races (Warf, 2006).

Anderson (1991) also notes that even before exploration and colonialism, wealthy Europeans defined themselves as superior to those living elsewhere. While during the exploration and colonialism, the non-wealthy in colonizing countries defined themselves as superior to the people in the colonies. "Colonial racism was a major element in that conception of 'Empire' which attempted to weld dynastic legitimacy and national community. It did so by generalizing a principle of innate, inherited superiority on which its own domestic position was based to the vastness of the overseas possessions, covertly (or not so covertly) conveying the idea that if, say, English lords were naturally superior to other Englishmen, no matter: these other Englishmen were no less superior to the subjected natives" (Anderson, 1991 quoted by Fouberg *et al.*, 2009).

Pertinently, one of the easiest ways to define the 'other identity' is through the skin colour because it is visible. In building our own identities, an easy way to determine who we are identifying against is by the colour of skin. What the general society typically calls a 'race' is in fact a combination of physical attributes in a population. Differences in skin colour, eye colour, and hair colour are variations within the human race. These differences are the result from a long history of adaptation to different environments. It is understood that the sunlight stimulates the production of melanin, which protects skin from damaging ultraviolet rays of the sun; the more melanin that is present, the darker the skin will be. That is why, humans living in tropical region with maximum sunlight have darker skin colour.

5.2 Classification of Human Race

Many geography textbooks have illustrated that how race was used as a factor to classify people. The classification of Linnaeus (1758) is a pioneering first classification of races based on the continents, viz. American, African, European and Asiatic. Blumenbach (1806) modified it to Caucasian, Mongolian, American, Ethopian and Malay. Griffith Taylor's classification is another popular work on the classification of races of mankind by taking cephalic index and hair structure as the basis of classification.

5.2.1 Griffith Taylor's Classification of Race

Taylor (1921) in his work on 'The Evolution and Distribution of Race, Culture, and Language', published in *Geographical Review journal* has based his classification mainly on two criteria, viz. cephalic index (number expressing the ratio of the maximum breadth of a skull to its maximum length) and hair structure. The description of the habitats of different races is based on his Zones and Strata Theory, i.e. 'Evolution from the Map'. It was believed that the evolution of human races took place in Asia before the last ice-age. Migrations caused differential racial features and cultural artefacts like of Homo sapiens (Fig. 5.1). "If there is a centre where evolution is taking place, then after a considerable time, the various differentiated classes will be found to be arranged in zones, so that the most primitive is at the margin, and the advanced at the centre of the series of zones. Thus, the earliest class will have covered the greatest area in its migrations, but buried in the deepest stratum under the latest strata at the centre of evolution. This is the Zone and Strata concept which is also referred as 'Age and Area' concept by biologists" (Taylor, 1921).

The classification divides the human races with subsequent explanation of Mongolian race, Mediterranean's, Australoids, Alpines, Nordics, Negroids and Negtritoes (Table 5.1).

a. **Mongolian race:** The main features of Mongolian race are brachycephalic (short skull), straight to wavy hair, yellow complexion, medium stature, oblique eye with an epicanthic fold. This race is further classified into two sub-groups: (i) Early Mongoloid, and (ii) Late Mongoloid. Early Mongoloids are spread in most of the Asia covering Central Asia, Korea, Japan, China, the sub-Himalayan region and north-eastern states of India. Late Mongoloids extends from the Alpine region of Switzerland to Manchuria region in China covering the central zone (Fig. 5.2).
b. **Mediterranean race:** The physical traits of Mediterranean race are mesocephalic (medium skull), wavy or curly hair, light brown complexion and medium stature. Their cradle land is Mediterranean region of Europe. They migrated to different parts of the earth including Egypt, Iraq, Iran, India, North and South America.

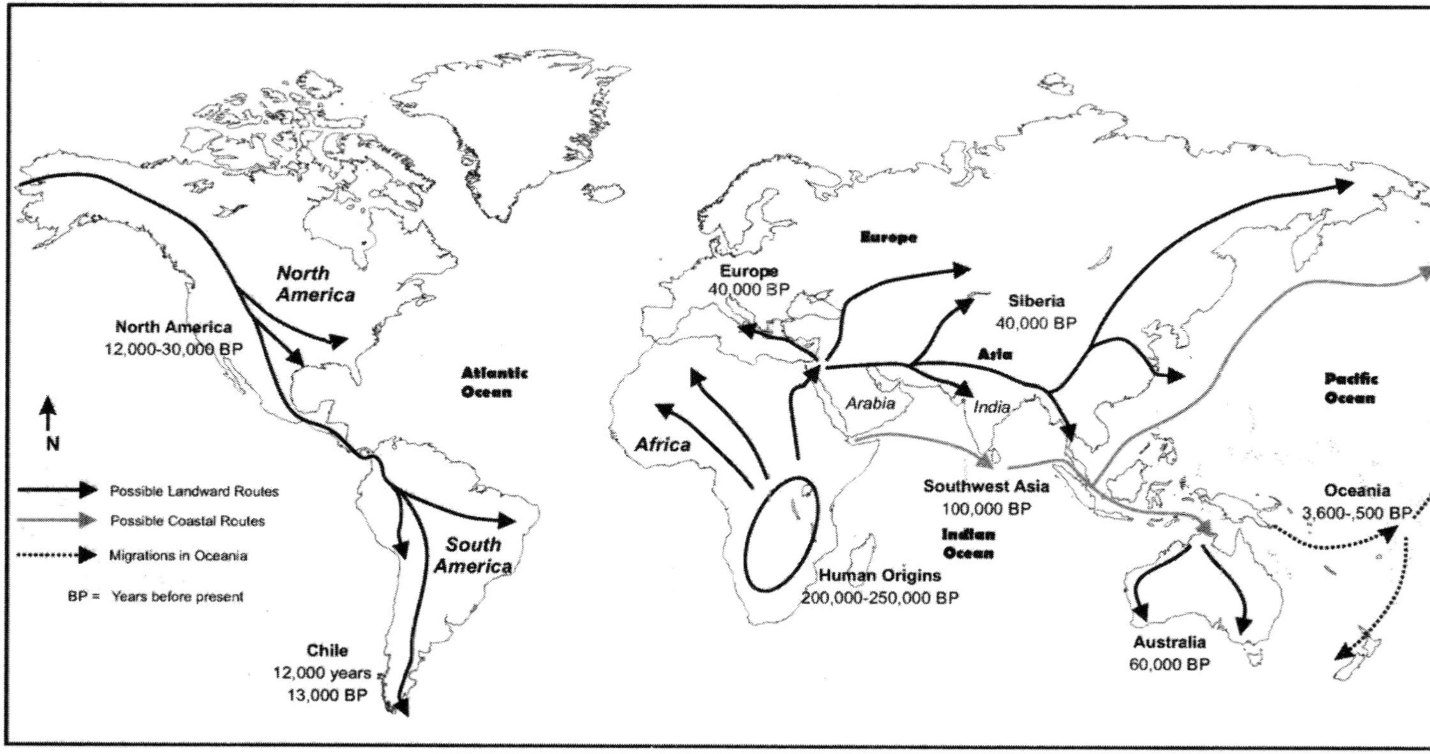

Fig. 5.1: Migration of Homo Sapiens
Source: Based on wikimedia Creative Commons.

c. **Alpine race:** The typical physical feature of Alpine race is brachycephalic (shorter skull), mesorrhine nose (small and straight nose with wide nostrils), wavy hair, light brown colour and medium stature. Their cradle land is the Alps region of Europe. They occupy a transitional position between the Nordic in north and Mediterranean in south. Swiss, Slav, Magyars, Fins and Sioux covering Switzerland, Poland, Russia, Ukraine, Hungary, Finland and other European nations belong from this race.

Table 5.1: Five Major Races (after Taylor, 1921)

Sl. No.	*Race*	*Head Index*	*Hair*	*Habitat*
1.	Latest Migrations a) Late Alpine Mongolian	88-83	Straight or Wavy	Central Zone and highest stratum. Extend from Swiss Alps to Manchuria
	b) Early Alpine Mongolian	83-80	Straight or Wavy	Second zone and second stratum in cradle land. Covers most of Asia and Central Europe.
2.	Mediterranean (variants Nordic Nesiot)	80-77	Wavy to curly	Submarginal zone, North Africa, South Asia, fringe in North Eurasia, South West Europe
3.	Australoid (variants : Pre-Dravidians & Veddah)	76-73	Wavy to curly	Marginal zone in peninsular India, Australia
4.	Negro	74-70	Frizzy	Marginal Zone in Southern Africa and Melanesian islands
5.	Negrito Farthest Migrations	About 80	Frizzy	Most Marginal zone and lowest stratum. Inaccessible forests or deserts or islands of Africa and South East Asia

Source: After Taylor, 1921.

d. **Nordic race:** Mesocephalic, Curly wavy hair, blond hair, blue eyes and long stature are characteristic physical features of the Nordics. They are also called by some scholars as 'bleached Mediterranean' who migrated from Mediterranean region to the Baltic region (Scandinavia, Estonia, Latvia, Lithuania). These racial features are also found in North West India and Pakistan. Anthropologists consider Nordic and the Mediterranean races as the sub-groups of Caucasoids.

e. **Australoids:** The Australoids appear to be dolichocephalic (long skull), wavy to curly hair, dark brown to black in complexion and short stature. Their cradle land is Australia from where they migrated to Eastern Asia, India, East Africa, North America and Patagonia. The pre-Dravidians in South India and Sri Lanka are Australoids. They differ from Negroids on the basis of their hair colour.

f. **Negroids:** Negroids have physical features, most of which are associated with the Negritoes. Dolichocephalic (long skull), ulotrichi (wooly, tightly curled hair), flat nosed and dark are some of their physical features. Negroids are divided into two categories: (a) African Negroes and (b) Oceanic Negroes. African Negroes

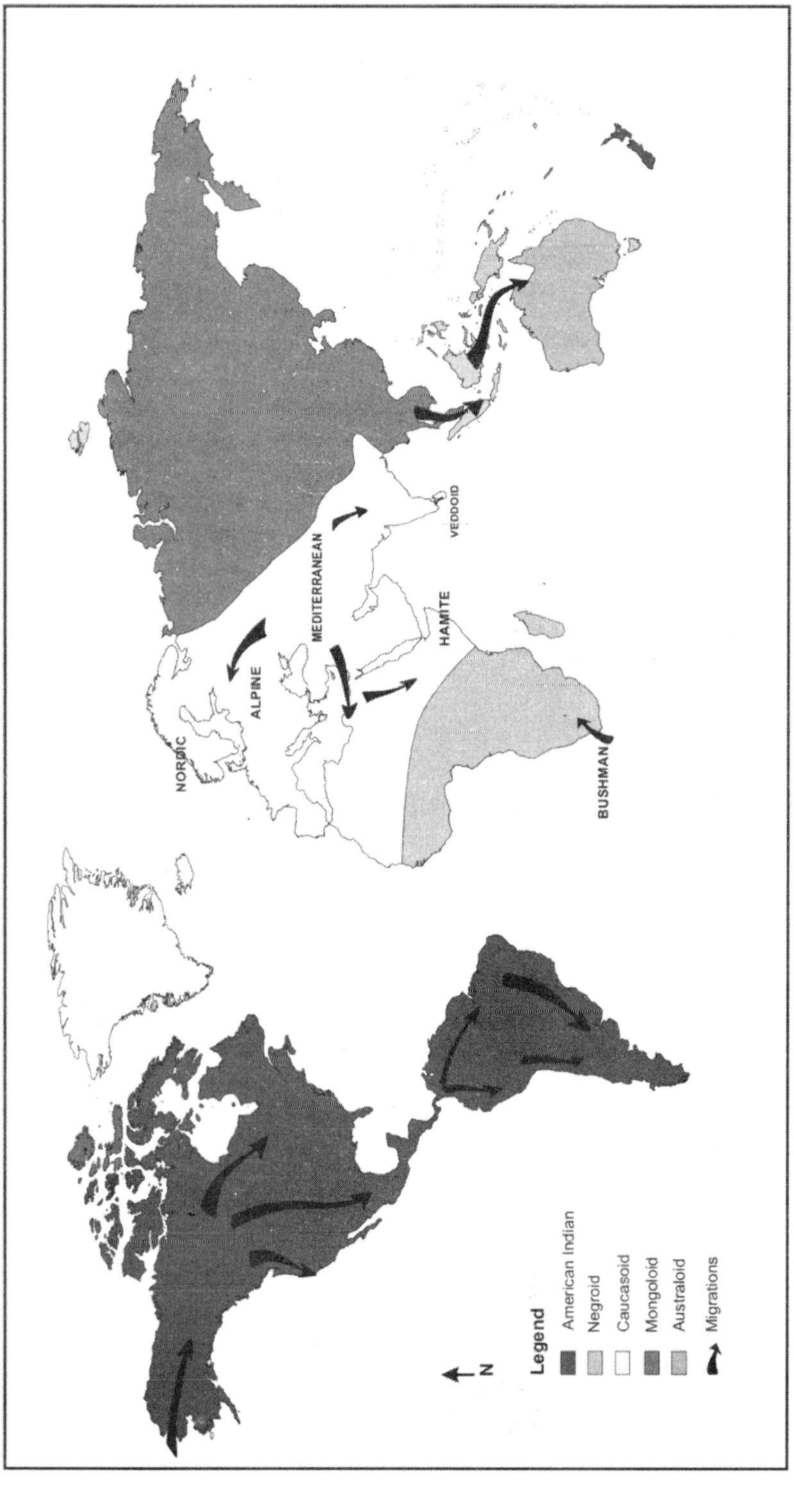

Fig. 5.2: Distribution of Races in 1500 AD
Source: Singh (2009).

comprised the Negroes from West Africa, Cameroon and Congo were transported to USA as slaves of whites to work on agricultural fields. The southern Africa also constitutes of African Negroids. Papuans of New Guinea, Melayesians of Melanesia, Semangs of Malaysia and Aetas of Philippines fall under the category of Oceanic Negroes.

g. **Negritoes:** The Negritoes are short in stature, flat nosed, woolly haired, dolichocephalic and black people. Most anthropologists accept Asia as a place of origin for Alpine, Mediterranean and Australoid races. However, Taylor was of view that Asia was also the cradle land of the Negritoes and Negroes who migrated to Africa. Blache (1922) has also highlighted the distribution of the Negritoes in scattered groups in Philippines, Malay Peninsula and Andaman Islands.

Taylor is also of view that Negritoes are relic of a very ancient type of man, contemporaneous with Neanderthal Man.

5.3 Race in India

Culture operates at various levels of society: nation, industry, occupation, corporate and organization (Groeschl and Doherty, 2000). Lenartowicz and Kendall (1999) observe that most existing approaches to study culture use nations that are convenient to define but usually represent broad unit of analysis. They suggest that culture-based research should identify and examine multiple subcultures within a single country.

India is a country with economic, caste, ethnic, religion and linguistic diversities (Stern, 2003). The recognition of India as a single culture unit could lead to wrong comprehension of the phenomenon and lead to erroneous decisions. India is a multicultural country with multiple groups and subgroups. India is home to several thousand ethnic groups, tribes, castes, and religions. "Like any other plural society, India offers a cauldron where the processes of unification as well as of fragmentalization are unceasingly taking place" (Bhasin, 2007). This presents a situation of cultural, biological and environmental richness and diversity, and one where the constant interactions between communities are aiding the formation of bridges, thus creating a sense of unity (Bhaskar, 2007). It is in these terms that India offers an ideal case for examining unity in diversity from both, biological and socio-cultural perspectives.

There have been different classifications on the people of India following different thresholds. Based on the reliability and standardization of the measurements, Guha's classification (1935) has been widely accepted.

5.3.1 Guha's Racial Classification (1935)

In 1935, Guha from the Zoological Survey of India attempted a classification of race. The Census of India (1931) published this classification. The classification was based on an analysis of 29 characters and 63 crude coefficients of racial likeness of different measurements of 2511 persons belonging to 34 groups. The survey done by him was claimed to have the great advantage of standardization of the anthropometric techniques. The application of Karl Pearson's coefficient of racial likeness was done to ascertain the biological relationships among the different populations of India. According to Guha (1931) there are 6 main races with 9 sub-types are found in India, which are discussed below in detail:

(a) The Negritos: Morphologically Negritos have dark brown to dark black skin colour, woolly hair, small, rounded, medium or long form of the head. The forehead is bulbous, the supraorbital ridges are smooth and the eyes are dark in colour. Negritos have a straight, flat and broad nose and their stature is very short in height or Pygmy. Negritoes are represented by the Kadars, Pulayans (Kochi and Travancore), Irula, Toda and primitive tribes of Wynad. Other tribes like Jarwa, Ongy, Nicobari, Shompen of Andaman & Nicobar Islands also belong to this group. They are considered to be indigenous habitant of India. It is considered that the Negritos are one of the earliest races in India.

(b) The Proto-Australoids: Proto-Australoids have features like dark brown skin colour, the hair is dark coloured, wavy and curly in form, long (Dolichocephalic) head, less developed and slightly retreating forehead. The supra-orbital ridges of Proto-Australoids are prominent, dark coloured eyes, broad nose which is depressed at the root and a short stature with delicate limbs. The morphological features of Proto-Australoids is wavy hair which is different from the Negritos who are having frizzly or woolly hair. Proto-Australoids are located in central region, paritularly, Chhotanagpur Plateau and Telangana region. It is represented by Urali (Travancore), Baiga (Rewa), the tribal groups—Chenchu, Kannikar, Kondh, Bhil, Santal, Oraon also belong to this group.

(c) The Mongoloids: Mongoloids are characterised by straight hair, obliquely set eyes showing epicanthic fold, scanty hair on body and face, flat face with prominent cheek bones. They are represented by two groups—(1) Palaeo-Mongoloids which are further categorised into (a) Long-headed and (b) Broad-headed, and (2) Tibeto-Mongoloids:

1. **Palaeo-Mongoloids:** These are of two types:
    a. *Long-headed:* The long-headed Palaeo-Mongoloids possess dark to light brown coloured skin, dark colour straight form hair, long (Dolichocephalic) head, short and flat face, supraorbital region is faintly developed, prominent cheekbones, medium nose form and stature. The people of sub-Himalayan Region represented by the tribal groups of Assam (Sema Nagas), Nepal (Limbus) and tribes of north-eastern hills like Bomdila, Abor, Miri, Dafla and Mismi constitute long-headed Palaeo-Mongoloids.
    b. *Broad-headed:* Broad-headed Palaeo-Mongoloids have dark skin colour and hair, broad (Brachcephalic) head, obliquely set eyes which show marked epicanthic fold, medium nose and height. They are represented by Lepchas of Kalimpong and hill tribes—Chakmas, Maghs of Chittagong.
2. ***Tibeto-Mongoloids:*** The features of Tibeto-Mongoloids are light brown skin colour, dark and straight hair, the head form is broad (Brachycephalic) and massive, the face is long and flat. The eyes of Tibeto-Mongoloids are oblique having marked epicanthic fold, the nose shape is long to medium and they are tall in stature. The Tibetans of Bhutan, Sikkim, Himachal and Ladakh are representing this type.

(d) The Mediterranean: They have been categorized in three different racial sub-types:

1. ***Palaeo-Mediterranean:*** They are considered as very ancient people.

Morphologically Palaeo-Mediterranean have dark skin colour and dark hair with a wavy to curly hair form, long (Dolichocephalic) head form and narrow with bulbous forehead. Their face is narrow with pointed chin, dark eyes, small and broad nose. Besides, the stature is medium height. The Tamil Brahmans of Madurai, Nairs of Kochi and Telugu Brahmans are representing Palaeo-Mediterranean. The Dravidians of South India show the preponderance of this type.

2. ***Mediterranean:*** Morphological features of Mediterranean include light skin colour, dark coloured hair, long (Dolichocephalic) head with arched forehead, long face having well-developed chin, eyes having dark brownish to dark colour, nose form is narrow and prominent and stature is medium to tall and slender body built. The Numbudiri Brahmans of Kochi, Brahmins of Allahabad, Bengali Brahmans, and Marathas are representing Mediterranean. The people of this group are inhabitants of Uttar Pradesh, Maharashtra, Bengal, and Malabar.
3. ***Oriental Mediterranean:*** The Oriental types represent all most all the characteristics of the Mediterranean type except the nose form which is long and convex. Punjabi Khatris and the Pathans are the representative of Oriental Mediterranean. The people of Punjab, Sind, Rajasthan etc. are representative of this group.

(e) The western broad headed people of Brachycephals consisting of three types:

1. ***The Alpinoids:*** Alpinoids possess morphological features like light coloured skin, dark brownish to dark colour hair and wavy in form, the head is broad (Brachycephalic) with rounded occiput, round face, dark brown colour of eyes, prominent nose; medium stature and body is thickly set. The representatives of this group are Bania of Gujarat, Kathi of Kathiawar, and the Kayasthas of Bengal.
2. ***The Dinarics:*** Morphological features of Dinarics are darker skin colour, dark hair, broad (Brachycephalic) head with rounded occiput and high vault, long face, dark coloured eyes, receding forehead, very long and often convex nose and stature is tall height. This type is represented among Brahmans of Bengal; Kanarese Brahmans of Mysore and the inhabitants of Bengal, Odisha, and Coorg. It is considered that Alpino-Dinaric people have entered India through Baluchistan, Sind, Gujarat, and Maharashtra into Kannada and then Sri Lanka. Dinaris have also been observed in the Indus Valley site, Tinnevally, Hyderabad.
3. ***The Armenoids:*** The Armenoids have most of the morphological features similar to that of Dinaric. A difference is that they are having more prominent, narrow and aquiline nose and occiput is more marked. Parsis of Bombay are best representative of this group.

(f) The Nordics: Nordics possess *skin* of fair complexion, brown to dark colour hair which are wavy in form, long (Dolichocephalic) head, protruding occiput and arched forehead, long and straight face and a strong jaw. The eyes of Nordics have a bluish tinge coupled with fine and narrow nose. Their stature is tall with powerfully built body structure. The inhabitants of Northern India, mainly the people of Punjab, Rajasthan are representative of this group. People belonging to this group are scattered over the mainland.

Therefore, all the six major racial groups are scattered all over the country.

5.4 Racial Discrimination

Early work in geography took race as a biological fact and used this so-called fact to map the geographic extent of racial differences. At that point of time, race and place were considered to be so interconnected that the thought prevailed that particular places have a particular type of climate that produces a particular type of racial characteristics. This knowledge framework was known as environmental determinism. It was dominant till early 20th Century. The mapping of racial difference in turn served to reinforce the idea of race as a biological fact and to reinforce racist beliefs and practices. This also played an important role in colonialism and Nazism. However, recently many geographers have turned to the spatial analysis of race and ethnicity, revealing that race and racial inequality are far from biologically given natural categories; rather, they are social products of domination and subordination that play out unevenly over space and time (Warf, 2006).

From the mid-1960s onward, American geographers in particular became explicitly interested in issues of race. This shift coincided with the reinvigoration of the US civil rights movement, which drew attention to the ways in which Afro-Americans had been systematically discriminated against by structures of white privilege. This also coincided with a movement within geography to make the discipline more socially relevant (Warf, 2006). As a result, geographers began to engage with social problems based on racism such as residential segregation, exclusion to access of public spaces, gerrymandering, and the creation of ghettos. For example, Massey and Nancy (1988) have outlined five types of residential segregation prevalent in cities of US.

Since problems surround the concept of race, ethnicity has been widely adopted as an alternative term and analytical concept. Ethnicity is a social construct as compared to race which is a biological construct. The concept of ethnicity as an identity originates from the notion that people are closely bounded, even related, in a certain place over time. The word *ethnic* comes from the ancient Greek word *ethnos* meaning 'people' or 'nation'. Stuart Hall explains, "Where people share not only a culture but an *ethnos*, their belongingness or binding into group and place, and their sense of cultural identity, are very strongly defined" (Fouberg *et al.*, 2009).

It is further explained that ethnic identity is historically constructed like all cultural identities and is often considered natural because it implies ancient relations among peoples over time. Ethnicity is a common cultural background having common language, traditions, beliefs, behaviour etc. For example, in USA, there are several ethnic groups like Hispans from Spain, Swiss Americans from Switzerland, Italians from Italy and so on.

5.5 Summary

The concept of race originates from historical classification of people according to phenotypes that were linked to different genetic makeup or blood. Race is a major division of humankind, having distinct based on physical characteristics. Taylor's classification of races is based upon two criteria, cephalic index and hair structure. Taylor also mentioned about the races. Race being considered as a biological fact, has given rise to the practice of racism. This gave rise to racial discrimination, genocide, segregation and exploitation based on the race. Since problems surround the concept of race, ethnicity has been widely adopted as an alternative term and analytical concept. Ethnicity is a social construct as compared to race which is a biological construct.

Review Questions

1. Explain the concept of race and racism.
2. How relevant is the classification of race presented by Griffith Taylor?
3. Is the concept of race operational in India? Discuss.
4. What is the difference between race and ethnicity?
5. Racial discrimination is making the concept of race problematic. Elaborate.

Analytical Questions

1. Is the concept of race operational in India? Discuss.
2. Racial discrimination is making the concept of race problematic. Elaborate.

Chapter 6
Religion and Tribes

6.1 Religion: Meaning and Definitions

Religion lies at the foundation of the culture as they reflect identity. Religion knows neither frontiers nor geographical barriers, however, tribal religion is an exception. Leong and Morgan state that religions originally grew up as a response to the way of life of a group of people. This chapter focuses on the geographical manifestations of the religious beliefs. The religion values are important to understand the variety of ways that people organise the landscape. As a major facet of culture, religion leaves a strong imprint on the physical environment.

Religion is a difficult concept to be defined. But some scholars have attempted to define its contours. Stoddard and Prorak (2004) define religion as 'a system of beliefs and practices that attempt to order life in terms of culturally perceived ultimate priorities'. Stoddard and Prorak explain that the idea of 'perceived ultimate priorities' is often expressed in terms of 'should' like people explain and justify how they and others 'should' behave based on their religious beliefs. From eating habits to dress codes, religion sets standards for how adherents 'should' behave. Similarly, Otto (1999) defines the essence of religious awareness as awe, a unique blend of fear and fascination before the divine. The main characteristics of religious life are: traditionalism, myth and symbol, concept of salvation, sacred places and objects, sacred actions (rituals), sacred writings, sacred community (monastic order), and the sacred experience.

All societies have value systems, common beliefs, understandings, expectations and controls—that unite their members, and distinguish them from other different cultural groups. This form of value system is termed as religion that involves a system of worship and faith in the sacred and divine. Adding further religion manifests itself in variety of ways. A form of religion can be seen in the worship of the souls of ancestors who are thought to inhabit natural objects, such as mountains, animals, or trees, another form could be a belief that a particular living person possesses special and supernatural abilities, and in the belief in a deity or deities as practiced in the great world religions. In some places, societies are so infused with religion that religious tradition strongly influences behaviours during waking hours through ritual and practice and even during periods of sleep in prescribing the orientation of the body (Fouberg *et al.*, 2009).

The conversion, migration, missionary efforts and conquest have been the major reasons of spread of major religions of the world beyond the lands of their origin. The cultural landscape is marked by religion most obviously by places of worship, cemeteries and statues and symbols. Figures 6.1 and 6.2 are some examplcs of such places of worship.

Fig. 6.1: A Christian Place of Worship (Church) in Moscow
Source: Authors.

Figure 6.2: Temple of Confucius, Beijing
Source: Authors.

Other more subtle symbols of religion dot the landscape as well. The presence or absence of stores selling alcohol or of signs depicting the do's and don'ts for devotees reflect the prevailing religious views. Religion is also proclaimed in modes of dress (veils, turbans), personal habits (beards, ritual scars), food habits, clothing and shelter. The outward display of religious beliefs often reveals the inward structure of a religion. For example, in 1991, the Pakistan government proclaimed that possessing a beard would be a condition for the appointment of judges. The beard requirement is an outward display of religion, and it also shows the inward structure of Islam in Pakistan, where women are kept away from the place of power and decision making. Another example can be of the religious restrictions on food that may affect the kinds of animals that are raised, being revered or those being forbidden. Further, some religions like Sikh Khalsa Panth follow various rules of observance such as prohibiting the cutting of one's hair.

Human geographers are particularly concerned with the interaction between religion and the landscape. Religion as a culture rallying point—recognizes God as an object of worship, love and reverence—leaves a strong imprint on the natural environment. Religion may be studied as a geographic process with a point of origin, pattern of diffusion and current distribution across the earth's surface. The relationship between the environment and religion is evident from the fact that religious content may be derived from the events in physical environment. A quote from Guru Granth Sahib can be mentioned here *"Pavan guru, paanee pitaa, Maataa dharat mahat"* which means that Wind is the teacher, Water is the father, and Earth is the great mother. In fact, like other cultural characteristics, religion is a source of pride to the people and an identification of a distinct culture. This intense identification with one's religion has led to conflicts between different religious and secular political organizations.

The basic task of human geographers is to study the process of diffusion of religions from one location to another and resulting in a distinctive spatial distribution. The distribution of a particular religion is generated by process of spatial interaction, as religion is diffused from a point of origin and follows a distinctive pattern of communication networks. Fact of the matter for the geographers is that this process of diffusion of a religion is important because it is a major force in spreading of cultural values. Apart from the process of diffusion of religion, human geographers also explore the impact of religion on social and cultural practices of a region. The impact of religion upon landscape and resource management is also significant. Contemporary studies show that the economic impact of religion is enormous and people of different religions and ethnicity living in the same environmental conditions, nevertheless, utilise their resources differently.

6.2 Origin of Major Religions of World

Throughout, a large part of human history, virtually all religions were either animistic (belief that inanimate objects, such as mountains, boulders, rivers, and trees, possess spirits and should be revered) or polytheistic (worshipping more than one deity), or both. Around 3500 years ago, Zoroastrianism, a monotheistic religion developed in Southwest Asia. Some scholars believe that the monotheism of late Judaism, Christianity, and Islam can be traced to the influences of Zoroastrianism. It is also believed that Judaism was the first monotheistic religion. Nonetheless, Christianity and Islam are known to spread monotheistic ideas throughout the world and have marked a theological shift from a long dominance of polytheistic beliefs in many parts of the world.

It was around 500 B.C., four major hearths of religion and philosophy developed in the world (Fig. 6.3). The hearth of Greeks is along the northern Mediterranean. The hearth of Hinduism has its origin in South Asia along the Indus river valley. Judaism came from a hearth on the eastern Mediterranean and from a hearth on Huang Ho river valley, came the Chinese philosophy. These early established religions and philosophies impacted other

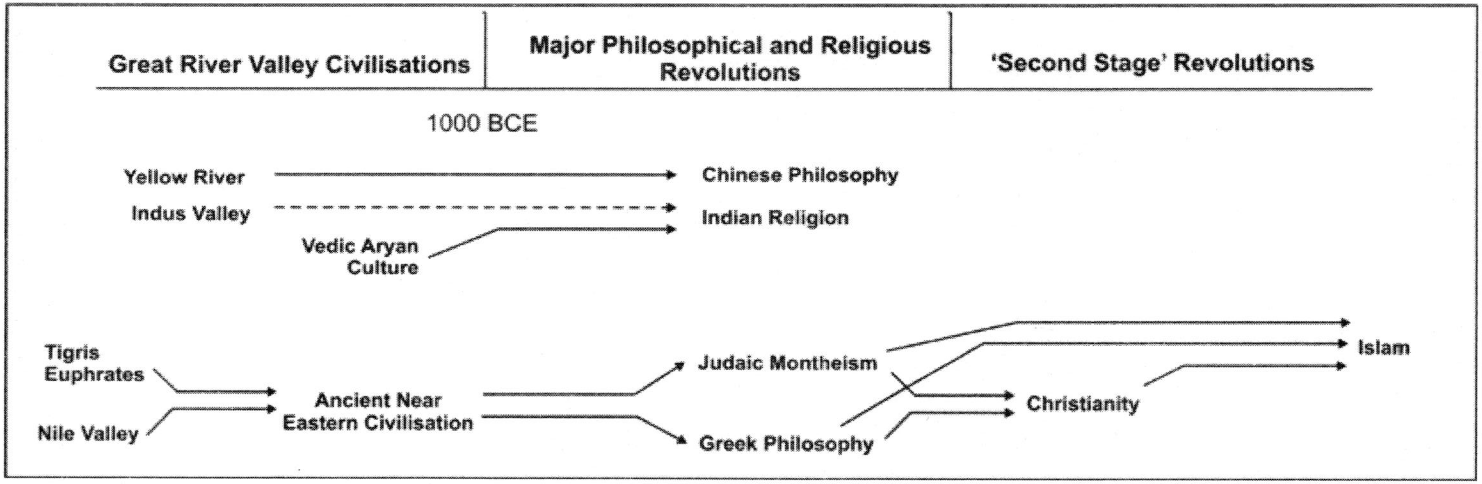

Fig. 6.3: Hearths of Major World Religions

Source: Adopted from Fouberg *et al.* (2009).

religions. For instance, the two religions with the greatest number of adherents in the world today Christianity and Islam, were both influenced by Judaism and Greek philosophy.

6.3 Classification of Religion

Based on the spatial scale a classification of the religion is given below. Universalizing religions are spread over a large area, while the tribal religion covers a limited area, with ethnic religion holding an intermediate place.

6.3.1 Universalizing Religions

These include Christianity, Islam and Buddhism. These are the faiths that claim applicability to all humans and that seeks to spread their beliefs through missionary works, conversion and conquest. Membership in universalizing regions is open to anyone who chooses to make some sort of symbolic commitment, such as baptism in Christianity. This is irrespective of nationality, ethnicity or previous held religious belief.

6.3.2 Ethnic Religions

Ethnic Religions have strong territorial and cultural group identification. One joins the ethnic religions on the basis of one's birth or by adoption or a cultural identity. These religions do not convert others. An ethnic religion is an integral element of a specific culture. Hinduism and Japanese Shintoism are examples of ethnic religions.

6.3.3 Tribal or Traditional Religions

Tribal or traditional religions are special forms of ethnic religions distinguished by their small size, unique identity with localized culture groups, closer ties with the nature and not yet influenced by the modern society. These religions are believed to be Animistic culture. Animism believes that life exists in all objects, from rocks and trees to lakes and mountains. For them, rocks, mountains, trees are the abodes of dead, spirits and God. An example can be sited of Dongria Kondh tribe worshipping Niyamgiri Hills in Odisha as 'Niyam Raja'.

6.4 Major Religions of the World

The section elaborates upon major religions of the world like Christianity, Islam, Hinduism, Buddhism and Judaism. The history, characteristics and spatial distribution of the major religions are discussed below.

6.4.1 Christianity

History and Characteristics

The religion with the largest number of adherents globally is Christianity (Table 6.1 and Figure 6.4). It was founded in the first century AD by Jesus of Nazareth (Palestine).

According to the Christian teachings, Jesus is referred as the son of God, placed on Earth to teach people how to live according to God's plan. Jesus of Nazareth was born in Bethlehem, and during his lifetime, he travelled through the eastern Mediterranean region preaching, performing miracles, and making followers. Christians celebrate Easter on the day Jesus rose from the dead after being crucified. Easter also known as Resurrection Day is celebrated on third day (Sunday) after the day of crucifixion which is named 'Good Friday'. According to Christian Holy text, the crucifixion of Jesus fulfilled an ancient prophecy and changed the fate of followers of Jesus—giving them eternal life. This marked the foundation of the faith of Christianity. Christianity is a monotheistic religion and is a split from Judaism.

Christianity in fourth century A.D. became the official religion of Roman Empire. Pope in Rome was the successor of St. Peter who was Christ's chief disciple and gradually Pope became widely recognized as the supreme authority in the church hierarchy. The first split in Christianity happened between the Roman Catholicism and Eastern Orthodox. At the end of the third century, the Roman Emperor divided his empire for the purposes of governance. However, his divisions left a lasting impression on the region and the religion. When the Roman Empire declined and broke up, the western region, centred on Rome, went into difficult times. The eastern region, with Constantinople (now Istanbul in Turkey) at its heart became the new focus of the Byzantine Empire (also referred as Eastern Roman Empire). Christianity thrived here and spread into other areas of the world. This split into west and east at the end of the Roman Empire became a cultural fault line over time. It was formally recognized in 1054 CE when the Roman Catholic Church (centred in Rome) separated from the Eastern Orthodox Christian Church (centred in Constantinople).

Eastern Orthodox Church: The Eastern Orthodox Church suffered blows when the Ottoman Turks took control of Constantinople in 1453 and when the erstwhile USSR suppressed Eastern Orthodox churches in the twentieth century. Today, the Eastern Orthodox Church remains one of the three major branches of Christianity. This denomination of Christianity is experiencing a revival in former Soviet areas now.

Roman Catholic Church: The Roman Catholic Church has the most followers of all Christian denominations. It claims to have more than 1 billion adherents. The Catholic Church with its centre in Rome believes in the infallibility of the pope in interpreting teachings of Christ and in formulating ways to navigate through this life. The power of the Roman Catholic Church was at peak in the Middle Ages, when the Church controlled sources of knowledge and corridors of power. It worked in conjunction with monarchs to rule much of the Western Europe. During the Middle Ages, authorities of church wielded their power in an autocratic manner and distanced themselves from the masses.

During the fifteenth and sixteenth centuries, John Huss, Martin Luther, John Calvin, and others challenged teachings of Roman Catholicism and the practices of the Church's leaders, which lead to the Protestant Reformation. The Protestant sect of Christianity composes the third major branch of Christianity—Roman Catholicism. Some countries in Europe such as Switzerland are divided into Catholic and Protestant regions. The Catholics have a highly developed spatial hierarchy system. The basic unit of geographic organization in the Catholic Church is 'diocese'. The Catholic world is divided into several thousand 'dioceses', each administered by a Bishop. Further, a diocese is spatially divided into 'parishes', each headed by a priest. Several dioceses are grouped into a province, headed by a bishop who is designated as 'Archbishop'. The Archbishops are subordinate to the Pope, who is also the bishop of Rome—a diocese (Husain, 1999). The climate, terrain and topography have affected the burial practices. The Christians bury their dead in a specially designated area known as cemetery. The Christians burial practices can be traced back to origin of religion. There were underground passages, known as catacomps, which were used to bury early Christians in ancient Rome. Catacomps also provide protection for the faithful at the time when the religion was still illegal. After religion was legalized, the Christians started burying their dead in the yard around the church (Husain, 1999).

Spatial Distribution

Christianity is most widely dispersed religion as its followers are found in different geo-ecological settings. Christians number around 2.2 billion, or about one-in-three (31.4 per cent) people worldwide (Table 6.1). About half of all Christians are Catholic. An estimated 37 per cent of Christians belong to the Protestant tradition which includes Anglicans as well as independent and non-denominational churches. The Orthodox group, including the Greek and Russian Orthodox, make up 12 per cent of Christians. And people who belong to other traditions that view themselves as Christian (including Christian Scientists, Mormons and Jehovah's Witnesses) make up about 1 per cent of the global Christian population (Pew Forum's Report Global Christianity, 2011).

Table 6.1: Size and Projected Growth of Major Religious Groups

Religion	*Population 2010*	*% of World Population (2010)*	*Projected Population (2050)*	*% of World Population in 2050*	*Population Growth (2010-2050)*
Christians	2,168,330,000	31.4	2,918,070,000	31.4	749,740,000
Muslims	1,599,700,000	23.2	2,761,480,000	29.7	1,161,780,000
Unaffiliated	1,131,150,000	16.4	1,230,340,000	13.2	99,190,000
Hindus	1,032,210,000	15.0	1,384,360,000	14.9	352,140,000
Buddihists	487,760,000	7.1	486,270,000	5.2	–1,490,000
Folk Religions	404,690,000	5.9	449,140,000	4.8	44,450,000
Other Religions	58,150,000	0.8	61,450,000	0.7	3,300,000
Jews	13,860,000	0.2	16,090,000	0.2	2,230,000
World Total	**6,895,850,000**	**100**	**9,307,190,000**	**100.0**	**2,411,340,000**

Source: The Future of World Religions: Population Growth Projections, 2010-2050, Pew Research Centre, USA, 2015.

There are around 430 million Christians in Europe and the former Soviet Union; approximately 355 million in North and Middle America; approximately 310 million in South America; perhaps 240 million in Africa; and an estimated 165 million in Asia.

6.4.2 *Islam*

History and Characteristics

Like Christianity, Islam, can also be traced back to a single founder, in this case, Prophet Muhammad who founded Islam in the 7th Century C.E. around at Mecca. Islam emphasises upon monotheism. Muhammad believed Allah had already revealed himself through other prophets including Judaism's Abraham and Christianity's Jesus. However, Muhammad

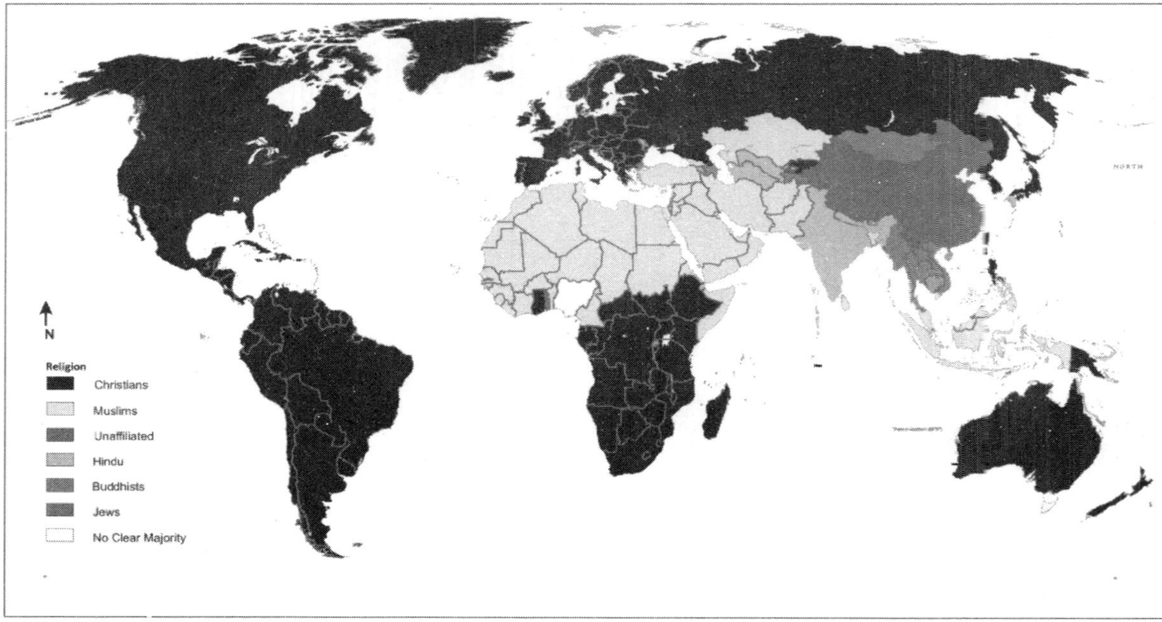

Fig. 6.4: Spatial Distribution of Religions in World

Note: Countries are coloured according to the majority religion. Darker shading represents a greater prevalence of the majority religion. Note: Nine countries have no clear majority: Guinea Bissau, Ivory Coast, Macau, Nigeria, Singapore, South Korea, Taiwan, Togo and Vietnam.

Source: Global Religious Landscape Report, 2012.

came to be viewed as the one true prophet among Muslims (Fouberg *et al.*, 2009). He spoke the verse of the 'Quran' based on the revelations directly from the God. Quran came to be known as the holy book of Muslims.

The Muslim creed consists of five articles of faith: belief in God, in angles, in Quran, in the Prophet, and in the day of Judgment. All Muslims have to practice the five essentials of Islam: (1) to recite the profession of faith in God, (2) to observe the five daily public and collective prayers, (3) to pay *zakat* (purification) for the support of the poor, (4) to fast in the month of Ramdan, and (5) to perform *Haj* (pilgrimage) if physically and financially possible (Husain, 1999). The faith dictates behaviour in other spheres of life as well. Islam forbids alcohol, smoking, and gambling.

Islam is divided, principally, between Sunni Muslims (the great majority with 90 per cent of Muslim population) and the Shi'ite or *Shiah* Muslims (concentrated in Iran). There are smaller sects of Islam which include Wahabis, Sufis, Salafists, Alevis, and Yazeedis etc. The religion's main division between Sunni and Shiah occurred almost immediately after Muhammad's death. The dispute on the succession was the primary cause of this division. Muhammad died in 632 CE, and some considered that Muhammad's son-in-law, Ali was the rightful heir to the Prophet's caliphate (area of influence). However, others preferred different candidates who were not necessarily related to Muhammad. This ensuing conflict was marked by murder, warfare, and disagreements.

Eventually the Sunni Muslims prevailed and the Shiah Muslims, the followers of Ali, survived only in some areas. However, in the 16th century, the state patronage to Shiah Islam by the Iranian (Persian) dynasty made Shi'ite Islam the only legitimate faith of that empire. This gave the strength to Shi'ite branch of Islam and created the foundations of its present culture region centred on the state of Iran. It is important to note that Sunni Muslims believe in the effectiveness of family and community in solving life's problems while the Shi'ites believes that the 'Imams' are the sole source of true knowledge and deputed by Allah.

Mosque is a place of worship in Islam where the entire local community offer prayers (referred as *salah* or *salat* and *namaz*). The mosque is organised around a central courtyard. The very important component of the mosque is '*Mihrab*'. It is a semi-circular niche in the wall of a mosque that indicates the *qibla*—the direction of the Mecca and hence the direction to which all Muslims should face when praying. Minaret, an another distinctive feature of mosques, is the place where the *muazzan* performs *azaan* (the Muslim call for prayers). Hasan-II Mosque in Morocco has the world's tallest minaret at 210 m.

Spatial Distribution

Muslims number around 1.6 billion; representing 23 per cent of all people worldwide (Table 6.1). Muslims are concentrated in the Asia-Pacific region, where six in ten (61.7 per cent) of all Muslims reside (Fig. 6.5). Many Muslims also live in the Middle East and North Africa (20 per cent) and sub-Saharan Africa (16 per cent). The remainder of the world's Muslim population is in Europe (2.7 per cent), North America (less than 1 per cent) and Latin America and the Caribbean (also less than 1 per cent) (Pew Research Centre, 2012). Although a majority of the world's Muslims live in Asia and the Pacific, only about one in four people (24 per cent) in that region are Muslims. By contrast, the Middle East-North Africa region has an overwhelmingly Muslim population (93 per cent), but they represent

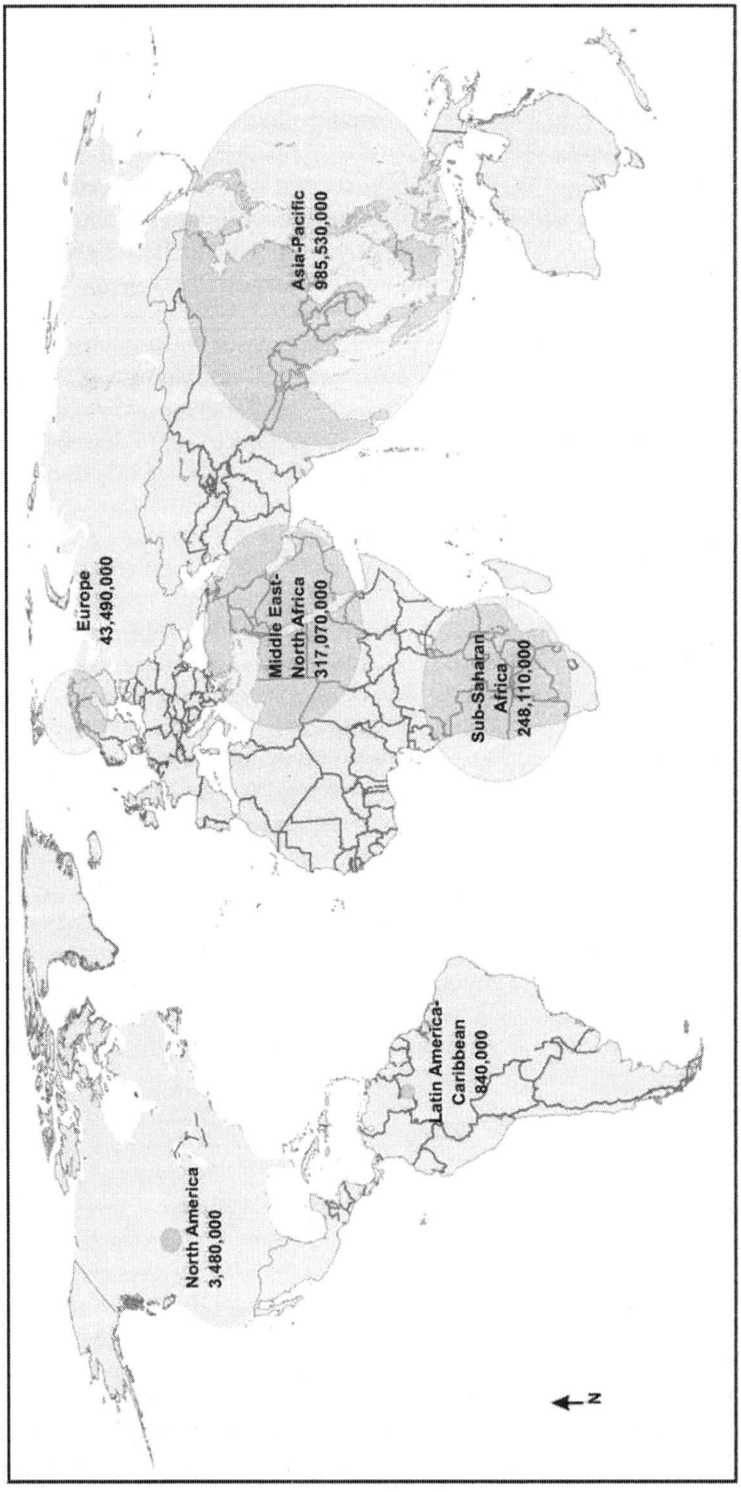

Fig. 6.5: Regional Distribution of Muslims
Source: Global Religious Landscape Report, 2012.

only about 20 per cent of the world's Muslims. Muslims also make up about three in ten people in sub-Saharan Africa, 6 per cent of those who live in Europe, 1 per cent of North Americans, and less than 1 per cent of the population of Latin America and the Caribbean.

Pew Research Centre, USA in its report presents that the 10 countries with the largest number of Muslims are homes to two-thirds (66 per cent) of all Muslims. The largest share live in Indonesia (13 per cent), followed by India (11 per cent), Pakistan (11 per cent), Bangladesh (8 per cent), Nigeria (5 per cent), Egypt (5 per cent), Iran (5 per cent), Turkey (5 per cent), Algeria (2 per cent) and Morocco (2 per cent). Although Muslims are a minority in India (14 per cent of the total population), India nonetheless has one of the largest Muslim populations in the world (in numbers).

The role of Islam in organization of space is significant in India. The impact of Islam in India is profound in places like Aligarh, Ajmer, Deoband, Lucknow, Hyderabad, Rampur, Ahmedabad and Patna. The Muslim rulers gave Mohmedan names to the new settlement established by them or renamed the ancient towns. Example, Shahjanabad, Akbarpur, Allahabad and Aurangabad.

6.4.3 Hinduism

History and Characteristics

Hinduism is an age old religion and in terms of number of followers ranks third after Christianity and Islam as a world religion (Table 6.1). The term 'Hindu' was derived from the river or river complex of the northwest India, the Sindhu. Sindhu is a Sanskrit word used by the inhabitants of the region, the Aryans in the second millennium BCE. Hinduism has its origin in the Indus river valley, now which lies in Pakistan. Therefore, the term Hinduism has geographical connotation attached to it rather than religious. Probably, the term 'Hindu' does not go back before the 15th and 16th centuries when it was used by people to differentiate themselves from followers of other traditions like Muslims. At that time this term may have simply indicated groups united by certain cultural practices such as cremation of the dead and styles of worship. The 'ism' was added to 'Hindu' only in the 19th century in the context of British colonialism and missionary activity (BBC, 2014).

Hinduism is a unique religion among the other world religions in a number of ways. The religion does not have a single founder, a single theology, a single holy text or any agreement on its origins. The Supreme Court of India defines Hinduism as a 'way of life'. Most Hindus believe in a Supreme Being—'*Brahman*'. He is the absolute God, a universal soul. The expressions of this Supreme Being are represented by the multitude of deities which emanate from Him. Hindus believe in the existence of a cycle of birth, death, and rebirth, governed by *Karma* of an individual. Hindus believe that the soul passes through a cycle of successive lives and its next incarnation is always dependent on how the previous life was lived. Hinduism is considered to be a tolerant religion believing in peaceful co-existence and acceptance of all faiths. This is evident from the fact that Hinduism has never expanded itself through invasion or forceful aggression in the history of the world. Believing in the noble idea of '*Vasudaiva Kutumbakam*' (World is one big family), it embraces all other ethnicities with harmony, compassion and brotherhood.

The Hindu religion is devoid of any central hierarchy unlike Christianity and Islam where the Pope is the leader of worldwide Catholic churches in Christianity and Islamic

Caliphs and Imams of mosques are stewards in Islam, respectively. It needs to be highlighted that though most Hindus recognize the sacredness of the Vedas—*Rig Veda, Sama Veda, Yajur Veda* and *Atharva Veda,* but there is no single holy book. If we elaborate about the Vedic texts, Veda is a Sanskrit word meaning 'knowledge'. These scriptures have not mentioned the word 'Hindu' but many scriptures discuss *dharma,* which can be rendered as 'code of conduct', 'law', or 'duty'. Hinduism is a conglomeration of beliefs characterized by a great diversity of institutional forms and practices. The caste system originated around 1500 BCE when Aryans invaded the Ganga plains in India. There came the four fold classification. *Brahmins* were the priests, *Kshatriyas* were the warriors, *Vaishyas* were the businessmen and *Shudras* did the menial jobs like scavenging and cremation. Gradually, *Shudras* were being considered untouchables or outcastes by the people from upper castes. They had no rights. With independence of India, the new Constitution abolished untouchability and gave equal rights to all irrespective of caste.

Spatial Distribution

There are about 1 billion Hindus in the world, representing 15 per cent of the global population (Table 6.1). Major traditions within Hinduism include Vaishnavism, which is devoted to worship of the god Vishnu, and Shaivism, organized around worship of the god Shiva. Because of a lack of census or survey data on subgroups of Hindus in most countries, however, reliable estimates of the size of the traditions are not available. The highlights that Hinduism traces its roots to the Asia-Pacific region, where the overwhelming majority of its adherents (more than 99 per cent) reside as displayed in Figure 6.6. Indeed, Hinduism is the most geographically concentrated of the eight religious groups analyzed in this report. Less than 1 per cent of Hindus live outside (Global Religious Landscape Report, 2012).

An overwhelming majority of Hindus (94 per cent) live in one country, India. The largest population of Hindus outside India are in Nepal (2 per cent of all Hindus) and Bangladesh (1 per cent). Hindus form a majority in just three countries: Nepal (81 per cent), India (80 per cent) and Mauritius (56 per cent) (Fig. 6.6). The followers of Hindu religion organize their space in a peculiar manner. It is important to understand that as an ethnic religion of India, Hinduism is tied to the holy character of the Indian landscape. The most of holy sites in India are river banks, coastlines, springs and waterfalls. As discussed earlier that Hinduism has no central authority, the relative importance of shrines is established by traditions and not by doctrine. Therefore, Haridwar, Amarnath, Vaishno Devi, Tirupati etc. attract pilgrims from the entire country. Many of the temple cities develop around a temple, as their centre. Madurai, Tamil Nadu where Meenakshi temple is located is an example. The caste system has also an impact on the growth of human settlements. There are inferior and superior cardinal directions in the Hindu religion. The upper castes, for example occupy the western, northern or eastern sides of the village while the *Shudras* (lower caste) are allowed to settle in the southern side of a settlement.

6.4.4 Buddhism

History and Characteristics

Buddhism was founded by Gautam (Siddhartha) around 2500 years back. The four sights or four events in Siddhartha's life made him deeply shaken by the misery he saw around

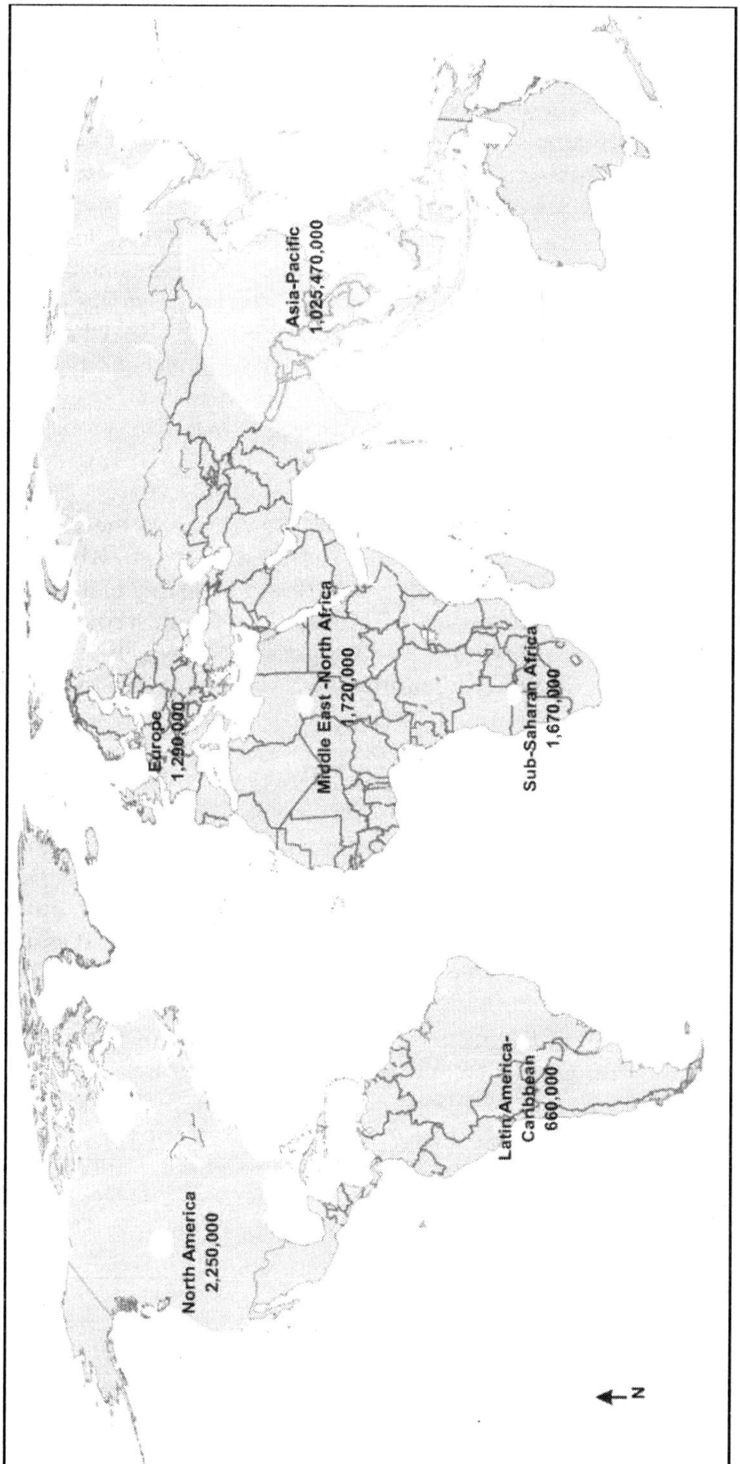

Fig. 6.6: Regional Distribution of Hindus

Source: Global Religious Landscape Report, 2012.

him, which contrasted sharply with the luxury and wealth in which he had been raised. This compelled him to transcend on his spiritual journey ultimately achieving the enlightenment. Siddhartha came to be known as Buddha (the enlightened one). He spoke against Hinduism's caste system. He preached salvation which could be attained by anyone irrespective of his or her caste. He articulated that enlightenment would come through knowledge, especially self-knowledge. Enlightenment can be achieved by elimination of greed, craving, and desire, being honest and by never hurting another person or animal.

In 489 BCE, after Buddha's death at the age of 80, the faith expanded slowly until the middle of the third century, when the Emperor Asoka became a convert. King Asoka ruled a large and powerful Indian state extending from Punjab to Bengal and from the Himalayan foothills to Mysore. Apart from ruling his kingdom in accordance with the teachings of Buddha, he also sent missionaries to carry Buddha's teachings to distant places. As a result, Buddhism reached to south in Sri Lanka and later advanced towards west in the Mediterranean region. It also spread over the north into Tibet, and east into China, Korea, Japan, Vietnam, and Indonesia, over a span of about ten centuries. However, Buddhism diffused to distant land but it began to decline in its region of origin. During Asoka's rule there were more Buddhists than Hindu adherents in India, but after Asoka's period the strength of Hinduism reasserted itself. Today Buddhism is practiced by relatively few in India, but still thrives in Sri Lanka, Southeast Asia, Nepal, Tibet, and Korea. Along with other faiths, it also survives in Japan (Fouberg *et al.*, 2009). *Pagoda* is a sacred structure of Buddhism. It is a tower with tiers and each tier having eaves (edges of the roof which overhang from the wall). Buddhism has suffered on Asian lands that have come under communist control. At many places, their traditional rights and privileges of monasteries have been abolished.

Buddhism's various branches have an estimated 488 million adherents, with Mahayana Buddhism and Theravada Buddhism claiming the most disciples (Table 6.1). Theravada Buddhism is a monastic branch of Buddhism that exists in Sri Lanka, Myanmar, Thailand, Laos, and Cambodia. It holds that salvation is a personal matter, achieved through good behaviour and religious activities, including periods of service as a monk or nun. Mahayana Buddhism is practiced in Vietnam, Korea, Japan, and China. This sect believes that the salvation can be aided by appeals to holy sources of merit. The Buddha is regarded as a divine saviour. "Mahayana Buddhists do not serve as monks, but they spend much time in personal meditation and worship. Other branches of Buddhism include the Lamaism of Xizang (Tibet), which combines monastic Buddhism with the worship of local demons and deities, and Zen Buddhism, the contemplative form that is prevalent in Japan" (Fouberg *et al.*, 2009).

Spatial Distribution

Buddhism, during the last two centuries has diffused over many areas of the world. There are about 488 million Buddhists worldwide, representing 7 per cent of the world's total population as of 2010 (Table 6.1). Buddhism began in Asia, and the vast majority of all Buddhists (nearly 99 per cent) still live in the Asia-Pacific region. Only two other regions—North America (3.9 million) and Europe (1.3 million)—have more than 1 million Buddhists (Global Religious Landscape Report, 2012). Although the majority of Buddhists live in Asia and the Pacific, only about one in eight people (12 per cent) in that region are Buddhists. About 1 per cent of North Americans are Buddhists. In each of the other four regions, Buddhists make up less than 1 per cent of the population.

All 10 countries with the largest Buddhist populations are in the Asia-Pacific region, and these countries collectively are home to the lion's share (95 per cent) of all Buddhists. Half (50 per cent) of the world's Buddhists live in one country, China. The largest Buddhist populations outside China are in Thailand (13 per cent), Japan (9 per cent), Burma (Myanmar) (8 per cent), Sri Lanka (3 per cent), Vietnam (3 per cent), Cambodia (3 per cent), South Korea (2 per cent), India (2 per cent) and Malaysia (1 per cent) (Global Religious Landscape Report, 2012).

6.4.5 *Judaism*

History and Characteristics

Judaism is the belief system of the Jews. The roots of Jewish religious tradition lie in the teachings of Abraham (first patriarch of Judaism). He is credited with uniting his people to worship only one God when the most of the societies still worshipped a multiplicity of gods. According to Jewish beliefs, Abraham and God have a covenant in which the Jews agree to worship only one God, and God agrees to protect his chosen people, the Jews.

The history of the Judaism is filled with upheaval (Fouberg *et al.*, 2009). Moses led Jews from Egypt, where they had been enslaved, to Canaan, where an internal conflict developed and the nation split into two parts—Israel and Judah. Israel was subsequently wiped out by enemies, but Judah survived. Later it was conquered by the Babylonians and the Assyrians. The Jews regrouped to rebuild their headquarters, Jerusalem, but again fell victim to a series of foreign powers. The Romans destroyed their holy city in 70 CE and drove the Jews away. This led to scattering of the Jews adherents to the faith in other parts of world. Most of, unfortunately, the Jews have been the victims of the horrendous Nazi campaign from the 1930s through World War II, when the Nazis established concentration camps and gas chambers to kill around six million Jews.

Spatial Distribution

An interesting fact is that the scattering of Jews after the Roman destruction of Jerusalem is refered as the 'diaspora'. This term now signifies the spatial dispersion or migration of members of any ethnic group or nationality and has been widely used in academia and politics. There are about 14 million Jews around the world, representing 0.2 per cent of the global population (Table 6.1). While Jews historically have been found all around the globe, Judaism is highly geographically concentrated today. More than four-fifths of all Jews live in just two countries, the United States (41 per cent) and Israel (41 per cent). The largest remaining shares of the global Jewish population are in Canada (about 3 per cent), France (2 per cent), the United Kingdom (2 per cent), Germany (2 per cent), Russia (2 per cent) and Argentina (between 1 per cent and 2 per cent).

6.5 Religious Landscape

The imprints of religion upon the cultural landscapes is evident with houses of worship such as churches, mosques, synagogues, gurdwaras and temples; with cremation grounds and cemeteries; with stores selling religious goods; and even with services like accommodation provided to religious adherents. The architecture of these places varies with time, location, cultural context and religious subdivisions. Mosques in Saudi Arabia differ from those in China, and the Hindu temples of north and south India contrast with each other. Notwithstanding these variations with the cultural settings, the structures identified within a particular religion incorporate common symbols.

When adherents voluntarily travel to a religious site to pay respects or participate in a ritual at the site, the act of travel is called a pilgrimage (Fouberg *et al.*, 2009). It is known as a '*tirtha yatra*' in Hinduism, '*Hajj*' (pilgrimage to Mecca) in Islam. Geographers are interested in the act of pilgrimage and its impacts on place, people, culture, and environment. Most interestingly, the holy places of pilgrimage in Hinduism are derived from the physical geography of India. It has been said that natural features most likely to rank among the holiest shrines in India are riverbanks (Rubenstien, 2010).

Sacred sites are places which are given special significance by people as locations of sanctity. Members of a religious group may define a space or place as sacred out of either reverence or fear. There exists a relationship between sacred places and the topographical features. The confluence of rivers, the source of origin of rivers, hot springs and mountain tops are often assigned sacred importance. For example, in Hindu tradition, Allahabad is considered sacred for its *Triveni Sangam*—the confluence of three rivers (two physical rivers as Ganga and Yamuna, and the invisible Saraswati River). Major places of pilgrimage in India are located mainly on mountains, hilltops, along rivers and seacoasts (Figure 6.7).

In India, according the recent Census (2011), the Hindu population constitutes the maximum (Table 6.2). These are mainly concentrated in the major states of India like Uttar Pradesh, Madhya Pradesh, Bihar, Rajasthan, Gujarat, Maharashtra and so on. In India, the second largest religion after Hindus is Muslims constituting one-seventh part. These are mainly found in Uttar Pradesh, Bihar and urban centres of the country. The Christians constitute 2.3 per cent of the total. Sikhs are 1.7 per cent of the total population and majority of them are in Punjab and Delhi.

6.6 Religion and Territorial Conflicts

Religious beliefs frequently reinforce political feelings about possession of an area. Religious beliefs and histories can bitterly divide peoples who speak the same language, have the same ethnic background, and even living together for years. Such divisions arise not only between people adhering to different major religions but also among adherents of the same religion. Religious conflicts usually involve more than differences in spiritual practices and beliefs.

Table 6.2: Religious Composition of India, 2011

Sl. No.	*Religion*	*Population*	*Per cent*
1.	Hindu	966257353	79.8
2.	Muslim	172245158	14.2
3.	Christian	27819588	2.3
4.	Sikh	20833116	1.7
5.	Buddhist	8442972	0.7
6.	Jain	4451753	0.4
7.	Other religions and persuasions	7937734	0.7
8.	Religion not stated	2867303	0.2
9.	**Total**	**1210854977**	**100**

Source: Census of India, 2011.

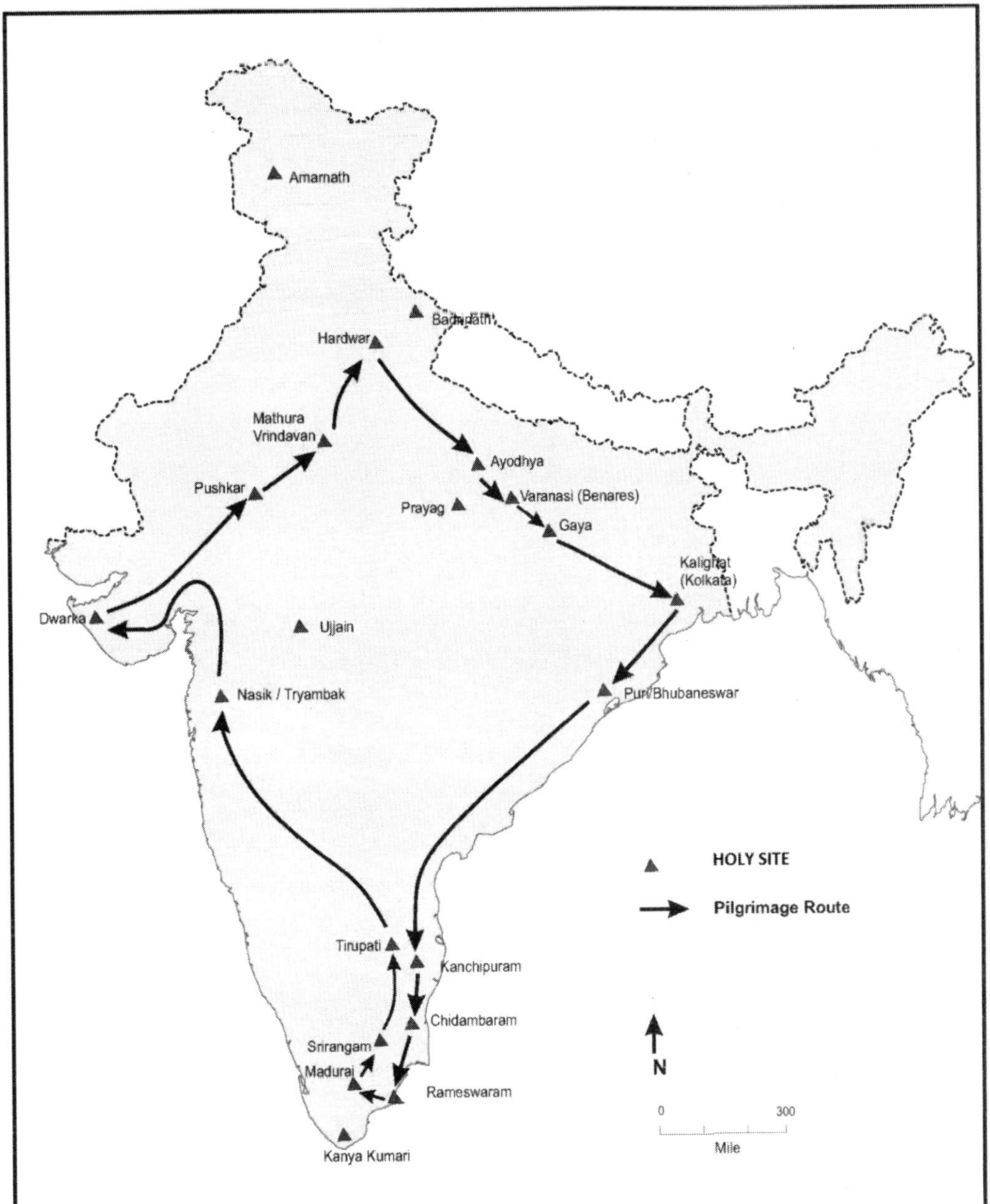

Fig. 6.7: Major Hindu Pilgrimage Sites and Routes in India
Source: Based on Stoddard, *et al.*, 1986.

Religion often functions as a symbol of set of cultural and political differences. The religious conflict in Northern Ireland also called as 'The Troubles' is not just about different views of Christianity, similarly, the conflict between Hindus and Sikhs in India has a strong political as well as religious dimensions. Territorial disputes become bitter when one of the contending groups believe that it is promoting the 'true' religion and spatially intrude upon the territory controlled by others. History has witnessed such events including wars, in which religion was a strong justification for spatial and cultural expansion by groups. Examples are the religious wars in seventeenth century Europe between the Catholics and Protestants.

It is important to discuss for the readers a case study of Jerusalem, as the bone of contention. The ancient city of Jerusalem (administered by Israel) is sacred to Jews, Christians, and Muslims. All three groups trace their origin to Abraham in Bible, but the religions diverge in ways that have made sharing the same territory difficult for them. Jews saw Jerusalem as sacred before the birth of Jesus. For Jews, Jerusalem is sacred and calls it as the Promised Land. Jews gather in the place to remember the story of Abraham and the destruction of the temples and to offer prayers. For Christians, Jerusalem is sacred both because of the sacrifice Abraham was willing to make of his son at the Temple Mount and because Jesus' crucifixion took place outside of the city's walls. In the seventh century, Muslim armies took control over the city from the Byzantine Empire. Muslims regards Jerusalem as their third holy city after Makkah and Medina. Muslims believe Muhammad arrived from Mecca and then ascended into heaven.

6.6.1 The Conflict of Israel and Palestine

The region of Israel and Palestine is embroiled in one of the most violent religious conflict in the world today. In the aftermath of World War I, European colonialism reached to a region that had previously been controlled and fought over by the Jews, Romans, Christians, Muslims, and Ottomans. A newly formed League of Nations (a precursor to the United Nations) recognized British control of the land, calling the territory as Palestine. At that point, the vast majority of people living in the land were Muslim Palestinians. The British government aimed to create, in Palestine, a national homeland for the Jewish people. This British policy created imbalance in the region. Civil war erupted immediately, and, by 1947-48, Jews and Palestinians engaged in open warfare. In the wake of World War II and the Holocaust, many Jews moved to the region. Shortly after the war, the British mandate ended, and the newly formed.

The newly established United Nations partitioned Palestine into two independent states—one Jewish controlled Israeli state and other Muslim controlled Palestinian state. Jerusalem was intended to be an international city, administered by United Nations. Palestinians and Israelis were to live in non-contiguous states. The surrounding Arab states reacted violently against the new Jewish state. Israel survived through numerous wars in which Palestinians lost their lands. As a consequence of war and the consolidation of the Israeli state, Palestinians migrated or fled to refugee camps in neighbouring Arab states. In the 1967 Arab-Israeli War, Israel gained control of the Palestinian lands in Gaza, the West Bank, and the Golan Heights. The international community calls these lands the Occupied Territories. Israel returned the Sinai Peninsula to Egypt in exchange for a peace treaty in 1979. During the last three decades, the Israelis built Jewish settlements throughout the West Bank, gradually the city of Jerusalem expanded eastward into the West Bank (razing Palestinian houses along the way) to gain more control of the territory. Moreover, the Israeli government severely restricts new settlement by Palestinians, even on lands in the Palestinian zones of the West Bank. Events in the early and mid-1990s began to change this religious-political mosaic as self-government was awarded to Gaza and to small areas inside the West Bank. Palestinian Arabs were empowered to run their own affairs within their zones. In September 2005, the Israeli government changed its policy towards the Gaza Strip. Israel evacuated the settlements that had been built there, burned down the buildings that remained, and then granted autonomy to Gaza. Palestinians now have greater freedom within the Gaza Strip, they are economically isolated and the standard of living has dropped. Today, the Israeli government tightly controls the flow of Palestinians and goods into and out of the West Bank and Gaza Strip. Gaza is surrounded by fences, and in some places a wall—with land mines in certain areas and dust road to show footprints. It is been argued that Palestinians continue to fight a war against the Israelis—by using terrorism. Palestinian attacks against Israelis threaten the everyday lives of the Israeli people; no place in Israel is safe from the threat of terrorist attack. Similarly, in the aftermath of a terrorist attack, the Israeli military hunts the suspects, shedding blood in Palestinian neighbourhoods.

While summing up on the situation in Israel and Palestine it can be commented that the prospects for peace in the region is very low. Despite of some signs that violence by both sides is abating, there is not a flicker of hope, in the short-run that even a truce is in the offing. The conflict over the small territory of the Holy Land is amplified by the sentiment of both Israelis and Palestinians that they have a historic right to the land; by the violence inflicted on each other by both sides.

6.7 Tribes

The history of tribal groups in Indian society is very long and complex in character. More than 700 different tribal groups are identified for administrative and census purposes and referred as Schedules Tribes. Padel (1992) states that the "census, which started in 1871 in British India, distinguished the tribal population from Hindus and their religion, as 'animism' from Hindusim." Morse (1992) quotes Ghurye (1962) who sought to avoid any emphasis on tribals indigenous status to oppose the British policy of divide and rule and considered them as a part of Hindu society. Ghurye called them "Backward Hindus"—a highly negative view of tribal culture.

Baviskar (1992) based on wide field experiences in Madhya Pradesh has come to the fore that "the notion of 'tribe' in the Indian context has been hard to pin down because of the porosity of the boundary between tribe and non-tribe, both of which have existed side by side for the centuries" (Baviskar, 1992). Nevertheless, the geographical isolation of many tribal groups made the creation of Scheduled Tribe category an easier case than what might it could have been. Many scholars have stated that the tribal's resisted integration, moved across large geographical areas, suffered economic, administrative and armed upheavals, over centuries. Himalayan tribal communities Gujjars—Bakkarwals perform transhumance (seasonal migration of people and their livestock) in search of food.

World Bank (1982) defines tribal people as ethnic groups typically with stable, low energy, sustained-yield economic systems, as exemplified by hunter-gatherers, shifting cultivators, herders or fishermen. The tribal groups exhibit in varying degrees of: geographically isolated or semi-isolated; unacculturated or only partially acculturated into the societal norms of the dominant society; non-monetized or only partially monetized; production largely for subsistence, and independent of the national economic system; ethnically distinct from the national society; non-literate and without a written language; linguistically different from the wider society; identifying closely with one particular territory; having an economic lifestyle dependent on the specific natural environment;

possessing indigenous leadership, but little or no national representation, and few political rights individually or collectively, partly, because they do not participate in the political process; and having loose tenure over their traditional lands, which is not accepted by the dominant society nor accommodated by its courts; and having weak enforcement capabilities against encroachers, even when tribal areas have been delineated.

Bhil tribe constitutes a majority of Scheduled Tribes in Indian subcontinent. Bhil usually use bows and arrows, and it is believed that their name emerged from the Dravid word "*billu*" which means bow and arrow. A Sanskrit text in 1100 AD describes 'Bhils' as barbarian people, living on plunder and found in the mountains along the Narmada river (Graham, 1852 quoted in Whitehead, 2010). The British applied the term 'Bhils' to a large group of hill tribes who resided in the western regions of the Satpura and the Vindhya mountains, inhabiting parts of Madhya Pradesh, and southern Rajasthan, as well as eastern Gujarat (Deliege, 1985 quoted in Whitehead, 2010). They were also often referred to as *junglijati* (wild people), during the colonial period (Skaria, 2001). Resource depletion, combined with their spatial isolation, has to a large extent allowed tribals to maintain a structural distance from modern cultural institutions which has given rise to a unique way of life of Bhils (Baviskar, 1995).

The tribal communities do not define themselves based on administrative state boundaries rather by the physical geographical boundaries. In tribes of Narmada valley, women and men are given equal status. Gender relations, involving control by women over some common property resources, are relatively more egalitarian than in plains upper-caste households (CSS, 1997). However, men make the major financial decisions of the household, but women do possess a certain degree of economic freedom. As women had access to the local resource base and to minor forest produce, they could raise small amounts of money by selling these. The requirement of money in everyday life was very limited which has also limited the extent of women's dependence on their men.

The natural environment has supported the subsistence economic activities of the tribals. Common property resources (CPRs) have traditionally been the basis of the tribal economy, as forests provide a source of berries, edible gums and timber for consumption and sale. In fact, the tribal world is known for their animistic beliefs. By animism, they believe in the attribution of a living soul to plants, living creatures, object and natural phenomenon. Bishnois of Rajasthan considered Blackbuck as a reincarnation of their Guru Bhagwan Jambaji. Recently, Bishnois were strongly in the favour of prosecution of actor Salman Khan in Blackbuck poaching case. Another instance is of Dongri Kondh tribals of Odisha. Dongri Kondh worships mountain god Niyam Raja which presides over the Niyamgiri hill range in Odisha. The tribe protested against the multinational firm Vedanta Resources which was planning to extract the estimated $ 2 billion-worth of bauxite that lies under the surface of the hills.

6.8 Classification of Tribes Based on Geographical Location

Census of India (2011) mentions about 10.42 crore Indians notified as 'Scheduled Tribes' (ST) which constitutes 8.6 per cent of the country's population. Madhya Pradesh has the highest Scheduled Tribe population (14.7 per cent). Meghalaya has the lowest (2.5 per cent). Haryana, Punjab, Chandigarh, Delhi, Goa and Pondicherry have very little tribal population. Classification of tribes based on four zones is presented below:

6.8.1 Zone 1: Northern and North Eastern Zone

Tribal people are spread across the sub-Himalayan region and mountain valleys encompassing Shimla in the western part of the Himalayas and Lushai hills and Mishmi hills in the Eastern Himalayas which extends further till Myanmar. Indian tribes of this belt belong to the Mongolian stock. It covers Assam, Arunachal Pradesh, Meghalaya, Nagaland, Tripura, Manipur and Mizoram, Eastern Jammu and Kashmir, Himachal Pradesh, Uttarakhand and the mountainous West Bengal.

In North East India, Paro-Barokachari is the strongest tribe in Assam numerically, and then comes Miri and Mizo. The hill districts, i.e. Mikir Hills and North Cachar Hills are predominantly inhabited by Scheduled Tribes. In the plains, Goalpara, Darrang and Kamrup districts possess large number of Scheduled Tribes. In Manipur, the highest distribution of Scheduled Tribes is found in Manipur west districts followed by Manipur east district. The major tribes inhabiting the region are Anal, Kabui, Gangte, Zarao, Moyan-Mansang etc. In Meghalaya the most important tribes are the Khasis, Garos and Jaintias. Mizo, Pawi and Lakher tribes are of importance in Mizoram. Nagaland is inhabited by Naga tribes.

Himachal Pradesh has Gaddi tribes that resides in snowy ranges between Chamba and Kangra; Kinner tribes, settled in Kinnaur; Pangwal group in Pangi region of Chamba district; and Lahulis that occupy Lahul-Spiti. Uttarakhand is represented by the Jaunsari, Bhotia, and Raji tribes. Bhotias are a late introduction in the Scheduled Tribes following the setback they suffered after Indo-China war.

6.8.2 Zone II: Central Zone

The Chhotanagpur Plateau is inhabited by many tribal communities like the Bhumij, Gond, Ho, Oraon, Munda, Santhal, Bhil etc. These tribal groups belong to Proto-Australoid group. These groups occupy the mountain belt between Narmada and the Godavari—the central barrier that divides the north from the Peninsular India has provided a shelter for these tribes from very ancient times. It includes West Bengal, Madhya Pradesh, Chattisgarh, Jharkhand, Odisha and Maharashtra. This region further extends to the Santhal Pargana (Bihar) in the east, Hyderabad in the South and Rajasthan and Gujarat with a strong Bhil population in the West. Bhuiya, Baiga, Dharua, Gaaro, Ho, Koli, Lodha etc. are some of the populous tribes. The Baiga appears to be a branch of the great Bhuiya tribe of Madhya Pradesh. Baiga means a sorcerer or medicine man. Rajasthan has Banjaras, Moghias and Sathiyas as important tribes. They mostly inhabit the region of Thar Desert.

6.8.3 Zone III: South-Western Zone

Andhra Pradesh, Karnataka, Kerala, and Tamil Nadu lie within this zone. The Western Ghats are occupied with the Chenchus, Irulas, Kadars, Ketas, Kurumbas, Jedas etc. having Negrito, Caucasoid, and proto-Australoid features. These tribal groups are concentrated in the southern-most parts of the Western Ghats stretching from Vindhyas to Cape Comorin.

6.8.4 Zone IV: Tribes of Andaman and Nicobar

There are various scattered tribal groups like the Andamanese, the Onges and the Sentinelese found in the Andaman group of Islands. These tribes have an affinity with the Semangos and Sakais of Malaya, the Vedas of Sri Lanka and other Negrito groups of South-East Asia. Shornpens and Nicobarese are other tribal groups belonging to Mongoloid stock. They are confined along the eastern and south-eastern coast of Great Nicobar island. They are also reported from the banks of Dagmar, Alexandra and Galathoa rivers respectively. Nicobarese are highly unevenly distributed and found only in the two islands, the Car Nicobar and Chowra.

6.9 Summary

Robert Stoddard and Carolyn Prorak define religion as "a system of beliefs and practices that attempts to order life in terms of culturally perceived ultimate priorities. Religion on the basis of spatial relevance is classified into Universalizing Religions, Ethnic Religions and Tribal or Traditional Religions. Christianity is the universalizing religion with most adherents in Western Hemisphere. Islam and Buddhism are universalizing regions with most of the adherents in Asia. Hinduism is the largest ethnic religion with India having majority of followers. Human geographers are particularly concerned with the interaction between religion and the landscape. Religion marks cultural landscapes with houses of worship such as churches, mosques, synagogues, *Gurdwaras* and temples; with cemeteries and cremation grounds dotted with religious symbols and icons; with stores designated to sales of religious goods; and even with services provided to religious adherents who travel to sacred sites like accommodations. Religious beliefs frequently reinforce political feelings about possession of an area. The Middle East has been a battleground for Jews, Muslims and Christians for a long time. Jerusalem is a bone of contention for these major religions as important religious structures of Jews, Islam and Christianity share the same space. With no sign of truce in offing, there is very low hope for peace in the region.

The history of tribal groups in Indian society is very long and complex in character. On the basis of geographical location, tribes in India are classified into four zones.

Review Questions

1. Discuss the interrelationship between religion and landscape.
2. How the major religions of the world had their origin?
3. Explain the history, characteristics and spatial distribution of the major religions of the world.
4. Discuss the religion and territorial disputes with a case study.
5. Explain the meaning of tribe.
6. Present a classification of tribes in India.

Analytical Questions

1. Discuss the religion and territorial disputes taking a case study of your country/ neighbouring country.
2. Analyse the tribal struggles taking the case study, in context of water (*Jal*), forest (*Jangal*) and land (*Jameen*).

Chapter 7

Language

7.1. Introduction

Language is one of the fundament of culture which shapes our very thoughts. Language reflects evolution of a culture, what a culture values, thoughts of people in a culture, and describe, and experience other cultural underpinnings. In fact, proverbs, medicine formulae, prayers, folk tales, Vedic hymns, songs and genealogies are some of the forms of language taken as culture preserving instrument. Language is an important medium to convey our feelings, expression, desire and thoughts. A language is a set of sounds and symbols that are used for communication. But language is also an integral part of the culture, reflecting and shaping it. It is an important medium of socialization. The importance of language in cinema can be gauged by analysing the trajectory of Indian Bollywood Cinema, from its first silent film 'Raja Harishchandra' to the present movies with lyrics, dialogues and songs. Adding further, human beings also communicate their expressions through either body language alone or in combination with vocal sounds or words. Example of using body language could be the nodding of the head by students in front of their teachers.

Earth's heterogeneous collection of languages is one of the most glaring examples of cultural diversity. Language is like a traveller's luggage—people carry it with them when they move from one place to other. They keep incorporating new words into their own language when they reach new places, and they contribute to the existing language at the new location. Variants of a standard language along regional or ethnic lines are called dialects. Differences in vocabulary, syntax (the way words are put together to form phrases), pronunciation, cadence (the rhythm of speech), and even the pace of speech all mark a speaker's dialect (Fouberg *et al.*, 2009). For Example, Awadhi, Brij Bhasha, Khari Boli are all dialects of Hindi language.

The boundary between linguistic differences can be shown on a map by a line called an Isogloss. Such a boundary is rarely a simple and clearly demarcated line. Usually, outlying areas of usage extend beyond the isogloss (Blij *et al.*, 2006). Fuzzy isoglosses signify that either the dialect has expanded or contracted. Linguists who study dialects examine pronunciations, vocabularies, use of colloquial phrases, and syntax to determine isoglosses (Fouberg, *et al.*, 2009). At the global scale, we classify languages into language families. A language family is a group of languages descended from a common ancestral language that existed long before the recorded history. This family relationship between languages is able to establish through similarities in their vocabulary and grammar. The language families are divided into sub-families (sub-branches within a language family), where the commonalities are more definite and the origin is more recent (Blij *et al.*, 2006). To simplify the categorization of the languages and dialects for students, it can be stated that the individual languages cover a smaller extent of territory, while the dialects cover the smallest extent of territory.

A language needs a group of people among whom the means of communication is that language. This group of people who communicate in certain language may be described as a 'speech community'. In the course of time, several speech communities are formed, each occupying a geographical contiguous space (Ahmad, 2012) as evident from Fig. 7.1 like Language A and Language B. It clearly represents that how in the case of language C, divergence of dialects is happening leading to formation of new languages.

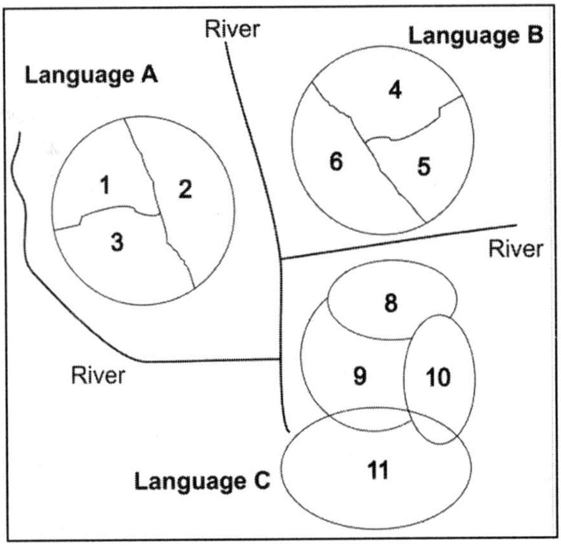

Fig. 7.1: Graphical Representation of Language Divergence over Space

Notes: (1) Territory of language shown as A, B, C.
(2) Dialect areas shown as 1, 2, 3.......11.

7.2 Language Formation

In the process of classifying languages and knowing about the language formation, linguists and linguistic geographers study relationships among languages and look for similarities and differences within and among the languages. More than two centuries ago Sir William Jones, an English scholar living in India, undertook a study of Sanskrit. Sanskrit is the language in which ancient Indian religious and literary texts were written. Jones discovered that the vocabulary and grammatical forms of Sanskrit has a striking resemblance to the ancient Greek and Latin. Jones made a proposition that Sanskrit, Greek and Latin have some common source, which, perhaps, no longer exists (Jones, 1970). In 1700, this idea of Jones was considered as a revolutionary notion. During the nineteenth century, Jakob Grimm, a scholar, suggested that sound shifts[1] might prove the relationships between languages in a scientific manner. His view was that the related languages have similar consonants, but these are not identical. He believed these consonants would change over time. He demonstrated in his work on German language that hard consonants, such as the *v* and *t* in the German word *vater*, softened into *vader* (Dutch) and *father* (English).

The linguists made an assumption based on Grimm's ideas that if consonants became softer over the time and due to sound shifts, they would become harder when went backwards. This backward movement might reach the original hearth and original language. Based upon Jones's notions and Grimm's ideas, the first major linguistic hypothesis was deduced that proposed the existence of an ancestral Indo-European language called Proto-Indo-European (Fouberg *et al.*, 2003). This discovery of a Proto-Indo-European language would connect us with the hearth of ancient Latin, Greek, and Sanskrit. A single Proto-Indo-European hearth would link modern languages from Scandinavia to North Africa and from North America through parts of Asia to Australia.

German linguist August Schleicher was the first to draw an analogy between the world's language families. Schleicher suggested that the new languages emerge through the process of language divergence. This process occurs when the spatial interaction among speakers of a language breaks down, then the language first fragments into dialects and then into distinct mother tongues. The process of language divergence has happened between Spanish and Portuguese, which have common origin. Further, languages are formed not only through divergence, they also emerge through the processes of convergence and extinction. If people with different languages have consistent spatial interaction, there are high chances of language convergence. As a result, two or more languages can collapse into one. Example, Wutun language is a mixture of Chinese, Tibetan and Mongolian languages spoken in Qinghai province in China.

Not only new languages are formed through divergence and convergence of different languages, but also many languages disappear or become extinct. Languages become extinct through two ways; first, when all the speakers perish due to spread of disease or invasion, second, when the descendants choose to use another language as a result of cultural assimilation, abandoning the language of their ancestors in favour of other lingua franca. *Latin* is a prominent example of extinct language. In fact, the process of language extinction does not occur overnight; it takes place across generations.

It is important that based on tracking the divergence, convergence, extinction, and original locations of the Proto-Indo-European languages, linguists and geographers are of the view that the hearth of the Proto-Indo-European language was in the vicinity of the Black Sea or east-central Europe. From this hearth, Proto-Indo-European languages and speakers have dispersed in different parts of the world. Furthermore, by analyzing the sequence of the disperson of the Proto-Indo-European language, linguists and geographers can deduce about the sequential development of social, economic and cultural lives of the speakers. Therefore, based upon the reconstructed vocabulary of Proto-Indo-European, it was discerned that the language dates back to a people who used horses, had developed the wheel, and traded in many goods.

7. 3 Linguistic Classification

There are numerous languages in the world. The diversity of languages is simplified when we recognize them among related families. The following is the classification of linguistic families:

7.3.1 Indo-European Language Family

The Indo-European Family comprises Indian, Persian, Armenian, Germanic, Italic, Albanian, Balto-Slavic and Celtic languages. First speaker of Indo-European language, which can be called Proto-Indo-European were Kurgans, whose homeland was in steppes to the north of Caspian Sea near Volga River. All the Indo-European languages share common words or the words whose origin has common roots. It was found that there is common word base for winter and snow but not for ocean, signifying that original speakers of this family probably lived in cold climate but did not came into contact to oceans.

Germanic Languages Sub-family

Germanic family includes English and belongs to the Indo-European language family. It has three branches—North Germanic, East Germanic and West Germanic. The North Germanic branch includes the Scandinavian languages (Danish, Icelandic and Swedish). The main East Germanic branch language is Gothic which got extinct. The language died because the descendants of Gothic tribe were converted to other languages through political dominance. The West German branch includes German, Yiddish, Anglo-Saxon, Old Saxon, Dutch and Flenish languages. English is most widely spoken West Germanic language. Its origin dates back to 1500 years and is a fusion of languages spoken by three tribes, viz. Angles, Jutes and Saxons who invaded England. English was diffused around the world through colonization of America, Australia, New Zealand, Africa and Asia.

Latin Linguistic Language Sub-family

The Latin linguistic family also known as Romance language includes languages like French, Italian, Spanish, Portuguese, Catalan and Romance. Romance languages evolved from Latin spoken by Romans 2,000 years ago. There was a growth in importance of Latin language as Roman armies conquered new provinces and made them part of their vast empire. Following the collapse of Roman Empire in fifth century, there was decline in communication among former provinces which eventually created regional variations of Latin. After several hundred years, residents of various parts of former Roman Empire spoke languages like Spanish, Portuguese, French, Italian and Romanian. Like English, some of these languages have achieved worldwide presence because of the colonial practices of the native speakers. French is the language of France and it has been adopted as a national language in Switzerland, Canada and several countries of Africa. Portuguese, apart from Europe holds great importance in Latin America because of the colonial activities of Portugal.

Balto Slavic Languages Sub-family

This is other language sub-family in the Indo-European branch. The Slavic languages are generally divided into east, west and south. Eastern Slavic language like Russian is widely used. It is spoken by about 240 million people, including 80 per cent of the Russian population of Russia. The importance of Russian increased in twentieth century with the rise in the power of former USSR. The two other important languages of this family are Ukrainian and Byelorussian (white Russian). The other West Slavic languages include Polish,

Czech and Slavik.

Indo-Iranian Language Sub-family

The Indo-Iranian family includes more than one hundred individual languages which are spoken by about 800 million people. The branch can be divided into two—(a) an eastern group—Indic—including speakers from Bangladesh, India and Pakistan, and (b) western group—Iranian. Hindi is widely spoken in India. Though it has several dialects, but there is one single script—Devanagari. Urdu is a principal language of Pakistan. It is spoken much like Hindi, but uses Arabic alphabets. Hindi and Urdu are considered a single one known as Hindustani. Another language Bengali is spoken in Bangladesh and adjacent areas. Important to highlight is that India has over 1500 languages and twenty two official languages (recognized by Constitution of India) explained in succeeding section. Iranian languages include Farsi in Iran, Pashto in Afghanistan, Kurdish by Kurds in Iran, Iraq and Turkey. These languages have Arabic letters. Besides, Sinhalese spoken in Sri Lanka is also language from Indo-Iranian family.

7.3.2 Sino-Tibetan Language Family

This family has languages of the Peoples Republic of China and many smaller nations of South East Asia. Mandarin is widely spoken in China by about three-fourth of the total population. There are four other spoken languages in China—Cantonese, Min, Wu and Hakka.

In addition to the Chinese languages, Sino-Tibetan language family includes a second branch known as Tibeto-Burman, used in South East Asia. Thai, Myanmari, Japanese and Korean are languages from this family.

7.3.3 Semito Haemetic Languages

Semito Haemetic languages include Hebrew and Arabic languages. The significance of these languages can be gauged from the fact that these languages were used to write the holiest books—the Judaeo-Christian Bible and the Islamic Holy Quaran. Arabic is official language of twenty nations of South West Asia and North Africa, from Morocco to the Arabian Peninsula. Hebrew is limited to Israel.

7.3.4 African Languages

There is no definitive count for number of different languages in Africa but nearly 1000 distinct languages and dialects have been accounted in Africa. Hausa, Yorubo and Ibo are widely used languages in Nigeria and Swahili is the official language of Tanzania and East African nations.

7.4 Spatial Distribution of Languages

The spatial distribution of languages of the world is most complex. About 50 per cent of the world population speak at least one of the ten major languages (Table 7.1). Distribution of these major languages covers a large part of the earth surface. Thus, distribution of

Table 7.1: Major Languages of the World

Rank	Language	Population Size (in million)
1	Chinese	1311
2	Spanish	460
3	English	379
4	Hindi	341
5	Arabic	319
6	Bengali	228
7	Portuguese	221
8	Russian	154
9	Japanese	128
10	Lahnda	119

Source: Eberhard *et al.* (2019).

languages has two main characteristics—first, the areal size of the regions is not consistently proportional to the population size of language. For example, Chinese is spoken by maximum population but the area where Chinese dominate is much smaller than the combined area making up the English language region. The second characteristic is the languages do not necessarily match administrative boundaries. There are languages spoken in more than one country. For example, English is a primary language in many countries while Hindi is a major language in only one country—India. It is a generalized picture showing regional distribution of dominant languages. In general, the world is divided into various major language families (Fig. 7.2). The Indo-European language family covers the large extent of territory and has maximum number of speakers. English, an Indo-European language is the most widely spoken language of all languages in the world.

7.5 Languages in India

India provides a unique mosaic of languages and presents an impressive example of socio-linguistic unity (Fig. 7.3). As a student of geography, it is important to understand the geographical patterning of languages in the South-Asian region. This has to be understood in the context of space relations that India and South Asia has with other parts of the Asia. Indian subcontinent marks a southward projection into the Indian Ocean. The overland connections with the West and Central Asia, Tibet, China and South East Asia have brought the linguistic influences in the South Asia in general and India in particular. It is evident that the languages spoken in Baluchistan, Pakistan-Afghanistan border, Kashmir, Gilgit and Baltistan have a strong affinity with the languages spoken in regions beyond Hindu-Kush Himalayas. The people residing in remote Himalayan areas of Ladakh and Himachal Pradesh speak Tibeto-Chinese languages. Similarly, the north-eastern region is influenced by the Myanmar and Indo-China and speaks Sino-Tibetan or Tibeto-Burman languages. The north Indian plains speak languages of Indo-European family while the peninsular India in the south has retained its Dravidian speech. Lying between the Indo-European and Dravidian families are the tribes speaking Austric languages located in the hills of central India.

The linguistic heterogeneity of India can be classified within the four language families: Indo-European, Dravidian, Austro-Asiatic and Sino-Tibetan (Tibeto-Burman) (Table 7.2). Over the millions of years, these families have carved for themselves niches in the Indian

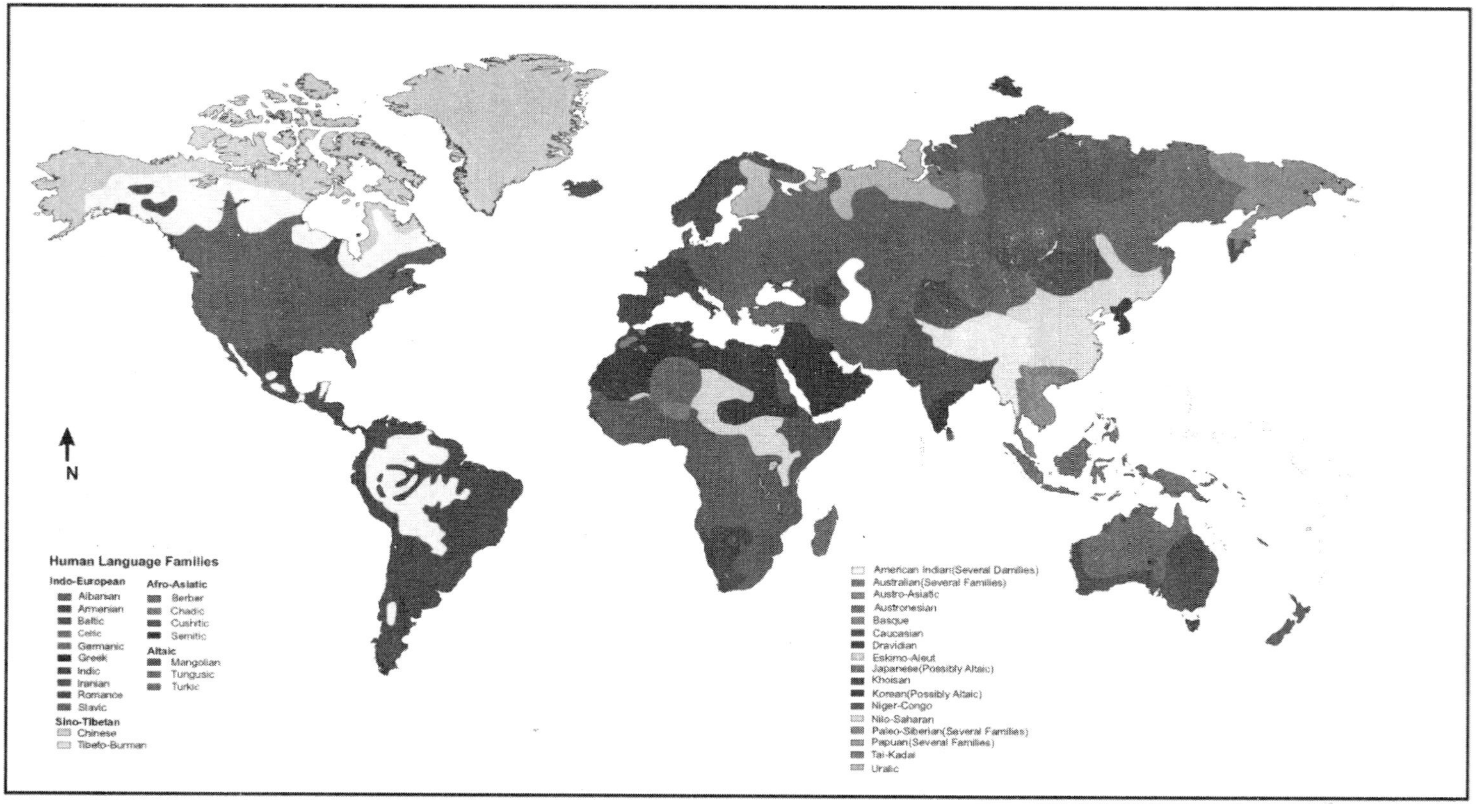

Fig. 7.2: World Language Families Map

Source: Online Resource on Introduction to Linguistic Analysis, University of Massachusetts Amherst, 2011 accessed on 1st December 2016.

Weblink: http://people.umass.edu/~nconstan/201/Language%20Families%20World%20Map.png

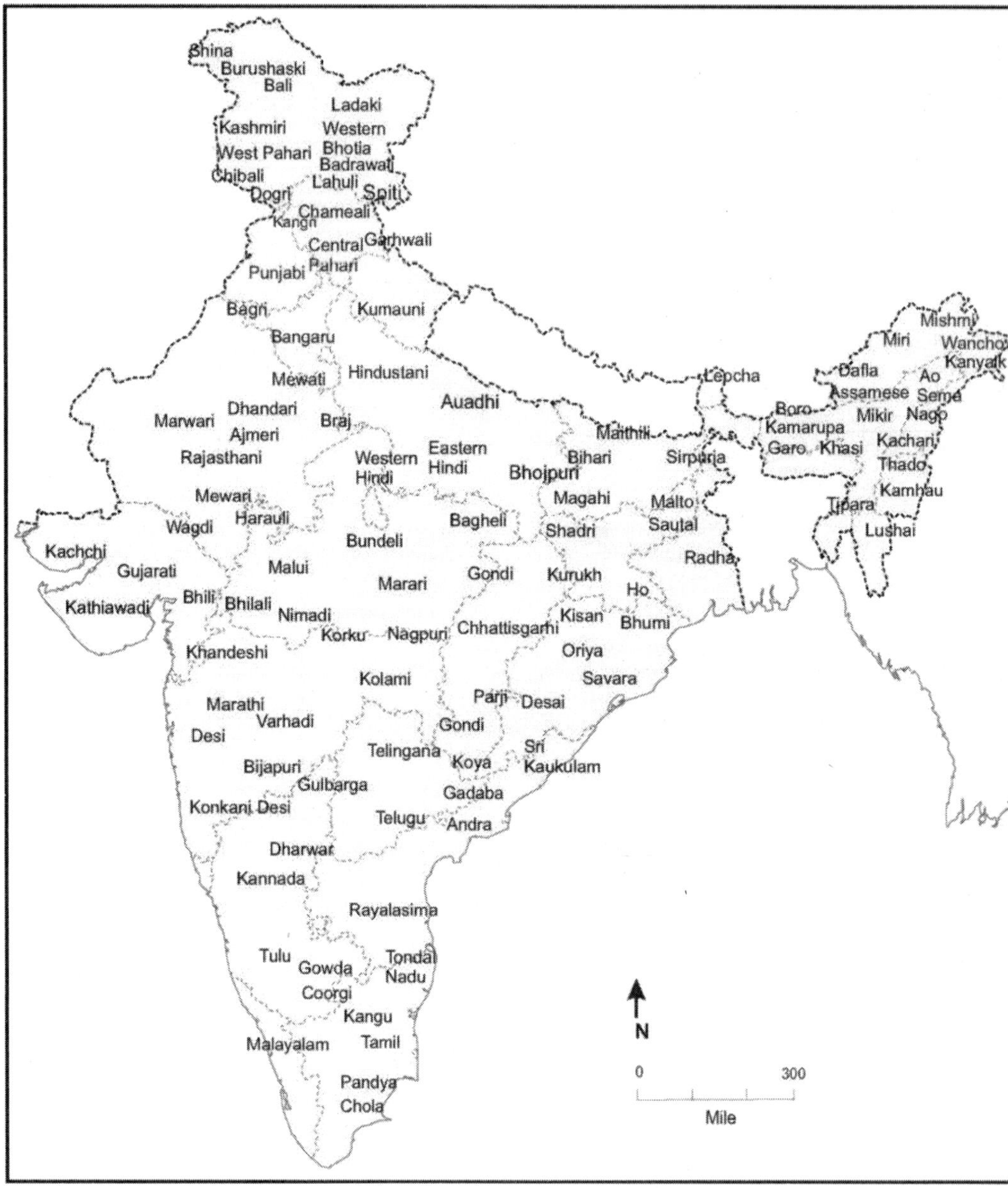

Fig. 7.3: Linguistic Variations in India

Source: Based on Stoddard, *et al.* (1986).

social space in different parts of the country. The variety of languages and dialects are spoken in India. A glance over it proves the age old Hindi saying "Kos Kos Par Badle Paani, Char Kos Par Vani" which translates to "Every 3 km, the taste of water changes; every 12 km, the dialect changes". India has thousands of dialects spoken across the length and breadth of India.

Table 7.2: Broad Classification of Modern Indian Languages

Family	*Sub-family*	*Branch/Group*	*Geographical Area of Language*
Indo-European (Arya)	Indo-Aryan	Iranian	Outside India
		Dardic	Jammu and Kashmir
		Indo-Aryan	Jammu and Kashmir, Punjab, Himachal Pradesh, Uttar Pradesh, Uttarakhand, Rajasthan, Haryana, Madhya Pradesh, Bihar, Odisha, West Bengal, Assam, Gujarat, Maharashtra, Goa
Dravidian (Dravida)		South Dravidian	Tamil Nadu, Karnataka, Kerala
		Central Dravidian	Andhra Pradesh, Odisha, Madhya Pradesh and Maharashtra
Sino-Tibetan	Tibeto-Myanmari	Tibeto-Himalayan	Jammu and Kashmir, Himachal Pradesh, Sikkim
		North Assam	Arunachal Pradesh
		Assam-Myanmar	Assam, Nagaland, Manipur, Mizoram, Tripura, Meghalaya
	Siamese-Chinese		Outside India
Austric (Nishada)	Austro-Asiatic	Mon-Khmer	Meghalaya, Nicobar Islands
		Munda	West Bengal, Bihar, Jharkhand Odisha, Assam, Madhya Pradesh, Chhattisgarh, Maharashtra
	Austro-nesian		Outside India

Source: Ahmad, 2012.

7.6 Summary

A language is a collective of sounds and symbols that is used for communication. Language is one of the fundament of culture which shapes our very thoughts. Language reflects evolution of a culture, what a culture values, thoughts of people in a culture, and describe, and experience other cultural underpinnings. Variants of a standard language are called dialects. Languages are classified into families, branches and sub-groups. About half of the world population speak at least one of the ten major languages. The diversity of languages is simplified when we recognize them among related families—Indo-European language family, Sino-Tibetan language family, Semito-Haemetic languages and African languages. Indo-European language family is divided into eight branches. Hindi and English belong to this family. Nearly half of the world speaks in languages of Indo-European family. India enjoys a great linguistic heterogeneity owing to its peculiar geographical position.

Note

1. A sound shift is a slight change in a word across languages within a sub-family or through a language family from the present backward towards its origin. For example, Italian, Spanish, and French are all members of the Romance language sub-family of the Indo-European language family. One way linguists and linguistic geographers can determine this is by looking at sound shifts for single words across time (all three languages are derived from Latin) and across languages. For example, the Latin word for milk, lacte, became latta in Italian, leche in Spanish, and lait in French. Even if linguists did not already know that Italian, Spanish, and French are languages rooted in Latin, they could deduce a connection among the languages through the sound shifts of particular words.

Review Questions

1. Language is one of the cornerstones of culture. Elaborate.
2. Explain the process of language formation.
3. Give a classification of languages.
4. India is a linguistically heterogeneous nation. Discuss.
5. Explain the important role of language in human society.

Analytical Questions

1. Explain the important role of language in human society.
2. "It is better to study major international languages like English rather than minority languages for the sake of regional identity." Discuss.

PART 3

Population and Migration

Chapter 8
Population Distribution

8.1 Introduction

Distribution of population over the earth surface is one of the most important issues in recent time, because man has brought tremendous changes over the earth surface. At present, man is the single most important powerful geographical factor transforming the earth surface at an unparalleled pace. Scientists are at the threshold of achieving superconductivity, which will usher in revolutionary changes in global civilization. Man has tool to change the climatic conditions. The scientific achievements have resulted into acid rain, global warming, atmospheric pollution, ozone depletion and nuclear radiation and have further threatened to destroy nature's ecosystem across the world. Thus, the study of human population and its spatial pattern is of vital importance. A study of population and density distribution holds huge implication for geographers, as its understanding clutches the key to examine whole demographic character of a geographical place or city. Demko (1970) suggested that the land and people create two significant elements of an area and, therefore, the ratio between the two is of fundamental interest to all academicians concerned with population studies.

8.2 Methods to Show Population Distribution and Concentration

First of all, difference should be made between population distribution and population density. The distribution is more locational, which means how people are distributed in a particular area, while the density is more proportional which talks about individuals per unit area or volume. The former discusses to the spatial pattern within which the population finds its location like linear, dispersed, nucleated, agglomerated etc. and the latter shows the ratio between the size of population and the area. Thus, once one is addressing distribution, the focus is more for the pattern of spread of population and when one is dealing with density, the concern is more for some kind of man-land ratio. There are many means that of describing the spatial distribution of population and lot of techniques are developed to portray population distribution and population density. Demographers, geographers, sociologists etc. have all created their contribution in developing the means to explain population distribution and concentration. The easiest way of measuring population distribution has been *percentage* distribution, whereby the percentage of individuals living in the geographic areas of a given class has been computed. As an example, in order to have an idea of spatial spread of India's population one will simply calculate the percentage of country's population living in each state and union territory. The sum of all such percentages will total up to 100.

Similarly, another common practice has been to list the geographic areas of a given class into *Rank* Order. A further comparison of ranking from census to census can highlight the temporal trends in distribution and the redistribution tendencies, if any. Geographers have made use of this technique more in case of urban population. The geographers have also shown some interest in calculating some sort of an average point for population distribution within a country or an area. The most popular measure in this regard is the *median point*; the mean point also often called the centre of population. The median point of population in any area has been calculated with the help of median lines. The median lines are two orthographic lines each of which divides the concerned area into two parts, each having equal number of inhabitants. The median lines are drawn conventionally perpendicular is known as the *median point*. Such median point can be calculated for a country at different points in time with a view to understand the redistribution tendencies in its population through time.

The mean point of population or the centre of population may be defined as the centre of gravity of population of an area, implying the point upon which the plane would balance if it were a plane without weight and the population distributed thereon, each individual being assumed to have equal weight and to exert pressure on the central point proportionate to his distance from the point. Thus, mean point, unlike the median point, is influenced by the distance of an individual from it. The centre of population need not to fall in a density settled part of the country. The point of minimum aggregate travel has been defined as the point, which can be reached by all individual with the least total straight line travel. This concept has fairly obvious application to location theory, i.e. estimating the optimum central location for, say, a service.

The concept of population potential as developed by Stewart and Warntz (1958) applies to accessibilities of a point to the population. If the influence of each individual at a point is considered to be inversely proportionate to his distance from it, the total potential of population at the point will be the sum of the reciprocals of the distances of all individuals from the point. Thus, it was concluded that population potential is a measure of nearness of people to a point. It assumes that the influence (or accessibility) is inversely proportional to the distance. Thus, using this technique, contours of population potential can be compound and drawn for a country or a continent.

8.3 Factors Affecting Population Distribution

The regional disparities in the population distribution and density are governed or affected by a variety of physical, economic, social and political factors. Thus, all the factors affecting the population distribution may broadly classify into four major categories discussed in Table 8.1.

8.4 Population Distribution in World

In the initial phase of human history and pre-history, the human population grew at a snail speed. The hazardous climatic conditions, the migratory character of hunters and gatherers,

Table 8.1: Factors Affecting Population Distribution

Factors	*Sparsely Populated Areas*	*Densely Populated Areas*
PHYSICAL FACTORS		
Landforms	Rugged mountain where tempe-rature and pressure decrease with height; active volcanoes (The Andes); high plateau (Tibet) and worn down shield lands (The Canadian Shield)	Flat low land plains are attractive to settlements (The Netherland and Bangladesh) are areas surrounding some volcanoes (Mt. Etna and Java).
Climate (Temperature, amount of Precipitation and length of growing season)	Areas receiving very low annual rainfall (The Sahara Desert); areas having a long seasonal Drought or unreliable, irregular suffering rainfall (The Sahel countries); areas suffering high humidity (The Amazon basin); very cold areas, with a short gro-wing season (Northern Canada).	Areas where the rainfall is reliable and evenly distributed throughout the year; with no temperature extremes and a lengthy growing season (North-west Europe); where sunshine (The Costa del Sol) or snow is sufficient to attract tourists (the Alps); and areas with a monsoon climate (South-east Asia).
Vegetation	Areas such as the coniferous forests of northern Eurasia and Northern Canada, and the rainforest of the tropics.	Areas of grassland tend to have higher population densities than places with dense forest or desert.
Soil	The frozen soils of the Arctic (The permafrost in Siberia); the thin soils of mountains (Nepal); the leached soil of the tropical rainforest (The Amazon basin); also increasingly large areas are experiencing severe soil erosion resulting from deforestation and overgrazing (The Sahel).	Deep, humus-filled soils (the Paris Basin) and, especially river deposi-ted silts (the Ganges and Nile Delta) both favour farming.
Water Supplies	Many areas lack a permanent supply of clean fresh water; mainly due either to insufficient, irregular rainfall or a lack of money and technology to build reservoirs and wells or lay pipelines (Ethiopia).	Population is more likely to increase in areas with a reliable water supply. This may result from either a reliable, evenly distributed rainfall (northern England) or where there is the wealth and technology to build reservoirs and to provide clean water (California). Places with heavy seasonal rainfall (the monsoon lands of Southeast Asia) also support many people.
Diseases and Pests	These may limit the areas in which people can live or may seriously curtail the lives of those who do populate such areas (Malaria in Central Africa).	Some areas were initially relatively diseases and pest-free; others had the capital and medical expertise to eradicate those which were a problem (the formerly malarial pontine marshes, near Rome).
Resources	Areas devoid of minerals rarely attract people or industry (Para-guay).	Areas having, or formerly having, large mineral deposits and/or energy supplies (the Ruhr) often have major concentrations of populations; these resources often led to the development of large-scale industry (the Pittsburgh region, USA).
Accessibility	Areas where it is difficult to construct and maintain systems tend to be sparsely populated, e.g. mountains (Bolivia), deserts (the Sahara) and the forests (the Amazon basin and northern Canada).	Areas where it is easier to construct canals, railways, roads and airports have attracted settlements (the North European plains), as have large natural ports which have been developed for trade (Singapore).
Economic Factors	Areas with less developed, subsistence economies usually need large areas of land to support relatively few people (although this is not applicable to South-east Asia). Such areas tend to fall into three belts; tundra (the Lapps), deserts fringes (the Rendille) and tropical rainforest (shifting cultivation).	Regions with intensive farming or industry can support large numbers of people on a small area of land (Netherlands).
Demographic Factors (fertility, mortality and migration)	The rate of natural increase in the developed countries of the West is much lower than that in the developing.	Countries like India, Pakistan, China, Indonesia etc. have high density of population because of high rate of fertility and diminishing mortality.
Political Factors	Areas where the state fails to invest sufficient money or to encourage development—either economically or socially (the interior of Brazil)	Decisions may affect population distribution—e.g. by creating new cities, such as Brasilia; by opening up 'pioneer' lands for development, as in Israel.

Source: Authors.

and the poor nourishment were all unfavourable for the growth of population.

The most conspicuous feature of the world's population distribution is its unevenness and highly irregular spatial distribution. Such unevenness has been established through kinds of estimates. Approximately, 80 per cent of the world population is concentrated in 20 per cent of the world's total land area. It has been pointed out that more than 90 per cent of the world's population is confined to the northern hemisphere, while the rest is on continents of the southern hemisphere and the latitudinal distribution of population offer sharp differences in concentrations. For instance, 0-20° N latitudinal account for about 10 per cent of population of the world mainly in Asia, 20°-40°N zone claims more than 50 per cent of the world population again mainly in Asia, 40°-60°N latitudes have about 30 per cent of the world's population mainly in Europe and only less than 1 per cent population lives in regions north of 60°N latitude. Trewartha (1969) estimated that about half of the world's population occupied less than 5 per cent of the total area and the remaining half was spread over 50-60 per cent area. Similarly, inequalities have been observed in vertical distribution of population also. Trewartha found that vertical distribution of population was highest in South America (644 metres) and lowest in Australia (95 metres). Broadly, about four-fifth of the world's population lived within 500 metres from the sea level.

Interestingly, both crowded and sparse concentrations were found in traditional as well as technically advanced societies, in new as well as old worlds, and in tropics and temperate regions; Belgium and Holland of western culture of mid-latitudes; and Egypt of riverine, arid environment, High latitudes, on the other hand, were devoid of significantly high densities. Broadly, dense concentration of population was largely confined to East Asia, South Asia, Western Europe and north-eastern US by comparison, very low densities were typical of more extensive areas. Large territories covering drought regions, cold regions in the high latitudes, high altitudes lands, and wet typical lands were nearly empty lands of the world.

Hence, the world has been divided into two type of area: permanently inhabited lands (*ecumene*); and uninhabited, intermittently inhabited or very sparsely inhabited parts (non-*ecumene*). However, it is not an easy task to demarcate a precise boundary between the two types of areas because no compact continuous surface of either type exists. Thus, the boundaries separating *ecumene* from the non-*ecumene* are vague and complex. Though the great ice caps of Antarctica and Greenland are more complete and continuous non-*ecumene*, yet much of the non-*ecumene* is in the form of isolated unoccupied, intermittently occupied regions of varying size and is confined to desert wastes, cold barren, high mountains, swamps, primeval forests of the tropics and sub-arctics. It is estimated that about one-third of the total land area was barren waste, either cold or dry, with no settlements. While the movements of European people into the thinly peopled areas during the historic past led to significant shrinking of the non-*ecumene*, such a squeezing of the size of the non-*ecumene* was less typical of the present, due to serious obstacles. About 55-60 per cent of the total area of the continents could be classified as *ecumene*. These obstacles are basically climatic in origin, though drainage, soil, rough terrain, wild vegetation are often the auxiliary factors. Thus, the highest, the steepest, the coldest, the driest and the windiest lands continue to be the emptiest lands due to serious defects in their resource base. Not that the entire *ecumene* was equally crowded, there existed wide variations in the degree of population concentration within the *ecumene*. The variation within the *ecumene* were largely cultured conditioned and were related to socio-economic factors. About three-fourth of the world's population was confined to four major clusters, two of which are in Asia, one in Europe and one in North America.

The largest cluster is Primary cluster claiming about one-fourth of the world's total population was to be found in the East Asia encompassing China and Japan. This cluster of population was, thus, based at about 35°N latitudes (Table 8.2). The second largest cluster of population was tropical and claimed another one-fourth of the world's population. The tertiary cluster comprises the countries of South East Asia, Africa and other parts of the world.

Table 8.2: Population Distribution in World

Primary Cluster	*Secondary Cluster*	*Tertiary Cluster*
Major population cluster of the world, comprising 70 per cent of world population. 1. South Asia comprising Gan-getic Plains, Brahmaputra Plains and delta 2. East Asia—humid regions of China, Japan, Korea and Taiwan. 3. Counties of North-west Europe includes Netherland, Belgium, Luxemburg, Ger-many, Denmark and Britain. 4. United States of America	1. California—Pacific coast of western USA 2. South-eastern plateau of Eastern Brazil 3. Uruguay—Paraguay la-Plata river basin 4. Africa—Guinea coast 5. Asia—Java and Indonesia	1. South East Asia—river basins and coastal lowlands 2. Africa—Mediterranean regions, Nile valley 3. High Basin of Mexico 4. Form knots in and around urban and industrial settle-ments and also areas of agricultural settlements. 5. All urban industrial settlements of the world apart from primary and secondary concentration areas.

Source: Authors.

In recent scenario, the population of world reached 6,625 billion in 2007 and has crossed 7.0 billion around the close of the year 2011 and had reached 7,058 billion in 2012. Of these only 17.6 per cent was confined to more developed regions including North America, Europe, Japan, Australia, New Zealand and CIS countries. The less developed regions comprising Africa, Latin America, Asia, Malaysia etc accounted for over three-fourth (82.4%) of the world's total population (Table 8.3).

The increasing gap between the population of less developed countries and more developed countries is due to the large gap in growth rate of population between the two types of world. The latest population facts show as many as 267 births take place every minute in the world, out of which only 26 births take place in more developed countries and as many as 241 births take place in less developed countries. Accordingly, 385,046 people's births were being added to the population of the world at present per day, the corresponding figures for more developed and less developed realms are 38,147 and 346,899 persons per day, respectively. This is the reason why the gap between the populations of less developed and more developed countries is widened. It explains the continuously declining share of developed countries in the world's total population. Other indicators contributing to this widening of gap between the two types of world includes number of deaths, number of infant deaths and rate of natural increase.

It can also be concluded that out of every 10 births taking place in a minute in the world, 9 births take place in the less developed countries (Table 8.3). But in case of deaths,

Table 8.3: Population Distribution in Developed and Less Developed Countries (2012)

Population		World	More Developed Countries	Less Developed Countries
		7,057,075,000	*1,243,018,000*	*5,814,057,000*
Birth Rate	Year	140,541,944	13,923,718	126,618,226
	Day	385,046	38,147	346,899
	Minute	267	26	241
Death Rate	Year	56,238,002	12,191,662	44,046,340
	Day	154,077	33,402	120,675
	Minute	107	23	84
Natural Increase	Year	84,303,942	17,32,056	82,571,886
	Day	230,970	4,745	226,224
	Minute	160	3	157

Source: World Population Data Sheet, 2013.

out of every 5 deaths taking place in a minute in the world 1 death takes place in more developed countries and 4 in the less developed countries. It means that the gap in birth rates in less and more developed countries was much more than that in death rate. In terms of natural increase out of every increase of 50 persons in the world as many as 49 persons were being added to the less developed countries and only 1 per cent to the population of more developed countries.

8.5 Regional Distribution of Population

The population distribution gives a broad idea but it is necessary, however, to consider the regions too, in order to get better knowledge. The regional distribution of the world population clears that there are certain regions which are densely populated and other areas which seem to be empty and underpopulated. On the basis of distribution of population, the areas of the world may be classified into following four categories.

8.5.1 Highly Populated Areas

About 90 per cent population of the world lives in Northern hemisphere, most of which are concentrated in following 5 large human agglomerations: (1) East Asia (China, Japan, Korea, Taiwan, Hong Kong etc.); (2) South Asia (India, Pakistan, Bangladesh, Sri Lanka); (3) South-East Asia (Indonesia, Vietnam, Philippines, Thailand, Myanmar, Malaysia etc.); (4) Western Europe (UK, France, Germany, Poland, Netherland, Spain, Portugal, Italy etc.); and (5) Eastern Anglo-America (USA and Canada).

1. East Asia Agglomeration

It is the largest agglomeration of population in world. It claims a population of 1.6 billion or nearly 24 per cent of the world with a population of 1,298.84 million or 21.03 per cent of the world population (2005). Recent trends indicate slowing down of its population growth due to successful attempts in population planning as well as impact of industrialization and urbanization. The vigorous implementation of one child per couple has belied the Chinese code as scared duty. The present annual growth rate of China has declined to 1.1 per cent. China's dramatic growth in labour-intensive exports, higher economic growth propelled by market economy, health care and family planning programmes have guided its demographic transition but the Chinese population is far from evenly distributed; its south eastern coastal region and the alluvial river basin have witnessed heavy concentration of population (70%), while its frontier lands are still empty (30%).

China is basically rural but being less tropical than South Asia it has at its disposal a large collection of plants which enables it to have varied combinations of crops to be raised. It has large plain areas with fertile soils. In China, energy is completely devoted to cultivation. There is no rearing of animals, no grass fields. Nothing intended for feeding animals, seeing that man directly needs all the harvest. In the Chinese diet, there is neither milk nor meat, except some pork and poultry" (Perpillou, 1986). The most of the population in China is unevenly distributed and does not cover the area uninterruptedly. Highest population density is found in eastern plains of the country. The fertile valleys of Hwang Ho, Yangtze King and Tsekiang are very densely populated regions.

Japan is the only developed and industrialized country of Asia. It is highly populated with average density of population 337 persons/sq. km (Table 8.4). Its three-fourth population is concentrated in the island of Honshu. Japan is having 128 million people accounts for nearly 2.00 per cent population of the world. South Korea (50 million) and North Korea (25 million) are also densely populated having density of population 506 and 205 persons/sq. km, respectively.

2. *South Asia Agglomeration*

The second largest agglomeration of population is South Asia which claims a population of 1.5 billion. India is the second most populous country of the world with a population of 1,276 million (2010) and its decadal growth rate (1991-2001) is 21.34 per cent. Its population policy has not yielded desired results and demographic explosion is telling upon its economic development and social progress.

Distribution of population in India follows the amount of rainfall and fertility of the soil. Northern plains and coastal areas are much densely populated whereas the interior areas of the southern plateau and the arid and desert areas in north-west are sparsely populated. With an average density of about 378 persons/sq. km, the population of India is extremely irregular in its distribution. People swarm mainly in the Ganges valley which contains about 60 per cent of the population of the whole country swing to density of population above 500 persons/sq. km.

Pakistan is the second most populous country of South Asia. It has a population of 159.19 million (2005) which is less than the population of Uttar Pradesh but its fertility rate is 5.4 against India's rate of 3.3. Hence, its decadal growth is also higher than that of India. During 1975-2005 Pakistan population has increased from 70.3 million to 159.19 million.

Bangladesh ranks third in South Asia, with a population of 141.34 million (2005). Its fertility rate is 3.3 (against 4.9 in 1990), much lower than that of Pakistan. That is why its growth rate of population is also lower than that of Pakistan. Other countries of South Asia have low population (Nepal: 27.07 million, Sri Lanka: 18.8 million).

3. South-East Asia Agglomeration

It has a population of 545 million which is much higher than that of Europe (510 million). Its most populous country is Indonesia with a population of 270 million (WDR, 2019). In 1961 Indonesia had a total population of 97 million of which 63 million were concentrated in Java and Madura whereas the remaining islands accounted for 34 million only, its fertility rate is 2.7. It is predominantly a Muslim country but its rate of growth is lower than that of Pakistan.

South-east Asia lies as a transition zone between East Asia and South Asia and seems to be a third but small region of population concentration. Indonesia (248.5 million), Philippines (96 millions), Vietnam (89.7 million), Thailand (66 million), Myanmar (53 million) and Malaysia (30 million) are the countries with sizable population. *Philippines, the deltas of Mekong, Menam, Irawaddy and Java Island are densely populated areas.* All these countries are developing and agrarian countries where people are engaged mostly in rice production and plantation agriculture. Singapore is certainly the economic pole of the world. In a short spam of 40 years it has transformed its economy from the Third world to First world and stands next to Japan in Asia. It is certainly the pivot of the ASEAN economy and could withstand the regional economic crisis which crippled Indonesia, Thailand and Philippines. Singapore has taken its fallen rate very seriously, and has even announced 'Baby Bonus' for the parents having a second or third child and paid maternity leave for the third-time mothers.

Table 8.4: Country-wise Population Distribution in Highly Populated Agglomeration (2019)

Country	*Population (millions)*	*Percentage Share in World Population*
China	1433	19.0
Japan	1268	1.8
South Korea	51.22	0.7
India	1366	17.9
Pakistan	216	2.7
Bangladesh	168	2.2
Indonesia	270	3.5
Philippines	108	1.3
Vietnam	96.4	1.3
Germany	83	1.1
France	65	0.9
United Kingdom	67	0.9
United States	329	4.4
Canada	37.4	0.5
World	**7720**	**100**

Source: World Development Report, 2019.

4. Western Europe Agglomeration

In 1950 its population was 290 million which rose to 510 million (2001). The boundaries of the European agglomeration may be extended to 60°N Latitude, but its demographic axis is certainly 55°N Latitude. It has a favourable climate. This while region, bathed on the north by sea which is open for most of the year, has had an attraction for neighbouring peoples for the last ten centuries at least, today it is highly urbanized and industrialized region and has experienced the stationary demographic phase with low birth rates and low death rates. Their fertility rates are below the replacement level of 2.1 (Italy 1.2, Greece 1.3, Germany 1.3, Sweden 1.5, Portugal 1.5, Netherland 1.6, France 1.8, and Ireland 1.9). It is characteristics of development industrialization and urban society where attitude to the value of children and family size have drastically changed.

5. Eastern Anglo-America Agglomeration

As compared to the other population agglomerations, the Europe Anglo-America is the smallest in population size. It is much akin to the West European agglomeration in terms of modernization, industrialization and urbanization. Today the USA has a population of 329 million (2019) and is the third most populous country after China and India but accounts for 4.63 per cent of the world population (Table 8.4). During 1990s it has outstripped other developed countries in population growth because its fertility rate (2.1) is higher than that of other developed countries which have also provided substantial immigrants to the USA. The eastern coast of the USA. has turned into a gigantic megalopolis. The manufacturing belt extending from the great lakes to the Carribbean Sea is throbbing with industrial and urban activities and has its veritable projection in the adjustment of north-eastern Canada also. Another human agglomeration has developed in California, New York (30.1 million), the largest city and followed by Los Angles (16.7 million).

8.5.2 Moderately Populated Areas

In between the densely populated major areas and the sparsely populated areas lie transition zones have moderate population distribution. Apart from the above described five major regions of population agglomerations, there are many isolated and scattered nuclei of dense population. Among these small areas of small agglomerations important are Mexico and Central American countries, and Argentina in Latin America, Nigeria, east African countries, South Africa and Egypt in Africa, South-East part of Australia and countries of Eastern Europe.

Mexico is the second most populous country of North America with a population of 118 million. Mexico City is the second largest city of the world with a population of about 20 million. Argentina has a population of 40 million. In Africa, Nigeria is the most populous country with 148 million people. Logos in Nigeria with a population more than 15 million is the seventh largest city of the world. Egypt has a population of 85 million which is mostly confined to the Nile valley with sparsely populated areas in the marginal Sahara Desert. The coastal country of Ghana has a population of 26 million. In Eastern Europe Russian Federation (143 million), Ukraine (46 million), Romania (21 million), Greece (11 million), Belarus (10 million) are the countries which have population above 10 million.

8.5.3 Low or Sparsely Populated Areas

Like other parts of the world, in Asia also the regions that seem to be shunned by people are arid lands, the lofty mountains, dense forests and the cold polar ice caps. The deserts and arid lands extending from Arabian plateau to the Central Asia through Iran and Afghanistan form the greatest blank spaces in the distribution of population. Countries lying in these regions are sparsely populated. Saudi Arabia, Yemen, Oman, Iraq, Iran, Afghanistan etc. in South-West Asia, Thar Desert in Pakistan and India and Kazakhstan, Uzbekistan, Turkmenistan, Tajikistan, Kyrgyzstan in Central Asia are sparsely populated. The areas of extreme cold laying both in the southern and northern hemisphere are the second most sparsely populated regions of the world. Among them Antarctica, occupying an area of around 12.5 million sq. km, is virtually a non-ecumene where barely a few hundred scientists are living in their research stations. Besides, there are other permanently frozen lands in Canada, Eurasia, Greenland and Iceland where the total population is less than 5 lakh. If we add the cold high mountain regions then the total area of these frozen lands is nearly 25 per cent of the earth's area. Next come deserts (Sahara, Kalahari, Dead Hearts of Australia, Patagonia, Inter-montane Deserts of USA, Arabian Deserts, Gobi, Thar, Takla Makan, Karakum and Kyzikum etc.) which claims nearly 20 per cent of the earth's surface and are virtually empty lands with very sparse populations. The main problem with settling of deserts and arid lands is the deficiency and non-availability of water. The deserts form the greatest blank spaces in the distribution of population, because in the absence of water there can be no vegetation, and consequently, no food for human being or beast.

8.5.4 Ice Caps and Cold Regions

The second most sparsely populated are the areas of extreme cold, both in the northern and southern hemisphere. The Arctic region and the Antarctic continent are the regions of serve cold in which winters are dreaded, gloomy and long. The continent of Antarctica is almost exclusively uninhabited. In the Tundra region of Arctic, the hunting and fishing peoples live, who are a few in numbers. In fact, only a few seal-hunting Eskimos have been able to penetrate northward up to 82°N. Wherever, minerals are available men have settled there to exploit them, e.g. iron-ore in Gallivare (Sweden), gold in Yukon valley of Canada and Fairbanks and Fort Yukon in Alaska. Lofty mountains are almost uninhabited and population becomes sparser with altitude on mountains. The areas above 2500 m in the Himalayas, Alps and Rockies are almost uninhabited. Hot and wet tropical lands of Latin America (Amazonia), Africa (Congo Basin), and South-East Asia (excepting Singapore and Java) are also sparsely populated regions. These regions are covered by dense evergreen rainforest.

8.6 Continent-wise Population Distribution of World

According to the data available from United Nation Organization (UNO) and the above discussion, it is very clear that the world population distribution is highly uneven. Of all the continents Asia alone contributed about 61 per cent population of the World. Africa with 13 per cent population was the second largest continent of the world followed by Europe (12%), North America (7%), South America (8%) and Oceania (1%).

8.6.1 Asia

Asia is the largest continent of the world occupying about one-third land area of the world. As population is concerned, it is very large continent because about 61 per cent population of the world live in Asia alone. In 2018, total population of Asia is 4536 million accounting for approximately 60 per cent of the world's total population. The distribution of population in Asia is very uneven. In East Asia, South Asia and South-East Asia, some areas are very highly populated (already explained in regional distribution). But in contrast many areas are either very sparsely inhabited or are totally uninhabited. On the basis of general distribution pattern and density of population areas of Asia may be classified into following three categories:

There are two clear-cut areas of large and dense population: (i) East Asia including China, Japan, South Korea, North Korea and Taiwan, and (ii) South Asia comprising India, Pakistan, Bangladesh, Nepal, Bhutan and Sri Lanka. In between these two large human agglomerations, the third agglomeration of population lies in South-East Asia which is relatively small in size and is scattered. China, Japan, South Korea and North Korea are highly populated countries in East Asia. China with 1433 million people (Table 8.5) is the most populous country of the world. Nearly 19 per cent people of the entire world live in China alone. China is basically rural but being less tropical than South Asia it has at its disposal a large collection of plants which enables it to have varied combinations of crops to be raised. It has large plain areas with fertile soils. In China, "energy is wholly devoted to cultivation. There is no rearing of animals, no grass fields. Nothing intended for feeding animals, seeing that man directly needs all the harvest. In the Chinese diet "there is neither milk nor meat, except some pork and poultry" (Perpillou, 1986). The great multitude of population in China is unevenly distributed and does not cover the area uninterruptedly. High density of population (more than 500 persons/sq. km) is found in eastern plains of the country, however, overall it is 152 persons per sq. km in the country (World Population Prospects 2019). The fertile valleys of Hwang Ho, Yangtse King and Tsekiang are very densely populated regions. Major countries of South Asia are India, Pakistan, Bangladesh, Nepal and Sri Lanka. India according to population is the second largest country of the world after China (Table 8.5). It has 1366 million people to reside here accounting for about 18 per cent of the world's population. Its average density of population is 454 persons per sq. km. India is primarily an agrarian country and its more than 60 per cent people depend on agriculture and live in rural areas. There are many towns and large cities and industrial centres but agriculture and rural base yet dominant. South-east Asia lies as a transition zone between East Asia and South Asia and seems to be a third but small region of

Table 8.5: Population Distribution and Population Density in Major Countries of Asia, 2018

Country	*Population (in millions)*	*Percentage of the World*	*Density of Population (Persons Per Sq km)*
China	1433	19.0	152
India	1366	17.9	454
Indonesia	270	3.5	147
Pakistan	216	2.7	275
Bangladesh	168	2.2	1239
Japan	127.3	1.8	348
Philippines	108	1.3	357
Vietnam	97.4	1.3	308
Turkey	76	1.1	107
Iran	82	1.1	50

Source: World Population Data Sheet, 2018, World Population Prospects, 2019.

population concentration. Indonesia (270 million), Philippines (108 million), Vietnam (97.4 million), Thailand (69 million), Myanmar (54 million) and Malaysia (32 million) are the countries with sizable population. Philippines, the deltas of Mekong, Menam and Irawaddy and Java Island are densely populated areas. All these countries are developing and agrarian countries where people are engaged mostly in rice production and plantation agriculture.

The distribution of population in western Asia and interior parts of South-East Asia is neither dense nor sparse and therefore, these are moderately populated areas. Moderately populated countries include Turkey and coastal countries of Mediterranean Sea in West Asia and Cambodia, Laos, Myanmar and Malaysia in South-East Asia. Average population density of Turkey is 107 persons/sq. km. About 76 million people live in Turkey accounting 1.12 per cent population of the world. Most peoples of these countries are concentrated in low lands or the river valleys and sea coastal areas. In South Asia, southern parts of Pakistan and semi-arid region of Rajasthan and the interior parts of southern plateau in India are moderately populated regions.

Low and sparsely populated areas are also found in Asia. These regions seem to be shunned by people are arid lands, the lofty mountains, dense forests and the cold polar ice caps. The deserts and arid lands extending from Arabian plateau to the Central Asia through Iran and Afghanistan form the greatest blank spaces in the distribution of population. Countries lying in these regions are sparsely populated. Saudi Arabia, Yemen, Oman, Iraq, Iran, Afghanistan etc. in South-West Asia, Thar Desert in Pakistan and India and Kazakhstan, Uzbekistan, Turkmenistan, Tajikistan, Kazakhstan in Central Asia are sparsely populated.

8.6.2 Europe

Temperate climate and advanced economy of Western Europe is quite favourable or population concentration. Before nineteenth century, North-West Europe had predominantly agrarian economy and was densely populated. After Industrial Revolution, the European economy has gradually transformed into an industrial-urban economy. Now all the countries in North-West Europe are developed and industrialized countries dominated by urban economy. The areal size of most of the Vest European countries is small and natural resources are limited and have been exploited but they technologically very advanced, since last few decades, the populations of these countries have been stationary or are growing very slowly due to low fertility rate. Central European countries are included in this category of moderate population. European Russia, Ukraine, Romania, Greece, Hungary, Poland, Austria, Bulgaria, Albania, European Turkey etc. are the countries having moderate population size.

About 10.4 per cent (513 million) population of the world live in Europe. Its some parts are densely populated and many parts are sparsely populated. Its northern and eastern parts are sparsely populated but western and middle parts are either densely populated or moderately populated. Highly populated areas are North-western countries of Europe including Germany (82 million), France (66 million), United Kingdom (65 million), Italy (60 million), Spain (47 million), Netherlands (17 million), Portugal (11 million), Belgium (11 million) and Sweden (10 million) have considerable huge population (Table 8.6).

In these countries, density of population ranges between 50 and 125 persons/sq. km. The areas covering northern most and cold regions of Norway, Sweden, Finland and Russia are sparsely populated. A very few people mainly some tribals are found there. Average density of population in Norway (15), Finland (17), Sweden (22) and Russia as a whole (9) is below 25 persons/sq. km. Except only some including Sweden, Belarus, Greece, Ukraine, Spain etc. countries of this region experience density above 100 persons per sq. km. Population densities of Netherlands and Belgium are 405 and 367 persons/sq. km. In Germany (226), United Kingdom (263) and Italy (200) it is more than 200 persons per sq. km. (Table 8.6).

Table 8.6: Population of Major Countries of Europe

Country	*Population (in millions)*	*Percentage of the World*	*Density of Population (persons/sq km)*
Russia	144	2.0	9
Germany	82.5	1.1	226
France	66	0.9	117
UK	65	0.9	263
Italy	60	0.8	200
Ukraine	46	0.6	75
Spain	47	0.6	92
Poland	39	0.5	123
Romania	21	0.3	90
Netherlands	17	0.2	405

Source: World Population Data Sheet, 2018.

8.6.3 *Africa*

In the context of population, Africa is the second largest continent of the world after Asia. About 1100 million people live in this continent accounting for nearly 15.41 per cent of the world's population. The most conspicuous feature of the population distribution of Africa is its unevenness and highly irregular spatial distribution. Average density of population for entire Africa continent is near about 43 persons/sq. km. (World Populations Prospects, 2019). The population in Africa is concentrated in few limited areas apart from each other while its large areas are shunned by human beings because of arid expanses and dense equatorial forests. Waterless expanses, the deserts form the greatest blank spaces in the distribution of population. Sahara Desert in the northern Africa and Kalahari Desert in the southern Africa are either very sparsely populated or are without human beings. These deserts are inhabited only at isolated points where there is water.

The density of population in deserts is very slight. In the Libyan Desert it is 4 persons in per square kilometre. But in some oases the population is too great for local resources like precious metals, petroleum and other valuable minerals. A large area of central Africa (mainly Congo basin) is covered by dense rainforests and it is very difficult to form settlement there. Today the great forested areas of Congo basin have a very scattered population. In Africa, large areas remain uninhabited or nearly so, while relatively small points swarm with people. The example of such islets of dense population is found in the larger oases in the deserts of Africa. There rare spots afford many advantages that compensate for the drought around.

There are six small areas of relatively dense population which are fertile and have more or less alluvial soil, a warm, sunny climate and a supply of water for irrigation. Such areas are found in the lines of oases and in coastal lands. Following are the six densely populated areas in Africa.

Egypt situated in the eastern part of the Sahara desert is a large centre of population. It has 100 million populations with a density of population 98 persons/sq. km (World Population Prospects, 2019). In Egypt, area stretching along the Nile valley, represents a tiny area swarming with people. "In early times Egypt was acquainted with efficient agricultural methods and the practice of organized, collective irrigation. From the middle of the nineteenth century a prodigious increase in population followed the increase in cultivable land due to permanent irrigation." From 4.5 million persons in 1850 the population rose to more than 14 million in 1927 and to more than 100 million today. So Egypt is called 'Gift of the Nile'.

A cluster of population is found in the areas adjacent to the **Guinea coast**. It includes Cameroon, Nigeria, Benin, Togo, Ghana, Cote d'Lvoire and Liberia. Nigeria with more than 195 million people is the most populous country of Africa. Its density of population is 215 persons/sq. km. Ghana (29 million) with density above 130 is also densely populated.

South Africa and southern Mozambique forms the third moderately populated region. About 57 million people live in South Africa and about 29 million people live in Mozambique. South Africa is most developed country of Africa and its economy is based on mining, industry and agriculture.

A stretch of land along Atlas Mountain in **North West Africa** is also considerably populated. Situated along Mediterranean Sea, it is in the effect of Mediterranean climate. The countries of Morocco (36 million), Algeria (42 million) and Tunisia (11 million) are found concentrated in this small region.

Madagascar also seems to be little centre of population concentration with 26 million population and a density of 45 persons/sq. km.

8.6.4 North America

North America with population about 579 million is the fourth most populous continent after Asia, Africa and Europe. About 7.8 per cent of world population is found in North America. Main concentrations of population are in the eastern coastal plains of USA and Canada, in Maxico and Central America. North America has a very short history of human habitation. It is settled by Europeans mostly during seventeenth to early twentieth centuries. At present USA with a population of 316 million is the third most populous country of the world. It shares about 4.4 per cent population of the world (Table 8.7). Major population of United States is concentrated in coastal plain states. It is highly urbanized and industrialized

Table 8.7: Population of Major Countries of North America

Country	*Population (in millions)*	*Percentage of the World*	*Density of Population (Persons/sq. km)*
United States	329	4.4	33
Mexico	118	1.6	60
Canada	35	0.5	4
Guatemala	15	0.2	141
Cuba	11	0.15	102
Haiti	9	0.14	375

Source: World Population Data Sheet, 2018.

country. Mexico is second most populous country of North America with 118 million population accounting for about 1.60 per cent population of the world. It has average density of population 60 persons/sq. km. Mexico City is the second largest city of the world. Canada is a large country but its most areas are either very sparsely populated or completely uninhabited. Having 35 million population Canada is ranked on third place among the countries of North America.

8.6.5 South America

Like North America, South America is also newly inhabited continent. It is populated by emigrants mainly from southern European countries: Spain, Portugal and France. Present population of South America is nearly 401 million (about 5.6 per cent of the world population). Its major lands are very sparsely populated and some forested or deserted areas are without man. Main concentration of population is found along sea coasts particularly in Venezuela, Ecuador, Colombia, Brazil, Argentina, Uruguay, Paraguay, Peru and Chile. Brazil is the most populous country of South America with 196 million people accounting for 2.75 per cent of the world's population. It is the fifth most populous country of the world after China, India, United States and Indonesia. It is a sparsely populated country having density of population 23 persons/sq. km. It is emerging as an economic power also. Having a large land area and multiple resources it is capable of supporting for more people at a much higher level. It had a population of 52 million in 1950 which crossed 196 million mark in 2013. Its population is concentrated mainly in resource-rich north-eastern coastal region. Other populous countries in tropical South America are Colombia (48 million), Peru (31 million), Venezuela (30 million), and Ecuador (16 million). Average density of population in these countries ranges between 20 and 50 persons/sq. km. In all these countries, population is concentrated mainly in coastal areas (Table 8.8).

Table 8.8: Population of Major Countries of South America

Country	*Population (in millions)*	*Percentage of the World*	*Density of Population (persons/sq. km)*
Brazil	196	2.75	23
Colombia	48	0.76	42
Argentina	41	0.57	15
Peru	31	0.4	24
Venezuela	30	0.42	33
Chile	18	0.25	23
Ecuador	16	0.22	58
Bolivia	11	0.15	10
Paraguay	7	0.09	17
Uruguay	3	0.04	19

Source: World Population Data Sheet, 2018.

Argentina is third most populous country of South America with 41 million peoples. Its capital and port Buenos Aires with 13 million peoples is the tenth largest city of the world. Other temperate countries including Chile (18 million), Bolivia (11 million), Paraguay (7 million) and Uruguay (3 million) have population below 20 million. In these countries density of population does not exceed 22 persons/sq. km (Table 8.8).

8.6.6 Australia

Australia is the most sparsely populated continent. It is settled by only 23 million peoples accounting for only 0.32 per cent of the world's population. Its average density of population is only 3 persons/sq. km. In Australia, only limited parts of New South Wales and Victoria in the south-east are moderately settled regions. Tasmania is also moderately populated having density over 20 persons per sq. km. The vast area of Australian desert is almost uninhabited due to extreme aridity and lack of water. Gold mines have caused the growth of mining towns of Kalgoorlie and Coolgardie in the western part of Australian desert and drinking water is supplied from outside the region as far as 1000 km.

The distribution of world's population during the next few decades is expected to remain similar to the present pattern. The main reasons may be that the international law and politics do not permit free migration from one country to another country. Secondly, the sparsely populated areas have adverse climate and generally poor in resource potentials. World population will likely to rise by 50 per cent and reach around 11 billion by 2100. Reaching an estimated of 8 billion people in 2024 and 9 billion by 2040, while the 7 billion milestone was reached in 2018. The percentage share of population in different continent likely to change in different time periods, for example, Asia will be having 54.2 per cent of the total world's population which will go to decrease by 43.6 per cent in 2100, which can be the effects of low fertility rate, changes in population policy and social reasons. China with 1,433 million inhabitants (2018) was the most populous country of the world (Table 8.9). Its population was more than the total population of all the developed countries put together. India with a population of 1,366 million (2018) ranked second and was followed by USA (329 million), Indonesia (270 million) and so on. In 2018 China, India, USA, Indonesia etc. were the top ten most populous countries in the world, yet each one of them was at different stages of demographic transition. India was experiencing the demographic trap, China has almost succeeded in stabilizing its population, Pakistan, Bangladesh, Nigeria, Brazil etc. were still held up in the explosive second stage of the demographic transition. According to future projections, soon India was expected to acquire the top ranking position in the world in terms of population size. It is estimated that by 2050 India's population would reach 1,691 million while China will be shifted to second rank with a population of 1,311 million (Table 8.9). Prospects of large scale expansion of population in the cold, mountainous, arid or hot and wet climates seem to be dim. These areas remain inhabited

Table 8.9: Top Ten Most Populous Countries, 2018 and 2050

Country	*Percentage share in World*	*Population (in millions) 2018*	*Country*	*Projected Population (in millions) 2050*
China	19.4	1,433	India	1,691
India	17.9	1,366	China	1,311
USA	4.4	329	USA	423
Indonesia	3.4	270	Nigeria	402
Brazil	2.8	194	Pakistan	314
Pakistan	2.7	216	Indonesia	309
Nigeria	2.4	153	Bangladesh	226
Bangladesh	2.3	168	Brazil	213
Russian Federation	2.0	144	Congo	194
Japan	1.0	128	Ethiopia	166

Source: World Population Data Sheet, 2018.

by the indigenous groups that have adjusted to the harsh conditions over many centuries or by the outsiders who are busy in mineral extractions, military trainings and research activities.

8.7 Density of Population

Density of population is a quantitative measure that presents a ratio between the population of a region and its corresponding geographical area. It is used usually for comparative studies of population distribution. Geographers have been making more frequent use of the concept of *density of population*. It is simple concept of relating population size to the land area with a view to assessing crudely the pressure of population upon the resources of the area. Thus, it is a measure of the incidence of population concentration and is generally expressed in terms of persons per square kilometre (sq. km) or per square mile of land area rather than of gross area (land and water). The numerator in this calculation is population and the denominator is area.

Geographers, by way of manipulating the numerator or denominator, have derived various types of densities having a varying degree of utility in different situations. The objective has been to arrive at a better understanding of the population-resource relationship. These ratios have been called arithmetic density, physiological density or nutritional density, agricultural density, economic density etc. Clarke (1971) rightly observed that despite of some handicaps in these ratios, the concept of density of population is most revealing and is a useful tool in the analysis of the diversity of man's distribution in space.

8.8 Spatial Patterns of Population Density

The contemporary pattern of density of population in the world is largely a reflection of the history of settlement of different parts of the world and to some extent an expression of the carrying capacity of various regions. On the whole, World had an average density of 52 persons/sq. km, the sharpe differences between different countries say Singapore (6773 persons/sq. km) and Australia (3 persons/sq. km) notwithstanding. The less developed countries displays a general density of 70 persons and the more developed countries a density of only 27 persons. Thus, in comparison to the more developed countries, the less developed countries continue to be more crowded parts.

From among the various continents, the continent of Asia, which had oldest civilization of the world, undoubtedly was the most densely populated continent in the world. It had an average density of 169 persons/sq. km. Europe, with an average density of 32 persons/sq. km was only a distantly second raking continent in this regard. It was followed by Africa (35), South America (22), North America (16) and Oceania (3) in this order (Table 8.10). The spatial pattern of density of population in world reveals that although world, on an average, had a density of 52 persons/sq. km, there exist vast regional contrast in spatial pattern of population density (Fig. 8.1). The variation in densities is too prominent ranging from 2 persons/sq. km to 36,356 persons. Leaving these extreme cases apart, vast territories of the world in every continent still display a comparatively low density of less than 30 persons/sq. km. On the basis of variation in density pattern the world can be divided into four major areas.

Table 8.10: Density of Population in Selected Countries of World

Area/Country	*Density of Population (Persons/sq. km)*
World	52
Area of High Density	
Bangladesh	1088
South Korea	506
Netherland	405
Rwanda	422
India	328
Areas of Medium Density	
Romania	90
Spain	92
Greece	85
Cambodia	80
Malaysia	90
Areas of Low Density	
Guinea	48
Italy	46
Cameroon	45
South Africa	43
Columbia	42
Areas of Very low Density	
Bolivia	10
Chad	10
Russian Federation	9
Libya	8
Australia	3

Source: World Population Data Sheet, 2016.

8.8.1 Areas of High Population Density (Above 100 persons/sq. km)

The density of population in the countries which belong to Asian and European agglomerations of population is found high. Most densely populated areas lie in these human agglomerations. Bangladesh, South Korea, India, Lebanon, Japan, Israel, Sri Lanka, Philippines, Vietnam, Pakistan, China, Thailand, Indonesia etc. in Asia are highly populated countries having density over 100 persons/sq. km. In European countries *of* high population density include Netherlands, United Kingdom, Germany, Italy, Switzerland, Denmark, Czech Republic, Poland, France etc.

8.8.2 Areas of Moderate Population Density (51-100: persons/sq. km)

The moderately populated countries carry population densities between 50 and 100 persons/ sq. km. Such areas are found in almost all inhabited continents except only Australia. Continent-wise countries of medium density are given below:

- Europe: Romania, Spain, Greece, Ukraine, Ireland, Croatia, Bosnia and Herzegovina, Bulgaria, Georgia, Lithuania, Uzbekistan etc.
- Asia: Cambodia, Malaysia, Myanmar, Turkey, Jordan, United Arab Emirates etc.
- Africa: Ethiopia, Kenya, Egypt, Morocco, Tunisia, Benin, Sierra Leone, Burkina Faso, Senegal etc.
- Latin America: Costa Rica, Honduras, Mexico etc.

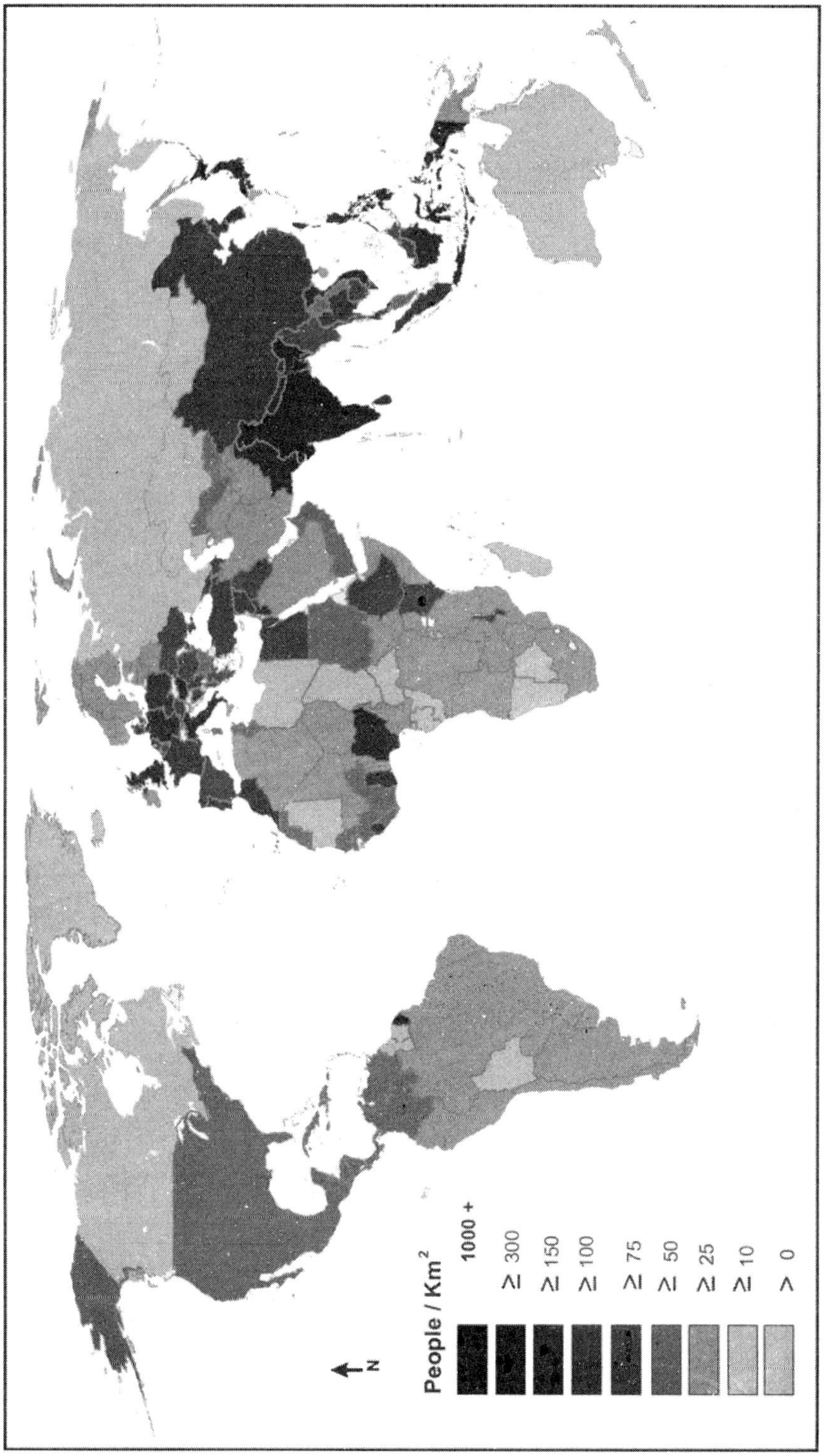

Fig. 8.1: World Pattern of Population Density, 2015

8.8.3 Areas of Low Density (11-50 persons/sq. km)

In the world context, the population density from 11 to 50 persons/sq. km is considered as low density. Countries falling under this category are: Ecuador, Panama, Peru, Brazil, Chile etc. in Latin America; Tanzania, South Africa in Africa; Tajikistan, Saudi Arabia in Asia.

8.8.4 Areas of Very Low Density (Below 11 persons/sq. km)

Very low density of population is found in mountainous country of Bolivia (Andes mountain in South America), in cold countries of Russia and Canada, in Chad, Libya and Mauritania lying in Sahara Desert, in arid country of Kazakhstan in Central Asia, and in Australia having two-third of its area as deserted land and in densely forested country of Central African Republic which occupy a large area of Congo basin. Thus, very sparsely populated regions are arid expanses, the polar caps, lofty mountains and dense forests.

Thus, East Asia and South Asia, were the world's two most populous countries, China and India, are located, which together constitute the world's largest belt of very high densities were more than 240 persons/sq. km. While the factors of long history of settlement and long period of population explosion may have contributed to very high density of population in countries of South Asia. Large parts including Australia, Canada, Most of South America, Northern Europe and Eurasia, Majority of African countries all have a population density of less than 30 persons/sq. km where the factors of history of settlement, supporting capacity of land, climatic and soil conditions, immigration/emigration volume, political economy, development strategy have played a significant role in different parts of low population density belts in the world (Table 8.10).

8.9 Population Distribution and Density in India

The development processes taking shape in the less developed countries under the stress of explosive state of demographic transition have often initiated redistributed tendencies in the spatial patterns of employment opportunities. Consequently, there are qualitative changes in the distributional pattern of population in these countries. Some of the typical characteristics of India's and its distribution that carry wide range of political, social and economic implications, both at national and international level include huge population base (844 million in 1991), ethnic multiplicity and rural bias and unevenness in its distribution.

8.9.1 Population Distribution

In its distribution, the Indian population had an overwhelmingly rural bias. Over three-fourth (76.6%) of its population lives in the countryside, largely, in agglomerated settlements. It is only Kerala and the Himalayas that the dispersed settlements occur (Spate and Learmonth, 1954).

According to Census (2011) reveals that from among the various states of India, Uttar Pradesh was the most populated state (Fig. 8.2) with a concentration index of 3.62 and Sikkim was the less populated state with a concentration index of 0.01 only. Among the Union Territories, Delhi emerges as the most crowded (5.70) and Lakshadweep the least

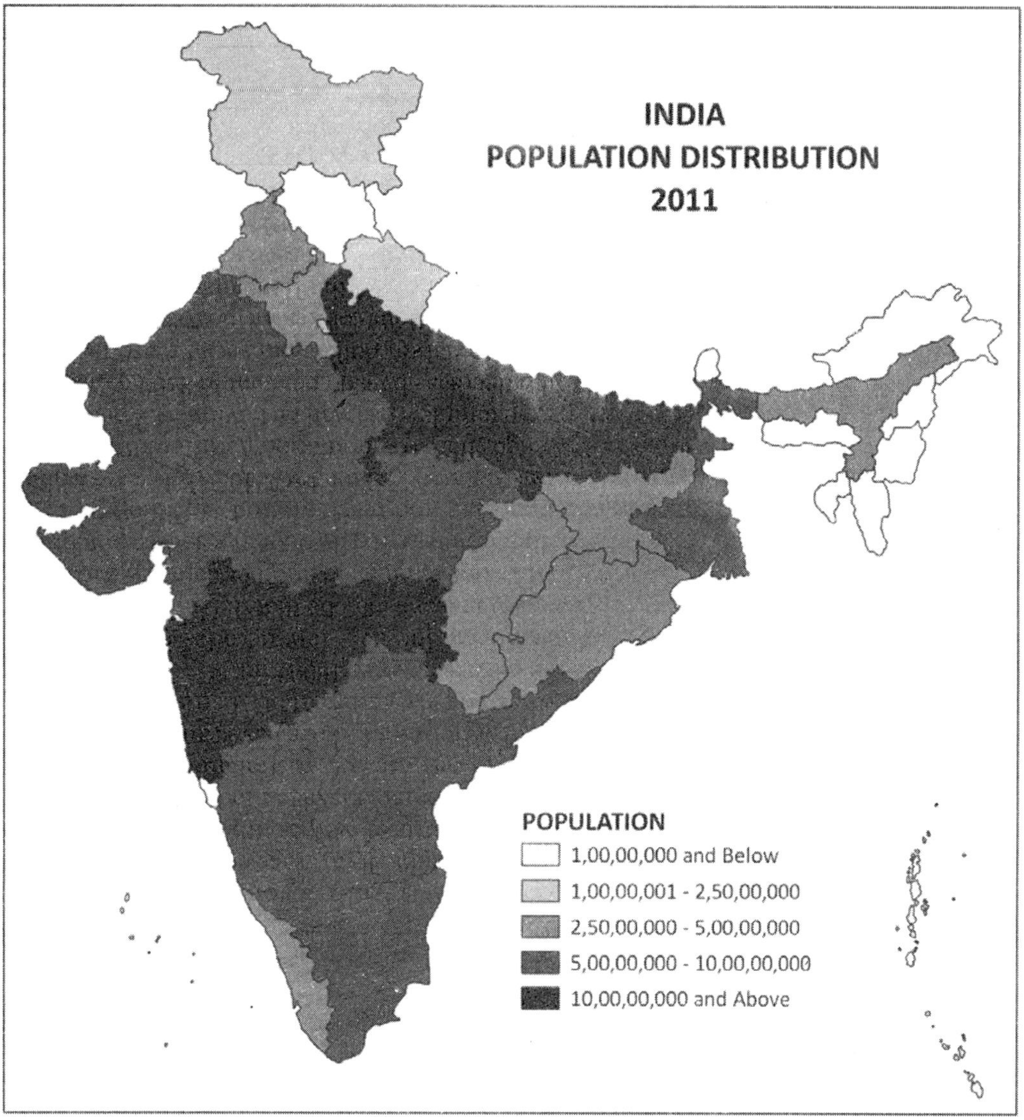

Fig. 8.2: Population Distribution in India, 2011
Source: Census of India, 2011.

crowded (0.04). Besides, Uttar Pradesh, there were nine more states, which displayed a relatively high degree of concentration of population. These include Bihar (2.27), Maharashtra (2.04), West Bengal (1.78), Andhra Pradesh (1.74), Madhya Pradesh (1.70), Tamil Nadu (1.58), Karnataka (1.21), and Rajasthan (1.11). In all these states the index of concentration was more than unity signifying that these were relatively more thickly populated states. By contrast, the hill states of Sikkim, Nagaland, Meghalaya, and Manipur, Tripura in Northeast and Himachal Pradesh and Kashmir in Northwest had extremely low population as well concentration index of less than 0.2. Other states displaying relatively low population includes Haryana, Punjab, Assam, Kerala and Odisha.

Interestingly, the border zone reveals contrasting patterns. The areas adjoining China and Burma have low population concentration, while those bordering with Pakistan, Nepal and Bangladesh show high population concentration. A low concentration index of less than 0.5 was observed in about 106 districts. These districts were confined to the Himalayas in the Northwest and the northeast and to the central highlands in Madhya Pradesh. A few of such districts were scattered in the Thar Desert, in the rain shadow areas of Peninsula, and on distantly located islands and the Bay of Bengal and Arabian Sea.

Apart from these major areas, a number of highly urbanized and industrialized districts spread out in different parts of the country, also displayed high incidence of population concentration. The recent expansion of administrative, transportation, general services and growth of commercial activities have made their own contribution to the process of population concentration in most of these districts.

With increasing population of the country, the density of population has also been increasing (Table 8.11). The latest census of 2011 has shown that now country has a general density of 382 persons/sq. km in comparison to the density of 325 in 2001. During 2001-2011 there is an addition of 57 persons/sq. km which denotes an additional burden of 57 persons/sq. km area of the country within only 10 years. This increase is more than double the existing density of population of USA (28), the most developed country of the world.

8.9.2 Patterns of Population Density

Within the country there is great variation in the spatial pattern of density, the maximum density of 11,297 persons/sq. km is recorded in Delhi followed by Chandigarh (9252) and Puducherry (2598), while minimum density of 17 persons/sq. km is found in hilly state of Arunachal Pradesh. On the basis of so wide range of population density, all the states and union territories may be classified into following three categories:

Table 8.11: Trends and Change in Population Density in India, Selected States and UTs

States/Union Territories	*1981*	*1991*	*2001*	*2011*	*Changes 2001-2011*
India	216	267	325	382	57
West Bengal	615	767	903	1,029	126
Bihar	402	685	881	1,102	299
Uttar Pradesh	377	548	690	828	138
Punjab	333	403	484	550	66
Maharashtra	204	257	315	365	50
Sikkim	45	57	76	86	10
Mizoram	23	33	43	52	9
Arunachal Pradesh	8	10	13	17	4
Delhi	4,194	6,252	9,340	11,297	1,957
Chandigarh	3,961	5,632	7,900	9,252	1,352
Puducherry	1,229	1,698	2,030	2,598	568
Andaman & Nicobar	23	34	43	46	3

Source: Census of India, 2001 and 2011.

1. Areas *of High Population Density (More than 500 persons/sq. km)*

This category includes such states and union territories of the country where the density of population is more than 500 persons/sq. km. Thus, however, 13 states and union territories are included in this category. Delhi has highest density with 11,297 persons/sq. km followed by Chandigarh (9252), Puducherry (2598), Daman and Diu (2169), and Lakshadweep (2013). From among major states Bihar (1102) occupied the first rank followed by West Bengal (1029), Kerala (859) and Uttar Pradesh (828). All these have density above 800 persons/sq. km. The presence of very high level of population density in Delhi, Chandigarh and Puducherry is mainly due to dominance of urban agglomerations there. Other states and Union territories under this category are Dadra and Nagar Haveli, Haryana, Tamil Nadu and Punjab.

2. Areas of Moderate Population Density (Between 150-500 persons/sq. km)

This category is characterized by population density between 150 and 500 persons/sq. km and spreads over 13 states of India. It is a transitional region between the zones of high density and low density. It includes major parts of the peninsular India incorporating the states of Jharkhand, Goa, Maharashtra, Andhra Pradesh, Karnataka, Gujarat, Odisha, Madhya Pradesh and Chhattisgarh. Punjab and Haryana in the north-west and Uttarakhand in Himalayan region is also included in the category of moderate density. The vast expanse of the moderately cultivated and thinly irrigated areas of southern India exhibit moderate population density

3. Areas of Low Population Density (Less than 50 persons/sq. km)

The category of low population density includes the most of the mountainous states such as Nagaland, Himachal Pradesh, Manipur, Meghalaya, Jammu and Kashmir, Sikkim, Mizoram and Arunachal Pradesh. Andaman and Nicobar Islands are also sparsely populated region with density of population below 50 persons/sq. km. The negative areas such as the deserts, mountainous and hilly areas and dissected plateau without much potential for agricultural or industrial development have very low density of population and remain very sparsely populated.

8.10 Summary

The single most striking fact about the world population is that it is not uniformly distributed. Moreover, the population distribution has continuously changed in space and time, with migration and varying rates of population growth. By contrast, three types of climates, cold, dry and hot-wet have been found to be the most hostile to man. The cold lands, the dry lands and the hot-wet regions, thus constitute the chief non-*ecumene* areas of the world. The recent history has witnessed appreciable expansion of settlements within the dry lands with the development of irrigation techniques. Two major suggestions of desalinization of sea water and augmenting the normal rainfall with cloud seeding techniques have often been made to dry land reclamation a possibility for future population expansion and management of resources.

Review Questions

1. Explain various factors affecting the population distribution with examples.
2. Describe regional distribution of population in world.
3. Why distribution of population in Asian continent is highly populated than western developed continent? Evaluate.
4. Discuss the regional patterns of population density in World.
5. Analyze the population distribution pattern in India.
6. "Population density patterns in India is highly uneven." Comment.

Analytical Questions

1. How population density of USA and DR Congo affects the national development of both the countries in different ways. Discuss.
2. Assess how the population distribution in the largest city in your state/province has changed over the last 30 years and name three factors that brought these changes over the time.

Chapter 9
Population Growth

9.1 Introduction

The population is the primary element of any area. One can never think of a state or country without a resident population. The population also play an essential role in modern economic development. It is the most potent resource which can alter the entire face of the country if utilised potentially. Population study is concerned not only with the population variables but also with the relationship between population variables such as social, economic, political, biological, genetic and geographical and, further, the interrelationship between those variables. It includes both qualitative and quantitative aspects of the human population.

Population studies were not given much preference in the past. But at present days people of different field require the information about population, so its importance is increasing day by day. Population education is very valuable at present to be a successful geographer, sociologist, politician, administrator and environmentalist. Its study is very important in various fields to like to do social work, to develop the economic field, to do political work, different administration work and to make rules and regulation. The growing consciousness among the social scientists about the necessity for exploring the trends in population change may be attributed to: (i) the recent population explosion resulting in a great demand for food-stuffs and other resources; (ii) the world economic recession on 1980-83; (iii) widening gap between per capita income of developed and less developed countries; and (iv) Increasing environmental damage; and Increasing population pressure upon the limited resources of the less developed world. Population studies, thus, are pivot to the region's demographic dynamism. The understanding of population in an area holds the key to the understanding of the entire demographic structure of the area.

9.2 Meaning and Measures of Population Growth

The concept of population change and the increase is often used to connote the change in the number of inhabitants of the territory during a specific period, irrespective of the fact whether the change is negative or positive. Such a change can be measured both regarding absolute numbers and regarding percentage. A "natural population increase" occurs when the birth rate is higher than the death rate. While a country's population growth rate depends on the natural increase and migration, world population growth is determined exclusively by the natural increase.

The growth of the population is often calculated for ten years. This period normally synchronises with the inner-census period. Such a growth rate calculated with the help of actual population counts is known as actual rate of population growth. Population geographers have often made use of the natural rate of growth of population. This natural rate of growth of population is obtained by dividing the difference between the births and deaths of the population at the beginning of the period and multiplying it by hundreds. It implies that while in case of natural growth rate only the births and deaths are taken into accounts, in case of actual growth rate the factor of migration is also taken into consideration. Both actual and natural rates of population growth have been subjected to spatial portrayal and interpretation by the geographers. It is easy to determine the change in absolute numbers by subtracting the numbers of inhabitants at an earlier point in time from that of at a later point in time, the measurement of percentage change poses a little problem.

The growth of population in percentage is calculated by dividing the absolute change by the population at an earlier date and multiplying it by hundred. Logically, the denominator should be mid-period population, but since the mid-period population will have to be estimated, therefore, the growth rate is normally calculated by using the actual population size at the beginning point under review.

9.3 Factors Affecting Population Growth

Fertility, Mortality and Migration are the three basic components of population change. In order to calculate the magnitude of population change in an area, it is essential to measure fertility, mortality and migration precisely.

9.3.1 Fertility

Fertility refers to the occurrence of birth. However, it is different from fecundity which refers to the reproductive capacity of women during her entire reproductive period. It is not very easy to measure fecundity, but the measurement of fertility does not pose many problems. Various measures of fertility have been coined. These include crude birth rate, general fertility rate, child women ratio, fertility ratio, total fertility rate etc.

Determinants of Fertility

The attributes that shape the fertility behaviour of a population in an area have been probed more by sociologist than by population geographers. The spectrum of factors determining fertility is significantly wide and the range may vary from the basic biological factors of the race to such social constraints as the political ideology. The basic determinants of fertility include fecundity; age at marriage, duration of the marriage, marriage system, sexual habits etc. besides these, there is a long list of other factors, which make their contribution in influencing the fertility patterns of a population. For convenience, we may classify these factors into four broad categories of biological, demographic, socio-cultural and economic.

World Patterns of Fertility

One of the most popular measures of fertility is the crude birth rate. The data on the crude birth rate of different countries covering almost the entire world is made available by the United Nations through its various publications. The 2004 World Data sheet brought out by the United Nations reveals that the world had an average birth rate of 21 per thousand. The crude birth rate for the less developed regions of the world was more than two times that of the developed regions. The developed countries have a birth rate of 11 per thousand while the corresponding figure for the less developed countries was 24 per thousand. From amongst the various continents, Africa continues to be far ahead of all the continents regarding crude birth rate. It had a birth rate of 38 per thousand. The continent of Latin America was the second-ranking continent with the birth rate of 22 per thousand. Asia, the most populous continent, ranked third with an average birth rate of 20 per thousand. It was followed by Oceania 17 per thousand and North America 14 per thousand and Europe 10 per thousand.

9.3.2 *Mortality*

Mortality has been defined as permanent disappearance of all evidence of life at any time after birth taken place. Death can occur only after a live birth has occurred. Therefore, for mortality, all deaths before births are to be excluded. Not all countries follow this definition recommended by United Nations. In countries like Equatorial Guinea and Morocco, infants who die within 24 hours of birth are classified as still births. In countries like Algeria, French Guinea and Syria, infants who are born alive but die before the end of the registration period, which may last, in some cases, for a few months, are considered still births.

Determinants of Mortality

The causes of mortality vary both in space and time. Spatially different regions are at different stage of socio-economic development and technological advancement, therefore, the cause of mortality varies from one part of the world to another. There is a large variety of factors that determine the mortality pattern in the world. A broad distinction has been made between *endogenetic* (biological) and *exogenetic* (environmental) factors. The *endogenetic* factors are essentially biological in nature, which cause death due to rapid alternations in the functioning of human body. The diseases of the circulatory system, the diseases that may cause infant mortality and cancer are some of the typical example of this category. The *exogenetic* factors that are environmental in nature comprise the environmental influences giving rise to infections pulmonary and digestive diseases. The environmental conditions which have their link largely with climate (Sharpe temperature, excessive cold, excessive heat) have been found to have adverse effect on the human body. The role of such factors is most prominent in case of countries, which are at low level of technological advancement. Broadly speaking, a country passes from a preponderance of *exogenetic* factors to a complete dominance of *endogenetic* factors as it evolves demographically. Besides that, broadly the mortality rates in an area may be governed by its demographic structure, social advancement and economic development. Demographically, the age structure is most prominent. Other demographic factors like sex composition and degree of urban development are also significant. Socially, incidence of infanticides, restrictions on widow remarriage, adequacy of medical facilities, general conditions of nutrition, housing and sanitation, literacy standards and religious beliefs are important. Among the economic factors, the standard of living or per capita income and type of economy are considered significant. Besides, the factors like natural calamities, wars, epidemics, food shortage also cause mortality on a large scale as and when these come.

World Pattern of Mortality

It was in 1962 that the United Nations had hoped that within a decade or two, the vast majority of the world's population will have an expectation of life at birth of 65 years or more. The World Population Data Sheet, 2012 reveals that the crude death rate, for the world as a whole, was 8.0 per thousand. There was little to differentiate between the mortality rates of the developed regions and less developed regions. The developed countries had a death rate of 10 per thousand and less developed countries had a death rate of 8 per thousand. Thus average death rate of more developed countries was higher than that of less developed countries.

9.3.3 Migration or Mobility

The third major components of population change referred to earlier was migration. While the measures of fertility and mortality have been discussed at length in the preceding pages, the measurement of migration is not that easy in the absence of direct data on migration. While the place of birth data do help in giving some information on the magnitude of in and out migration, the main problem arises when migration, the main problem arises when migration and mortality are to be integrated. Wunsch and Termote (1978) have successfully demonstrated that the magnitude of migration varies significantly when mortality probability is taken in account. They have discussed the measures of migration at length in their book '*Introduction to Demographic Analysis*'. For geographers, it is not merely a reallocation of human resources but is a process, which has a three-fold impact: (i) on the area experiencing in-migration, (ii) on the area experiencing out-migration; and (iii) on the migrants themselves. Whenever migration takes place, in whatever form, it modifies the area or origin, the area of destination as well as the way of life of the migrants. Beaujeu-Garnier (1966) rightly remarked that area which people out-migrate, the area to which they in-migrate and the migrants themselves never the same. Migration may be permanent, temporary or seasonal. It may take place from rural to rural areas, rural to urban areas, urban to urban areas and urban to rural areas.

Determinants of Migration

Migration is a complex phenomenon and an enquiry about the motives behind it is the most difficult part to analyze of the process of migration. With regard to the determinants of population, distinction has been made between push and pull factors. Push factors make the place or origin seem less attractive for reasons like unemployment, poor living, political turmoil, unpleasant climate, natural disaster, epidemics and socio-economic backwardness. The pull factors make the place of destination seem more attractive than the place of origin for reasons like better job opportunities and living condition, peace and stability, security of life and property and pleasant climate.

Migration Distribution in World

In the classical world, international migration were considered as voluntary, rational attempts of the human beings to maximise utility and to attain uplift. Recently, not only the number of persons involved in international migrations had decreased significantly but also the purpose of migration has undergone a change. The number of international migrants worldwide has continued to grow rapidly over the past fifteen years reaching 244 million in 2015, up from 222 million in 2010, 191 million in 2005 and 173 million in 2000. Between 2000 and 2005, the international migrant stock grew by an average of 2 per cent per year. During the period 2005-2010, the annual growth rate accelerated, reaching 3 per cent. Since then, however, it has slowed, falling to around 1.9 per cent per year during the period 2010-2015. High-income countries host more than two-thirds of all international migrants. As of 2015, 71 per cent of all international migrants worldwide, equal to 173 million international migrants lived in high-income countries. Of these, 124 million migrants were hosted in high-income OECD countries, while 49 million migrants were living in other high-income non-OECD countries. Only 29 per cent (71 million) of the world's migrants lived in middle- or low-income countries. Of these, 61 million resided in middle-income countries and 9 million in the low-income countries.

9.4 Phases of World Population Growth

In England, some economists including Wallace (1753), Adam Smith (1766) and Robert Malthus (1798) tried to study the trend of population growth systematically but these efforts were too fragmentary. Every matter relating to population growth previous to the nineteenth century has almost no scientific value. The first modern census was held in Sweden in 1749 but it was not complete. The United States had their first systematic census in 1790, Great Britain and France in 1801 and Russia in 1897. The First Census in India was held during 1869-72.

The present distribution of mankind in the world is the result of universal diffusion of human species from earliest times. It is estimated that during 99 per cent of human history, the world population remained scanty and sporadic. The rapid growth in population began from mid of the eighteenth century. The time span of population growth in the world is classified into following time periods.

9.4.1 Ancient Period (Prehistoric Time to 4000 B.C.)

There is no direct and documented evidence to know the growth, pattern and density of population of the world during this era. The scholars of population studies have, however, estimated the population of the past on the basis of circumstantial evidence. For example, agriculture was unknown before about 8000 B.C.; prior to that all humans groups made their living by hunting and gathering. Not more than 52 million sq. km of the earth's total land area of about 150 million sq. km could have been successfully utilized in this way by our early ancestors. From this assumption and the population density figures of hunting and gathering tribes of today, it has been estimated that the total population of 8000 B.C. was about 5 million (Durand, 1974).

In Ancient period the world population remained scanty and sporadic. It can be attributed to the fact that because people were nomadic herders. Most areas were unoccupied and population was sporadic with blank spaces here and there and was about stationary. The growth rate of world population must have been about 0.00001 per cent per annum (Maurya, 1989). However, the world population gained momentum during the Neolithic age when, the Agricultural Revolution eased man's relationship with his environment by modifying the harshness of natural surroundings. The information had been passing from generation to generation and his transmission of knowledge about hunting, gathering, method of food preparation and even identification of enemies helped in the expansion of agriculture and consequently the growth of population.

At the time of birth of Christ the estimated world population was about 300 million, of which India and China each claimed 60 million, Egypt (30 million), Mediterranean Europe (30 million) and the remaining population was sprinkled in other parts of the world. By 1000 A.D. the world population stood at 375 million and could rise to 500 million by 1650 (NCERT, 2018).

9.4.2 Medieval Period (4000 B.C. to 1650)

During the medieval period of human history, agriculture has started taking the shape of business and there was more emphasis on trade and commerce. This helped the formation of city-centred society, which had important demographic consequences. The rise of city-centred society, associated with improvement in farming, led to a fairly continuous belt of densely populated land, which stretched from the Mediterranean Sea across Southwest Asia to India and by way to the Central Asia to China. The usual course of population growth, at this time, was marked by a gradual growth for a short period followed by a sudden decline. During comparatively normal times, unhampered by wars and crop failures, the death rates would remain unchanged and would be slightly higher than the death rates, population tend to gather some surplus, which would serve as insurance against a calamity. There has been a very slow growth rate of population which continued for long time from 4000 BC to 1500 (Table 9.1). The main characteristics of population of the world in medieval period prior to the industrial revolution were high death rate, high infant mortality rate, short life expectancy, periodic famines and vulnerability to epidemics. Consequently, there were Sharpe periods of population decline followed by short-term revival. In such a way the population was growing with very slow pace. The medieval period experienced a considerable growth and development of towns and cities and the consequent increase in the demand and supply of consumer goods particularly of agricultural products. By the end of medieval period, in 1650 the world population reached about 550 million.

Table 9.1: World Population Growth in Medieval Period

Year	*Average Annual Growth Rate (%)*
4000 B.C.	0.01
01 AD	0.15
1000	0.08
1500	0.27

Source: Weeks (2002).

9.4.3 Modern Period (1650 to Present)

The modern period of rapid growth began after 1650. The industrial revolution and the medical revolution pushed the world population to one billion by 1850. The Industrial revolution in Europe and North America created a new industrial urban society in which agriculture and other primary activities began to decline and activities related to manufacturing (secondary) and services (tertiary) began to take an increasingly important role. In this period, the population was attracted to migrate from rural to urban areas and the productivity per capita increased substantially. The world's population has greatly increased in last three centuries but the rate of growth increased sharply only after 1900.

The growth rate of population in the medieval period moved at a snail's pace for thousands of years reached at its peak in 1970 (Table 9.2). The average annual growth rate of population in 1970 was the highest 2.07 per cent and the doubling period of world population had reached its lowest of 33 years. Prior to that, the doubling period of world's population at the time of beginning of Christian era was 463 years. It rose to 906 years by 1000 AD. Since then it continued to suffer a steep decline to the extent that by the dawn of industrial revolution in the West it had declined to 203 years. In the post-industrial period, there was a consistent decline in the doubling period of population due to sharp decline in mortality rates first in industrial countries and later on in the selected less developed countries of the world as well. However, the year 1970 marks another significant divide in the world's growth rate of population as it started declining due to increasing control on fertility even in large sized developing countries.

Table 9.2: Growth of World Population (1650-2013)

Year	Population (millions)	Increase (millions)	Increase (percentage)	Annual Growth Rate (percentage)	Doubling Period (years)
1650	550	-	-	-	-
1750	720	170	30.9	-	203
1800	930	210	29.2	-	163
1850	1330	400	43.0	-	129
1900	1660	330	24.8	-	118
1950	2510	850	51.2	1.0	47
1960	3000	490	19.5	2.0	52
1970	3650	650	21.7	2.1	33
1980	4400	750	20.5	2.0	41
1990	5300	900	20.5	1.9	44
2000	6100	800	15.0	1.6	55
2010	6860	860	14.1	1.3	67
2013	7138	278	4.0	1.2	-
2019	7706	568	48	1.07	-

Source: United Nations Population Reference Bureau, 2019.

A rapid acceleration in population growth is the product of decline in mortality and the widening gap between the birth rate and death rate. The gap between the births and deaths increased steadily for about 200 years. Consequently, by the middle of 20th century, the population of the world reached 5 billion mark. This shows that while it had taken the world more than one million years to reach one billion mark in 1804, the next billion was added in just 120 years (1927). The third billion was added in 32 years (1960) and the fourth billion came in just 15 years (Fig. 9.1). The fifth billion mark was reached in 1988, i.e. just in 13 years. Implying that the last billion was added in lesser than 12 years. The future growth of world population is estimated to be 8 billion by the year 2048.

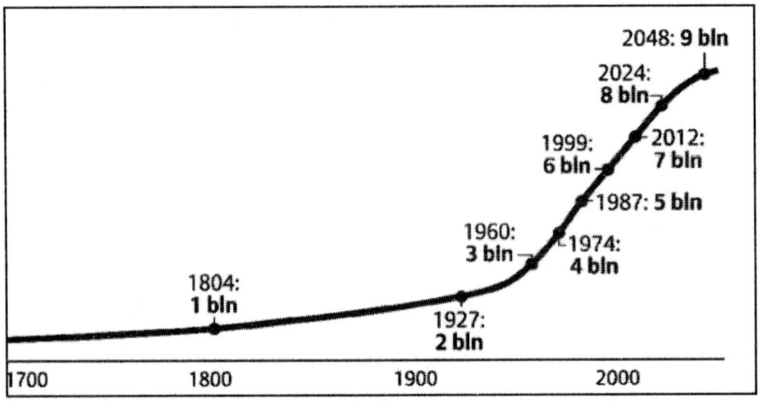

Fig. 9.1: World Population: A Historical Growth Chart

Source: Based on UN World Population Prospects.

9.5 World Pattern of Population Growth

After going through the phases of population growth in world, it is worthwhile to study its growth in different continents to find out how the growth rates varied from continent to continent and population growth in different parts of the world can be compared. During 1800-2015 the world's population has grown from 905 million to 7138 million experiencing 612 per cent increase (Table 9.3). During the same period the increase in population was experienced 573 per cent by Asia (597 to 4302 million), 285 per cent by Europe (192 to 740 million), 952 per cent by Africa (90 to 1100 million), 8052 per cent by North America (6 to 557 million), 2331 per cent by South America (19 to 401 million) and 5731 per cent by Australia (1 to 35 million).

Table 9.3: Growth of Population According to Continents (in millions)

Year	*Asia*	*Africa*	*Europe*	*North America*	*South America*	*Oceania*	*World*
1650	327	100	103	1	12	2	545
1750	475	95	144	1	11	1	727
1800	597	90	192	6	19	1	905
1850	741	95	274	26	33	1	1170
1900	915	120	423	81	63	6	1608
1950	1377	122	572	166	166	13	2416
2000	3780	830	680	440	340	32	6102
2013	4302	1100	740	557	401	38	7138
2019	4601	1308	747	366	401	42	7713

Source: World Population Data Sheet, 2019.

9.5.1 Asia

About 350 years ago (1650) **Asia** was most populous continent. At that time its population was 327 million accounting for more than 60 per cent population of the world. This ratio is maintained today also. Its population increased four times during 300 years (from 1650 to 1950) and became 1377 millions. The rate of population increase was high during preceding 63 years and it touched the level of 4302 million in 2013. Rate of average annual increase was 1.9 per cent during 1980-85, 1.6 per cent during 1990-95 and 1.2 per cent during 2000-05. These data show the trend of decreasing growth rate since 1980. China, with about one-fifth of the world's population, and India, with about one-sixth. Because of its higher fertility, India's population is expected to pass China in the coming century. The annual growth rate is found 2.0 per cent or above in some other Asian countries like Saudi Arabia (2.3), Pakistan (2.3), Philippines (2.0) and Nepal (2.0). It is high in context of Asia (1.3) and World (1.2).

9.5.2 Africa

Africa is the second most populous continent after Asia with 1100 million people (2013), 13.8 per cent of the world's population. Two 17th Century writers, Riccioli and King, had both made guesses of 100 million for Africa's population and Willcox assumed that this population was maintained for the next two centuries. Africa's population is growing faster than that of any other continent and its share of the world's population is expected to rise. Most countries of Africa during 1990-95 were experiencing an average annual growth rate of over 3.0 per cent which could be explained only through their high fertility rates and sharply declining mortality rates. Having so high growth rate, the population of Africa is expected to double by 2050. During 2000-07 the average annual growth rate of population experienced by some African countries including Chad (3.0), Congo (3.0) and Uganda (3.2) was above 3.0 per cent. Over a dozen countries were experiencing an average annual growth rate of population between 2.0 and 3.0 per cent.

9.5.3 Europe

Europe is the third most populous continent with 740 million population (2013), about 11.4 per cent of the world's population. Probably there is no country in Europe which is growing faster than 1.0 per cent annually. There are only few countries like Norway (0.7), Italy (0.6), France (0.7), Austria (0.5), Greece (0.4), Denmark (0.3), which experienced annual growth rate 0.3 per cent or above but below 1.0 per cent during 2000-07. A number of European countries since beginning of the present century are experiencing continuous decline in their population. Negative annual growth rate of population during 2000-2010 is recorded by Norway (–0.7%), Romania (–0.6%), Russia Federation (–0.5%), Belarus (–0.4%). In such countries mortality rates are not very high but fertility rates are extremely low even infant mortality rate is also very low.

9.5.4 North America

North America has grown very fast from 1900 onwards and has reached to 557 million in 2013 (Table 9.3). During the second half of the century, the average annual rate of population growth for North America was 3.65 per cent the highest ever recorded. This was partly due to continuous immigration from European countries and partly due to early marriage and extremely high marital fertility. After economic recovery and the end of the war, North America experienced "baby boom". The rate of population growth began to increase and the continued to go up till 1960, after which the birth rate started declining, resulting in a decreased rate of population growth. The area including Mexico and Central America and complete South America is known as Latin America because most of the countries of this region use predominantly Latin Language.

9.5.5 South America

Most of the countries of South America recorded a population growth rate ranging between 1.0 and 2.0 per cent per annum, which by and large was the result of low mortality and low fertility. Among South America, countries except only Uruguay (0.1%), most of the countries experienced annual growth rate of 1.0 per cent or above but below 2 per cent. Such countries include Mexico, Argentina, Chile, Peru, Brazil, Colombia etc. Anglo-America comprises highly developed countries. Birth rates and death rates of these countries are very low (below 10 per thousand) but birth rate is slightly higher than that of death rate. The population growth rates of USA and Canada are considerably higher than those European countries mainly due to coming immigrants from throughout the world for employment and other purposes.

9.5.6 Oceania

Australia, New Zealand, Papua New Guinea and Island of Pacific Ocean grouped together to be called Oceania. Australia and New Zealand are considered developed countries and are dominated by European people and Western culture. Papua New Guinea and other islands of Pacific Ocean are less developed. During 2000-2007 Australia and New Zealand both experienced the growth rate of 1.3 per cent per annum in their population. Fertility and mortality in these countries are low but fertility is somewhat above the mortality that make possible a slight growth in population. It is clear from the above discussion that in the 21st century population contribution of developing countries, particularly of Asia, Africa and Latin America will further increase and that of the developed countries will decrease. Australia, New Zealand, Papua New Guinea and Island of Pacific Ocean grouped together to be called Oceania. Australia and New Zealand are considered developed countries and are dominated by European people and Western culture. Papua New Guinea and other islands of Pacific Ocean are less developed. During 2000-2007 Australia and New Zealand both experienced the growth rate of 1.3 per cent per annum in their population. Fertility and mortality in these countries are low but fertility is somewhat above the mortality that make possible a slight growth in population. It is clear from the above discussion that in the 21st century population contribution of developing countries, particularly of Asia, Africa and Latin America will further increase and that of the developed countries will decrease.

It is interesting to note that large territories of the European world have recorded a decline in their population during this period. It is because of their mortality rates being higher than the fertility rate. The revival of high mortality in these countries is dangerous because of Infant Mortality Rate in all such countries is extremely low. Rest of the Europe too had the lowest growth rate of less than 1 per cent. By contrast, highest growth rate of population was to be found in the continent of Africa, where in this period most of its countries were experiencing an average annual growth rate of over 3 per cent. The Islamic world from Asia too was not far from Africa in this regard. Most of Muslim countries of Asia also continue to record a population growth rate of 2 to over 3 per cent per annum. These apart, the countries like Mexico, Panama, Venezuela, Bolivia, Paraguay, Vietnam, and Cambodia etc. are some of the non-Muslim countries of the world where too the growth rate was above 3 per cent per annum (Figure 9.2). In all these countries the fall in mortality had got well established, while the fall in fertility was yet to make its mark. In most of these countries, the urban population grew at much faster rate than its rural counterpart, signifying some contribution of rural to urban migration in their intra-country regional pattern of population growth.

However, by 2011, the spatial pattern of growth of population in the world has undergone tremendous changes (Fig. 9.2). The comparison between Figures 9.2 and 9.3 reveals that the shades have become much lighter. In all most every part of the world the annual growth rate has declined considerably. The number of countries having more than 3 per cent per annum growth rate has declined significantly and such countries are more confined to East Africa. Similarly, the decrease in population has become more widespread in European countries. Countries of North America also have a growth rate of less than 1 per cent, same in case of Australia and New Zealand. The two most populous countries of the world, China and India now have below replacement level natural increase.

9.6 Population Growth in Developed and Developing Countries

The countries of the world can be dichotomously classified into two categories in accordance with certain indicators of social and economic enhancement, the developed and developing. The population of developing countries was growing faster than those of developed countries until 1950. After 1950, the situation has reversed mainly due to restrictions on international migration. Average annual growth rate was recorded 1.1 per cent in the population in developed countries during 1950-1975. This growth rate decreased to 0.8 per cent during 1975-2005 and is expected to be 0.5 per cent during 2005-2016. The overall growth rate in developed countries is quite lower than half of developing countries during last 30 years. Only some large countries like Australia, Canada and United States has experienced average annual population growth rate of 1.0 per cent or slight above (Table 9.4). Most of the developed countries are growing at very slow rates, i.e. even below 1.0 per cent. The average annual population growth rate has not exceeded even 0.5 per cent in Norway (0.5%), France (0.5%), Switzerland (0.5%), Japan (0.5%), Finland (0.5%), Poland (0.4%), Sweden (0.3%), United Kingdom (0.2%), Russia Federation (0.1%), Hungary (-0.1%).

Since 1950, developing countries have been growing more rapidly than those of developed countries. The data on population growth by UN reveal that the average annual population growth rate of developing countries was recorded 1.9 per cent during 1975-2005. This figure was only 0.8 per cent in the case of developed countries in the same period. Almost all the countries of Asia (except only Japan), Africa and Latin America are the constituents of the developing countries. The average annual population growth rates in Sub-Saharan Africa (2.8%), South West Asia (2.6%) and South Asia (2.1%) are higher than 2.0 per cent.

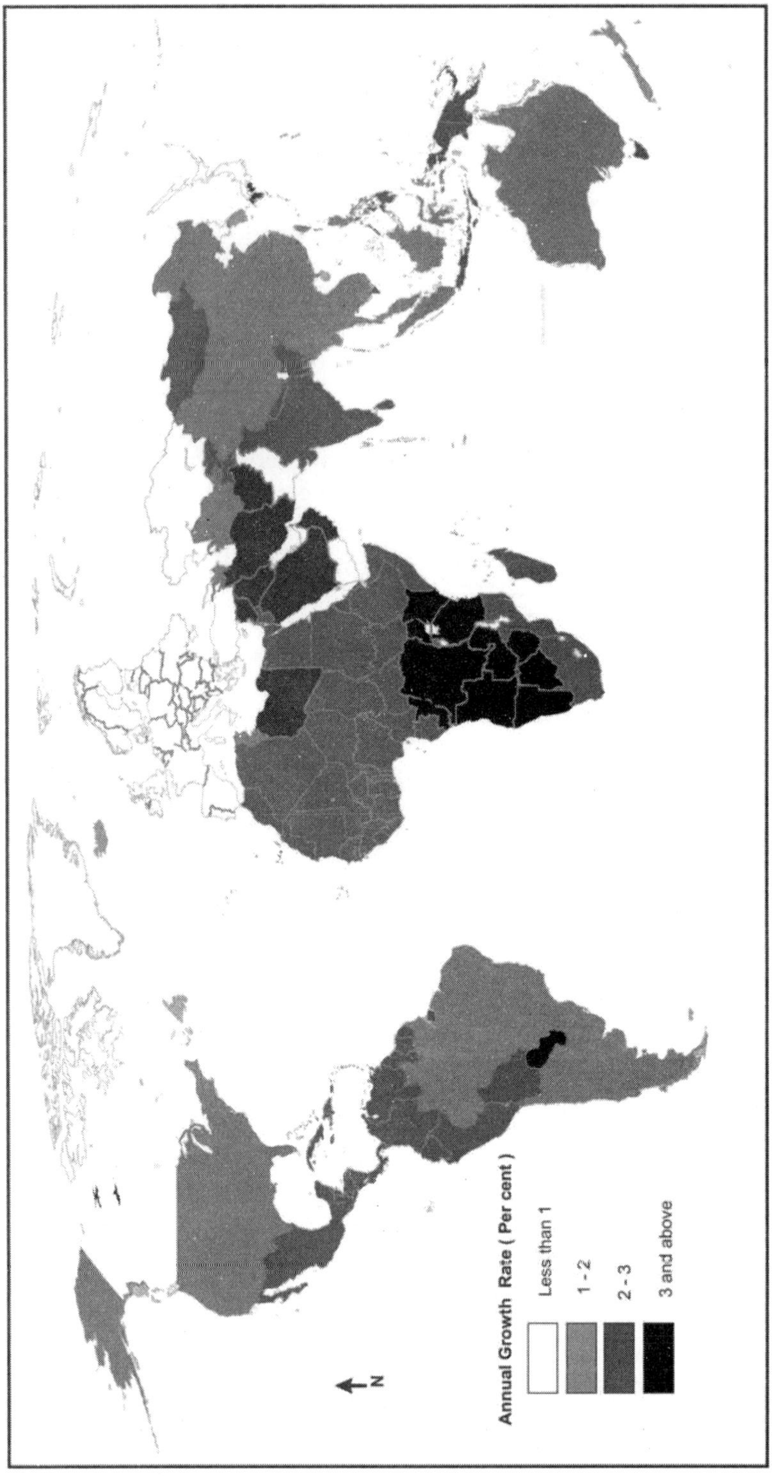

Fig. 9.2: Population Growth Rate in World, 1990-2000

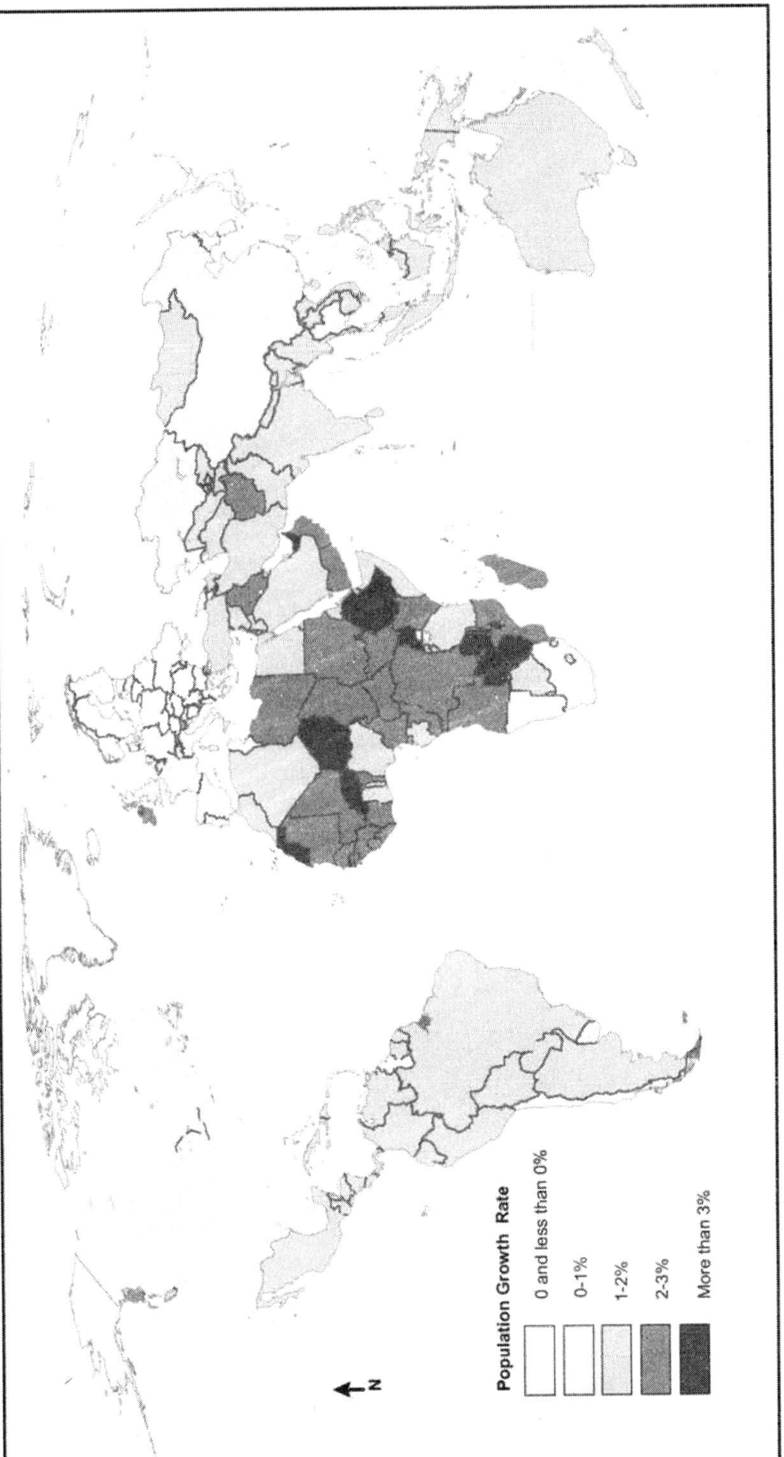

Fig. 9.3: Population Growth Rate in World, 2011

Table 9.4: Average Annual Population Growth Rate in Selected Developed and Developing Countries

Countries	Annual Population Growth Rate (in percentage) 1975-2005	Annual Population Growth Rate (in percentage) 2005-2016
Developed Countries		
Australia	1.3	1.0
Canada	1.1	0.9
Iceland	1.0	0.8
Netherland	0.6	0.2
France	0.5	0.4
Japan	0.5	–0.1
Poland	0.4	–0.2
Developing Countries		
Saudi Arabia	3.9	2.1
Yemen	3.6	2.9
Nigeria	2.8	2.2
Pakistan	2.8	1.9
Sudan	2.6	1.9
Costa Rica	2.5	1.4
Bangladesh	2.2	1.6
India	2.0	1.4

Source: Human Development Report, 2016.

As per the World Development Report (2007), the low income countries have increased their population from 1,384 million (1980) to 2,353 million (2005) claiming 36.6 per cent of the total world population whereas the middle income countries have increased their population from 2,217 million (1980) to 3,073 million (2005) claiming 47.7 per cent of the world population (Table 9.5). The demographic scenario of the high income countries presents a contrast; they have increased their population from 825 million (1980) to 1,011 million (2005) and their share in total world population has declined from 18.6 per cent (1980) to 15.7 per cent (2005). Most of the low income countries lie in Asia, Africa and Latin America where the incidence of poverty, malnutrition and ill health is high. The middle income countries have experienced population explosion because of high birth rates and declining death rates. The high income countries have very low birth rates and very low death rates.

Table 9.5: World Population Growth by Income Group

Group	Population (millions)		Percentage to Total	
	1980	2005	1980	2005
Low Income Countries	1,384	2,393	31.3	36.6
Middle Income Countries	2,217	3,073	50.0	47.7
High Income Countries	825	1,011	18.6	15.7
Total	**4,426**	**6,438**	**100**	**100**

Source: Human Development Report, 2016.

The factors involved in the natural rate of population change are considered, the average birth rate of developed countries is observed to be much lower (11 per 1000 population) than that of the developing countries (27 per 1000 population). However, some of these countries have death rates higher than their birth rates, e.g. Germany. This had led to the negative rate of population growth, resulting in dwindling of the population size (Table 9.6). A considerable decline in the death rate in the developing and less developed countries began in 1950s. By improving health interventions even in rural and poor settings, infant mortality rate in these countries were brought down significantly. Consequently their average life expectancy improved from 41 to 62 until 2000. Thus, as a consequence of sharp decline in death rate (mortality) and nominal decline or no decline in birth rate (fertility), most of the developing countries experienced an unprecedented growth in their populations. It is noteworthy that birth rate continued to remain at a high level in most of the developing countries like India, China, Bangladesh, Nigeria, Ethiopia, Kenya etc.

Table 9.6: Crude Birth Rates and Death Rates for Selected Countries

Country	*Birth Rate*	*Death Rate*	*Infant Mortality Rate*
Germany	10	11	4
U.K.	12	10	5
U.S.A	14	9	7
Canada	11	7	5
France	13	9	4
Australia	13	7	5
Japan	9	8	3
China	15	8	30
India	24	8	56.29
Bangladesh	30.01	8.4	72.4
Pakistan	30.42	8.45	62.6

Source: Human Development Report, 2016.

The population growth is the result of the interplay of fertility, mortality and migration which vary in response to economic development, cultural achievement, technological progress and historical factors. The spectacular increase in population in North America, Latin America, Africa and Oceania can be accounted by the influx of immigrants and the slow increase in Europe is due to emigration. But recent high growth rates in population in Latin America, Africa and Asia are largely due to natural increase.

9.7 Population Growth in India

India has had a very chequered demographic history, more so during the 20th century. The Indian demographic history of the 20th century can be divided into three distinct period of stagnant growth. India's population is characterised by high growth rate. On an average it has been increasing at a growth rate of 1.95 per cent per annum against 1.8 per cent per annum for the world as a whole and 1.3 per cent for China. Although population estimates are available since 1750 the first census was undertaken in 1871 giving a population figure of 203 million. Thence onward up to 1901 the population growth rate was very slow varying between 0.09 to 1.1 per cent per annum. This was due to high mortality arising out of epidemics and famines. India's population has been steadily increasing from 361 million in 1951 to 1028 million in 2001. It has been seen that from 1951 to 1981, the annual rate of population growth was steadily increasing; which explains the rapid increase in population from 361 million in 1951 to 683 million in 1981 (Fig. 9.4).

Since 1981, however, the rate of growth started declining gradually. During this period, birth rates declined rapidly. Still 182 million people were added to the total population in the 1990s alone (an annual addition larger than ever before). It is essential to realise that India has a very large population. When a low annual rate is applied to a very large population, it yields a large absolute increase. When more than a billion people increase even at a lower rate, the total numbers being added becomes very large. India's current annual increase in population of 15.5 million is large enough to neutralise efforts to conserve the resource endowment and environment.

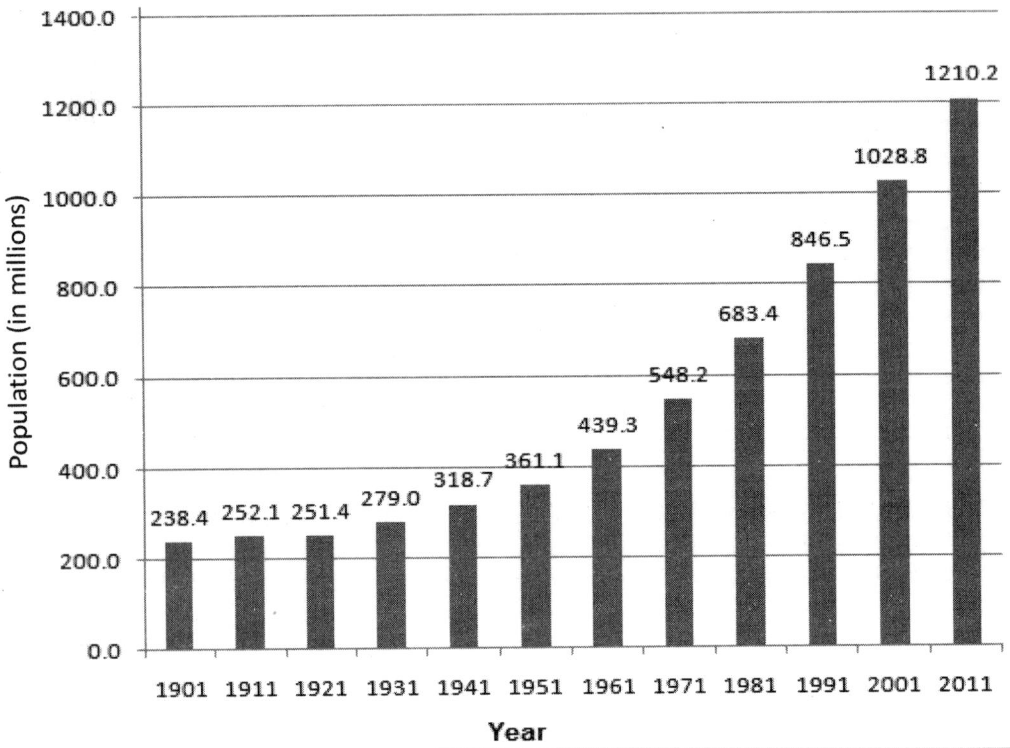

Fig. 9.4: India: Population Growth and Natural Increase during 1901-2011

Source: Census of India, 2011.

Going through the regional pattern of population growth of India (Fig. 9.5), the areas recorded high growth rate around 30 per cent include the entire north-eastern region, the arid and semi-arid parts of Rajasthan, the Terai zone of Uttar Pradesh and North-eastern Parts. Gosal (1961) attributes this rapid increase in these areas to large scale in-migration into these areas associated with development of industries, extension of irrigation facilities, reclamation of waste land, intensification of agriculture etc. By contrast, the slow growth rate of less than 20 per cent was experienced by large parts of Kerala, Tamil Nadu, Odisha, West Bengal and southern parts of India. These were the areas which experienced out-immigration due to severe population pressure and paucity of resources.

The regional pattern of population growth make a significant revelation that while in

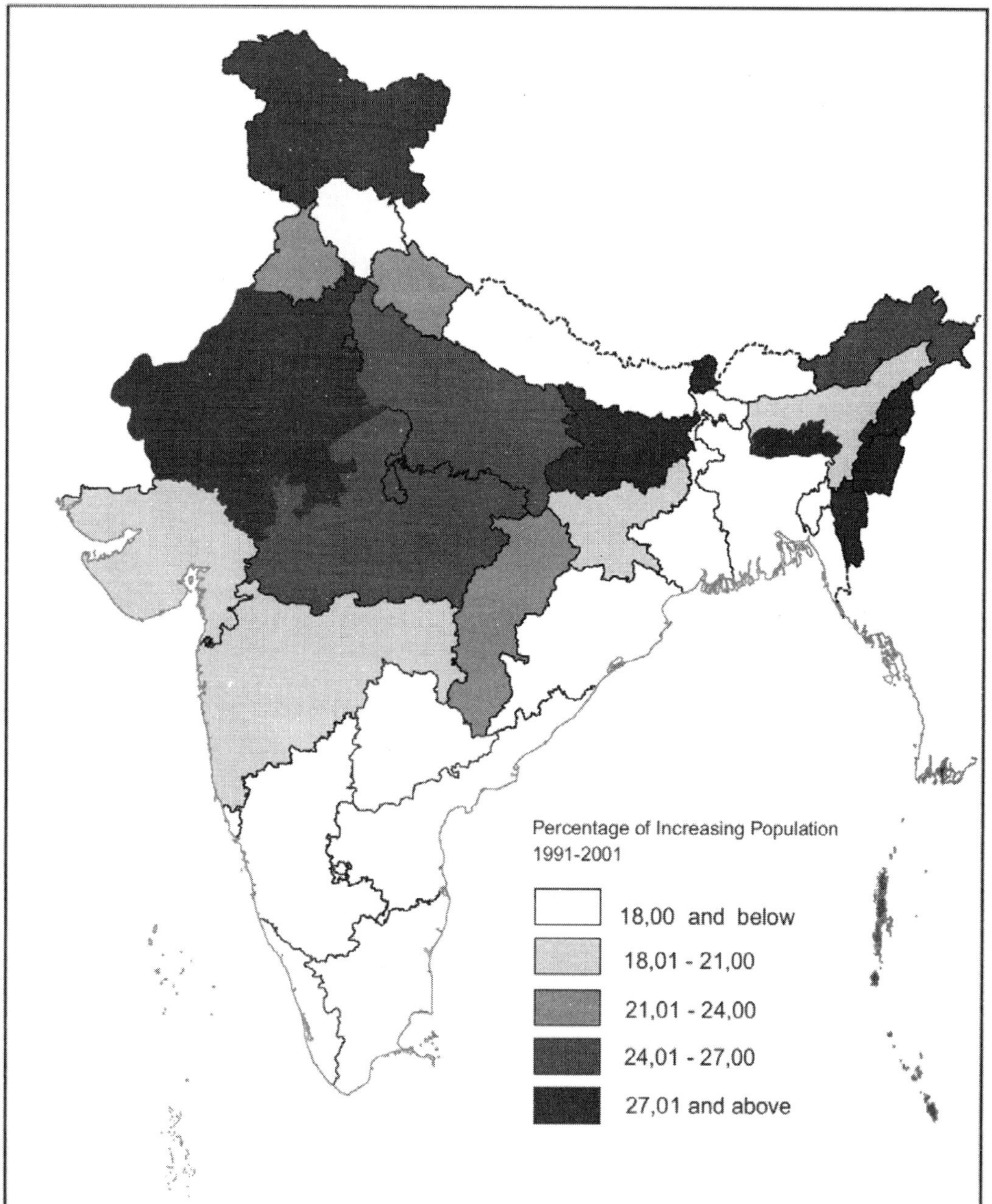

Fig. 9.5: Decadal Growth Rate of Population during 2001-2011
Source: Census of India, 2011.

some parts of the country the demographic transition has approached the final stage, in others, the fertility and mortality patterns are still in the early second stage of transition. Since the latter areas constitute not only the most crowded parts of the country but also the economically and socially backward parts of the country, therefore, their continuance in the second stage signals a serious warning for the country to formulate the policies with a view to generating rapid fall in the fertility rates of the country.

The declining trend of the growth rate is indeed a positive indicator of the efforts of birth control. Despite that, the total additions to the population base continue to grow, and India may overtake China in 2045 to become the most populous country in the world.

9.8 Future Projection

After reviewing the past trends of population growth, and after carefully examining population policies of most countries and evaluating their family planning programmes as well as their progress in the field of economic development, demographers have attempted to estimate future projections. According to the revised estimates by the UN Demographic Organization (2002), "the world population of 6.3 billion will rise to 8.9 billion in 2050 before peaking below 10 billion and possibly declining." It is based on the assumption that in developing countries the number of children per couple will fall below replacement level to 1.03 in place of the traditional norms of 2.1 because of the impact of HIV and lower fertility.

The estimated and projected world population levels are the product of divergent trends across the more developed and less developed regions. For developed regions, it seems that an era of population decline may not be too far into the future. According to the medium-variant (Constant rise) projection, the aggregate population of this region will rise from the year 2005 estimate of 1.21 billion persons to a peak of 1.25 billion around 2030, and will then fall to 1.24 billion by the end of the projection period, yielding a net addition of only about 25 million (Fig. 9.6). Only the high fertility variant (High rise) suggests continued growth in the population of the developed regions. If current levels of fertility were to be maintained, as assumed in the constant fertility variant, the population of the developed regions would fall below the medium-variant projection. The anticipation of some fertility increases in the medium variant for the very low fertility countries accounts for this result. By 2050, 56 countries will experience a negative population growth including all European countries, Japan and China. The population of developed regions as a group is expected to reach a peak of 1,617 million in 2020, then it will start a gradual decline and 2050 will be 2 per cent smaller than in 1998.

For the less developed regions, the expected trajectories all involve substantial further population growth. For example, the projection shows an increase from 5.3 billion in 2005 to 7.8 billion in 2050. The developing countries, with population 759 million in 2005, will witness continued increase under all fertility variants, attaining a total of more than 1.7 billion persons by 2050 in the medium variant. With continued current levels of fertility, that total would surpass 2.7 billion, and if fertility rates were to follow the high variant, the total population in the year 2050 would still reach close to 2 billion persons. Hence, the course for fertility decline remains of critical importance to the populations of the least developed countries.

As per the estimates 3 billion people will be added to the world population by 2050 by the developing and less developed countries. In 2050 India will be the most populous country with a population of 1.53 billion out exceedling China (1.39 billion). The third most populous country will be the USA (400.7 million), followed by Pakistan (348.7 million),

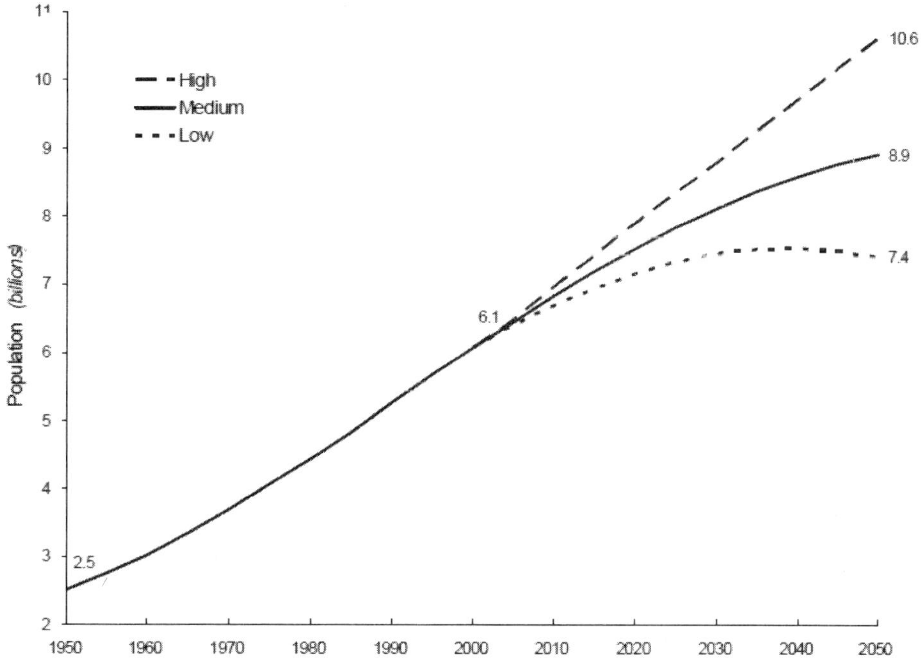

Fig. 9.6: Estimated World Population, (1950-2050)

Indonesia (293.8 million), Nigeria (258.5 million), Bangladesh (254.5 million). Japan will have a population of 109.7 million while Russia (101.4 million), Germany (79.1 million), UK (66.3 million) will have less numbers with an expected fertility ratio of 2.05 by 2050. Pakistan will boost 348.7 million people compared with 101.4 million in Russia (Table 9.7).

Table 9.7: Top Ten Most Populous Countries (2007 and 2050)

Country	*Population in (m) 2007*	*Country*	*Population in (m) 2050*
China	1,318	India	1,742
India	1,132	China	1,437
U.S.A.	302	U.S.A.	420
Indonesia	232	Indonesia	297
Brazil	189	Pakistan	295
Pakistan	169	Nigeria	295
Bangladesh	149	Brazil	260
Nigeria	144	Bangladesh	231
Russia	142	Congo	187
Japan	128	Philippines	150

Source: UN Demographic Organization, 2016.

Likewise, the path of fertility decline will make an important difference to the futures of the other less developed countries, a group that includes China, India, Indonesia, Brazil, Pakistan and other populous nations. The medium-variant projection for these countries indicates continued population growth, with their total rising from 4.5 billion persons in

2005 to 6.1 billion in 2050. Continuation of current fertility rates would add an expected 1.6 billion persons to the total population of these countries (relative to the medium variant), whereas the expected total would be only 632 million above the current population if the low fertility variant were to prevail. To sum up, for all less developed regions combined, constant fertility would imply total populations of 10.5 billion in 2050, well above the 7.8 billion produced by the medium variant. Overall, among all countries with a population of at least 100,000 in the year 2000, according to the results of the medium variant, 44 countries are expected to experience a reduction in population between 2005 and 2050, the majority of them located in the more developed regions.

9.9 Summary

At the end as a conclusion can be said that in the initial phase of human history and pre-history, the human population grew at a snail speed. The hazardous climatic condition, the migratory character of hunters and gatherers, and the poor nourishment were all unfavourable conditions for the growth of population. During the last ten thousand years, the growth of world population accelerated at distinct times. The agricultural and industrial revolutions were very important because population numbers and densities are at the heart of relationships between human and natural environment. Although the slowdown is not yet very pronounced, it represents a significant turn from the previous trend of growth at a progressively accelerating rate, whereby the number of earth's human inhabitants doubled and more than redoubled during the past two centuries. The climax in speed of multiplication seems now to have passed and the rate is expected to go on abating gradually in the future.

Review Questions

1. Define population growth? Explain various components of population change with suitable illustrations.
2. Distinguish between population growth and population distribution.
3. Describe trends and patterns in population growth in world.
4. Discuss and differentiate between the population growth in developed and developing countries.
5. Analyze the trends and patterns of population growth and its patterns in India.

Analytical Questions

1. Immigration affects population growth and economic development in USA? Analyze.
2. Analyze the changes in population of your native village since last 10 years.

Chapter 10
Population Composition

10.1 Introduction

A study of the structure and composition of population is an important aspect of study of population. The study of the structure and characteristics of population, which is also known as the study of the composition of population, covers this aspect of population studies, which embraces the following basic personal, social and economic characteristics or attributes of any population. Among various elements of population composition, sex composition, age composition, economic and occupational composition, ethnic and religious compositions are important. Age and sex of the population are the most significant demographic characteristics and biological attributes that are captured by a census of a population. Age and sex are two attributes that mostly affects an individual's role in society. The separate data for males and females is also important for various types of planning and for the analysis of other demographic characteristics such as natality, mortality, migration, marital status, economic characteristics etc. The balance between the two sexes affects the social and economic relationship within a community. Not only that, main types of planning, particularly planning of community institutions and services, manpower supply etc. are guided by the age structure of the populations.

10.2 Sex Composition

Sex is an easily identifiable characteristic. The number of women and men in a country is an important demographic characteristic. The ratio between the number of women and men in the population is called the sex ratio. In some countries it is calculated by using the formula:

$$\frac{\text{Male Population} \times 1000}{\text{Female Population}}$$

The sex ratio is an important information about the status of women in country. In region where gender discrimination is rampant, the sex ratio is bound to be unfavourable to women. Such areas are those where the practice of female foeticide, female infanticide and domestic violence against women are prevalent. One of the reasons could be lower socio-economic status of women in these areas. The number of males in the world as a whole exceeded marginally the number of females (Table 10.1). There were 993 females for every thousand males in the world. This may be attributable to the universal fact of masculinity at birth.

However, among the various continents, Europe, North America, Africa, were characterized by the preponderance of females. The continent of Latin America, Asia, and Oceania suffered from the paucity of females. Europe had the highest sex ratio followed by North America and Africa. Asia, on the other hand, had the largest deficiency of females.

Table 10.1: Continent-wise Sex Ratio

Continent/Country	Sex Ratio (Females/1000 Males)
1. Europe	1051
2. North America	1050
3. U.S.S.R.	1137
4. Africa	1017
5. Latin America	995
6. Oceania	983
7. Asia	960
8. World	993

Source: United Nations Demographic Organisations, 2016.

The data on spatial pattern of sex ratio in 2011 reveals that wide ranging disparity from one part of the world to another. Although on an average, the world had a sex ratio of 984 females per thousand males yet there were countries like Russia with 1140 females per thousand males and Saudi Arabia with less than 900 females per thousand males. This shows a significant variation in sex ratio. Considering the even ratio of thousand, the world can be divided into two sets of areas. One, where the number of females exceeded the number of males and, two, where the number of females falls short of number of males. It has been observed that with regard to sex composition the distinction between the developed world and less developed world is not that markedly sharp as it has been the case with other attributes discussed so far. The most developed continent of North America and the most backward continent of Africa display preponderance of females over males. Interestingly, in both these cases the sex composition is the product of high mortality rate among males, though the high mortality among males in the two continents may result from contrastingly different factors.

The world pattern of sex ratio does not exhibit variations in the developed regions of the world. The sex ratio is favourable for females in 139 countries of the world and unfavourable for them in the remaining 72 countries listed by the United Nations. In general, Asia has low sex ratio. Countries in Asia, like China, India, Saudi Arabia, Pakistan, and Afghanistan, have a lower sex ratio. On the other extreme is greater part of Europe (including Russia), where males are in minority. A deficit of males in the populations of many European countries is attributed to better status of women, and an excessively male dominated out-migration to different parts of the world in the past.

10.3 Age Composition

Age is an important factor which determines the physical as well mental capacity of people to engage themselves in economic and other activities. The United Nation has defined age as "the estimated or calculated interval of time between the date of birth and the date of census, expressed in completed solar years." The age structure influences the economic and social interactions, social attitudes and social and occupational mobility. Children up to the age of 14 years are considered as too tender to bear any physical and mental burden. Being immature, they cannot be entrusted with responsible jobs. Likewise, the persons above 60 years become too weak to undergo physical strain because of their old age and feeble health. They want to retire and rest in peace for the remaining period of life. Age structure is an important variable and also have special interest in the study of social relation within a community is affected considerably by the age structure. Not only that, many types of planning, particularly planning of community institution and services, manpower supply etc. are guided by the age structure of population. Age is an important variable in measuring potential school population, potential voting population, potential manpower, future population projections and projections for the requirement of teachers, doctor, technical hands, armed personnel etc. it is also important variable in the studies pertaining to mortality, fertility and other demographic characteristics, like dependency ratio etc.

The data on age may be defective and suffer from more serious handicaps and thus, warrant extreme caution in their utilization. The data on age are collected by asking the question either about the date of birth or about the exact age at the time of enumeration. The data on age at the time of enumeration may suffer from misreporting because of: (i) general illiteracy, (ii) ignorance about the date of birth; (iii) carelessness; (iv) preference for figures ending with zero, five etc. (v) preference for even ages; and (vi) prevalence of different calendars etc.

10.3.1 Determinant of Age Composition

There are three basic determinants of age composition of a population, these incudes fertility, mortality and mobility. Clarke (1971) rightly pointed out that these determinants of age structure are inter-dependent and any change in one of these may influence the other structure.

Fertility

The fertility rate (birth rate) determines the proportion of population (structure of population) in different age groups. In the developing countries of Asia, Africa and Latin America, which are characterized by high fertility or birth rates have large proportions (30 to 40%) in young age groups (0-14 years). In these countries, longevity of life (life expectancy) is short and consequently, the proportion of population in the old age groups (65+) is also not very large (below 5%). In contrast, the developed countries of Europe, Anglo-America, New Zealand and Japan with low fertility rates and with long expectancy of life have below 25 per cent of their populations in the young age groups (0-14 years). The proportion of population in the older age groups is relatively large (above 10%). It is noteworthy that most of the developed countries of the world have completed their demographic transition and possess age structure where the proportion of younger population is low and that of old people is high. In these countries, decreasing trend in fertility contributes to increase in the proportion in older ages.

Mortality

Mortality or death rate also affects the age composition of a population. However, its impact upon age structure depends largely upon the variations in mortality rates at different ages. High death rate adversely affects the proportion of population in a particular age group. Generally, when the death rate decreases in younger age groups, the proportion of children will tend to rise and that of the older population will tend to fall. When the death rate is low both among younger and older age groups (as in developed countries) it contributes to an increase in the proportion of population in the older age groups. In many developing countries of the world, the decline in mortality is sharper in childhood than in the older age group which has resulted in the swelling up (increase) of numbers in younger age groups (0-14).

Migration

Migration upon the age composition of a population can be analyzed in a similar way, but the specific impact of migration on age distribution is very much different from that of fertility and mortality because the migrants have their own typical age pattern as well as natural increase pattern. As the migrants tend to be relatively younger and possessing high rate of natural increase, their usual short term impact is the decline in the proportion of older adults and aged population. This youthful effect continues if the volume of migration is maintained.

Other Factors

These basic factors of fertility, mortality and migration apart, the age structure of a population is also influenced significantly by wars, catastrophe, natural calamities, population policies etc. the impact of wars is most pronounced on the age distribution as these take a heavy toll of young males. The elimination of males of a particular age group also affects the fertility, which in its own turn influence the age distribution. The irregularities in age distribution of a population, which arise due to wars, continue to remain there shifting from one age group to another until the complete elimination of that age group. Similarly, the natural calamities, catastrophe, and when they come, leave their own impact upon the age distribution until affected age group has lived its entire age. Certain population policies with far-reaching implications, as and when adopted by the country, also make their impact felt upon the age distribution of that country's population. For instance, the legalization of abortion in Japan immediately after the Second World War did result in squeezing of Japan's expanding population base of 0-4 years.

10.3.2 Method of Age Structure Analysis

Age data are usually available in the form of single years, that is, the number of persons in the population of age 13, 14, 15, 16 etc. for demographic analysis, however, age data are seldom used in this form. It is customary to classify them in five-year age groups, such as 0-4, 5-9, 10-14, 15-19, 20-24 and so on. The age data thus classified in mutually exclusive age groups are used for an analysis of the age structure of any population, and are also useful for a wide variety of analytical purposes. The age structure of any population is most commonly studied with the help of a single mathematical measure like the per cent distribution and an equally simple measure like the age pyramid. The other measures used for an analysis of the age structure are the average age (mean, median, and mode) and a few other indices based on the distribution of persons in various age groups.

10.4 Age-Groups

The age structure of a given country or region may be analyzed on the basis age groups. On the basis of physiological and economic activities, the population is generally classified into three groups: the young, the adults, and the old. Although there are no standardized break points, yet the ages of 15 and 60 years are the most commonly used break points in the developing countries and 15 and 65 years in the developed countries. The social, economic and political implications of these age groups and the geographical variation in their distribution are worthy of serious consideration.

10.4.1 The Young

Over the world, the young age group includes the population below 15 years of age. The proportion of population in this age group in any country is determined by the stage of demographic transition it is passing through. This proportion is large if the country is passing through the first or the second stage of demographic transition. It starts declining as the country approaches the late stage. It is the minimum when the country is in the final stage of demographic transition. It is interesting to note that while in the world as a whole about 30 per cent population is below the age of 15 years, the corresponding figures for the developed and the developing regions are 20 per cent and 36 per cent, respectively (Table 10.2). In Germany, the proportion of young population (below 15 years) is only 15 per cent. In Italy, UK and France the adult population is only 14 per cent, 18 per cent and 17 per cent (2001) respectively. Thus, there are wide regional variations in the proportion of young population ranging from less than 18 per cent in Europe to nearly 43 per cent in Africa and about 36 per cent in Asia and Latin America. In India, about 33 per cent of the total population is below 15 years of age. These regional variations are related with the fertility patterns of different countries. Countries that are characterized with high fertility rates have large proportions of young populations and *vice versa*. There seems to be a direct correlation between birth rates and proportion of young population. This age group is economically unproductive and the most expensive as it is to be provided with food, clothing, education recreational, health and medical facilities.

10.4.2 The Adults

The group of adults consists of 15 to 65 years in the developed and 15 to 60 in the developing

Table 10.2: Percentage Distribution of Population among Broad Age-Groups in the World

Region	*Age Groups*		
	0-14	*15-64*	*65+*
Developed countries	19.6	66.8	13.6
Developing countries	31.2	63.4	5.4
Least developed countries	42.0	54.8	3.2
World	28.5	64.2	7.3

Source: Human Development Report, 2010.

countries. Depending upon the life expectancy, the upper limit in the developing countries is 60 and that in the developed countries is 65. The adult age group is biologically the most reproductive, economically the most productive and demographically the most mobile (migratory). It supports the bulk of other age groups, it carries the burden of feeding, clothing, educating the young age group and of looking after the old age group. The developed countries have relatively high proportion of adult population. This adult age group is sometimes divided further into two sub-groups: (i) 16 to 34, and (ii) 35 to 59/64. The first sub-group of young adults is considered biologically most reproductive and economically more active than the second one of older adults.

10.4.3 The Old

The old age group consists of those who have achieved the age of 60 years in the developing countries and 65 or above in the developed countries. Such people are called as the senior citizens. The proportion of people in this age group, by and large, increases as the population of a country completes its demographic evolution. About 7.3 per cent population of the world as a whole is found under old age group (Table 10.2). Its proportion in the population of developed countries comes to be as high as 13.6 per cent. In contrast only 5.4 per cent and 3.2 per cent population of developing and least developed countries is found under old age groups. People in this age group, particularly, females are biologically non-productive and economically most non-productive.

10.5 Age Indices

The age composition of population may also be analyzed with the help of age indices. The calculation and use of age indices for analysing the age distribution is not very common. However, the calculation of such ratios holds significance for the purposes of manpower planning, growth of population analysis, migration analysis etc. The calculations of different age indices are based on the proportion of population in three broad age-groups: young's, adults and olds. According to the aim of the study following types of age indices may be used, namely (1) Ratio of young and adults, (2) Ratio of young's and olds, (3) Ratio of adults and olds, (4) Ratio of young and adults + olds, (5) Ratio of olds and youngs + adults, and (5) Ratio of adults and young plus olds.

Besides this, one most important type of age indices is Dependency ratio. This Dependency ratio is an index of age produced drain on a country's manpower potential. The total Dependency ratio is the number of persons under age 15 plus persons aged 65 or older per one hundred persons in between age group 15-64. This ratio talks about the sum of the youth dependency ratio and the old-age dependency ratio. (1) The youth dependency ratio focuses on the number of persons 0 to 14 years per one hundred persons 15 to 64 years. (2) The old-age dependency ratio is the number of persons 65 years and over per one hundred persons 15 to 64 years. This index presents the ratio of adults: young + olds and is very helpful in the analysis of an economy. Generally, the adult population is considered as active (working) population while children below 15 years and old persons of 65 years and above are dependent on active population. Following is the formula for the calculation of dependency ratio:

$$\text{Dependency Ratio} = \frac{\text{Young} + \text{Old Population} \times 100}{\text{Adult Population}}$$

Thus, the dependency ratio presents an index of non-working and working population in per cent. The dependency ratio is generally high in the case of developing and least developed countries of the world mainly due to large number of young population. Different age indices also can be represented graphically on the map which may help in the analysis of spatial variations in these indices.

10.6 Age-Sex Pyramids

One of the most commonly used methods of analysing age composition is the age pyramid, which is more commonly known as age and sex pyramid. The age-sex pyramids are constructed for depicting the age structure of a population along their vertical axis. In such pyramids age groups at a regular interval 'say 5 years', starting from 0 to 5 and ending according to the age structure of population under review are normally displayed. The horizontal axis of such pyramids represents the total population or the populations of males or females separately; the pyramid is divided vertically into two halves, right side representing the females and the left side representing the males. In some cases, the proportion of males and females in each respective age group is represented and in others the absolute numbers of males and females are represented. Since under normal circumstances, the number of persons in each successive year is less than that in the preceding year, the representation of age composition in this form gives it the shape of a pyramid.

The shape of pyramid varies from country to country depending upon the state of the demographic transition (Chapter 9) through which the country is passing. The shape is also significantly modified by a variety of factors like wars, epidemics, migration, baby boom etc. The countries which are in first stage (high birth rate and high death rate) of demographic transition have very broad base which narrowed upward rapidly presenting a concave shape to the sides of the triangles. The developing countries which are at the second stage (high birth rate and sharply declining death rate) of demographic transition show large base of the pyramid mainly due to high birth rate and sharply declining death rate. The developed countries which are at third stage of demographic transition represent a narrower base with about equally wide successive age groups tapping off gradually.

The shape is also significantly modified by a variety of factors like wars, epidemics, migrations, baby booms etc. Wars, epidemics etc. cause large scale abnormal deaths and distortions in the normal shape of the pyramid. Sometimes the distortion in age pyramid is the product of more than any single factor, so that it becomes difficult to clarify the role of each factor in forming a typical shape to a age pyramid. Similarly, migration also produces irregularities in normal shape of the age pyramids. Thus, the areas from which people of a particular age group move out, and also the areas to which these people move in, record irregularities in their respective age pyramids. Thus, the shape of age pyramids is so distinct that with practice one can interpret the irregularities in it with apt precision. However, although it is possible to infer a good deal about the demographic history of an area from the shape of the age pyramid, yet since the pyramid do not identify the specific factors affecting their shape, the knowledge about the history of the area is essential to understand

and interpret these irregularities. Moreover, sometimes to distortions in age pyramid are not the product of any single factor, it becomes difficult to identify the role of each factor in giving a particular shape to a pyramid.

10.6.1 Types of Age Pyramids

Different countries expecting typical socio-economic and demographic history may produce age pyramid of typical shapes and the specific historical events may find expressions in the irregularities in the bars of the pyramids in different states. For instance, a long history of low fertility and low mortality (as is the case with Sweden) may produce a barrel-shaped pyramid; the fluctuations in the number of births and deaths caused by the World War I and II (as was the case with France) may produce a number of irregularities in the age pyramid; the population policy like the legalization of abortions may result in decline in the number of births (as was the case with Japan) and may shorten the base of the pyramid to the extent that it may become shorter than the subsequent bars; and the length of the middle bars or upper bars of the pyramid may become excessively long or short in case of countries experiencing immigration or emigration, respectively. Based on observations of various countries, three major types of age-sex pyramids are identified (Fig. 10.1).

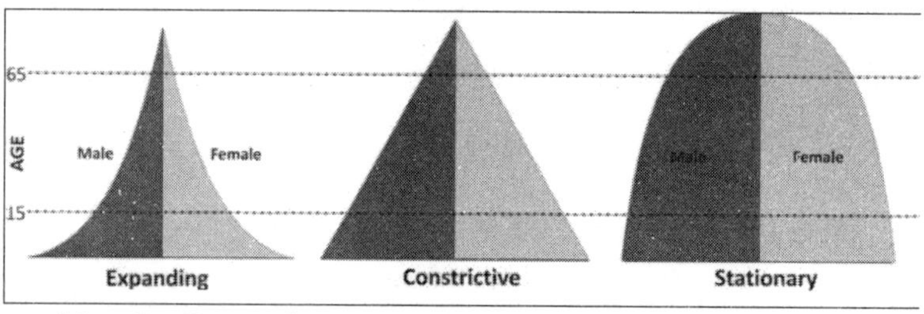

Fig. 10.1: Types of Age-Sex Pyramids

(a) Expansive

Population pyramids illustrate larger numbers or percentages of the population in the younger age groups. These types of pyramids are usually found in populations with very large fertility rates and lower than average life expectancies. The age-sex distributions of most of the Third World countries would probably display expansive population pyramids. For example, this age-sex pyramid of Afghanistan's population breakdown in 2015 represents a fast rate of 2.3 per cent annually, that represents a population doubling time of concerning thirty years (Fig. 10.2). we are able to see the distinctive pyramid-like shape to the current showing graph, that displays a high birth rate (Afghan women have on average 5.3 children, this is often the whole fertility rate) and a high death rate (life expectancy in Afghanistan from birth is simply 50.9).

(b) Constrictive

Population pyramids shows lower numbers or percentages of youngers. The age-sex distributions of the United Nations fall into this kind of pyramid. Within the United States, the population is growing at an awfully slow rate of concerning 0.8 per cent annually, that

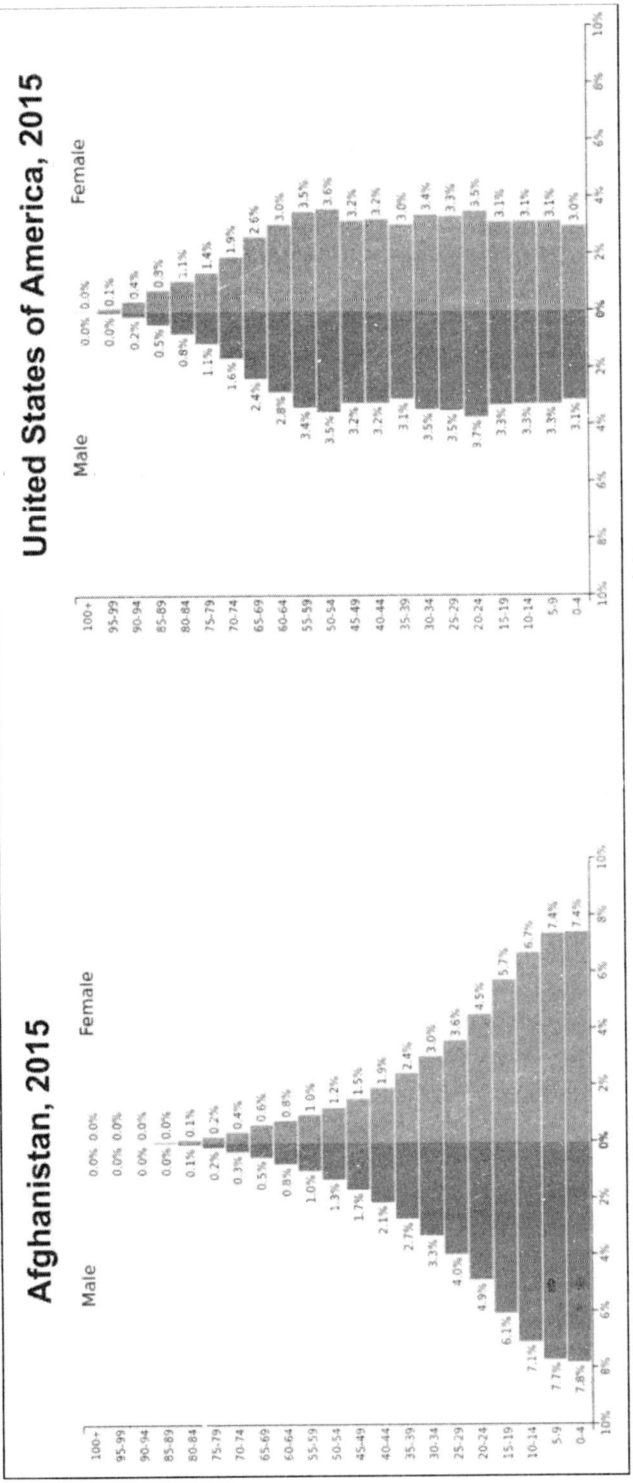

Fig. 10.2: Expansive Population Pyramid of Afganistan and Constructive of United States

represents a population doubling time of just about ninety years. This rate is mirrored within a lot of square-like structure of the pyramid. the total fertility rate within the United States in 2015 is estimated at 2.0, which ends up in a very natural decline within the population (a total fertility rate of concerning 2.1 is require for population stability). As of 2015, the only growth in the United Nations is from immigration. On this age-sex pyramid we are able to see that the quantities of individuals in their 1920s of each gender is considerably beyond the number of infants and children aged 0-9. Also, the lump can be seen within the pyramid between the ages of concerning 50-59, this massive phase of the population is that the post-World War-II. As this population ages and climbs up the pyramid, there will be a way bigger demand for medical and different geriatric services, however, with fewer young people to provide care and support for the aging baby boom generation. unlike the Afghanistan age-sex pyramid, the United States population shows a major variety of residents aged eighty and higher than, showing that raised longevity is far a lot of probably within the United States than in Afghanistan. Note the inequality between male and female aged within the United States—women tend to outlive men in each population cluster. Within the United States expectancy for men is 77.3 except for women it is 82.1.

(c) Stationary

Stationary population pyramids show somewhat equal numbers or percentages for almost all age sections. Of course, smaller figures are still to be expected at the oldest age groups. The age-sex distributions of some European countries, particularly, Scandinavian ones, can tend to make up this class like Japan (Fig. 10.3). Since 2005, Japan's population has been declining. In 2005 the population was 127.7 million and in 2015 the country's population throw down to 126.9 million. The Japanese population is projected to about 107 million by 2050. If current predictions hold true, by 2110, Japan is anticipated to own a population under 43 million people. Japan has been taking their demographic state of affairs seriously but unless Japanese citizens start coupling and reproducing, the country will have a demographic emergency.

10.6.2 Utility of Age Sex Pyramid

In recent years, more varied use of pyramids has been made by population analysts. Pyramids have been drawn to represent economically active and economically inactive population and to represent actual consumption and production patterns of population in an age group. The idea is to correlate the incidence of working, production and consumption to the age of population. Age pyramid or age and sex pyramid may be used as a tool in the analysis of a population. Such pyramids provide a beautiful diagrammatic representation of the relationship between age structure of a population and economy (Valentey, 1978). Seeing the shape of an age pyramid a population geographer or other social scientist may explain the typical socio-economic and demographic history of the concerned population.

10.7 Age-Sex Pyramid Pattern in World

Age composition of population in different countries of the world may be easily analyzed

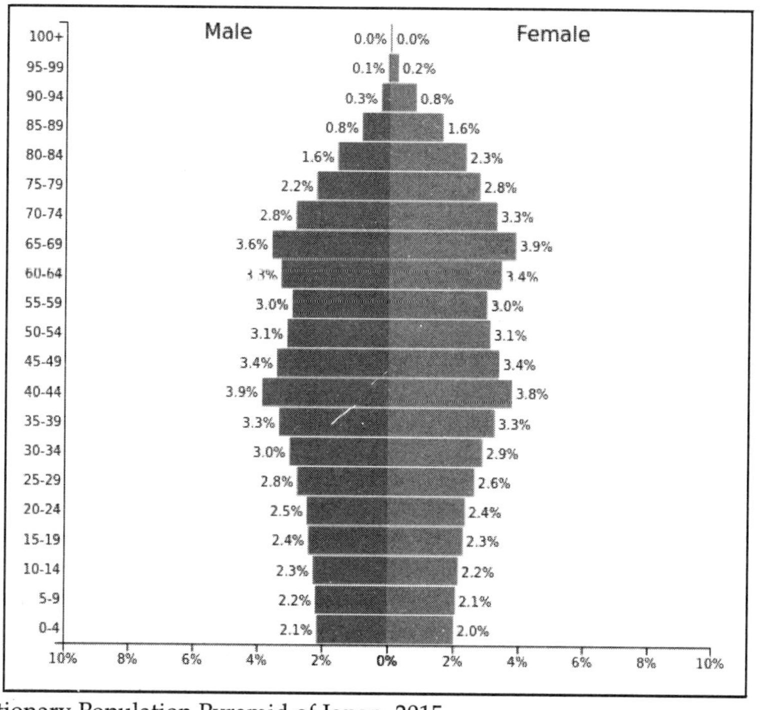

Fig. 10.3: Stationary Population Pyramid of Japan, 2015

with the help of broad age groups. The proportions of young population and of the old population are inversely correlated with each other (Table 10.3). It is noteworthy that there is very little variation in the proportion of adult population, but there are great variations in the proportions of young age group and old age group. It is quite evident from Table 10.3 that, 30 per cent population of the world was below 15 years of age. The corresponding figures for developed and developing countries were 17 and 33 per cent respectively. In most developed countries of the world, proportion of young population is below 20 per cent. Examples include Japan (14.1), Italy (14.1), Germany (14.6), Ukraine (15.4), Russia

Table 10.3: Age composition by Major Regions of World

Area/Country	*Percentage of Population*	
	Below 15 Years	*65+ Years*
World	30	7
More Developed Countries	17	15
Less Developed Countries	33	5
Africa	42	3
North America	21	12
Central America	36	4
South America	31	6
Oceania	25	10
Europe	17	15
Asia	30	6

Source: Population Reference Bureau, 2010.

(15.7), Austria (15.8), Sweden (17.7), Canada (17.9), Netherland (18.3), France (18.2), Denmark (18.8), Norway (19.7) etc. On the contrary, in many least developed countries, ratio of young population is as high as above 40 per cent, like Uganda (50.4), Niger (49.0), Mali (48.3), Zambia (46.0), Angola (46.6), Ethiopia (44.8) and Kenya (42.9).

Thus, the disparity in the proportion of population below 15 years of age in the two types of countries, the developed and the less developed, was attributable to the differences in the stage of their fertility transition. The developed world has completed its fertility transition and had reached a low level of fertility, sometimes even below their mortality levels. By comparison, most of the countries in the less developed realms were still in the explosive second stage of the demographic transition, adding large number of children to their population every year, thanks also to their large population base that has already emerged due to the prolonged second stage of their demographic transition coupled with long history of settlement.

Data also explains that the proportion of population below 15 years of age was almost ubiquitously above 40 per cent on the continent of Africa. Within Africa, Zaire (48.0), Kenya (47.7), Angola (47.1), Nigeria (45.6), Ethiopia (44.4), along with many other countries displayed above 40 per cent proportion of children displayed above 40 per cent proportion of children in their populations, while South Africa (37.3) in the south and Egypt (38.0) in the North displayed a proportion only marginally below 40 per cent. Outside Africa, Children's proportion exceeds 40 per cent in Islamic Asia—Yemen (46.7), Pakistan (44.3), Jordan (43.4) and Afghanistan (40.8); in South America, Paraguay (43.3) and in Central America—Nicaragua (46.0). A comparison brings out very clearly that these are the areas where the total fertility rate per women still soared at a high level of 4 to 5 children per women. The World Population Data sheet brought out in 2004 reveals that various parts of the World were contrastingly different from each other with regard to the stage of their ageing process. On an average 30 per cent of the world's population was still below 15 years of age signifying that large parts of the most populated world were still in the early stages of the demographic transition experiencing large annual increment in their populations. Similarly, on an average, only 7 per cent of the world's people were above 65 years of age, implying that ageing process too was still slow in case of most of the populous regions of the world.

From among various continents Africa had the highest percentage (42%) of population below 15 years of age. On the contrary its proportion of aged population 65+ was lowest (3%). Central America (36%), South America (31%) and Asia (30%) were other areas having considerably high proportion of their population below 15 years of age. There are the regions where a large number of countries are still in the explosive stage of demographic transition. Continuing high fertility rates in these countries have been resulting in large annual increments in their populations. In consonance with their stage of demographic transition, their average life expectancy was low and hence the proportion of their population in 65+ age group was low. In case of Central America only 4 per cent of its population was reported to be above 65 years of age and in case of both South America and Asia the corresponding figure was 6 per cent. It implies that the process of aging in all these areas was slow and their average life expectancy was below 65 years. However, Japan, the most developed country of Asia, was the only exception in Asia. About 19 per cent of its total population was above the age of 65 years. It had the highest percentage of 65+ age group population in the whole world. Japan also had the distinction of having lowest

(14%) proportion of its population below 15 years of age in the world. It not only compared well with the other developed countries of North America, Europe, Oceania but also excelled them in this regard.

However, by 2007 the world as a whole had only 28 per cent of its population below 15 years of age. The corresponding proportion of this population in the less developed and more developed countries was 31 per cent and 17 per cent, respectively. Recently published data sheet by Population Reference Bureau (UN) has revealed that the world on an average had about 8 per cent of its population in the 65+ age group category and in the coming decades such proportion was likely to improve further. The industrially developed countries had more than 16 per cent of their developed population in 65+ age group while the corresponding proportion in case of less developed countries was only 6 per cent.

From among various continents, Europe had about 16 per cent of its population in 65+ age group. Europe was followed by North America (13%), Oceania (7%), Latin America (7%), Asia (7%) and Africa (3%). Thus, the continent of Africa had lowest life expectancy and Europe had the highest life expectancy. It is projected that by 2050 the world will have 16 per cent of its population in the 65+ age group (Table 10.4). In case of more developed countries such as proportion may increase only to 9 per cent by 2050. By 2050, the proportion of population, above 65 age group in Europe may increase to 21 per cent. It will be followed by North America (18%), Oceania (15%), Latin America (10%), Asia (10%) and Africa (4%). Similarly, by 2050 the developed countries may have 26 per cent of their population above 65 years of age, while in case of less developed countries such proportion may reach 15 per cent. The average for the world as a whole may reach around 16 per cent. From among different continents Europe has 28 per cent of its population above 65 years of age would continue to have highest life expectancy. It may continue to be followed by North America (21%), Oceania (19%), Latin America (19%), Asia (18%) and Africa (7%) in this order.

Table 10.4: Percentage of Senior Citizen (65+ years)

	2012	*2025*	*2050*
World	8	10	16
Industrial Countries	16	21	26
Developed Countries	6	9	15
Europe	16	21	28
North America	13	18	21
Oceania	7	15	19
Latin America	7	10	19
Asia	7	10	18
Africa	3	4	7

Source: Population Reference Bureau, 2010.

The life expectancy in most parts of the world is increasing gradually. Such an increase in the life expectancy is likely to be slowest in case of the continents of Africa where most of the countries are still in the explosive second stage of the demographic transition. The countries with highest life expectancy are Japan, Singapore and a large number of Western countries, while the countries with lowest life expectancy are confined to the continent of Africa (Table 10.5).

The average for the world in this case was more close to the less developed world, as vast majority of the world's population lived in the less developed regions. Among the

Table 10.5: Countries with Highest and Lowest Life Expectancy

Country	*Life Expectancy (Years)*	*Country*	*Life Expectancy (Years)*
Japan	83	Swaziland	33
Australia	82	Botswana	34
France	82	Losatho	36
Iceland	82	Zimbabwe	37
Sweden	82	Zambia	38
Italy	82	Malawi	40
Switzerland	82	Angola	41

Source: Population Reference Bureau, 2010.

various continents, the dependency ratio was the highest in Africa. It was 91.4 in case of sub-Saharan Africa. It was followed by Arab states (74.3), South Asia (68.1), Latin America (61.5), East Europe and CIS countries (51.2), East Asia (47.5) etc. in this order. Thus, true to their contrast in terms of fertility patterns, the less developed and the more developed world presents contrast in terms of total dependency ratio also. Naturally so, as the total dependency ratio is the function of fertility behaviour. Data on dependency ratio reveal interesting trends in the dependency ratio in the coming 20 years or so. The dependency ratio for the world as a whole is expected to decline from 59.6 in 1997 to 50.6 in 2020. During the same period, while the dependency ratio in case of less developed countries is likely to decline from 62.5 to 50.7, in case of most industrialized countries it is expected to increase from 49.7 to 52.7. It is to be viewed in the context of the fact that the ageing process in case of less developed countries is adding to the share of their working population. By comparison, the ageing process in case of industrialized countries is adding more to their population of above 65 years of age.

The pyramids of the developing countries have broad based and steeply sloping sides, indicating a large proportion of children and young persons and a small proportion of old people in the population. But on the other hand, developed countries are almost rectangular in shape, with a slight sloping at the older ages. These pyramids indicate a lower proportion of children and a higher proportion of the adults and the elderly in the population (Fig. 10.4). It is, therefore, ironically to observe that countries, in the sense having long histories, such as India, Egypt and China, have very "Young Population", while comparatively young countries like the United Kingdom, France, Sweden and United States have "Old Population". It has been observed by demographers that the age structure of the developed countries has undergone several changes over the years and that the present age structure of many developed countries is markedly different from what it was in the past.

The trend in the number of older persons in the world is dominated by the fast growth of the older population in the less developed regions, where the size of the older population is 554 million in 2013, which is five times greater than in 1950 (108 million). The number of older people in these regions will further triple by 2050 to attain 1.6 billion. The speed of change in the more developed regions has been impressive too, but significantly slower than in the less developed regions. The older population of the more developed regions tripled between 1950 and 2013, from 94 million to 287 million, and it will increase further in coming decades, reaching 417 million in 2050.

Until almost hundred years ago, the age structure of various populations of the world did not vary much. All countries had typical pyramid shaped age structures, representative

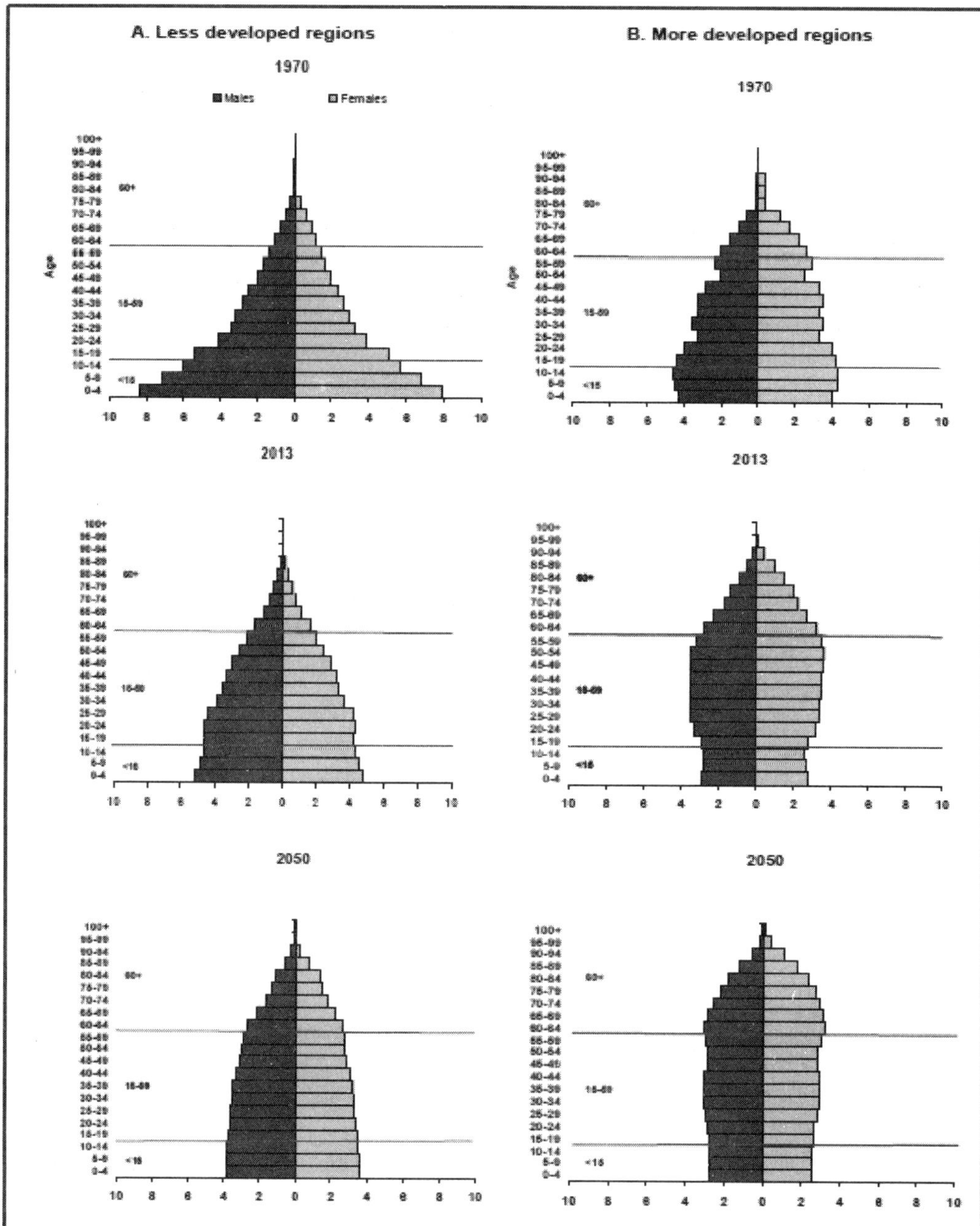

Fig. 10.4: Population Pyramids of Less and More Developed Regions of World
Source: UNDY, 2015.

of high fertility and high mortality. During the course of the past two hundred years, however, industrial developed populations have experienced substantial changes in their age structures; their populations have become older, that is, the proportion of older persons in the population has markedly increased. For instance, in 1990, the proportions of children under the age of 15 and that of old persons above the age of 64, were 33.25 and 5.3 respectively in Sweden. At the beginning of the 20th century, the corresponding proportions were 32.5 and 8.4. In 2000, the proportion of children under 15 decreased to 20.8 and that of old persons above 64 increased to 13.8. Similar changes have taken place in the age structure of the populations of France, England and Wales, United States, Norway, Russia, Germany etc. it may, therefore, be concluded that the populations of these countries have become 'older' during the course of 50 to 100 years. Correspondingly, the dependency ratios have undergone changes in these countries and have become lower.

10.8 India: Age-Sex Pyramids

The age structures of the populations of the developing countries like India have changed only slightly. The proportion of children under 15 and that of old persons of 65 and above were 39.0 and 2.5 respectively. Even after 50 years, there has been no significant change in these proportions. The Indian age-sex structure in 2000 is a good example of the classic pyramid shape. In fact, the proportion of children under 15 has increased to 42.1 and that of old persons to 2.8. The median age of the Indian population was 21.7 in 1901, 21.6 in 1921, 21.4 in 1951, 19.5 in 1961 and 19.0 in 1971 and 29 in 2010 (Fig. 10.5). It thus becomes clear that, in contrast to the populations in the Western developed countries, which have become "older", the Indian population has become slightly "younger".

The age group 0-14 is further sub-categorized into the age groups 0-4, 5-9 and 10-14. This can be seen that in many of the age groups, Male-Female variation within the age distribution of population are negligible except in the combined age-group of 0-14, 15-59, 60+ and 65+. Within the age-group 0-14, Male population is concerning simple fraction over feminine, whereas within the age-group 60+ as also 65+, percentage of Female is 0.7 per cent more than Male. The proportion of young children in the age group 0-4 and also the proportion of population in the age group 0-14 are higher in rural than in urban areas both for Male and Female. A higher proportion of Male and Female in the working age group 15-59 live in urban areas as compared to rural areas.

India's dependency ratio in 2000 stood at 65.0 but is expected to decline significantly to 47.3 by 2010. It signifies that India's fertility transition has entered the most critical phase. With accelerated decline in fertility in coming years, India is likely to improve its life expectancy at birth and increase the share of its population in the working age group of 15-65. The share of India's population in the age group of below 15 years may suffer a further decline during 1997-2015 and the share of country's population in above 65 years of age would increase but only marginally.

10.9 Summary

Population composition is very relevant and important as social relations within a community are affected considerably by the age structure. Trewartha (1953) rightly remarked that the proportion of the two sexes is fundamental to the geographic analysis of an area because it is not only an important feature of the landscape but it also influence the other demographic elements significantly and as such provides an additional means for analysing the regional landscape.

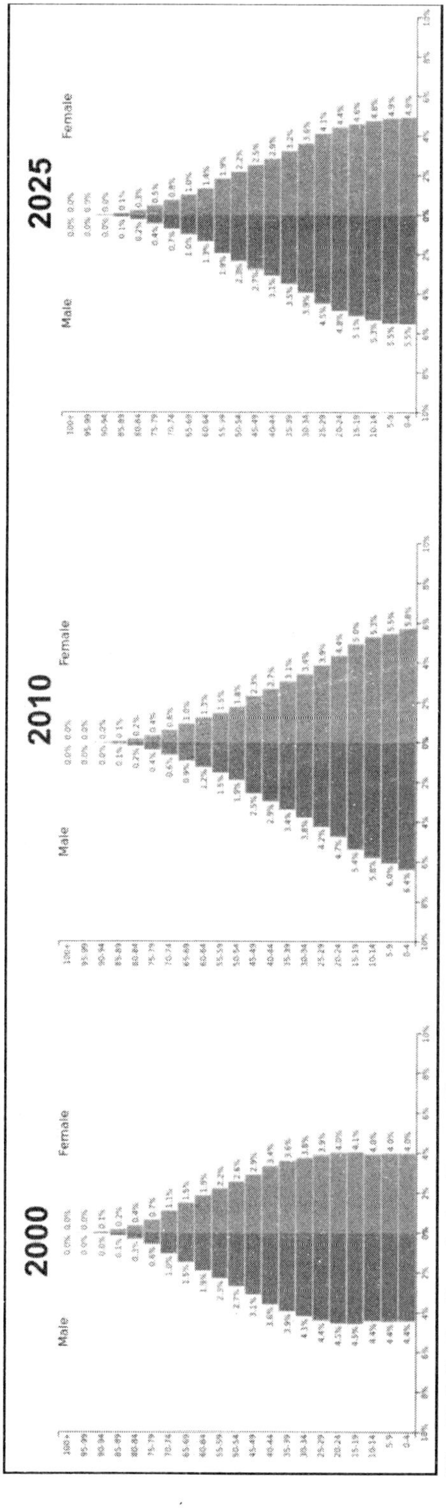

Fig. 10.5: India: Population Pyramid

Review Questions

1. What do you mean by age composition? How 'age composition' is an important component of population.
2. Explain types of age-sex pyramids with suitable illustration.
3. What is the relation between age composition and development in world?
4. Describe dependency ratio. How it affects social and economic structure.
5. Explain importance of age-sex pyramids.
6. What do you understand by distribution of age-sex pyramids at the World level?

Analytical Questions

1. Prepare a sketch of population pyramid of your city/state. Explain the reasons behind its shape and structure.
2. The shape of population pyramid of China has been changed significantly over last 10 years. Discuss.

Chapter 11
Migration

11.1. Introduction

Migration is the third component of population change, the other two being mortality and fertility (already discussed in earlier chapters). The nature of migration as a factor affecting population size is different from that of mortality and fertility. For one thing, migration is not a biological variable, while both mortality and fertility operate within the biological framework, through social, cultural, economic and political factors do exercise some influence on it. Migration on the other hand, is entirely determined by the wishes of the persons involved, though in exceptional cases this may not hold true. Usually, each migratory movement is deliberately made and an element of human violation is involved in the decision to move. Migratory movement are, therefore, a produce of the social, cultural, economic, political and physical situations and circumstances in which individuals and societies find themselves.

11.2 Defining Migration

Different scholars have tried to define the concept of migration distinctly because of their different approaches. While geographers have emphasized on the time and space significance of mobility, sociologists have laid stress on social consequences of mobility whereas importance to economic aspect of migration has been given by the economists. Literal meaning of "Migration" is "shifting of people or an individual or group of individuals from one cultural area to another, which may be permanent or temporary". In Webster's dictionary, the term has been defined as "the act or an instance of moving from one country, region to settle in another". Secondly it as defined as "an act of moving from one area to another in search of work". According to many individuals, the simplest meaning of the word migration can be a simple shift in the physical space. But, it would be interesting to note that meaning of migration is changing simultaneously with the passage of time. Now-a-days, both the scope and definition of migration have become more complicated, i.e. only mobility in physical state cannot define the concept of migration. The United Nations Multilingual Demographic Dictionary defined migration as follows: "Migration is a form of geographical mobility or spatial mobility between geographical unit and another, generally involving a change in residence from the place of origin or place of departure to the place of destination or place of arrival. Such migration is called permanent migration and should be distinguished from other forms of movement which do not involve a permanent change of residence."

11.3 Causes of Migration

Migration of population is a complex phenomenon and to know about the motives or reasons behind it is not easy. The factor controlling migration varies considerably from region to region and also from person to person. There are two types of factors responsible for the process of migration called push factors and pull factors. Pull factors operate in areas of out-migration and compel the people to migrate to other areas. Such factors repel the people from it. Push factors include war, floods, drought, epidemics, volcanic eruption, earthquake, unemployment, poverty, religion, conflict etc. Pull factors are that that operate in areas of in-migration and attracts the people to these areas. There are many factors in an area that attract more people to it and hold the people of the area. Pull factors include availability of various facilities of requirement such as employment, opportunities, educational facilities, security, facility of entertainment, social, religious and cultural attraction etc. Further, the causes of human migration are numerous which may be classified into following groups.

11.3.1 Physical Factors

Human migration is influenced by physical features, which vary according to time and space. Migration has been influenced from time to time by physical catastrophe such as volcanic eruptions, earthquakes, landslides, soil erosion, climatic fluctuations etc. Whenever people come across such problems, like frequent flood or drought conditions, they prefer to move from their place of origin or birth. People in early days used to consider epidemics as a vital force in driving people from one region to another. But with the development of medical science these forces have become insignificant. During summer season people of plains in tropical regions get attracted towards the health resort towns for improving health conditions. In a same way, people from colder regions move out to the warmth of the coastal areas. Even today the role of physical factors has not become insignificant, although the scientists are in a position to bring modification in natural conditions. To settle even in unsuitable conditions, scientists have developed air conditioners, they have invented disease resistance plants, animals, crops etc. Today even in deserts there are irrigation facilities that have been developed and have been made suitable for agriculture and human habitation. Punjab is an ideal example for this.

11.3.2 Economic Factors

The most important factor of all the factors that motivate people for migration is the economic factor. People migrate from hilly regions or mountainous regions to fertile plains. During pre-industrial era, people migrated from one place to another because of the absence of cultivable land. Because of population growth per capita share of land reduced, it became difficult for rural people to maintain their families with inadequate agricultural land. Therefore, members of the family generally advise their family members to earn money by migrating to urban centres. Industrialization is also considered an important migration motivating factor. Before industrialization, village cottage industries were providing job opportunities to few persons. But with the development of industries, growth of urban centres got encouraged having adequate employment opportunities. Before industrialization the life of the people in rural areas was the same in developed as well as developing countries. Along with this, development of transport and communication has remarkably influenced migration. Migration flow and its rate have increased with the help of transport and communication. Previously people used to confine their movement to short distances as there was least development of transport. With the increase in transport facilities the distant movement of people has also increased. So, now people started migrating to even inaccessible areas of previous times. Because of the development of transport, people started commuting on daily basis rather than migrating and settling in a short distance area.

11.3.3 Social Factors

Significance of social factors cannot be overruled as one of the important reasons for migration. People's migration is induced by social customs, traditions, social prejudices etc. Rural areas have old and traditional social customs and these customs are not linked to young generation. Certain people of rural areas remain so orthodox that they do not want to do any changes in their traditional social customs and manners. If by chance any individual tries to break these customs and traditions, he will be socially outcasted and then it becomes difficult for him to live in that particular environment. This situation ultimately leads to the migration of that individual from his place of birth to the place of destination, where he can enjoy his social freedom. Migrations due to marriage hold the highest share among all migrations. A girl has to migrate from her parents' house to her husband's house after getting married. People in olden times used to arrange marriage of their son/daughter within a short distance of area, so that they can move easily but with the development of transport and communication this distance has increased. Also, those people who prefer to go for inter-caste marriage are disliked by fellow villager's and in such scenario, they have to move out from their region of birth to take shelter in urban areas. People living in rural areas in religious oriented countries are more rigid in terms of religious principles and guidelines. People are forced socially as well as morally to follow traditional, religious customs. Moreover, people are not allowed to express their independent thinking and practice. People who try to express their independent thinking will be expelled socially because of which they will be forced to move out of that setting which ultimately leads to their migration to urban areas. People of rural areas are not only bounded by religious, social or customs of the village but they are also bounded by the restrictions of the joint family. These people sometimes get disguised with the joint family rules and regulations and decide to move out and go out to an urban area to live an independent life.

Urban areas provide better conditions for social development. Facilities of education are easily and adequately available here. Parents send their kids from rural areas to urban areas for better education, better social thinking and bright future. Sometimes, people prefer to migrate to urban areas so that they can avail themselves of proper educational facilities. Moreover, providing education to a girl child in rural areas is a problem partly because of the lack of girl school and colleges and partly because of the environment of rural areas.

Apart from all these factors people have become more conscious about comfortable and luxurious life. To lead a comfortable and luxurious life is not possible in rural areas because even today rural areas are not connected well by rail, road, electric lines, telephones etc. Even today villages are deprived of even basic essential facilities like tap water, medical facilities etc. but all these mentioned services are easily available in urban areas.

11.3.4 Demographic Factors

Those factors that motivate people to move from one region to another include uneven distribution of population, imbalanced growth of literacy and uneven growth of population etc. are known as demographic factors. People migrate from the places having high density coupled with low per capita land share to the places with less population and adequately cultivable land. In this respect, migration is also considered as a process of equalizing unequal distribution of population. Because of this both qualitative as well as quantitative aspects are determined. Human migration is also influenced by birth rate and death rate. Areas where there is low birth rate experience shortage of labour and therefore, attract migrants. Birth rates have been controlled by many developed countries because of which in spite of automation they face inadequate labour supply. So, all this leads to the movement of people towards the area having inadequate labourers.

11.3.5 Political Factors

These factors cannot be ignored while studying migration. It plays an important role in motivating people to migrate from one region to another. Histogenic accounts of different countries reveal several incidences of human migration based on political grounds. Because of political restrictions migrants of different countries were prohibited to settle in Australia, due to this reason it is still sparsely populated. Likewise, many other developed nations have put restrictions by changing immigration laws and prohibited mass movement of people. In certain countries migrants are not treated at par with their own citizens. Even if the government tries to facilitate migrants the local people of that area force these migrants to leave their countries. People have moved from one time to time from one region to the other in forms of refugee, political asylums etc. at the times of international wars and treaties. World War I and its after-effects caused large scale migration. The population transfer between India and Pakistan after partition is an ideal example of political effect on migration.

11.4 Consequences of Migration

Migration is an important means of cultural diffusion and social interaction which exercises three-fold impact: on the area of immigration, on the area of emigration and the migrants themselves. The results of migration of people may be favourable or unfavourable to the environment, society and economy of the place of its origin and destination. The main consequences of migration are to be discussed here.

11.4.1 Brain Drain and Brain Gain

Human capital flight is an Economics term equivalent to the Sociology term, brain drain, which refers to the emigration of intelligent, well-educated individuals to somewhere for better pay or conditions, causing the place they came from to lose those skilled people, or "brains". Brain drain occurs when scientists, engineers, doctors, IT-professionals and other intellectuals migrate to another country for higher studies, to undertake research activities, to get better job and work experiences which they are not getting from their country of origin. India is a very prominent source for supply of professionals. Elites and highly qualified professionals from India are placed all over the World. India is very rich in resources including human resources. India needs to put these resources to optimum utilization to bring amazing results for the country. The intellectuals which India loses every year can help in the effective utilization of our natural resources. Government needs to take timely and effective efforts to bring these resources back to India.

Brain gain can be generally defined as a form of brain drain where human capital moves in reverse from the developed countries to the developing ones. These migrants may accumulate savings; develop skills which could later be utilized in their home countries. The dot-com bubble, sub-prime crises, 9/11 attack, attack on students in Australia and related issues; in contrast the resilience shown by India made many of these migrants come back home. The expertise of these talented migrants can be used for the establishment and management of enterprises. Brain gain also results in increased capital flows into the country of origin, which can be used for the better utilization of resources. The returning entrepreneurs can also help India in making a distinguished position in the international markets.

11.4.2 Talent Shortage

Migration results into talent shortage in the home country. The educated crowd instead of serving their own country prefers to work for the developed nations for the sake of better pay and standard of living or any other reason. This is evident in India also especially in the field of medical services. Rural areas face acute shortage of medical practitioners. Also, there is huge demand of IT professionals in Telecom software companies which is unfulfilled. Most of the available professionals prefer to go to abroad to meet the requirements of software companies abroad. This results in the crunch for professionals in these sectors.

11.4.3 Cross Flow of Knowledge and Information

Thanks to the Indian Diaspora they have become a means for the exchange of thoughts, skills, ideas and practices across the nations. This has helped India becoming an innovative centre especially for IT development. Naturally these resources contributed to the development process in India. In addition to the direct financial advantage Indian Diaspora especially highly qualified ones bring other benefits such as image improvement for the country, knowledge transfers, access to new markets, business networks.

11.4.4 Financial Resources

Migration results in remittances. Indians who are earning abroad in foreign currencies send back money home for their families and to fulfil their liabilities. They also travel to and forth and along with them they bring foreign earnings to their country. Estimated at 30 million with a presence in 189 countries, the Indian Diaspora produces an annual economic income of about $ 400 billion, almost 30 per cent of India's GDP. There has been a steady increase in remittances from US$ 15.8 billion in 2001-02 to US$ 70 billion in 2011-12. This is highly encouraging and shows the significant aspect of brain gain to our economy. Indian Diaspora has also resulted in increased demand for Indian products in foreign market. This has further helped in the increased consumption of various products of Indian origin which now is equally liked and demanded by Indian and foreign markets. Indians settled abroad are now investing in various businesses in the form of FDI. This has helped in establishing a business network which helps in facilitating capital circulation between India and other countries.

11.4.5 Impact on Physical Environment

Mobility has been exerting its influence on physical landscape right from the beginning of human life. Intensity of impact changes temporally. In the wandering stage people were confined to gathering eatables from the forests rather than altering landscapes. Alterations started in landscape only when people started realizing the importance of domestication of animals, agriculture etc. Then they started the process of deforestation of land to start agriculture and this was first impact of migration on landscape. Initially people moved to fertile plains with suitable climate. But as the population kept on increasing, people started moving towards less fertile lands in mountainous region, plateaus, and semi-arid areas and hence they brought significant changes in the physical landscape. People started cutting down forests in mountainous region to perform terrace farming and also developed irrigation facilities. Similarly, plateaus were also used. Early migratory population molested plateaus. Accessible areas were transformed into agricultural and pastoral lands. People reached here with less difficulty. Impact of migration can easily be seen on semi-desert and desert regions. Growing demands of people coupled with the development of science and technology enabled people to inhabit areas which were otherwise unsuitable for living. Also, in and out migrations in rural areas have considerable impact on physical landscape. Landscape transformation is much more in urban areas and industrial areas than rural areas.

11.4.6 Impact on Economic Activity

Impact of economic activity can be seen on all aspects and stages of migration. Economic activity plays a pivotal role in different stages of migration. People get motivated to move from one place to another for differential economy and with a lust for economic betterment. Migrants improve their economic status by getting better jobs at the place of destination. Significant changes can be seen in agriculture at the place of origin. During different phases of agricultural development impact of migration on agriculture can be seen distinctly. Earlier due to lack of permanent habitation people were practicing shifting agriculture, because of this significant change were brought in agricultural landscape. Also because of migration, methods of agriculture were also affected. Methods such as commercial farming, truck farming, dairy farming etc, involved in shifting agriculture underwent changes. Historical analysis of various crops and fruits shows that they are not native of the place where they are grown now. Migrants have brought them along with them from their places of origin. Plantations like coffee, tea, and sugarcane were originally produced in Abyssinian highland, China and India respectively. A change in resource utilization, technological innovations, and industrial development can be seen as a consequence of migration. Excessive migration encouraged people to tap all kinds of available resources to fulfil their increasing demands. Trade activities are also affected by the process of migration. For example, European movement towards the different parts of the world was trade oriented. They established their trade centres to gather raw materials.

11.4.7 Impact on Social Conditions

Impact of migration has been seen on different aspects of social life right from the beginning of human civilization. This has resulted in the social complexities and these complexities are well marked in social structure, standard of living and socialization pattern. Social structure is an essential framework of human relations. It refers to the fundamental social relations because of which society gets its basic forms and also it sets the limits of the action. An organized arrangement can be applied to a town in a distinguished manner, i.e. to the institutions, groups, situations, processes, social positions etc. social structure constitutes important social groups such as family, caste, class, marriage and religion. All these groups basics kept changing in the wake of migration. Family structure has been affected immensely due to industrialization, growth of scientific knowledge, and extensions of communications. Traditional joint family started disintegrating because of people's migration from villages to the cities, leading to a number of psychological, social and economic problems. Size of family experienced changes due to rural urban migration and urbanized composition.

11.4.8 Impact on Culture

Before getting into the details of impact of migration on culture, we should first be aware of culture and acculturation is Man's behaviour and the way of carrying his daily activities represent his culture. A culture consists of habits that are shared by members of a particular society, whether it is a primitive tribe or a civilized nation. The habits that are shared in a society fall into two major headings, i.e. termed as customs and collective ideas respectively. Modes of behaviour such as etiquettes and the techniques of manipulating material objects are included in customs. On the other hand, practical knowledge, religious beliefs and social values comes under category of collective ideas. Similarly, acculturation is a process of change in custom resulting from the contact of people of different cultural backgrounds. An individual may like to change his pattern of behaviour and activities. Transfer of culture and acculturation has been seen in history a lot, as history is full of migrations. People not only move into a new place but they also bring with them their own culture and try to maintain the same in their new environment. And in this whole process the culture of the place of destination starts changing. These changes can be observed in different elements of culture such as customs, manners, dress, language, values etc. There is a huge difference between cultural attributes of people in rural areas from urban areas.

11.4.9 Impact on Demographic Structure

The demographic structure of both the places, i.e. the place of origin and place of destination gets changed because of movement of people between these two places. Because of this movement several factors related to demographic features gets affected, i.e. population distribution, age composition, sex, literacy, occupational structure, fertility and mortality of people. Proportion of working force gets change because of migration proportion of working force increases at the place of destination as people move to urban areas for better economic status. In addition to this, occupational structure also changes. Nature of job at the place of destination is mainly responsible for the change in occupational structure. Migration also leads to occupational mobility, i.e. very few migrants will follow their traditional occupational patterns in towns. In fact, they adopt such occupations which provide them social position as well as higher earning. Changes of this kind can generally be seen in the people of backward community as they want to hide their traditional occupation.

11.4.10 Impact on Urbanization

Migration is closely related to urbanization. Important elements in urban dynamics are constituted by both internal and external migration. Migration as such is a precondition of the process of urbanization. Initially, migrants in the urban hands are raw but they become skilled over a period of time. And by obtaining skills, techniques and required knowledge they fit into a number of urban jobs. Migration is not only a prerequisite condition of urbanization but also a concomitant process of industrialization and subsequent expansion as well as proliferation of the cities. Also, migration affects public utility services very worst. Large scale arrival of migrants leads to increase in demands of facilities of transportation, health care, educational institutions, recreational centres such as cinema hall, club etc., water supply, sanitation and power supply. This condition can be avoided if towns are planned well.

11.4.11 Impact on Political Activities

Every sphere of life and day to day activities has been covered by political activities. All bug and small communities are being controlled by political activities. Political impact of migration is distinct in local, intra-national and international migration. National solidarity and integration have been consolidated by regional, interstate or intra-national migration and feeling of regionalism gets discouraged. People of different religious and cultures are brought together by regional movement of the people. This further leads to national integration as it includes cultural interaction, adaptation, acculturation and assimilation. Local administration of both the places, i.e. place of origin and that of destination gets affected due to rural urban migration. Lack of political participation of migrant is because of several factors, i.e. illiteracy, community adjustments etc. The exodus of rural people to the towns creates problems for local administration. If people migrate from key strata of population, it tends to disturb the structure and distribution of power in both the societies. Migrants generally began political activities from his place of work; there he tries to establish his relationship with his fellow persons on the basis of his ability and aptitude. They become members of organizations related to their profession and such participation in professional and occupational association paves way for his political activities and participation. All the professional and occupational organizations are directly or indirectly associated with political parties. Migrants who work in government organizations do not accept membership of political parties whereas people who do not work in government organization easily become members of political parties of their choice.

11.4.12 Impact on Biological Characters

Three most important elements of ecology are man, animal and plants, which are affected by migration. All these three elements are closely related to environment and any change in environment leads to change in them. There is a considerable change in environmental conditions of any two regions. Migration of people is also influenced by the environmental conditions. Also, migrants bring modification in the existing environmental conditions by exploiting resources, deforestation, development of industries etc. And because of these activities land and water get affected very much. Two main factors that are responsible for pollution of water are industrialization and urbanization.

11.4.13 Impact on Discovery and Exploitation

Migration of human beings and their exploration are totally interdependent. In ancient times, main motive behind migration was ration of new areas, things etc. also during primitive times people use to wander from one place to another in search of livelihood., then started discovery for land and natural resources, this further motivated people to move from one place to another. In this way process of migration got influenced due to ongoing explorations. This quest leads to the discovery of new continents, along with the discovery of new resources at the newly found place. In this way migrants found new land and resources to live on.

11.5 Types of Migration

Migration has been classified on various bases. Some of them are discussed below.

11.5.1 Migration Types based on Motivation

On the basis of motivation, migration may be classified as Economic and Social migration.

Economic Migration

It is caused by economic determinants of migration. Such migration is mainly governed by economic factors including general resource base of the area, availability of fertile arable land, employment opportunities etc. The depressed economic condition and poor employment opportunities in the rural areas of Bihar and Eastern UP are generating tendencies of out migration for West Bengal, Punjab, Haryana, Delhi, Gujarat and Maharashtra.

Social Migration

It is generated by social custom, religious faith, socio-cultural contact, desire for social upliftment etc. females migration from the place of residence of their parents to the place of residence of their spouses is special type of social migration. This category of migration also includes the movement of people for pilgrimage places.

11.5.2 Migration Types based on Time

On the basis of time period, migration may be permanent, temporary, periodic or seasonal and daily.

Permanent Migration

In permanent migration, the migrants do not return their native place in future. The large-scale migration of European people in eighteenth and nineteenth centuries for North and South Americas, Australia and New Zealand is the best example of permanent migration. In internal rural-urban migration, many people with their families leave their villages for ever and are settled permanently in towns and cities of the country.

Temporary Migration

In this type of migration people leave their residences for short time. The movement of people for tour purposes or for pilgrimage is the example of temporary migration.

Periodic/Seasonal Migration

In such migration, people move for other places in a definite time period of the year. Trans-humane practices by many tribes in hilly areas are the best example of seasonal migration.

Daily Migration

Daily movement of communities, in the morning from villages and residential towns towards industrial towns and big cities for daily work, and in the evening or night, a movement in opposite direction it can be seen. The daily movement of workers for their work place and of students for their educational institutions are the well examples of daily migration.

11.5.3 Migration Types based on Number Involved

On the basis of numbers of migrant, migration may be of two types: Individual and Mass Migration

Individual Migration

It is personal migration which involves only a person or his family. Motive of this movement may be social, religious, economic etc.

Mass Migration

It involves a huge number of people migrating from one place to another place particularly for long distance.

11.5.4 Migration Types based on Direction of Flow

In migration, people leave one place to another place temporarily or permanently. According to direction to move, migration is of two types: Immigration and Emigration.

Immigration

The migration in the context of place which is the destination of their move or where they are ultimately settled is called immigration. In America, incoming migrants from other continents called immigrants and this migration is termed immigration.

Emigration

The move of people from an area is called emigration or out migration. Out migration of people from European countries is termed as emigration in the European context. Thus, migration from rural to urban area is considered out migration for rural areas and immigration for urban areas. Likewise, transfer of people from Europe to Australia is called outmigration in Europe and immigration in Australia.

11.5.5 Migration Types based on Areal Size

The geographers should not be satisfied with migration classification based on these four above mentioned elements. Since geography is a spatial science, the parameter of area or space is most sacred and justified to any geographic classification of migration. On the basis of areal size or scale, migration may be broadly classified into two groups—(1) International Migration and (2) Inland Migration.

International Migration

In the international migration, people move from a country for the other country. Continental migration may also be included in this category. Migration of population from European countries to North America, South America, Australia, New Zealand and the countries of Asia and Africa is termed as international migration. Migration from China and Japan and India for south-east Asian countries is also the example of international migration.

Inland Migration

It involves the migration of people within the country from one region, area or place to another. The internal migrations are further classified into four types: (i) rural to urban migration, (ii) urban to urban migration, (iii) rural to rural migration, and (iv) urban to rural migration.

11.5.6 Based on Movement Patterns

Based on classifying people according to their social status, travel points and periodicity:

Step Migration

Migration initiating from a small settlement and moving towards a larger one, in the urban hierarchy, it has been a trend over the years. This includes a pattern of closer, not too destabilizing migrations from a person's place of origin to an ensuing destination, such as movement from a farm to a village, then to a town and subsequently to a suburb (if applicable) and finally into a city. This category also includes the movement of people from a smaller to a bigger city.

Circular Migration

Cyclical migration experiences between an origin and a destination with at least one migration and return. Migrants share their time between multiple (at least two) locations, with their family, work, etc. While the frequency of movement may vary along with the length of stay at the destination, a circular migrant spends significant periods of time at the origin and destination. Seasonal migration is a very common form of circular migration, driven by seasonal peaks in labour demand, mostly in agriculture. Return migration, on the other hand, refers to a one-time emigration and return after an extended stay outside the host territory.

Chain Migration

Migration of families at different stages of the life cycle, from one location to the next, who subsequently bring people from their home location to this new place, is known as chain migration. In theory, a chain of people constantly moves from place to place, supported by those who migrated before them.

11.5.7 Based on Decision-Making Approach

Based on classifying migration as voluntary or involuntary, given certain socio-political factors (e.g. the fear of ill-treatment attributed to race, religion, political affiliation, nationality or association to social groups; flight from war; conflict involving arms; civil war; natural or man-made disasters; famine) or developmental factors (e.g. substantial infrastructure projects, including airport, road, dam or port construction; the administrative clearance of urban projects; mining and deforestation; the creation of conservation parks/ reserves and other biosphere related initiatives, among others).

Voluntary Migration

Based on a person's free will, initiative and desires to live in a better place and to improve their financial status, among other factors.

Involuntary Migration

Involuntary migration is based on a person's is being forced out of their home due to certain unfavourable environmental and political situations. This can be further classified as: reluctant/impelled/imposed migration. It happens when a person is put in a situation that encourages relocation or movement outside their place of residence. Another is forced migration which happens when a person is unable to return home (refugee), or undergoes a legal procedure to qualify as a refugee in the host country (asylee), or is forced to leave their home due to a conflict or development but does not cross any boundaries (internally displaced person).

11.6 Spatial Distribution of Migration

The distribution migration can be understood in three ways. It can be international, inland and seasonal.

11.6.1 International Migration

International migration is as old as human history, whether it is voluntary or forced upon people by famines, conquests and various types of persecutions. Unfortunately, because of the lack of precise information, the size and nature of such migrations are not exactly known. In the classical world, international migration was considered as voluntary, rational attempts of the human beings to maximise utility and to attain uplift. Recently, not only the number of persons involved in international migrations had decreased significantly but also the purpose of migration has undergone a change. In an analysis of International Survey data collected by the International Organization for Migration (IOM) from the Gallup World Poll for the period 2010-2015, 1.3 per cent of the global adult population, or 66 million people, were planning to migrate permanently within the next 12 months. One in three adults surveyed plans to migrate to a developing country, with the United States as the most popular destination followed by the United Kingdom, Arabia, France, Canada, Germany and South Africa. According to the World Gallup Poll data from 2013 to 2016, the desire to migrate has grown since the 2010-2012 period. Nearly 710 million people (14% of the world's adult) would like to move to another country if they had an opportunity.

The number of international migrants worldwide has continued to grow rapidly over the past fifteen years reaching 244 million in 2015, up from 222 million in 2010, 191 million in 2005 and 173 million in 2000. Between 2000 and 2005, the international migrant stock grew by an average of 2 per cent per year. During the period 2005-2010, the annual growth rate accelerated, reaching 3 per cent. Since then, however, it has slowed, falling to around 1.9 per cent per year during the period 2010-2015. High-income countries host more than two-thirds of all international migrants. As of 2015, 71 per cent of all international migrants worldwide equal to 173 million international migrants lived in high-income countries. Of these, 124 million migrants were hosted in high-income OECD countries, while 49 million migrants were living in other high-income non-OECD countries. Only 29 per cent or 71 million of the world's migrants lived in middle or low-income countries. Of these, 61 million resided in middle-income countries and 9 million in the low-income countries.

Nearly two-thirds of all international migrants worldwide live in Europe or Asia. In 2015, 76 million international migrants were residing in Europe, compared to 75 million in Asia. Northern America hosted the third largest number of international migrants (54 million), followed by Africa (21 million), Latin America and the Caribbean (9 million), and Oceania (8 million) (Fig. 11.1). In 2015, of the 244 million international migrants worldwide, 104 million (43 per cent), were born in Asia. Europe was the birthplace of the second largest number (62 million or 25 per cent), followed by Latin America and the Caribbean (37 million or 15 per cent) and Africa (34 million or 14 per cent). In 2015, India had the largest "diaspora" in the world (16 million), followed by Mexico (12 million). Other countries with large diasporas included the Russian Federation (11 million), China (10 million), Bangladesh (7 million), and Pakistan and Ukraine (6 million, each). Between 2000 and 2015, positive net migration contributed to 42 per cent of the population growth in Northern America and 32 per cent in Oceania. In Europe the size of the population would have fallen between 2000 and 2015 in the absence of positive net migration.

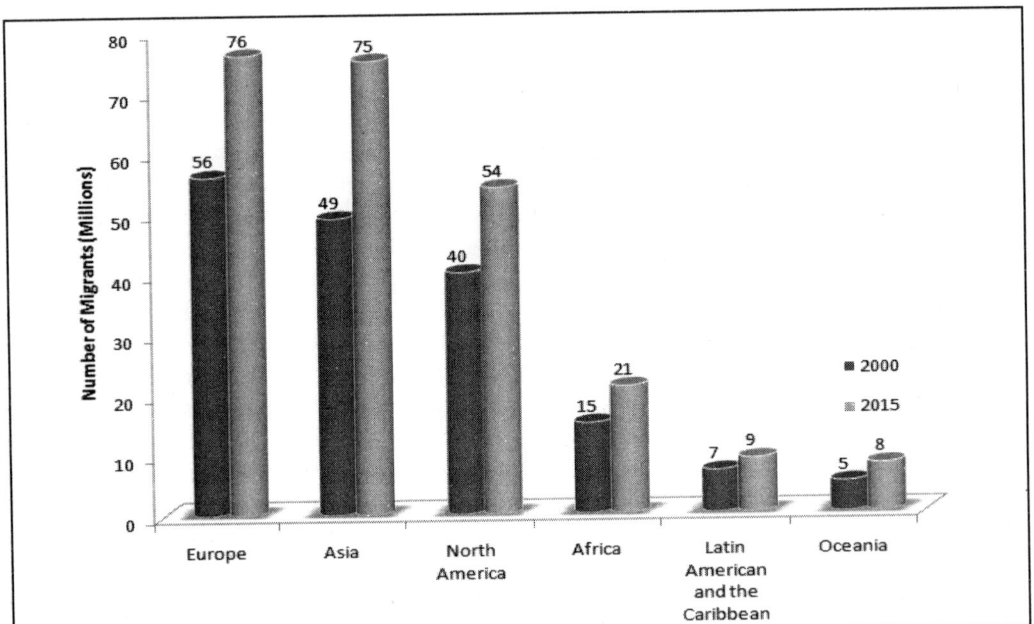

Fig. 11.1: Number of International Migrants by Major Area of Destinations, 2000 and 2015

Source: Based on Data of World Economic Forum, 2017.

11.6.2 Inland Migration

All types of human migration that take place between two different areas lying within the territorial jurisdiction of a country are distinguished as inland or internal migrations. Inland migration includes interstate migration (between two states) and intrastate migration (within state). The inland migrations are further classified into four types on the basis of rural and urban areas: (1) rural to urban migration, (2) urban to urban migration, (3) rural to rural migration, and (4) urban to rural migration.

Rural to Urban Migration

This type of migration carries the rural population to the growing towns and cities and it is more common in developing countries. It is caused by both rural push and urban pull forces. In developing countries, rural poverty is found to be greater than urban poverty and thereby, most of the rural people migrate to urban centres, mainly for their livelihood. The large rural to urban migration has various socio-economic, demographic and cultural consequences like high cost of living, shortage of housing and growth of slums, deterioration in the basic civic amenities and unemployment in urban centre.

Urban to Urban Migration

Inter-urban migration takes place between two urban centres. It is more common in the highly urbanized and developed countries of the West than those of developing and less developed countries of the East. Inter-urban migration is generated mostly by economic factors. Generally educated and skilled people and technician move from one urban centre to another with a view to improving their employment prospects. Big cities attracts such workers from other towns who have acquired sufficient qualifications and skills for their absorption in industrial and service sector. The vacuum caused by emigration from small urban centres is filled by the subsequent immigration from the local rural areas. Thus, inter-urban migration is an important factor promoting the process of metropolitan.

Rural to Rural Migration

Migration of people from one rural area to another is a common phenomenon in predominantly agrarian countries. Such migration is directed towards areas having much and better employment opportunities in agricultural works. In developing countries like India, in the force of rural to rural migrants, unskilled agricultural labourers are in majority. The areas with advanced irrigation facilities, reclamation of waste land, intensification of agriculture and demand for agricultural labourers attract rural people from backyard rural areas that are overpopulated and experiencing acute unemployment. Direction of such migration is from crowded areas of low agricultural productivity towards sparsely populated agricultural areas having much employment opportunities in agricultural sector.

Urban to Rural Migration

Urban to rural migration is not common compared to other type of migrations. Such migration takes place usually in the advanced stage of urban development from big cities due to over congestion. Urban to rural migration is not common in developing and less urbanized countries. It is the characteristic of industrialized urbanized developed countries particularly in North-west Europe and Anglo-America.

11.6.3 Seasonal Migration

It is a special type of human migration in which pastoral farmers move with their herds and flocks seasonally or periodically between two areas of different climatic regions. This practice is known as "transhumance". The practice of seasonal mountainous can be seen in the regions of Himalayas, Alps, Altai, Khingan etc. Bhotias, the tribal of Uttarakhand (India), are semi-nomadic people and practise transhumance. Khirgiz is a nomadic tribe of Central Asia which is the traditional land of pastoral monads. The nomads of Central Asia including Khirghiz live under arid conditions and migrate seasonally in search of water and pastures for their herds of sheep, cattle and horses. Khirgiz are the dwellers of southern Tien Shan and the Pamirs. A similar transhumance is also found in Swiss and French Alps in Europe.

11.7 Migration Theories

The quantitative revolution in geography in early 1960s brought a new realization among the geographers and stimulated them to formulate theories and models. The task of theory-building and model-development is not easy for population geographers, who deal with human phenomena which are highly dynamic and which change in their spatial and temporal dimensions with unusual rapidness. Moreover, it may be difficult to subject the individual human behaviour to a well-defined set of laws. The preceding pages have highlighted that the phenomenon of migration is highly complex phenomenon and the factors associated with the movements of people are still more complex. In this context, one is reminded of Humphrey's observation that migration was rather distinguished for its lawlessness than for having any definite laws.

In spite of great difficulties in theorization of the process of migration, the recent developments in this field of theoretical model building with regard to migration are quite encouraging. It may be pointed out here that theory building in the field of migration is almost a century old if Ravenstein's attempt (1885) is considered as the beginning point. Lee (1966) has forwarded a set of general theories and hypotheses concerning migration process on the lines similar to that of Ravenstein (1889). A comprehensive typology of migration has also been developed by Peterson (1958). Pryor (1971) in his monograph on *Internal Migration and Urbanization Stresses* on the significance of individual adjustive, institutional, adaptive and information diffusion factors for comprehending this residential relocation which takes place through migration. Gale (1973) while commenting on Rossi's (1955) life cycle hypothesis and Haggerstrand's (1967) ideas of temporal and spatial stationarity argues that although migration models definitely help in the search for pattern and order, yet there is no escape from simple descriptive studies. These models are deterministic in approach and try to establish relationship between migration and its explanatory variables.

Probabilistic models of migration, on the other hand, have been specifically designed for forecasting migration flows. With the help of such models it is asserted that future patterns of migration may be predicted (Rogers, 1966, Compton, 1969, Joseph, 1975). Woods (1979) sums up that such models are essentially of a descriptive and at best explanatory nature. Their function is not to interpret reality but to let it change along predetermined lines. Wolpert (1975) brought micro analytical perspective in model building, when he stressed upon the importance of human behaviour in the decision making process of the migrant. Gould and Prothero (1975), and Zelinsky (1971) have also made their contributions in the field of model-building with regard to migration. In the pages that follow, an attempt would be made to discuss briefly some of the popularly known laws and models describing and explaining the migratory behaviour of human population.

11.7.1 Ravenstein's Law of Migration

The first formal attempt on theoretical formulations on migration was made by Ravenstein (1885) when he gave the following laws of migration, which he derived from an analysis of inter-country movements within Britain in 19th century using census birthplace data.

1. **Migration and Distance.** Large number of migrants move to a short distance only... there takes place consequently, a universal shifting displacement of population, which produces 'currents of migration' setting in the direction of great centres of commerce and industry which absorb the migrants. Implied in this are: (i) distance-decay function; and (ii) preference for large centres of commerce and industry among long-distance migrants.
2. **Migration by Stages.** The inhabitants of the countryside surrounding a rapidly growing town flock into it; the gaps, thus, created in the countryside are filled up by migrants from remoter areas, until the attractive force of one of the rapidly growing cities makes its influence felt, step by step, to the most remote corner. The process of dispersion is the inverse of that of absorption and exhibits similar features.
3. **Streams and Counter-streams.** Each main current of migration produces a compensating counter current.
4. **Rural-Urban Differential.** The natives of the towns have low degree of propensity to migrate in comparison to their counterparts in the countryside.
5. **Preponderance of Females.** Among the short-distance migrants, the number of females is far more than that of males. This is due to the migration of females after marriage.
6. **Technology and Migration.** The magnitude of migration increases with the advancement of technology.
7. **Motives behind Migration.** Economic motives have a primary importance among various factors governing magnitude of migration.

Most of the laws forwarded by Ravenstein seem to have stood the test of time. Pryor (1969) found these laws to be largely valid in his study pertaining to experience of Malaysia and other countries.

11.7.2 Gravity Model

The role of population size and distance in determining spatial interaction had become formalized in 1930s and 1940s when Newton's Law of Gravitation was applied to population movements. Although it was John Q. Stewart who first pointed out the isomorphic relationship of population movements with Newton's Law of Gravitation (James, 1972), which later came to be known as Gravity model, yet it is believed that W.J. Reilly (1929) had already postulated in 1909 that the movement of persons between two urban centres would be directly proportional to the product of their population and inversely proportional to the square of distance between them (Reilly, 1929). Accordingly, the index of migration can be expressed as follows:

$$MI = K\frac{P_1 P_2}{d^2}$$

Where,

MI : Migration Index,
K : Proportionality Constant,
P_1 : Population size of settlement 1,
P_2 : Population size of Settlement 2, and
d : Distance between the two settlements.

The Gravity model, which was the first attempt to theorize population movement, gives a cross-section of macro-level interaction in a system of regions. It is argued that, this model, theoretically, is stationary in respect of time, space and direction. Just like the Newton's Law of Universal Gravitation, the gravity model also believes that the power of any area to attract migrants depends upon its size of its economic base. Of course, human beings are not molecules, but probability. The square of the distance being taken as denominator conveys that the number of migrants decreases increasingly with the increase in distance. This model did attract criticism from Harris on the plea that migration could not be considered independent of explicit societal decisions. Peterson (1958) complained that the model neglects the age and sex profile of the migrants. Gale (1973) considered it too simple a model to explain too complex a phenomenon. Taylor was most critical about Gravity model when he designated it as a crude physical analogy with no theoretical basis in social sciences (Taylor, 1977).

Recently, Foot and Milne (1984) stressed upon the inter-regional nature of migration flows and advocated that any comprehensive analysis of migration must be carried out in multi-regional framework interaction between all relevant regions and be specified and analyzed in a system-wide approach. Their extended Gravity model is based upon human capital theory where variables like real wage rates, unemployment rates are introduced as additional determinants of migration-decisions.

11.7.3 Principle of Least Effort

Several attempts have been made in migration research in search of a specific population size and distance relationship. In 1949, George K. Zipf regarded the movement of goods, information and people within the social system as an expression of his 'principle of least effort' (Jones, 1981), whereby inter-community movement is such as to minimise the total work of the system. Accordingly, the amount of movement between any two communities was expressed as under:

$$M_{ij} = K\frac{P_i P_j}{D_{ij}}$$

Where:

M_{ij} : Magnitude of Movement between any Two Communities i and j,
P_i : Population size of community i,
P_j : Population Size of Community j,
D_{ij} : Distance between i and j,
K : Proportionality Constant.

According to Zipf, the magnitude of migration between two cities was the function of distance separating them, where greater distance required greater effort to overcome the hurdles, and hence reduced the number of migrants. His formula when put to test in American cities did reveal an inverse correlation between distance and magnitude of migration. It is stated that Zipf's principle of least effort is not different from gravity model and was too successful in describing the population flows. This principle is also objected to the principle of least effort and wanted that the power of the distance in the formula be raised to more than one and less than two if the magnitude of migration decreases increasingly with the increasing distance.

11.7.4 Intervening Opportunities Model

In 1940, Stouffer introduced his concept of intervening opportunities. According to this model, linear distance was less important a determinant of migration than the nature of space, the distance should be considered in socio-economic rather than geometric terms. Thus, distance *per se* was not as important as the number of opportunities available. His basic hypothesis was that the number of persons moving for a given distance was directly proportional to the number of opportunities at that distance and inversely proportional to the number of intervening opportunities, i.e. the number of opportunities offered by places located in between the two places in question (Stouffer, 1940). It may be expressed as under

$$Y = K\frac{X^*}{X}$$

Where:

Y : Expected number of migrants from a place to particular concentric zone or distance band around that place,
X : Number of opportunities within this band,
X* : Number of opportunities intervening between origin and mid-way into the band in question, and
K : is the proportionality constant.

The actual opportunities are the kind that have attracted migrants and may include employment, environment, housing etc. Several studies that were conducted to test Stouffer's formula pointed out that in-migration represent only the opportunities or vacancies filled, so that in areas of employment expansion it will invariably underestimate the opportunities available.

11.7.5 Competing Migrants Model

In 1960, Stouffer refined his own intervening opportunities model which faced operational inflexibility, in the sense that it could cope with only migrations flow from a given centre to the surrounding distance bands. He also realized that the migration between the two places 'A' and 'B' was not the function of opportunities at B and intervening opportunities between 'A' and 'B' but was also a function of the number of competing migrants from elsewhere. Thus, he introduced another variable of competing migrants. Accordingly, the number of migrants from a city 'A' was a direct function of number of opportunities available at another city 'B' and an inverse function of the number of intervening opportunities between 'A' and 'B' and also an inverse function of other migrants that may compete from elsewhere for the opportunities at 'B'. The competing migrants were defined as the sum of out-migrants from all cities within a circle which had city 'B' as its centre and its distance from A as its radius (Jansen, 1969). Stouffer's refined formula was expressed as under (Galle and Taeuber, 1966).

$$Y = K\frac{X_o X_1}{X_b X_c}$$

Where:

Y : Number of migrants from city 1 to city 2,

K : Proportionality Constant.

X_0 : Number of all out-migrants from city 1,

X_1 : Number of opportunities at city 2 measured by total in-migrants,

X_b : Number of opportunities intervening between cities 1 and 2, measured by total in-migrants to a circle having as its diameter the distance from city 2 to city 1,

X_c : Number of migrants potentially competing for opportunities in city 2 measured by total out-migrants from all cities within the circle having city 2 as its centre and the distance between 1 and 2 as its radius.

Various studies conducted to test the validity of this model established that it was definitely an improvement over Zipf's model and in many cases a reliability index of over 90 per cent was observed. However, some of the scholars suggested the introduction of some sociological variables in the model like the status of the migrants.

11.7.6 Summary

Many of the young Indian scientists and technicians are working very hard to develop our country. It is the hard work and devotion of its human talent that India today could achieved the nuclear status as well as become a space power. There is no limit to development and progress, India needs the talent of all the Indian scientists and engineers settled abroad. They can play an important role in future progress of our country. Migration can be taken as one of the positive factors in the era of globalization which helps in the free flow and exchange of ideas, commodities, and technology along with talents. It has its own positives and negatives. In Indian context, as of today, migration has resulted into brain circulation. The migrants of yesterday are coming back and are creating new avenue for economic development. The situation is improving in IT, pharmaceuticals, bio-tech, and chemical field. The need of the time is to develop effective policy framework to attract the migrants which can then create substantial benefits for the nation.

Review Questions

1. Define migration. Explain different push and pull factors affecting internal migration.
2. Explain various types of migration with suitable examples.
3. Describe spatial patterns of migration in the world.
4. Explain the laws of migration given by Ravenstein.
5. Discuss the major theories which explain migration.

Analytical Questions

1. Identify three push and pull factors that shape the decision of students of your college/institution to migrate from their native places.
2. Identify environmental and economic factors in your country that might result immigration/emigration.

Chapter 12
Population Theories

12.1 Introduction

Since time immemorial, scholars and thinkers have concerned themselves with the population question. Of course, the points of view have differed, especially as they related to the size and growth of human population. A large and rapidly growing population has sometimes been considered to be desirable as a source of the nation's strength and wealth and as an essentially useful factor underlying technological development. It is, therefore, worthwhile to trace the development in thinking of scholars and the different points of views expressed by them with respect to population phenomena within the socio-economic-political context. The first thinker who took the question of population in a formal way was Malthus Thomas, who is well known for his theory of population growth (1798). Despite of criticism, Malthus attempted to give a scientific explanation of the growth of population which was largely based on the information available from capitalist countries. After that Demographic Transition Theory, developed in the 20th century, which gives a more cogent, logical and systematic explanation of population growth. The present chapter will look into both theories.

12.2 Demographic Transition Model

Demographic Transition Model is based upon the trends in mortality, fertility and natural increase. This model represents the process of change of countries from high birth rates and high death rates to low birth rates and low death rates as part of the economic development of a country from a pre-industrial to an industrialized economy.

Earlier demographers such as Landry (1909) and Warren Thompson (1929) had attempted to construct the typology to describe the transition in countries from high mortality and high fertility to condition of low mortality and low fertility. None of these demographers can, however, be called the father of the theory of demographic transition, for none made an attempt to explain these changes either in fertility or mortality. In 1945, F.W. Notestein (1945) explained demographic transition in an almost mature form, with explanations for the changes in fertility. The demographic transition theory of Notestein suggests a relationship between population change and socio-economic development. The theory is an idealized representation of the growth of population based on the experience of Western European countries' demographic evolution in 18th-19th century.

The theory of demographic regulations emphasizes that man is highly flexible and adaptable creature. He is capable of curtailing his fertility when the mortality decline yields faster population growth than the supporting capacity of the environment. The demographic transition theory is upon the trends in the mortality, fertility and natural increases in the more developed countries of the world since 18th century. Trewartha (1969) observes that the concept of demographic transition organizes the variety of population data into an orderly and coherent pattern with a view to integrating the spatial processes of change and the dimension of time.

Demographic transition theory can be used to describe and predict the future population of any area. The theory tells us that population of any region or country changes from high births and high deaths to low births and low deaths as society advancements and growth from rural agrarian and illiterates to urban industrial and literate society. These changes occur in stages which are collectively known as the demographic cycle.

12.2.1 The Forerunner

The first formulation within the English demographic literature is that by Warren Thompson, printed in 1929. He specified 3 varieties of countries with totally different rates of increase. The primary (Group A) were those with falling rates of increase and that were facing potential population decline, though mortality in these countries was low, their apace declining fertility presages 1st writing paper, and later a declining population. enclosed during this class were the countries of Western Europe and overseas countries that had been settled by immigrants of European origin.

Group B comprises countries within which each birth and death rates had fallen, however, wherever death rates had declined earlier and sooner than birth rates. As a result, their populations were growing terribly apace, till falling birth rates would originate a writing paper, then a declining population. Thompson recognized that their demographic scenario was reminiscent of that of nations in blood type some thirty five to forty years earlier. However, since death rates were currently falling sooner than within the past, rates of natural increase during this cluster were larger than those old earlier in countries in blood type.

Countries in Group C within which neither birth nor death rates were in check were classified as 'Malthusian'. Thompson advised that this cluster contained between seventy and seventy five per cent of the world's population. However, as a result of knowledge were typically distributed, he confined his analysis to 3 giant countries within which knowledge were available: Japan, Republic of India and Russia. He expected that increase in Russia would be abundant larger than in Republic of India, attributable to its abundant larger resource base. He thought that it would take 3 to four decades, before several of the countries in Group C entered in Group B.

The nature of the demographic transition and also the method though old will be abundant to clarify simply, however, human society ought to wherever its nowadays. Variations during this method additionally facilitate justify variations round the world now-a-days. As a result of the transition could be an international development, the actual fact that varied components of the planet area unit at totally different stages of the demographic transition, helps North American countries to chart a minimum of a part of the long-run course among the relative newcomers to that. Foretelling the long-run is usually risky and unsure, however, characteristic the transition as a pathway modification enables us to understand more clearly the contexts of change to come for many countries.

However, if we look at the data, they do not look as neat as this. For example, India and China started quite similarly on demographic front, but today China is far ahead of India in terms of GDP growth whereas Japan has long been in the group of top 12 developed countries. In fact, China had lower per capita GDP than India in 1960 and it continued up to late 1980s until which time India was ahead of China in terms of per capita GDP. In 1990s, China surged ahead India considerably and now it has per capita GDP double that of India. Similarly, the population as a whole and the age structure of Africa is quite favourable in demographic terms; even then, its economic growth forecast in the next 45 years is not promising.

There were three distinct parts of the theory:

1. Descriptive
2. Theoretical
3. Predictive

The first part was concerned with the simple description of the trends in mortality and fertility through time. The second part related to the casual mechanism that create the pattern of trends described in the first part and hence was purely theoretical. The third predictive part postulates as to what will happen in future.

12.2.2 Stages of Demographic Transition Model

The demographic transition theory is characterized by conspicuous stages. The four stages suggested by Demographic Transition suggests definitive characteristics associated with each stage in an almost cause effect relationship (Fig. 12.1).

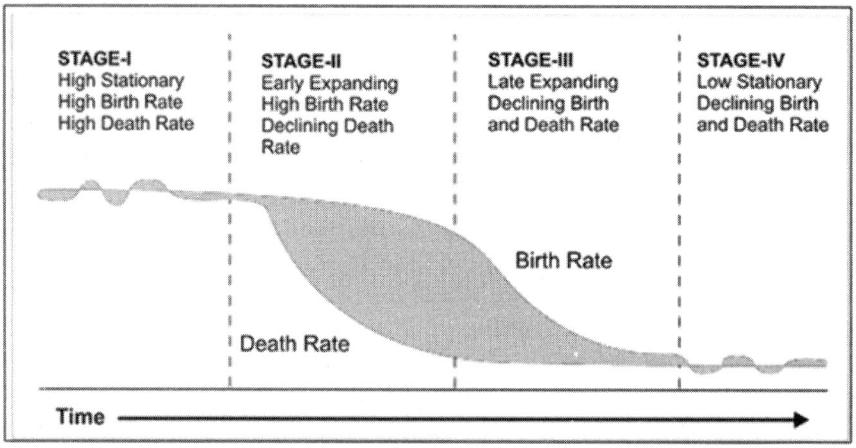

Fig. 12.1: Stages of Demographic Transition Model

In the first stage, the fertility is over 35 per thousand and is almost stable. The mortality in this stage is also high being more than 35 per thousand but its behaviour is erratic due to epidemics and variable food supply. So, basically this stage is characterized by high birth rates and death rates (about 35 per 1000) that fluctuate at a high level giving a small population growth. This stage thus postulates the stable and slow growing population which is characterized by agrarian primitive societies. It follows such production processes, that have high generation of wastes. manual labour is way valued. Poor technical ability, poor acquisition and low urban development is that the characteristic options found in these stages. during this stage, the country is backward and is defined by high birth and death rates with the result that the expansion rate of population is low. folks principally sleep in rural areas and their main occupation is agriculture that is during a state of stupidity.

There are many straightforward, lightweight and tiny goods industries. The tertiary sector consisting of transport, commerce, banking and insurance is underdeveloped. of these factors are answerable for low incomes and financial condition of the plenty. giant family is thought to be a necessity to enhance the low family financial gain. youngsters contributed to the economy of the family from associate degree early stage by carrying water, fuelwood, caring for younger siblings, sweeping, laundry dishes, getting ready food and doing a little works within the fields. The high rate of birth may be due any or all of the factors that are related to high fertility even these days in several less developed countries. With a high death rate among youngsters, there would be very little incentive in rural societies to regulate fertility except within the most unendurable of circumstances. The birth rates are high thanks to (1) No contraception or birth control, (2) High death rate such a large amount of youngsters die in infancy that parents tend to produce more additional therein hope that many can survive, (3) giant families are thought of as assets as a result of several youngsters are required to figure on the land, (4) youngsters are thought to be a signal of virility, and (5) Some faith encourages giant families. Besides this, death rates also are terribly high particularly among youngsters. The explanations for an equivalent are as follows: (i) Poor hygiene, (ii) very little data and provision of medical sciences, (iii) Diseases and plague within the type if epidemics oftentimes came about, and (iv) Shortage and unsure food provides light-emitting diode to famine, poor diet etc.

The first stage that is characterised by agricultural low financial gain economy is marked by comparatively stable birth rate at the utmost fertility level found in societies not having any data concerning mistreatment contraceptives, and also the death rate is found to fluctuate in response to conditions of prosperity or famines, epidemics and different disasters. About 100 years ago, all the countries of the world were at this stage of demographic transition.

The second stage of demographic transition is characterised by a high and gradually declining fertility of over 30 per thousands and a sharply reduced mortality rate of over 15 per thousands. Thus, second stage is characterized by high birth rates (35 per 1000), but death rate fall rapidly to about 20 per 1000, giving a rapid population growth. This stage leads to a fall in its death rate and an increase in population. In this expanding stage of demographic transition, while the improvement in sanitation and health conditions, general productivity and distribution system results in sharp decline in the mortality rate, the fertility maintains a high level, at least in the early second stage. As the second stage prolongs, the fertility also shows sign of gradual decline. The changes leading to this stage in Europe we initiated in the Agricultural Revolution of the 18th century and were initially quite slow. In the 20th century, the falls in death rates in developing countries tended to be substantially faster. Countries in this stage include Yemen, Afghanistan the Palestinian territories, Bhutan and Laos and much of Sub-Saharan Africa (but do not include South Africa, Zimbabwe. Botswana, Swaziland, Lesotho, Namibia. Kenya and Ghana which have begun to move into stage 3).

A consequence of the decline in mortality in Stage two is a progressively speedy rise in population growth (a "population explosion"), because the gap between deaths and births grows wider. Note that this growth is not because of rise in fertility (or birth rate), however, to a decline in deaths. this transformation in population occurred in north-western Europe throughout the nineteenth century caused by commercial revolution. During the second half of the 20th century less-developed countries entered Stage two, creating the worldwide population explosion that has demographers concerned today. Another characteristic of Stage Two of the demographic transition is a change in the age structure of the population. In Stage One, the majority of deaths are concentrated in the first 5-10 years of life, therefore, more than anything else, the decline in death rates in stage two entails the increasing survival of children and a growing population. Hence, the age structure, of the population becomes increasingly youthful and more of these children enter the reproductive cycle of their lives while maintaining the high fertility rates of their parents. The bottom of the age pyramid widens first, accelerating population growth. The age structure of such a population is illustrated by using an example from the Third World today.

The decline within the death rate in Europe began within the late eighteenth century in north-western Europe and spread over to the next 100 years to the south and east. Facts from Sweden clearly show this stage (and 2 different stages following it).

The third stage the growth rate starts getting lower and lower that what it was in the early expanding stage. This stage experience growth of urban and industrial society increased industrialization introduces mechanization which reduces manual labour requirement. With growing urban facilitation, the society starts having increased desires for material possessions and less desires for bigger families. By the third stage birth rates fall rapidly, to perhaps 20 per 1000, while death rates continue to fall slightly (15 per 1000 people) to give a slowly increasing population. In this stage, the role of fertility and mortality are reversed, the mortality is low and stable and fertility is low but fluctuating. Not only that, the set of socio-economic conditions associated with the first stage and the third stage and final stage of demographic transition are completely different. In the first stage, the society is traditional and primary, whereas in the third stage, the population is highly urbanized. The technical development is abundant, the deliberate controls on family size are common, the literacy and education levels are high and the degree of labour specialization is high.

This stage shows subsequent changes within the age structure of the population embrace a reduction within the youth dependency and eventually population aging. The population structure becomes less triangular associated a lot of like an elongated balloon, throughout the amount between the decline in youth dependency and rise in old age dependency there is a demographic window of chance which will doubtless turn out economic process through a rise within the magnitude relation of operating age to dependent population; the demographic dividend. However, unless factors like those Listed on top of are allowed to work, a society's birth rates might not drop to a low level in due time, which implies that the society cannot proceed to Stage Four and is barred in what's referred to as, a demographic entice.

Countries that have experienced a fertility decline of over 40 per cent from their pre-transition levels include: Costa Rica, El Salvador, Panama, Jamaica, Mexico, Colombia, Ecuador Guyana Surinam, Philippines, Indonesia, Sri Lanka, Turkey, Azerbaijan, Turkmenistan, Uzbekistan, Egypt, Tunisia, Algeria, Morocco, Lebanon, South Africa, India, Saudi Arabia, and many Pacific islands. Countries that have experienced a fertility decline of 25-40 per cent include: Honduras, Guatemala, Nicaragua, Paraguay, Bolivia, Vietnam, Myanmar, Bangladesh, Tajikistan, United Arab Emirates, Zimbabwe, and Botswana. Countries that have experienced a fertility decline of 10-25 per cent include: Haiti, Papua New Guinea, Nepal, Pakistan, Syria, Iraq, Libya, Sudan, Kenya, Ghana and Senegal.

In the fourth stage, both the birth rate (16 per 1000) and death rate (12 per 1000) remain low, fluctuating slightly to give a steady population. Highly industrialised and urbanized population is the characteristics features of this stage. Better technical knowledge, high degree of specialization and better education prevailing in this stage changes it into a modern society.

This occurs where birth and death rates are both low. Therefore, the total population is high and stable. Some theorists consider there are only four stages and that the population of country will remain at this level. The DTM is only suggestion about the future population levels of a country. It is not a prediction. Countries that are at this stage (Total Fertility Rate of less than 2.5 in 1997) include: United States, Canada, Argentina, Australia, New Zealand, most of Europe, Bahamas, Puerto Rico, Trinidad and Tobago, Brazil, Sri Lanka, South Korea, Singapore, Iran, China, Turkey, North Korea, Thailand and Mauritius.

The original Demographic Transition model has just four stages, however, some theorists consider that a fifth stage is needed to represent countries that have sub-replacement fertility. Most European and many East Asian countries now have higher death rates than birth rates.

There may be a further stage of demographic development. In an article in the August 2009 issue of Nature, Myrskyla, Kohler and Biliary show that previously negative relationship between national wealth (as measured by the human development index (HDI) and birth rates has become J-shaped. Development promotes fertility decline at low and medium HDI levels, but advanced HDI promotes a rebound in fertility. In many countries with very high levels of development (around 0.95) fertility rates are now approaching two, children per woman although there are exceptions, notably Canada and Japan.

12.2.3 Strength of Demographic Transition Model

The Model has several strengths which are discussed below:

1. It shows dynamic changes through different time periods.
2. It describes some countries such as UK, Germany, Italy and India well.
3. It has worked well for European and North American industrialised countries.
4. It has worked for some East Asian countries such as South Korea but this country has gone through the stages much quicker with the advent of technology for industrialization and overnight medicine.
5. It also highlights certain events and be used for explanations.

12.2.4 Limitation of Demographic Transition Model

The theory of demographic transition is widely accepted as a useful in describing demographic history. Its contribution is, however, considered to be of limited value. It is to be noted that this theory is based on the actual experience of the changes in the vital rates in Western countries during the various stages of their industrial and economic development. The critics of this theory, however, point out that the experience of the various European countries were not uniform, in the sense that the sequences of the stages as described in the statement of the theory were not the same. Recent studies reveal that, in Spain and in some countries of Eastern and Southern Europe, fertility decline occurred even when mortality was very high. In some countries like the United States, the growth rate in the post-transition stage was probably higher than in stage II and stage III of the demographic transition. Notestein's claim that fertility declined initially in urban areas is found to be untrue for some countries. For instance, countries with predominantly rural population, such as France, Sweden, Finland, Bulgaria, did experience decline in birth rates to the same extent as did some highly urbanized countries, such as England and Wales. Such exceptions suggest that the theory of demographic transition is only a broad generalization, which does not encompass the experience of even all the western countries. This theory is also cannot explain the phenomena of "the baby boom" in Western countries after the economic recovery and the Second World War.

Loschky and Wilcox (1974) assert that neither the theory is predictive nor its stages are sequential and inevitable. The role of man's technical innovations cannot be underrated, particularly in the field of medicine which by modifying the trends in mortality can bring in unexpected changes in the rate of natural increase.

1. The model was created in the 1920s and only studied population patterns in Western Europe and North America. Therefore, patterns experienced today in many different countries may be different.
2. Another criticism of this theory arises out of the fact that it does not provide a theoretical explanation of an important forces, viz. fertility, which brought about the demographic transition.
3. The exact nature of stage four is a much debated. Technological developments and scientific research is likely to have an impact on population levels in the twenty first century.
4. Social changes, such as increased migration play no part in Demographic Transition Model yet although other evidence suggests that migration can have a profound impact on a country's birth rate.
5. The model does not suggest any time scale and some countries will spend very little time in some stages compared to others.
6. Birth rates in several MEDCs have fallen below death rates. This has caused the population to decline which suggests that the model should have a fifth stage.
7. The Demographic Transition Model is Eurocentric as the model assumes that all countries pass through the same four stages. It now seems unlikely, however, that Africa and many other LEDCs will ever be industrialised. There are also variables and exceptions such as war that may lead to different results.
8. The model assumes the fall in death rate in stage 2 was due to industrialization. In

the UK, however, the death rate rose due to the poor conditions during the industrial revolution. The delayed fall in death rate in many LEDCs is due to the inability for people to afford healthcare. In many countries, the fall in birth rate has been slower in stage 3 due to opposition by religious organisations. Alternatively, in China, the birth rate has fallen sharply due to government intervention.

9. The timescale of the model, especially in several South-East Asian countries such as Hong Kong and Malaysia, is being squashed as they develop at a much faster rate than earlier industrialized countries. The UK stayed in stage 2 for over 100 years as social, economic and technological changes were introduced slowly and death rate fell slowly. In many LEDCs, death rate has fallen more rapidly because changes (i.e. the introduction of Western medicine) have taken place much more quickly. The birth rate has stayed high and so the population has increased rapidly.
10. The model does not include the impacts of migration. Countries that grew as a consequence of emigration from Europe (e.g., USA, Canada and Australia) did not pass through the earlier stages of the model.
11. Some countries arte developed but have high birth rates: this is due to culture, religion and not evidence of a poor, less developed country.
12. The model does not suggest any time scale and some countries will spend very little time in some stages compared to others.

It has, moreover, been asserted that the theory of demographic transition cannot really be called a "theory", for it does not fulfil an important criterion of any theory, that is, to extract fundamental processes from a phenomenon and identify crucial variables. This theory does not provide fundamental explanation of fertility decline, nor does it identify the crucial variables involved in the process of the fertility decline. Therefore, it does not have any predictive value.

12.2.5 Demographic Transition Model and Age Sex Composition

The decline in death rate and birth rate that happens throughout the demographic transition results in a radical transformation of the age structure. once the death rates decline throughout the second stage of the transition, the results primarily a rise within the child population. The rationale is that once the death rate is high (stage one), the infant mortality rate is extremely high, typically higher than two hundred deaths per one thousand child born. once the death rate falls or improves, this, in general, ends up in a considerably lower infant mortality rate and, hence, accumulated child survival. Over time, as cohorts accumulated by higher survival rates become older, there'll even be a rise within the range of older kids, teenagers, and young adults. this suggests that there's a rise within the fertile population that with constant fertility rates, can cause a rise within the range of kids born. this can more increase the expansion of the kid population. The second stage of the demographic transition, therefore, implies an increase in kid dependency.

12.2.6 Relevance of Demographic Transition Model in Contemporary World

Although the demographic transition model was conceived in simple terms, yet there were not clear threshold levels of development, which could be identified for the initiation of a regular fertility decline. As observed earlier, the concept was first evolved keeping in mid the demographic evolution being experienced by the Western countries. It is from there that it diffused spatially. In the present-day world, as would be true of any point in time, different countries of the world are at different stages of the demographic transition. According to Trewartha, this is largely due to the dual nature of man. According to him, biological man is the same everywhere and is engaged in the process of reproduction but, culturally man differs from one part of the world to another. It is the cultural diversity of man that gives rise to varying fertility patterns in different areas resulting in different stages in demographic transition.

There is, however, little evidence to suggest that all the countries in the transition had similar trends from high fertility and mortality to low fertility and mortality. In fact, both the sequential patterns of fertility and mortality and their timings have varied greatly from country to country. Similarly, though the pattern of demographic transition can clearly be recognised, yet the way it is derived from diverse socio-economic changes, it varies so much from country to country that it is difficult to say that the transition diffused from one country to another. It seems that the diffusion took place from one world to another. As it diffused from one type of world to another it also underwent certain modifications. The sequential patterns as well as the temporal span were never the same in Western Europe, East Europe and Third World. There has been a good deal of variety between these worlds and even within the countries belonging to the same world. It may not be out of place to elaborate upon the experience of these three worlds.

By and large the First World consisting of North-western Europe, North America, Australia, New Zealand, South Africa experienced the typical sequential pattern of fertility and mortality as visualised in the demographic transition model with a little bit of variety in demographic responses of individual countries. The transition was completed during the late 19th or early 20th century when the rest of the world still remained in the first stage. In the case of the First World it has often been parts stated that the fertility levels were never as high as being experienced by the other parts of the world. The demographic transformation here was coupled with the socio-economic transformation and technological advancement.

In the Second World consisting largely of Eastern Europe, the transition period began in the early decades of 20th century with Austria and Czechoslovakia first showing the signs of departing from the first stage. Interestingly, the Second World countries never experienced the explosive stage of population growth as was envisaged by the original transformation model. By 1940, most of the countries Second World comparing Austria, Ireland, Switzerland, and Finland countries of the Southern and South-eastern Europe crossed over to the third stage of transition. All these countries experienced only moderate population growth as the time spam between the fertility and mortality decline was too short. Japan also followed this pattern and entered the second stage of moderate growth in 1930s. The east while USSR joined this group in 1940s. Both of these countries crossed over to the third stage by 1950s. It reveals that both the sequential pattern and the time span of demographic transition experienced by the Second World countries very much different from the one experienced by the First World. In case of Second World countries, thus, neither there occurred a population explosion nor that opposed to the deliberate measure of controlling the family size. It expedited the process of fertility decline. Moreover, the accessibility to the modern medicines further helped in sharping a decline in mortality.

The experience of the Third World consisting of the remaining countries of the world was very much different from the First and Second Worlds. Relatively small sized countries of the Third World were first to experience the signs of explosive second stage. Gradually, the explosive second stage spread to the other smaller countries of Latin America, Africa, and Asia. The big countries like China, India, Indonesia, Pakistan, and Bangladesh entered the second stage of the transition only in 1950s. Mortality declined in large sized countries took little longer period to reach appreciably low levels. The necessary fertility regulations came quite late in case of big countries. Consequently, the great mortality declines were not accompanied by the moderation of fertility.

These points below showing the examples of developing and developed country's demographic situation and changes include:

1. A later (20th century) transition in LDCs (Least Developed Countries).
2. A faster decline in death rates (50 years *vs.* 150 years). Death control has been imported from MDCs and applied rapidly. In most LDCs childhood mortality remains high, but 1/3 to 1/2 what it was 50 years ago. However, the most rapid improvements have occurred in places in which female literacy has increased the most. Therefore, it is not simply the application of modern drugs that is responsible but, rather, behavioural changes that have improved survival (e.g. changes related to hygiene). These types of behavioural change are readily adopted because, in so far as they improve survival, they act to support traditional values that favour life over death in almost all societies.
3. A relatively longer lag between the decline in death rates and the decline in birth rates (death rates are lower before decline in birth rate starts). Fertility change requires a more conscious effort than mortality change and requires social and behavioural changes that conflict more with traditional values. This has been slower coming in LDCs because economic change has been delayed in many cases. The same economic pressures that existed in urban areas 100 years ago in MDCs (More Developed Countries) have been slower to develop in LDCs because many, particularly in Africa, remain very rural. Hence, attitudes and values have been slower to change.
4. Higher maximum rates of growth in LDCs: over 3.5 per cent growth per year at the height of stage 2 in Mauritius and Mexico compared to 1.3 per cent in the same stage in Sweden. Also, therefore, age structures are far younger in LDCs. These data yield doubling times of 20 years *versus* 55 years.

12.2.7 Demographic Transition Model in India

Census of India (i.e. Registrar General of India) suggests that increment is on the decline since 1991. The average number of children a woman expected was 3.8 in 1990, and this has fallen to 2.7 children per woman today (Bloom, 2011). The fertility and increment rates are declining rapidly day by day, India's population is projected to extend from 1.2 billion these days to an estimated 1.6 billion by 2050 due to the population momentum and this figure relies on UN's medium-fertility scenario (Planning Commission, 2008). Population momentum refers to a state of affairs wherever the massive cohort of women of reproductive age will fuel increment over subsequent generation, though every woman has fewer children than previous generations did. In addition, the drop by crude death (CDR) and birth rates (CBR) for the past four decades indicates that India is progressing towards a post-transitional section.

From Fig. 12.2 it is clear that from 1951 to 1991, the drop in CBR was less steep than the drop in the CDR. However, throughout nineties the decline in CBR has been less than the decline in CDR, that has resulted in a very reduced annual increment rate of 1.4 per cent these days (Planning Commission, 2008).

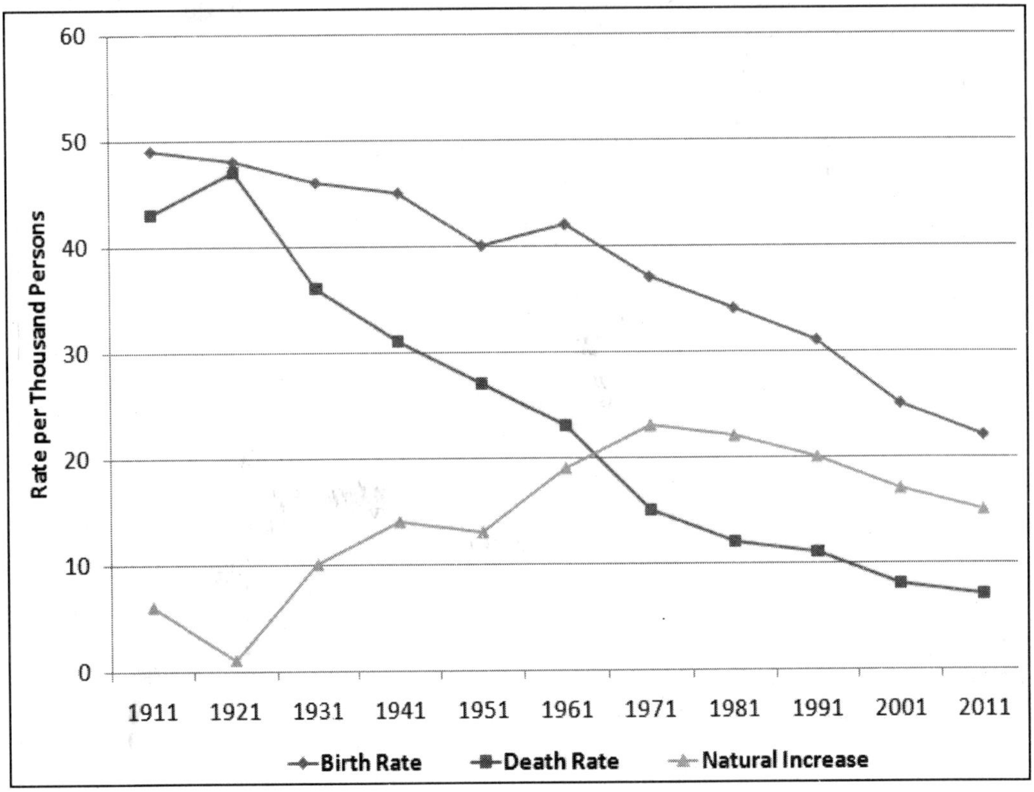

Fig. 12.2: India: Demographic Transition and Trend of Population

India's demographic transition is visible through population pyramid that provides knowledge on a nation's age structure. The pyramid helps portray the share of population in every age bracket, and in 1995, India had an awfully young population with many children between the ages of 0-15, whereas there have been only a few older people (Fig. 12.3). This gave India a typical pyramidic form shape wherever the massive base of young child indicated associate degree overall young population (Bloom, 2011). In 2015, India is blessed with a large range of population with the age bracket of 15-45 years (Fig. 12.3). Moving forward in time to years 2030 and 2050, United Nations' projections regarding India show that with the declining CBR and increment, the bottom of the population pyramid can shrink because the range of working-age people will increase relative to the youngsters and also the older. As of 2016 there are still a sizeable range of kids within the age-group of 0-15 years, that could be a result of the population momentum.

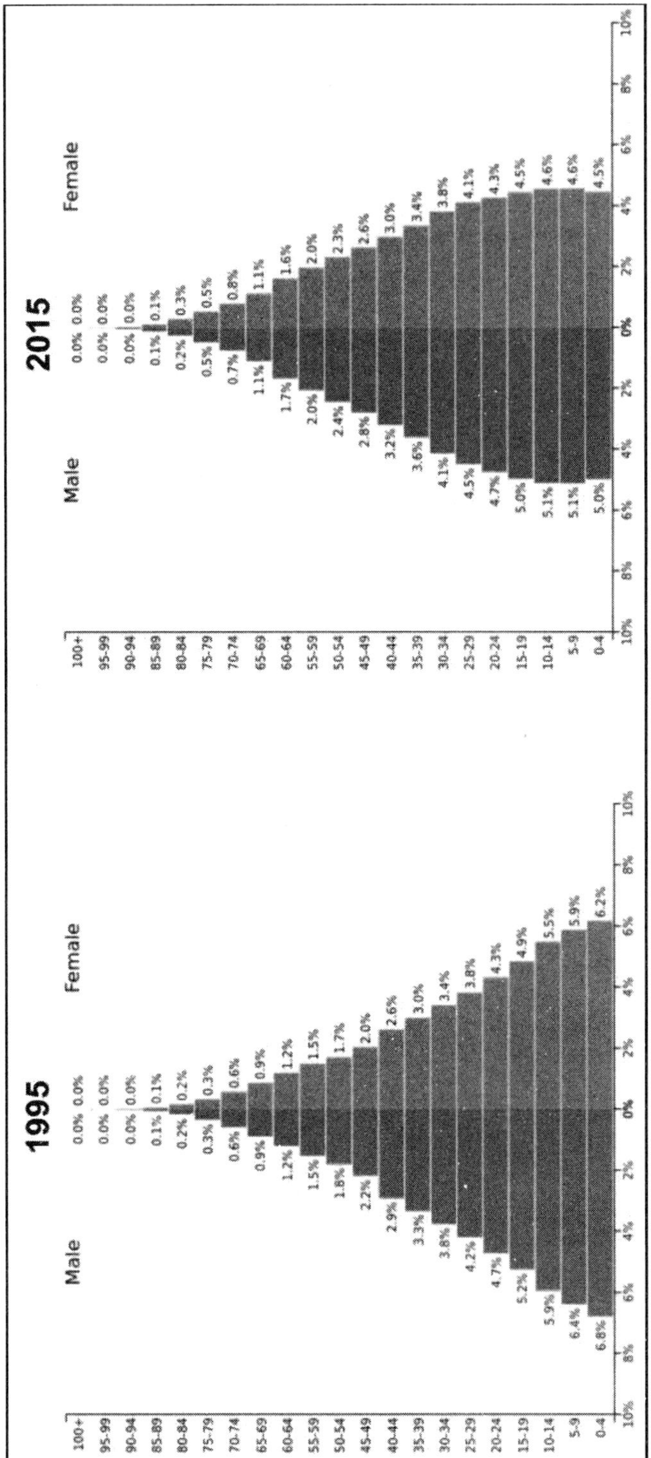

Fig. 12.3: Age-Sex Pyramid (Population Pyramid) of India, (1995 and 2015)

The concept of demographic dividend has been applicable to India, where the three phases of the demographic transition have created three unique age structures. In the first phase, the fertility is very high and mortality begins to drop, which we know was the case in India during the 1960s and 70s (with growth rate at 2.3 per cent). In the second phase, the fertility starts to decline at a fast pace leading to a reduction in the child population and one can see this trend occurring in India for the last four decades. However, due to the higher fertility of the past, India's population would continue to grow and will reach 1.6 billion by 2050 (population momentum). This period will include a large working age population and a lower dependency load. During the third phase, the dependency ratio will begin to rise as a result of higher old age population (60 and above), which also consumes resources in the form of health care, pension etc. The dividend is a term used to understand better the second phase of the age structure where the working age population will be higher than the growth of infant and child population growth, resulting in a reduced dependency ratio. By the year 2020, the large cohorts of earlier years will reach prime years of working and saving.

The age structure transition of dividend may result in economic process in a very few ways: (i) foremost, India will increase savings throughout this age structure transition. Once majority of the population are going to be operating, savings rate can increase. Citizenry save the foremost throughout their operating years and this accumulation of assets is important for achieving the demographic 'gift' (Bloom, 2011). The medium variant of India's increment implies that by 2030, India may reach East Asia's operating age magnitude relation and can be ready to match its per capita financial gain growth in line with the globe Bank (2010), India's annual rate of growth in real financial gain per capita averaged around four per cent throughout the last 3 decades and is quickly rising to East Asia's levels. this can be a major increase as a result of once East Asia was undergoing such ascent in average incomes, its rate was around half-dozen. Four per cent and current trends show that India's per capita financial gain growth is additionally change of integrity year once year (Bloom, 2011). (ii) Second, since there will be a decline in fertility, women can enter the labour force at increasing rates, which is able to facilitate increase the economic activity in India. A serious impediment to women's labour force participation has been high fertility and also the time spent on raising and caring for youngsters. Once there is a decline in fertility, women are a lot of inclined to enter the paid manpower leading to higher economic process throughout this era. (iii) Third, once there are fewer children to care for, people invest a lot of on their own health and on their few child, resulting in higher productivity and economic edges for the house. Health will drive economic process as a result of healthier manpower could be a lot of productive workforce and have higher savings rate thanks to anticipation of longer lives post-retirement. On the opposite hand, government will be in a very position to pay and invest in additional productive activities as a result of public outlay resources may be allotted off from children's education, infant health etc.

The theory of demographic transition is that the most acceptable theory related with population growth. It neither lays stress on food provide just like the Malthusian theory, nor will it develop a disheartened outlook towards population growth. It is additionally superior to the optimum theory that lays associate degree exclusive stress on the rise in per capita financial gain for the expansion of population and neglects the opposite factors which influence it. The demographic transition theory is superior to all or any other theories of population because it is supported by the particular population growth trends of the developed countries of Europe. Most of the European countries of the world have passed through the primary 2 stages of this theory and are currently within the end. Not solely this, theory is equally applicable to the developing countries of the world. Backward countries in a number of the African states are still within the initial stage whereas all the opposite developing countries of the world are in the transmutation stage 2. It is on the premise of this theory that economists have developed economic-demographic models so underdeveloped countries ought to enter the ultimate stage and attain the stage of self-sustained growth. Thus, this theory has universal relevancy.

12.3 Malthusian Theory of Population Control

Thomas Robert Malthus was the first person who propounded a systematic population theory in the end of 18th century based on natural law. Since then a number of scholars have attempted to search for some rules governing the growth of population. A number of theories were propounded during the nineteenth and twentieth century based either on natural law or social facts. The British economist and demographer Robert Thomas Malthus (1766-1834), was the first scholar to propound a population theory based on scientific and natural law. Malthus completed his higher education from Cambridge University and he was appointed as the economics teacher in a college of East India Company where he had been working till death (1834). Malthus travelled various West European countries and collected many important data in support of his population theory. Thus, Malthusian theory was based on his experience and observations. His motive was definitely humanitarian, as he was always thinking and trying about the welfare of humanity.

12.3.1. An Essay on the Principal of Population

Malthus (1798) published his first essay on population. The title of his essay read as "An Essay on the Principal of Population as It Affects the Future Improvement of Society, with Remarks on the Speculations of Mr. Godwin, M. Condorcet and other writers." As the title suggests, it was the first place a reaction to the utopian ideas concerning a perfect society. Malthus echoed a view similar to that of Robert Wallace, who, in this book Various Prospects of Mankind, Nature and Providence, published in 1761, had suggested that "the perfection of society carried with it the seeds of its own destruction" (Encyclopaedia Britannica, 1993). Malthus' first essay was very poorly drafted without any support of empirical evidences. He soon revised his arguments and published the second edition in 1803. Subsequently, another four editions of his essay were published posthumously in 1872. The revised editions were more meticulously drafted and were based on extensive study of works on related topics. However, the essence of his arguments on two basic propositions, first that food is necessary for human existence, and, second is that the passion between sexes is necessary and would continue in the present state.

12.3.2 Assumption of the Theories

While formulating his population theory, Malthus assumed following postulates:

- Food is necessary to the existence of human being and the population is necessarily limited by the means of subsistence.
- The person between the two opposite sexes is necessary and will remain nearly in this present stage.
- Law of diminishing return is applicable on agriculture.

12.3.3 Explanation of Theory

Malthus stated that the power of population to reproduce is indefinitely greater than the power in the earth to produce subsistence for population. "His interpretation was that population tends to increase always faster than the means of subsistence, thus absorbing all economic gains, unless uncontrolled by what he termed 'preventive' and 'positive' checks. He maintained that population, if unchecked, tended to increase at a geometric rate (i.e. 1, 2, 4, 8, 16……) while subsistence increased at an arithmetic rate (1, 2, 3, 4, 5………). Malthus concluded that the population doubles after every 25 years. According to him, in two centuries the proportion of population would be to the means of subsistence as 256 to 9, in three centuries as 4096 to 13, and in two thousand years the difference between the power of population to increase and the power of earth to produce subsistence for people. Malthus believed that the table of nature is laid for limited number of guests and those who come uninvited must starve.

Malthus thought and explained that the eagerness between the sexes led individuals to marry at a comparatively early age and would lead to such an outsized numbers of births that the population will increase sharply and doubles itself in few years if not checked by misery and vice. The widening gap between population and subsistence will certainly increase human tendency to press upon the means of subsistence. Consequently, the society gets divided into two categories of people: one rich and other poor who provides rise to capitalistic start.

Rich people are the owners of the means of production earn profit and accumulate capital. Rich people with the increased income enhance their consumption but do not like to increase their population as they feared of decline in their standards of living. On the other hand, the poor constituting the labour class are engaged to increase their population as their source of income depends only on man power. In such a way, the rich will continue to grow richer and the poor to grow poorer.

In the opinion of Malthus, the increasing gap between the population and resources or subsistence shall ultimately lead to the point where misery and poverty shall become inevitable. According to him when the growth of population reached that point, it could be kept in check only by war, vice and misery. "Yet the basis for the arithmetic growth of agriculture was never made clear. Moreover, in the 1817 edition of his book, Malthus paid considerably more attention to the curtailment of population increases through birth control that to the gloomy devices of war, vice and increasing human misery" (Haggett, 1983).

According to Malthus, fast growing population can be checked naturally or artificially. Excessive population can be checked naturally or artificially. Excessive population is controlled by two types of checks: the positive checks and the preventive checks. These checks in human population to prevent excessive growth relate to practices affecting death rate and birth rate respectively. His positive checks included wars, floods, earthquakes, diseases, hunger, poverty and particularly lack of food. His preventive checks included mainly moral restraint like postponement of marriage, self-control and in which he included birth control and abortion. Malthus observed the tension between population and resources as a major cause of misery of much of the human population. Malthus being a priest of the church and a religious teacher, was not, however, in favour of artificial contraceptive methods to prevent faster growing population, because their use did not generate the same drive to work hard as would a postponement of marriage. "he stressed the negative correlation between station in life and number of children and, in order to induce in the lower classes the self-control and social responsibility which he saw in the middle classes, Malthus asserted that the poor should be better paid and educated" (Rao, 1994).

A simple Malthusian check on population growth can be explained by imaging a fixed level called saturation level above which numbers cannot expand. At this level the population exactly equals the carrying capacity of the local environment. Peter Haggett (1983) explained that when the population growth approaches this ceiling, there are three conceivable situations:

1. The rate of increase may continue unchanged until the ceiling is reached, and then abruptly drop to zero.
2. The rate of increase may decline as it approaches the ceiling, eventually falling to zero.
3. The population may overshoot the ceiling periodically, only to be reduced by flood shortage and oscillate above and below the carrying capacity.

The chart below illustrates the process of increasing population with geometric progression and food supply with arithmetic progression starting from a balanced stage between population and food supply and ending at a new balanced stage between population and food supply. Thus, it explains the cycle of population growth.

Another topic of Malthus was poor law. At the time of Malthus, in England, poor law was in practice, under which the responsibility of the maintenance of the poor and disabled rested with the local community called *parish*. The charity to the poor and disabled used to be given out the fund generated in the form of taxes collected from the general public. According to Malthus, the law did more harms than good to the society. He was convinced that the law led to early marriage and high birth rates among the poor resulting in further worsening of food-population balance. He, therefore, strongly opposed the law and argued for its complete abolition. In place of charity to the poor, he recommended free use of yet uncultivated small tracts of land. He was thus, instrumental in the passage of the reform bills in 1834, which finally abolished the law (Rao, 1994).

12.3.4 Criticism of Theory

Malthus's view has been challenged in a great variety of wages. Some drawbacks of Malthusian theory are given below:

1. Malthus's basic premise on passion between the sexes has been criticised on the plea that the desire to have children cannot be mixed up with passion and desire for sex because the desire for sex is a biological instinct, whereas the desire to have children is a social instinct.

2. The application of geometrical growth rate for population and arithmetic growth for means of subsidence is also challenged. Actually, population has rarely grown in geometrical progression and means of subsidence have rarely multiplied in arithmetic progression.
3. The time span of 25 years assumed by Malthus as the doubling period for population is far away from reality because this varies very much from country to country depending upon the stage of its economic and demographic advancement.
4. Malthus was swayed by the supremacy of positive checks over preventive checks mainly because he believed about unnatural checks like delayed marriage, moral restrains, self-control on sex after marriage etc. He could not suggest of the use of contraceptives as on preventive checks which later become most popular and successful in controlling the population.
5. He could not realize even the biological limitation that a population is not able to grow beyond a certain limit.
6. Malthus is also criticized for ignoring the role of changing technology and consequent improvement in the level of subsidence and transformation in social and economic setup of society. He ignored the potential of industrial and technological revolution in increasing the means of subsidence. The economic and demographic history of modern Europe has disproved Malthusian thesis.
7. The Malthusian theory is based on the false hypothesis that the rate of increase of population remains invariable during many continued series of generations. This hypothesis has been denied by irregularities in the rate of population increase experienced by United States, France, Japan and many other countries of the world particularly by East European countries of the world particularly by East European countries.

Despite so many criticisms, the Malthusian thesis gained widespread currency during his lifetime. Malthusian principal of population has been successful in highlighting the urgency of maintaining a balanced relationship between population and means of subsidence. The success of Malthus's ideas owes much to the social and political condition prevailing in Europe at that time. The French Revolution has disillusioned intellectuals, and through the idea of the perfectibility of society was not given completely, people has begun looking for some realistic solutions to the prevailing situation of uncertainty. The ruling classes saw in Malthus their ideologue and their prophet, who had scientifically proved by the eternal law of nature that poverty was inevitable and not the product of any unjust social and political institution. His ideas have profound effects on the public policies; on the classical and neo-classical economists; and on demographers and evolutionary biologist.

12.4 Summary

The preceding discussion on the view of population and its change, growth and distribution can be summarised as follows. Malthus considered that man's nature shall inevitably lead to such a high fertility that there would be severe conflict between his fertility and the ability to produce subsistence. This conflict shall lead to perpetual poverty and suffering, which may only be reduced through preventive checks but could not be escaped. On the other hand, the theory of demographic transition is the most acceptable theory of population growth. It neither lays emphasis on food supply like the Malthusian theory, nor does it develop a pessimistic outlook towards population growth. It is also superior to the optimum theory which lays an exclusive emphasis on the increase in per capita income for the growth of population and neglects the other factors which influence it. The demographic transition theory is superior to all the theories of population because it is based on the actual population growth trend of the developed countries. Not only this, this theory is equally applicable to the world. Thus these both theories has universal applicability and usefulness in population growth.

Review Questions

1. Explain Demographic Transition Theory in detail with suitable illustrations.
2. Describe strength and limitations of Demographic Transition Theory.
3. Describe application of Demographic Transition Theory in world comparing with Indian context.
4. Critically evaluate the Malthusian Theory of population control.

Analytical Questions

1. Discuss the limitation of Demographic Transition Theory in explaining the population growth of Canada.
2. How far Malthusian theory is applicable in contemporary period. Explain taking two contrasting examples.

PART 4

Settlements and Urbanization

Chapter 13
Human Settlement

13.1 Introduction

The study of human settlements is most fundamental to human geography (branch of geography) because the shape of settlement in any particular region reflects the relationship of the human with their environment. Settlements are the function of interaction of man with his environment. A man constructs houses and develops settlements to protect themselves against the vagaries of weather and to live and enjoy a social life in peaceful manner. In fact, the settlement is one of the most essential steps of man towards adaptation to his physical environment. Few people live in isolation while most people of the world reside in some form of settlement where permanent collection of houses, buildings and inhabitants is found. Living in isolation or at greater distance from one another is though found around the world but living in groups and close to each in compact manner is a reality which is observed by most of us. Settlements occupy a very small percentage of the surface of the earth but exert a far greater influence on the culture of the world. Settlements are both the storage centres of the world's cultural heritage and the point of origin for the promulgation of innovative economic, social and political patterns. It is because of the cultural functions that the study of settlement is essential to human geography. In a nutshell, settlements are a prerequisite for social and economic development, in that no social progress for sustainable economic growth can transpire without efficient settlements systems and settlement networks.

A human settlement is defined as a place inhabited more or less enduringly. The houses may be designed or redesigned, buildings may be remodelled, functions may vary, but settlement continues to be present in both time and space since existence of human on this earth. However, the kind of settlement has changed over time from temporary to permanent. The Oxford Dictionary has several definitions for the term settlement and the one that comes closest to that of geographer is "is an assemblage of persons settled in a locality".

Human Settlement means the bunch of dwellings of any type or size where human beings live. For this aim, people may raise houses and other structures and command some area or territory as their support-base to economic activities. Thus, the process of development of settlement inherently involves assemblage of people and apportioning of territory as their resource base. Settlements vary in size and type and range from a hamlet to metropolitan cities. With size, the economic organisation and social structure of settlements changes and so do the ecology and technology of the settlements. Settlements are fundamental to development where people can actually live, learn and work in milieu of safety and comfort which leads to efficiency and are essential and elementary need. Settlements are also a parameter in a sense that they are the most noticeable expression of civilization's capability and potential to execute some of the basic needs of its members as they are the score of accomplishments as well as expose destitution, neglect and inequality.

The study of settlement has been one of the most notable themes of human geography. The term "settlement geography" is derived from the German "siedlunge geographic" (Singh, 1978) which concerns the study of optical indentations conceived by man upon cultural landscape in the process of occupation. In the inception, various settlement features carried simpler forms and relationship with the environment, with the growth of civilization and technical knowledge, the proportion of variability in their size, form and complexity of their relationship became overwhelming greater. As far as the size and spacing of Settlements are concerned, they could be small and meagrely spaced while they may also be large and closely spaced. The sparsely or meagrely located small settlements are called hamlets, villages or suburbs practice agriculture or other primary activities are the main function of economic structure. On the other hand, there are several but larger settlements which are termed as urban settlements perform various functions based on secondary and tertiary economic activities. This economic structure based functions in diverse range of settlement requires perfection in the study of evolution of human settlements and the understanding of the concerned surrounding environment as a whole. The present chapter deals with origin and development of settlement and classification of settlements.

13.2 Origin and Development of Settlements

The most fundamental purposes of existence of contemporary settlements is principally to subserve economic functions, but earliest settlements probably were established for other reasons necessary for survival. The definite reasons for the formation of the first and the very initial settlements are shrouded in enigma, as they occurred before recorded memoir. There are only rational presumptions on where and why permanent settlements embark. Human beings were nomads meaning wanderer, moving in search of food and water from place to place. They obtained food by gathering wild berries and roots and killing wild animals for their sustenance. Why the nomadic groups need permanent settlements is essential to probe here to seek explanations about the origin of settlement? No one comprehends the precise sequence of events through which settlements were established, but analysts offer two types of explanations, i.e. cultural explanation and economic explanation. A brief account of these factors has been given below in this section.

The cultural explanation of settlements in prehistoric settlements is that they may have been instituted for religious, educational, political, or military reasons. The earliest permanent settlements may have served as places to bury the dead bodies. After all, what could be sturdier than a burial pit? Nomadic groups may have had rituals and rites to honour the dead, perhaps memorial ceremonies on the anniversary of death. The basic and indispensable duty lead to having established a stable resting place for the dead, the group then might introduce priests at the site to perform the last appropriate observances. By the time recorded history commenced, one of the most permanent peculiarities of various settlements was the synagogue (house of worship). In fact, the tallest structures in the community were often the religious buildings until the invention of high-rises in the late nineteenth century. The settlements may also have served as a site to home women and children of their family, permitting the men to travel farther and faster in their search for food and other necessities. Women constituted household objects, such as pots, tools, and clothing as essential commodities. Even provisions to educate children were felt and made in the settlements. The political leaders of a group or a community choose to live permanently in the settlement, which may have been chosen for its strategic location to protect the land claims of the group. There was a creation of elaborate structures in the settlement to house the leaders. The settlement probably was also grown as a reliable base from which the society could maintain nearby food sources against competitors. As far as protection of people in settlement is concerned, soldiers were stationed in the settlements. It is believed that strong walls may have been erected surrounding the settlement to withstand attack. In this process the settlement thus became citadels, centres of military power. The wall proved an extremely effective defence for protection for thousands of years until the introduction of gunpowder and cannonballs that could destroy them.

Now the most basic requirement of spiritual, militaristic and political leaders and their dependents is food, which was furnished by the group through hunting and gathering. It is felt that there is growing necessity to store surplus food, and with this the settlements procured an economic role. The settlements develop into a warehouse to store an excess supply of food permanently. Settlement then grew as centre of agrarian economy because the people apprehended that they can grow the wild vegetable they accumulated and can nurture them from near. There is a progression of behavioural and cultural characteristics and changes, including the use of wild and domestic crops and of domesticated animals. People were capable of producing most of the food through planned agricultural practices and no longer had to endure by hunting and gathering. In addition to food, people needed tools, clothing, shelter, and other objects and settlements became centre of manufacturing. Men accumulated the materials needed to make different kinds of articles, including stones for devices and weapons, grass for containers and matting, animal hair for clothing and wood for shelter and heat. Everyone in group did not have access to the resources equally because the vegetation and animal species differed across the landscape due to variations of natural environment. This diversified patterns of flora and fauna has led the settlements to perform the function and become centre of trading.

In the above discussion, it is well evident that when the human settlement grew thousands of years ago, it was primarily a kind of rural settlement. The oldest remains that have been discovered of constructed abodes are remains of the sites of huts that were created of mud and branches around 17,000 BC at the Ohalo site (now underwater) near the edge of the Sea of Galilee. Around 10,000 BC in the Levant, it is revealed from literature that the Natufians also framed houses. Remains of settlements such as hamlets and villages become much more common after the domestication of animals and invention of agriculture. The evolution of site, growth and advancement of human settlements are closely determined by the possible physical elements of nature such as soil, water, forest and mineral resources. Depending on the nature, quantity and quality of resources, the settlements may be temporary, seasonal or permanent, and from the rural settlements, they may acquire the state of urban settlements to the modern day planned settlements.

13.2.1 Unstable Settlements

The population of nomads is about 3.5 per cent of the total population which lives in the temporary or unstable settlement (Husain, 2011). In fact, the permanent rural and urban settlements are the consequences of long progression over space and time. The hunting people, pastoralists, transhumant and the shifting cultivators have mostly movable dwellings or temporary settlements. This movable dwelling is in a way a kind of seasonal migration from one place to another. The basic reason behind movements of early people depends upon many factors such as harsh climatic conditions, availability of resources over a particular area, advantageous of locations like water availability etc. The nomads almost always pitch their tents within a small perimeter and make very closely knit kind of settlement known as encampments. An Encampment means a place with temporary accommodations consisting of huts or tents, typically for troops or nomads.

The word transhumance originates from French and derives from the Latin words trans 'across' and humus 'ground' meaning thereby moving across the ground. Transhumance developed on every inhabited continent. Some examples of temporary and unstable settlements are Khaimas of Badawins of Saudi Arabia, the camps of Kirghiz of Central Asia, the Kraals of African nomads, the transient structures of Jhumias (shifting cultivators) of North-East India and the *kothas* (houses) and *band* is (cattlesheds) of the Gujjars and Bakarwals of Jammu and Kashmir. Furthermore, the Mors of Vietnam and the Fans of West Africa (primitive cultivators) build close-set villages which they move, sometimes from season to season. This is very well apparent through literature that there were numerous instances of unstable settlements in past but it is not hard to believe that these kind of practices are still prevalent in some form in few pockets of harsh climates around the world.

Transhumance is a type of controlled nomadism or pastoralism, a seasonal movement of people with there are substantial cultural and technological variations and the underlying practices for taking advantage of remote seasonal pastures are similar. Everyone including the hunters, nomads and itinerant cultivators have extremely strong social cohesion. The cohesion sometimes gives a way temporarily to the form and site of the settlement and are modified accordingly. This persistent return to the same winter quarter secures the cohesion among the tribes and during summer season the tribes were relaxed of all the moral and religious bonds of the community. As is the case of Gujjars and Bakarwals of Jammu and Kashmir who practise transhumance also have a dual plan of settlement and dwelling. In the winter season, they settle in the valleys of Siwaliks where winters are moderate and pastures are available for their flocks and reside in close set villages. In the summer season, they along with their goats climb in the dhoks or margs (alpine pastures) of the Middle Himalayas located about 200 km away from their winter dwellings. During their this upward and downward journey, they pause at least at 10 to 12 conventional camping grounds to utilize the intervening pastures. In these summer pastures, they have to arrange temporary structures and shades to live. To avoid mutual inconvenience between the various *kajilas* (groups), the Bakarwals split into small sub-groups which camp independently. It is seen in above discussion that transhumance is prevalent and practiced world over. There is another category of people who also thrives on temporary settlements is discussed below.

The shifting cultivators are those who constantly have to clear new terrains, have to do strenuous work to remove the forests and to develop fields for cultivation. When the soil near the village is exhausted or looses its fertility, they move or abandon for a new sites for cultivation and many times they have to shift their settlements also. This primarily happens in shifting cultivation, an agricultural system in which parts of the land are cultivated temporarily, then abandoned and allowed to return to their natural vegetation while the cultivator moves on to another plot. The period of cultivation is usually discharged when the soil shows signs of exhaustion or, more commonly, when the field is invaded by weeds. The length of time that a field is cultivated is normally shorter than the period over which the land is allowed to regenerate by lying fallow. In some areas, cultivators use a practice of slash-and-burn as one element of their farming cycle. Slash-and-burn agriculture, or fire-fallow cultivation, is a farming process that comprises the cutting and burning of plants in a forest or woodland to create a field. Slash-and-burn farming is a form of shifting agriculture where the natural vegetation is cut down and burned as a process of clearing the land for cultivation, and then, when the field converts infertile, the farmer moves to a new fresh plot and does the same again.

The foregoing discussion clearly reflects that the unstable settlements are restricted in the difficult terrains of deserts and semi-desert areas, tundra, equatorial forests and mountainous areas. It is also circumscribed to the regions which experience harsh and severe climatic conditions. The total number of nomads and those who shift their dwellings and settlements frequently or seasonally is not very meagre but being less than 2 per cent of the total population of the world.

13.2.2 Stable Rural Settlements

The nomadic life of early humans in search of food played a key role in the nature of settlements. They used to live temporarily at a place and created unstable structures and settlements for themselves. At the times when man started domestication of animals and cultivation of crops, he felt the need to stay close and nurture the plants and animals for his advantage. So, eventually after living a life of nomad in search of food, the shelter is the most primary and basic need of man after learning to grow crops. The main reason to create stable houses or develop settlements is to protect themselves against the vagaries of weather and to enjoy the social life. In fact, the settlement is man's important step towards adapting himself to his physical environment. Most people of the world reside in some form of settlement—a permanent collection of houses and buildings. Settlement in which maximum people are occupied in agriculture, forestry, mining and fishery is known as a rural settlement. A rural settlement is often called an agricultural workshop. It cannot be segregated from the land whose use it ensures. Its type, shape and pattern are generally by the kind of work, the agricultural techniques and the way the soil is worked.

Most of the rural settlements of the world are stable and permanent. The rural areas are dominated by open countryside, extensive and vast land uses, comparatively low population densities and simple mode of life. It is often conjectured to be opposite to urban settlements. As per the data most of the world's settlements are rural as in 1960 there were twice as many people living in rural settings (2 billion) than urban (1 billion). Over the second half of the 20th century this gap bunged, not as a consequence of absolute declines in rural population, but due to rapid growth in urban areas. In 2007, rural and urban populations were approximately equal in size both at 3.33 billion people respectively. Since the crossing point in 2007, urban population has continued to increase rapidly whilst rural population has grown only marginally. In 2016 it is estimated that 4 billion people lived in urban areas and 3.4 billion in rural (https://ourworldindata.org/urbanization). Therefore, the most of world's settlements continues to be rural for some time. This increasing trend of urban population around the world will lead to more planned settlements or somewhat different from stable rural settlements is discussed in forthcoming paragraph.

13.2.3 Planned Settlements

The sites that are not instinctively chosen by villagers themselves, planned settlements are envisioned by governments by providing shelter, water and other infrastructure facilities on procured lands. There are planned villages in the newly irrigated areas of Ferozpur (Punjab) and Ganganagar (Rajasthan). These novel compact settlements are rectangular with an open space where the mosque, *gurdwara* or temple and shops stand. However, in the recent decades, attempts are being made to develop planned rural settlements. Examples of planned rural settlements in Australia, Israel, South Africa, Russia, Central Asian Republics, Germany, Sweden and India are numerous. The carefully planned rural settlements have numerous socio-economic and environmental advantages. Some of the benefits of the planned settlements are described. In the planned rural settlement, the use of land is judiciously planned, and only those crops are sown which may give higher agricultural returns. These settlements are planned systematically to give each family a reasonably good income and the land is equitably distributed among inhabitants. There are several economic advantages for the settlers in these planned settlements. They have assured a steady income and they come to areas where services such as roads, communication and electricity have already been provided. One of the most significant advantages of well-planned settlement is that they ensure that the land cleared is of a sufficiently good quality and that it is planted with the crops and social forestry—best suited to the soil and slope characteristics of the area. In unplanned settlements, the land cleared might be infertile or easily eroded.

In the planned settlements, their ways, their plans, their designs and their building materials are often far better suited to local needs, local incomes, local climatic conditions and local resources than the official, legal standards demanded by governments. Planned settlements are also cited to as "approved" settlements. These settlements sit on land demarcated as "development area" in the Master Plan (and the concerned Zonal Plan). At the time of construction, the housing units in these colonies comply with planning norms and measures and are fully sustained with infrastructures like water pipelines and sewerage systems. The housing constructed by the Delhi Development Authority (DDA) and Haryana Urban Development Authority (HUDA) are examples of this category of settlement.

13.3 Classification of Settlements

The classification of settlements has been approached in various ways. Settlements may be categorized by their function, size, morphology, number and density of houses etc. The most common classification is that of based on the function of settlements. It is accepted that settlements can be distinguished in rural and urban by function, but there is no accord on what exactly defines a village or a town. There is a divergence of opinion across the literature as to how and where to draw the borders between each type of settlement. A settlement where the population is extremely large or highly dense and has the peculiarities of a built environment (an environment that provides essential facilities for human activity) is known as urban. Urban areas are manifested in a planned and systematic way in the infrastructure establishment according to the process of urbanization and industrialization. Whereas the development in rural areas is seldom based on the availability of natural vegetation and fauna present in the region. The rural is more of a geographical region located in the outer parts of the cities or towns. A rural area is an open swath of land that has few homes or other buildings, and not very many people. There is vaster detachment from nature in urban areas due to the presence of the built environment by mankind. Conversely the rural areas are in direct connection with nature as they are influenced by physical elements. Despite this vague description of rural and urban areas the section below outlines various rudiments which distinguishes them.

13.4 Basis of Difference Between Rural and Urban Settlements

Most people have a clear impression of what the cities, towns, villages and hamlets in rural hinterland and countryside look like, both physically and in terms of the lives of the people who live there. This section describes some fundamental concepts of comparison of rural and urban areas for themes such as population size, economic aspects, social aspects, services and infrastructure, land use and administration. Several key methods have been suggested in trying to explain the difference between a village or rural settlement and a town or urban settlement to have clear cut understanding of the subject.

13.4.1 Population Size

The size of settlement can be represented through its area and population. A large area does not necessarily contain large population. The size of a settlement more often refers to its extent of population and not just its areal extent. Population size simply means the number of individuals in the population. The growth of a settlement, therefore, means a greater density of population. There is a wide inconsistency of views over the minimum size of population expected to enable a settlement to be termed a town, for example in Denmark it is estimated to be 250 people, in Ireland 500, in France 2,000, in the USA 2,500, in Spain 10,000 and in Japan 30,000. In India, the required population is 5,000. The population growth of urban centres depends on the functions of the city among others. The population size in villages in rural areas is often related to carrying capacity of the land. Generally speaking, where land is flat and fertile and agriculturally pleasing, villages tend to larger, for example, those in the river valleys of China and India as compared to rough terrain. In India, the regional variation of population size in villages is large as in population in a village in Himachal Pradesh is as low as 208 while villages in Uttar Pradesh has population over 10,000.

13.4.2 Economic Aspect

Rural settlements have traditionally been designated as places where most of the workforce is involved in farming or is engaged in other primary activities. The people in rural settlements are employed in primary occupations such as agriculture and animal husbandry. In contrast, most of the workforce in urban areas is engaged in secondary and service industries. However, many rural areas have now grown into commuter/dormitory settlements for people working in adjacent urban areas or, even more recently, a location for smaller footloose industries. Urban people are engaged in non-agricultural work, i.e. trade, commerce or service industry can be termed as secondary and tertiary activities. In the rural society, there is very limited scope for occupational mobility. In urban areas, there are many occupations, so occupational mobility is more as well as quite frequent. In the rural society, there is no division of labour as compared to the urban society where the division of labour and specialization in job allotment are always present or typical.

13.4.3 Service Provision

The services mean a system supplying a public need such as transport, communications, or utilities such as electricity and water. No matter where people and business enterprises settle, they anticipate the provision of certain categories of basic public and private services. Service provision is regarded as essential for the functionality of a modern family life. Intuitively, services provision in any area is there to support the daily lives of the citizens and enterprises. A certain level of public service provision is crucial in order to reduce social deprivation and in order to increase social inclusion (Berry, 2004). The importance of having a vibrant service sectors from the perspective that it ensures quality of life for citizens and it is necessary for the development of the economy. OECD further states that "The availability of an appropriate mix of private, public and voluntary services in all communities is an increasingly important factor in building a competitive and sustainable economy" (OECD, 2010). The provision of services such as schools, hospitals, shops, public transport and banks is usually limited and at times absent in rural areas. But urban areas are the hub in the provision of all the techno-scientific services of very high order. Unlike rural areas, urban settlements are defined by their advanced civic amenities, opportunities for education at higher levels, facilities for transport, business and social interaction and overall better standard of living. The supply formats of services may, however, still be different in rural due to smaller and more dispersed populations, longer distances and limited availability of delivery infrastructure. Socio-cultural statistics are customarily based on an urban population. The service production and provision is found to be like the one to reduce rural-urban differences. In earlier times the rural population was regarded as a fairly homogeneous population group, and yet in many respects different from the urban population. Today, the aspirations related to quality of life for rural citizens are converging with the aspirations of urban citizens (OECD, 2010; Moseley and Owen, 2008). The literature on rural lifestyles tends to state that the distinction between these two groups of citizens has become less weighty over time.

13.4.4 Land Use

Land use is the function of land—what it is used for. Land use varies from area to area. Land use is the sum total of arrangements, activities, and inputs that people undertake in a certain land cover type. Land use involves the management and modification of natural environment or wilderness into built environment such as settlements and semi-natural habitats such as arable fields, pastures, and managed woods. In rural areas (countryside) land use can include forestry and farming. In urban areas (towns and cities) land use could be housing or industry. The urban sprawl often infringes upon viable agricultural or productive forest land, neither of which can resist nor deflect the overwhelming momentum of urbanization. In rural areas, settlements are extensively spaced with open land between adjacent villages. Within each village, there may be individual farms as well as residential areas and probably small-scale industry. In urban areas, settlements are often packed closely together, and within towns, there is a greater infusion of land use with residential, industrial, services and open-space provision. While rural areas may develop randomly by natural vegetation and fauna available in a region, urban settlements are proper, planned settlements raised up according to a process called urbanization. Many times, rural areas are focused upon by governments and development agencies and turned into urban areas. Urban areas are developed in a planned and systematic way while development in rural areas is seldom, based on the availability of natural vegetation and fauna present in the region.

13.4.5 Social Aspect

When it proceeds to social mobilization, urban people are highly accelerated as they switch their occupation or residence frequently in search of better opportunities for their development. However, in rural areas occupational or territorial mobility of the people is comparatively less intensive and revolve around their homestead. Rural settlements, especially those in more outlying areas, tend to have more inhabitants in the over 65 age group, whereas the highest symmetry in urban areas lies within the economically active age group or those under secondary school age. While rural settlements are based more on natural resources and events, the urban population reaps the benefits of the advancements of man in the areas of science and technology and is not nature-dependent for its day-to-day functions. Businesses stay open late into the evenings in urban areas while sunset in rural areas means the day is implicitly over.

13.4.6 Administrative Levels

There is a local administrative institution like town area, notified area, cantonment area, municipal board, Municipal Corporation etc. in every town and city as a local controlling authority. But in rural areas, there is no such local authority, and they are controlled by district authorities under government. But in certain cases, the village is governed by a planning authority or by an elected body. For instance, Aymara villages in the Andes have the rigid social system in which land is communally owned and allocated to individuals by the village elders to ensure internal organization of villages. In India, Gram Panchayat is responsible and plays a central role in the arrangement, maintaining law and order. There are various ways of classification of settlements and may be categorized by their function, size, morphology, number and density of houses etc. By function, settlements are often arranged into two broad categories of rural and urban settlements. The types of classification according to the size of settlements may be very small, small, medium, large and very large and can be divided into the categories of the hamlet, village, urban village, town, city, metropolis and megalopolis. The smallest occupancy unit is called hamlet which consists of few houses. The village is a small rural settlement and village having urban characteristics is termed the urban village. The urban village is the just budding stage in the process of origin of town which expands further to form city, metropolis, and megalopolis are in hierarchical order in the formation of urban settlements. The settlements are also assigned on the grounds of morphology. The settlements have different shapes and forms according to topography and terrain. The pattern of settlements is determined by the layout and functional morphology. Depending on these, the settlements can be classified in the various shapes such as linear, circular, rectangular, square, radial, star, amorphous etc. Further settlements are also classified by number and density of houses. Previously it is mentioned that a hamlet or small village has some houses whereas, in a village of large size, the number of houses is much more. The compactness of settlement is measured by the open spaces or distances between the houses. In this manner, settlements are classified into dispersed, semi-compact and compact categories. All these categories may be found in rural areas, while all the urban settlements are usually compact, clustered and agglomerated and are neither dispersed or semi-compact.

13.5 Summary

Over the years, the concept of human settlements has been broadened to become a framework for an overall national socio-economic development in the context of formulating global shelter strategies. Settlements are an objective of development in that places where people can live, learn and work. So, with the present discussion in the chapter, it is recognized that these two human settlements are very different in many perspectives, regarding the density of human structures and the residents of that area. The standard of living in urban areas is greater in comparison to the rural areas. These are entirely different from each other by working, earnings, services, and population using geographical classifications.

Review Questions

1. Describe the origin and development of human settlements.
2. Discuss the various basis of classification of human settlements.
3. Give examples of unstable settlements and planned settlements.

Analytical Questions

1. Conduct online or library research and find three examples of unstable settlement due to the practice of shifting cultivation.
2. Discuss the planned settlement during the Mughal period in India.

Chapter 14
Rural Settlement

14.1 Introduction

Rural area means the area positioned outside the towns and cities found in the form of villages and hamlets. It is also defined as an area that is encompassing all population, housing, and territory not included within an urban area and whatever is not urban is considered as rural. These areas have low population and small settlements as compared to urban areas. These are most closely related to nature based deeds. They are dominantly based on primary activities such as agriculture, animal husbandry, fishing etc. Rural settlement as a pioneer habitat of the human beings is a living and functional space. A rural settlement means a rural location occupied by the rural inhabitants with their specific kinds of economic, social and cultural environment. Geographers look at the rural settlements as the agglomeration of human made habitat on the earth which is dependent mostly on primary occupational accomplishments. Rural settlements are the sites where people obtain their earning from the primary occupation, particularly, agriculture and some houses as well as population density remains less. The houses are built with the help of locally available raw materials. The present chapter deals with rural settlements and various bases of their classification and associated problems.

14.2 Classification of Rural Settlements

A valuable contribution was made by Meitzen (1895) in Germany at the end of the 19th century which was perhaps, the first exhaustive effort in the sphere of rural settlements. He classified the rural settlement of Europe in two categories of the nucleated village or individual homestead or separate dwelling. After the classic work of Meitzen which has provided the basis for the study of rural settlements, researches in the field of rural settlements began in various parts of the world. Later on many attempts were have been made to understand and analyze village shapes with respect to broaden the scope of settlement geography like King (1927), Ahmad (1952), Sinha (1976) and many others. They have applied various methods and techniques to identify broad settlement patterns in different areas. The types of the settlement are defined by the extent of the built-up area and distance between one house to another. Rural settlements are of several types, and the classification of rural settlement has been addressed in various ways. There are several bases on which one classify the rural settlements such as setting (site), proximity, function and shape (pattern) are expressed in this section.

14.2.1 Based on Setting

The classification of rural settlement by setting generally means according to the location of the village. Mainly villages are plain villages, plateau villages, coastal villages, forest villages and desert villages according to their location. The plain villages are scattered over vast flat or plain areas. The site is favourable for settling down due to easy access and fertility of land which is suitable for agriculture. The villages located in an area of relatively high-level ground than other areas of land surrounding it is known as plateau villages. This kind of villages provides the excellent resource and mineral base for the growth of settlements. It also has rich volcanic soils, allowing better crop production and increased population densities. The villages located near the coasts are known as coastal villages. This kind of villages provides ample opportunity for the seafood and growth of fisheries. When settlements are established in the forests are called forest villages and villagers here are dependent on forest produce and lumbering activities. Sometimes, people settle in desert areas besides knowing the difficulties of the climatic factors. The settlements in such deserts are called desert villages, but in these deserts too, people prefer to settle near water bodies and patches of vegetation.

14.2.2 Based on Proximity

The major types of settlements by proximity and distance are compact or nucleated settlements; semi-compact or semi-nucleated settlements and dispersed settlements. The various types of settlements classified according to this criterion are as follows:

Compact or Nucleated Settlements: Compact settlements are those settlements in which a large number of houses are constructed very close to each other (Fig. 14.1). These settlements develop along the river valleys and in fertile plains according to its advantages. Communities are closely knit and share common occupational accomplishments. A compact or nucleated rural settlement is based on farming and comprises houses, farm structures, areas for grazing animals and growing crops and other buildings such as religious centres surrounding the village buildings. The fields must be convenient to reach by the farmers and are positioned within a radius of two or three kilometres from the village structures and houses. Compact settlements are frequently located in the profoundly productive alluvial plains. The rural inhabitants of these fertile plains have settled firmly on the soil. Compact Settlements got established in the productive alluvial regions such as the Indo-Gangetic plains, the Hawang Ho valley, the valley of Nile etc. during the pre-historic period. These are some of the most densely populated regions of the world in which the nucleated or compact settlements dominate the landscape. One more feature of these compact settlements in India is that they have a high degree of separation and differentiation of the upper and lower castes. Each caste is allotted its specific location in the region. The market place and shops are always near the core of the village. The mosques or temples are also in the midst of the settlement. Apart from agriculturists, compact settlements are likewise observed in numerous of the hunting and fishing communities. The American Red Indians and many hunting and fishing tribe's world over are living in big villages because compactness is required for making, maintaining and handling fishing boats. Large villages are still many along the Brahmaputra and Hooghly rivers, where fishing entails cooperative management of the weirs and traps on the rivers.

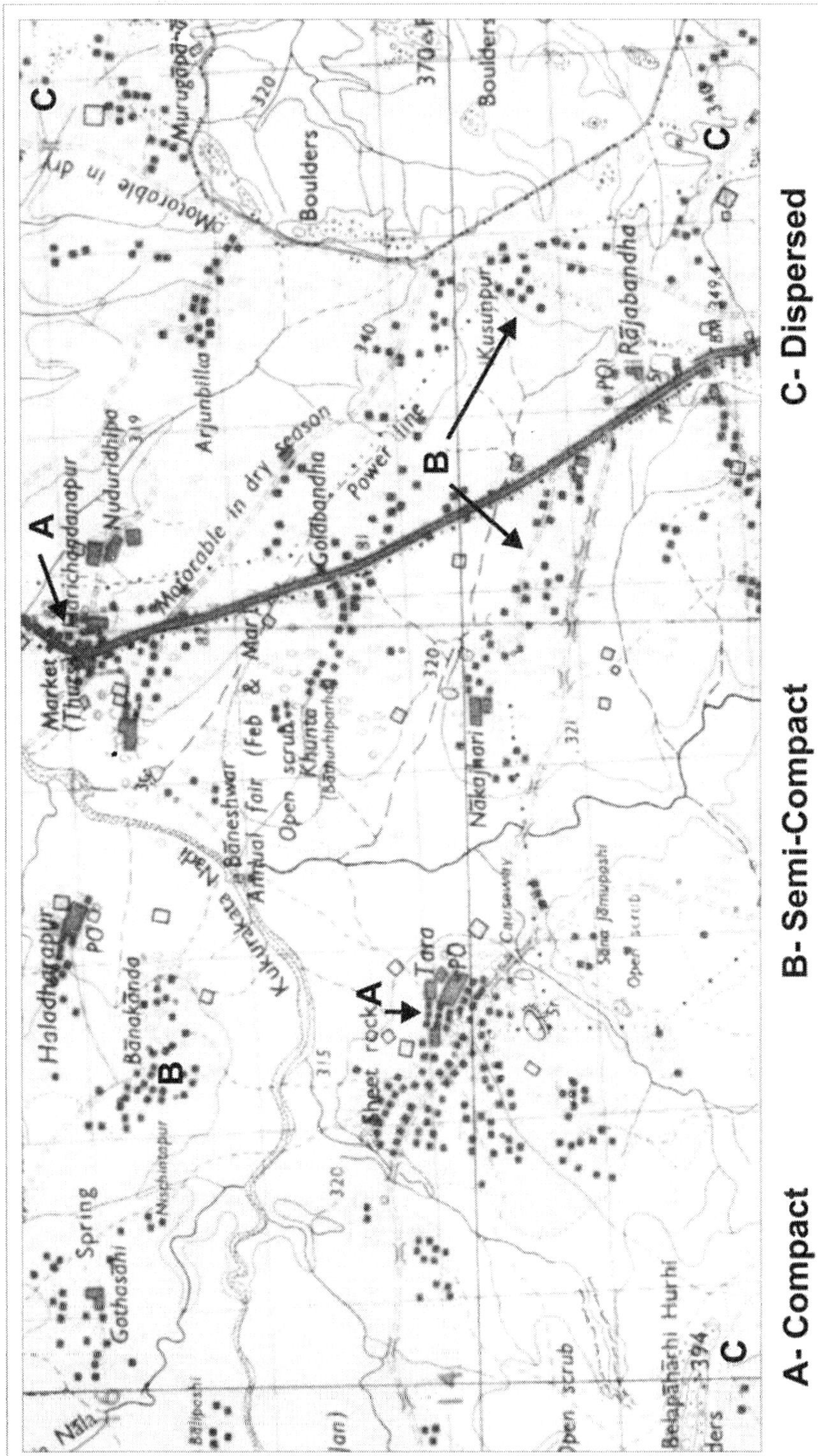

Fig. 14.1: Types of Settlements based on Proximity (Identified based on the Survey of India Toposheets)

Compact settlements are found in the plains or along the water bodies where soil, fish and other resources are rich. When the resources in the villages are poor and scanty, the size of villages is small and located close to each other. For instance, in the Aravalli tract, the Rajput settlements comprise of barely eight or nine houses. Contrary to this, the hunting and gathering Hottentots tribes of Africa exist in large compact settlements as their territories are well-endowed with the game and water holes. The resources and wealth of a country, however, are not static and with the shift in technology, the resource base also turns which leads to a transformation in the type and pattern of settlement. Intensive cultivation, which outlines the most scientific use of soil, has given rise to the greatest number of huge compact settlements. The archives of settlement very often prove that the addition of population in the agricultural communities and more demand for food have appeared into the intensification of cultivation. The rural settlement became more compact to accommodate exceeding people over minimum space. When there was not sufficient space to accommodate the accelerating number of individuals, many of them created their houses at a suitable neighbouring region and similarly established the new settlement on the pattern of their traditional village. This process can be seen everywhere in the Sutlej-Ganga plains. Many of the *purvas* and *majras* in the Ganga plain are the instances of settlements which are consequences of intensification of farming.

Compact settlements at the top of hills and ridges of Nagaland are the outcomes of the tradition of head-hunting in the past, where personages of each settlement have to depute volunteers from each household to work as the watchmen at nights fronting the invading head-hunters. Head-hunting is the system of taking and storing a person's head after killing the person. Head-hunting was followed in historical times in portions of Oceania, South and Southeast Asia, West and Central Africa, and Mesoamerica, as well as amid certain tribes of the Celts, the West Germanic tribes, and Scythians of ancient Europe. Although compact rural establishments may be noticed in all the intensively farmed plains and valleys of all the continents, their concentration is considerably immense in Northern parts of India, Eastern China, Egypt, Syria, Bangladesh, Pakistan, Myanmar (Burma), Java, Thailand, Sri Lanka, Nepal, Pakistan, Mexico, Brazil, Kenya and the North-western European plains.

Semi-Compact or Semi-Nucleated Settlements: The residences or houses are not well-knitted. Such settlements are characterized by a small but compact nuclear around which hamlets are scattered (Fig. 14.1). The semi-compact or semi-nucleated settlement is a transitional phase in the growth of a compact settlement. As the new technology is adopted, and the population increases, the scattered settlements start taking the shape of semi-compact settlements. For the growth of semi-compact settlement, no simple environmental explanation is acceptable. The emergence of such settlements differs from that of marginal productive lands to the highly fertile intensively cultivated lands. The only generalization about the semi-compact settlements is that in the arable lands and fertile plains the primary type of settlement was small and loosely nucleated and in fact lacked a pattern. Increase in population results in the growth of village and the number of houses increases. These houses spread on the open spaces and lead to the origin of semi-compact settlement which ultimately acquires the shape of a nucleated or compact settlement. Numerous instances of such settlements are observed in the east of Aravallis in the State of Rajasthan, in the hilly tracts of Madhya Pradesh, Arunachal Pradesh, Meghalaya, Manipur, Mizoram, Tripura, Sikkim in the Siwaliks and the valley of Brahmaputra and around Haridwar in Uttarakhand.

Dispersed Settlements: Dispersed settlements as the name indicates are the dwellings spaced far apart and usually interspersed with fields (Fig. 14.1). A cultural feature such as a site of worship or a market is main factor to binds the settlement together. Dispersed settlements are detected in the areas of severe climates, hilly expanses, thick forest stretches, grasslands, poor agricultural lands, areas of widespread agriculture and the areas where it is imperative that the farmer should survive on his agricultural land rather than in a distant village/settlement. One thing which may be stated about the dispersed settlements is that they are relatively recent in age. The Steppe grasslands of Kazakhistan, Uzbekistan, Turkmenistan, Kirgizistan, Russia-east of Ural are some of the striking cases of dispersed settlements which came into existence in the late 19th century and the early parts of the 20th century. The scattered settlements in various regions of the world like Prairies of USA and Canada, the Pampas of Argentina, the Velds of South Africa and the Downs (grasslands) of Australia have originated mostly around 200 years ago. In the desert and semi-desert regions of Rajasthan, in the forest lands of North-East India, the Siwalik, the side valleys of Jammu & Kashmir, the higher elevations of Himalayas and parts of the peninsular India, dispersed settlements commenced evolving during the medieval period. Such settlements are also observed in the underpopulated areas, such as Central Australia, New Zealand, Northern Canada, western parts of the USA, Scotland, Scandinavian countries, South-West Asia, the oasis of Sahara and the greater part of Africa excluding the coastal areas and irrigated tracts. There are, however, some areas of highly productive agricultural land and the right climate characterised with dispersed settlements. In such areas, the main reasons of scattered settlements are historical or socio-cultural. For example, if a village is overpopulated and grows enormous, the segment of its population moves the village to develop a recent settlement which is often a dispersed one. Such settlements may be observed throughout the plains of Northern India in between the two large compact settlements. Furthermore, when people relocated into the marshy land, *khadar* (new alluvial) tracts of rivers, or marginal upland farms, they normally built isolated farms rather than nucleated or compact settlements. This is mainly because, in the poor marginal lands, a larger area is needed for sustenance.

14.2.3 Based on Functions

The people residing in the rural areas, all over the world, are engaged and reliant on numerous primary occupations, viz. agriculture, dairying, cattle keeping, fisheries, forestry and mining. There may be kinds of villages such as farming villages, fishermen's villages, lumberjack villages, rural villages etc. The different types of villages by functions are outlined below.

Farming Villages: Agriculture is the most important occupation. Consequently, the functions of the maximum of the people of rural settlements are agricultural. Apart from the cultivation of crops and domestication of animals, the rural settlements perform other duties. Its religious place—mosque, temple, gurdwara or church—with one or two shops is a centre of religious and social activities. Some administrative and judicial functions are performed by the village panchayats in India and village councils in different countries. In the socialist countries such as Russia, Ukraine, Poland, North Korea and China, the village councils determine where and when certain crops should be sown, irrigated or harvested.

Fishermnn's Villages: In the rural settlements where fishermen prevail, the main activity is fishing. The fishing villages are located on rivers, lakes and sea coasts, and the people regard to the water rather than to the land to make their livelihood. Although the main o̯cupation of these villages is fishing this may be combined with some agricultural activity.

Lumbering Villages: There are various rural settlements in the forest areas in which the dominant economic activity is gathering of forest products and lumbering. Such villages are small in size and may be observed in the Taiga region, forest ranges of the sub-Himalayan terrain and hilly tracts like North-East India. In the forests where lumber jacking is on a massive scale, and timber industry has evolved, urban rather than rural settlements are more general.

Administrative Villages: The fishing, mining or lumbering villages are similar to agricultural settlements in which there are some shops and few small-scale administrative functions. They are different from towns, as do all villages, in the relatively narrow range of their activities and lack of commercial and industrial development.

14.2.4 Based on Patterns/Shape/Forms

The pattern of settlement has been defined as the relationship between one house and building to another. The pattern of settlement may be easily recognized by reading and observing the large-scale map, like that of the topographical maps prepared by the Survey of India or the Ordinance Survey of Britain. The term 'pattern of settlement' deals with compact and semi-compact settlements only as each of the dispersed settlements has its own and varied shape. The site of the village and the encompassing topography and ground influence the shape and size villages. In fact, the pattern of rural settlement is the outcome of a series of adaptations to the environment which has been going on for ages. Moreover, social and cultural factors such as caste structure of the people residing in a village and the functional requirements of the people also have a close bearing on its shape and size. In the valleys in mountainous areas, the pattern of settlement is linear, while in the fertile plains their shapes may be rectangular; near the lakes and ponds, the settlements are of the circular or semi-circular type, while at the crossroads, the configuration may be rectangular, circular or triangular. In unusual cases, the settlement pattern resembles the nebular form and so on. The river terraces resemble the staircase type. The location of the village, surrounding topography and terrain affects the shape and size of village settlements. There may be some geometrical forms and shapes such as linear, rectangular, circular, star, nebular shape, T-shaped village etc. are elaborated in section below:

Rectangular Pattern: Over 50 per cent of the world population lives in rural settlements, and most of the people inhabit the settlements of the rectangular pattern. Rectangular settlements largely occur in fertile alluvial plains and broad intermontane valleys (Fig. 14.2A). The alleys in the rectangular settlements are nearly straight, meeting each other at right angles at ninety degrees. The rural settlements of the Sutlej-Ganga plains, especially those which emerged on the crossroads, fall in this category. The well-planned settlements of Germany, Russia, Central Asian Republics, China, North and South Korea, Vietnam, Malaysia, Israel and France also fall under this group.

Linear Pattern: The Linear pattern is the most significant form of settlements. In the linear settlements, houses are organized along either side of a road, railway line, river or canal (Fig. 14.2B). Such settlements also develop along the edge of a valley, primarily in the mountainous areas, above flood level or along the coast. Difficult terrain and topography

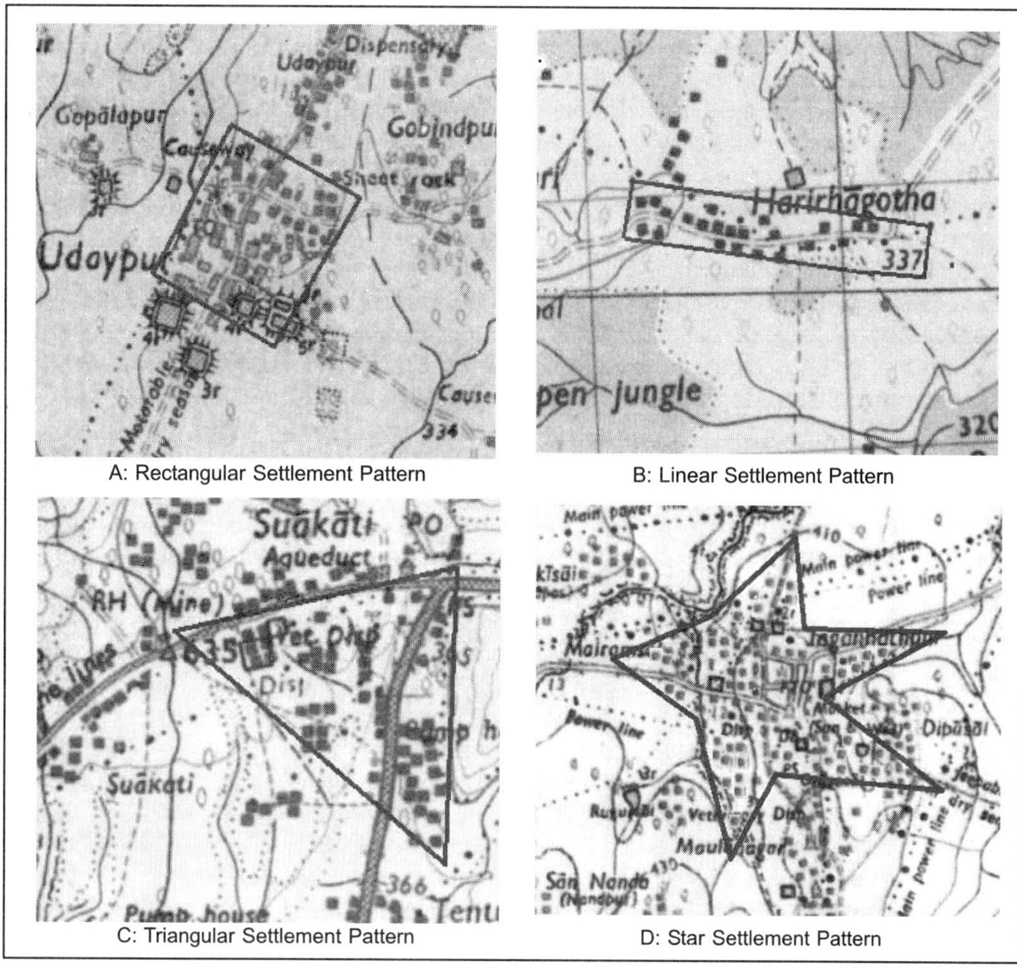

A: Rectangular Settlement Pattern
B: Linear Settlement Pattern
C: Triangular Settlement Pattern
D: Star Settlement Pattern

Fig. 14.2: Types of Settlements based on Shape/Pattern (Identified from Survey of India Toposheets)

chiefly regulate the evolution of linear settlements in the mountainous regions. Along the river banks and the road and railways, the flood and water level influence linear settlements. Such settlements are numerous in the Middle Himalayas, Alps, Rockies, Andes, Pyrenees, Pamir, Hindukush, Zagros, Elburz, Siwaliks and along the roads in the plains of Ganga-Yamuna Doab.

Circular and Semi-Circular Pattern: The fishermen and salt producers develop their settlements along the sea coasts and salt lakes, respectively. Since the people favour to stay near the water, they build their dwellings along the coasts and settlements here acquire the circular or semi-circular shapes. In the proximity of crater lakes and on the levees of ox-bow lakes, such settlements are located. The principal affair of the people of circular settlements is to earn their sustenance from the water either by hooking fish, water-nuts or by providing services to the recreators, picnic goers and aesthetic beauty lovers.

Triangular Patterns: Triangular patterns of rural settlement developed at the convergence of rivers. The rivers constrain the sidelong expansion of houses at the confluence. Consequently, the settlement acquires a triangular shape (Fig. 14.2C).

Star Patterns: The star-like settlements develop in the sites and places where several metalled or unmetalled roads converge. In the star-shaped settlements, houses radiated out along the sides of roads in all directions (Fig. 14.2D). This pattern is common to both villages and towns and is caused mostly by new development, spreading out along the major highways. This type of settlements is the characteristic of the countryside's of North-West Europe, plains of Yangtzekiang, Punjab province of Pakistan and the Sutlej-Yamuna plains.

Nebular Pattern: When the form of a settlement resembles a nebula, it is recognised as a nebular settlement. The composition of roads is almost circular which ends at the central location or the nucleus of the settlement. The size of nebular settlements is small, and they emerge from the house of the chief landlord of the village or the mosque, temple or church. There are several villages of this type in the Ganga-Yamuna Doab.

14.3 Problems of Rural Settlements

Rural settlements in the developing countries are in higher proportions and inadequately furnished with infrastructure. They portray a whole range of challenges and opportunity for planners. Supply and availability of water to rural settlements in developing countries is not satisfactory. People in villages, particularly in mountainous and arid areas have to walk long lengths and distances to fetch drinking water. The waterborne ailments such as cholera and jaundice tend to be a universal dilemma. The countries of South Asia bear conditions of drought and flood quite frequently. Crop cultivation sequences, in the deficiency of irrigation also undergo many sufferings.

The general inadequacy of toilet and garbage disposal facilities causes health-related emergencies. The design and use of building materials of houses differ from one ecological region to another. The houses constructed of mud, wood and thatch, remain susceptive to damage during heavy rains and floods and demand adequate preservation every year. Most house designs are typically defective in proper oxygenating. Furthermore, the design of a house includes the animal shed along with its fodder store inside it. This is intentionally created to keep the domestic animals and their food properly preserved from wild animals. Unmetalled roads and scarcity of modern communication interface create a unique intricacy. During the rainy season, the settlements continue to cut off and pose high-level difficulties in providing emergency services. It is further challenging to render enough health and educational infrastructure for their vast rural population. The problem is of the high level where houses are scattered over a large area. In the previous chapter, we have examined that how planned rural settlement has started evolving and they have many advantages. The planned rural settlements are, however, not free from disadvantages. Some of the disadvantages of the planned rural settlements are described herein further. In the early stages of planned settlements, the settlers have little freedom of action and the schemes and projects do not provide an immediate resolution to their problems as possibly they believed they would. Some homesteaders become disappointed and leave the scheme, but most recognise it is long-term advantages. Settlements are planned for a given number of families, based on the capability of the land to sustain them at a given income. Naturally, when they have children, not all the young people will be ready to live in the same areas. To surmount this dilemma, people will either have to move beyond from the area for future generations or will have to deliver the original settlement schemes the basis for trading and rural industries. The cropping pattern adopted may not be useful in the long-run. Generally, in planned rural settlements, cash crops are grown, and most of such crops are soil exhaustive. The merits of diversification and rotation of crops which enhance the fertility of soils by fixing nitrogen will not be available. These demerits of planned rural settlements may be subdued by adopting flexible and pragmatic planning as the number of people increases.

14.4 Summary

Rural settlement change in through time both in patterns and in functions. It is evident from the preceding discussion of nucleated and dispersed settlements that not only can shape of rural settlements change, but the whole pattern can change from nucleated to disperse or from dispersed to nucleated in certain circumstances. Such changes are still going on many areas, partly because of new developments in agriculture. In many regions, very rapid changes in rural settlements are taking place as a result of large-scale projects. The settlements are compact or nucleated or dispersed depending upon the spacing of settlements. Almost everywhere in the world, nucleated settlements are more common than dispersed. There are several reasons for this. Dispersed settlements, however, is almost always of relatively recent date and origin. The patterns of settlements are the relationship between one house and another house. The rural settlements have diverse shapes and sizes. They can be arranged in many patterns like in neighbouring valleys. The pattern is linear while in fertile plain their shape may be rectangular, near lakes and ponds, the settlement is of circular or semi-circular type. In exceptional cases, the settlement pattern resembles nebular form, and on the river, terraces resemble the staircase type.

Review Questions

1. Explain the concept of rural settlements.
2. Discuss the different basis of classification of rural settlements.
3. Discuss the patterns of rural settlements. Give examples.

Analytical Questions

1. Discuss the rural settlement pattern of refugee colonies and their associated problems.
2. Take the bird eyeview of rural settlement pattern in any mountainous region and any coastal plain region using Google map. Analyze the difference.

Chapter 15
Urban Settlements

15.1 Introduction

As discussed earlier in human settlements, urban stands for an area that is described by large human population with higher densities and vast human-built infrastructures in comparison to the areas surrounding it. City, towns, conurbations are examples of urban and this term cannot apply to villages and hamlets in rural hinterland. According to the Population Division of the United Nations Department of Economic and Social Affairs, "the urban population would grow to 6.4 billion by 2050, with 37 per cent of that growth to come from three countries: China, India, and Nigeria." The world is gradually becoming more and more urban than rural. In this whole process of urbanization the urban areas are being developed further to give best. The settlements in which most of the people are engaged in secondary, tertiary and quaternary activities are categorized as urban places. In other words, urban associates itself to the cities and towns. If urbanization is observed as a demographic process only, then urban places are those which exceed population size and density threshold limits. The size, density and occupations are the measures usually accepted in the census and other definitions of urban places, though the precise division through other parameters between urban and rural is arbitrary.

Urban settlements are such where the people derive their earning from the secondary and tertiary profession that is chiefly from manufacturing of goods as well as management. Here the density population, number of houses and number of people living in the area, all remain high. The houses built in the urban are mostly composed of concrete, and the materials are acquired from other places. Towns are of numerous different sizes, classifying from small country towns, sometimes smaller than village elsewhere, to large sprawling cities with several million inhabitants. The difference between towns and rural settlements is not only the size but the economic activities of their occupants. The dominant economic activities in towns and urban places concern to industries, trade, commerce and services. The definition of urban settlement is, nonetheless, a difficult one. Most of the countries define their urban settlements by a minimum qualifying size of the population. The size of the population may differ from one country to another country and from plain regions to the mountainous and the desert regions. The criteria of functions, administrative status, layout and amenities are also merged with the criterion of the minimum size of the population. The towns like villages must possess the fundamental requirements which make settlement possible here. These are availability of water and food supplies, shelter and building materials, and some protection against natural hazards, such as floods, landslides etc. However, this does not mean that any village can grow into a town easily. This does sometimes happen, but more often than not, towns and villages were developed separately because of their different dominant functions and the reliance of towns on certain advantageous situations. In the modern eras, villages may evolve and grow into towns as a consequence of residential and sub-urban development, but in the earlier times, town and countryside were quite separate. The causes for the development of towns are mainly historical, socio-cultural, economic and political. Which one of the factors are more important in the origin and growth of town is tough to say, but the experts of urban geography and town planning are of the opinion that traffic is the most important and the oldest factor responsible for the growth of towns. The classification of urban settlements is described in detail in the present chapter.

15.2 Classification of Urban Settlements

Some of the common basis of classification of urban settlements is the size of the population, occupational structure, administrative setup and location. Towns vary greatly regarding history, size, morphology, functions and demographic attributes. Urban centres are classified by their numerous attributes like growth stage, population size, functions, site and situation etc.

15.2.1 Classification Based on the Stage of Growth

Various scholars classified urban centres based on the stage of growth. For example, Mumford (1938) by cultural progress has determined following six stages of urban development: Eopolis, Polis, Metropolis, Megalopolis, Tyrannopolis, and Necropolis. According to this classification, a town is compared to a living organism and demonstrated how a single town resembles a whole civilization. He considers a town rising through first three stages and then sinking through another three. The first and the earliest stage is the eopolis. In this stage town is evolved from a village community. In this time the economy is based on agriculture. The second stage is polis envisages into a small urban unit of self-contained community. There is small market town with some manufacturing, trade and commerce activities. The third stage is metropolis or a mother city as it is the city with its full stature. It is applied to a very large city of dominant function with a large sphere of influence. It has high population density and large potentialities and developed infrastructure with full growth. The fourth stage is megalopolis refers to highly urbanized and bloated city where the material wealth dominates the life, standardized products replace the original art and evils of bureaucracy intensify. Due to all these it is beginning of decline of town and city. In other words due to the overgrown nature of the city, the problems begin to creep in all spheres of a city. The fifth stage is tyrannopolis and is an extension of megalopolis. Wealth demonstration and extravagance become the yardsticks of culture, oral apathy replaces good living, decay in military power and commerce and trade alternated between boom and depression. City shows drastic deteriorating situation. The last and sixth stage is necropolis meaning the city of the dead. This is so because the city is in worst state and unfit for dwellers due to war, famine, disease etc. The living conditions deteriorate badly and cultural institutions decay and municipal services decline and the city begin to resemble like shell due to shifting of people elsewhere. In this case the town may recover from its illness from long interval of time.

Geddes (1949) classified urban centres in four categories: Eotechnic, Palaeotechnic, Neotechnic and Biotechnic. This classification is based on social changes brought about by technical progress with the advances in human history. The eotechnic phase is characterised by the natural sources of power like wood, wind and water. The primitive technology was used and underdeveloped means of transport prevails. The manufacturing is done on the lines of cottage industry, using ubiquitous raw material and high labour input. They exhibit the scattered spatial pattern. The second phase is palaeotechnic marked by the beginning of use of coal as source of power and the development of iron and steel industry. There was not much advancement in transport system and was cost intensive. The industries here exhibit the compact spatial pattern. The factory system based on individual ownership is established using local raw materials for heavy and weight loose industries and serves fairly localized markets. The neotechnic phase is characterized by technological innovations and advancements in industry, agriculture and energy resources and transport system. This resulted in the introduction of electric power, combustion engines, the use of lighter and rarer material like aluminium and tungsten, regeneration of waste, invention of new gadgets etc. With these developments, manufacturing become well organized on large scale and the basis for mass consumption. Thus, the city is marked by tall buildings, traffic congestion, urban sprawl and degradation of infrastructure. The biotechnic is the last and most developed phase. The civilizations now dominated more by the biological sciences than by the physical sciences. The dwellers of these cities are more concerned about the environment of the city and its conservation.

15.2.2 Classification Based on Functions

As we have seen that city classification may be based on several factors but the most important and meaningful scheme of classification is based on the functions performed by a city. On the basis of dominant functions, towns and cities are organised into various functional classes. In the beginning, towns were hearts of administration, trade, industry, defence and religious importance. The importance of defence and religion as separating functions has declined over the years but other functions have subscribed the list. Now-a-days several novel functions, such as recreational, residential, transport, mining, manufacturing and new activities related to information technology is conducted on in specialized towns. Some of these functions do not necessarily require the urban centre to have any fundamental relationship with their neighbouring rural areas. Despite many towns displaying multiple functions, their dominant function is often referred. For instance, we think of Sheffield as an industrial city, London as a port city, Chandigarh as an administrative city, Oxford as an education hub and so on. Large cities have a preferably greater diversity in their functions. Besides, all cities are dynamic and over a period may promote distinctive functions. Most of the early nineteenth-century fishing ports in England have now evolved tourism centres. Many of the old market towns are now known for their manufacturing activities. Functional classification of towns endeavours to classify towns and cities according to their dominant economic functions, thereby identifying their roles within the urban systems. Most classifications based on function use employment and occupational data for this purpose. Such kind of data is prepared by applying simple and sophisticated statistical procedures such as standard deviation and principal component analysis techniques. These techniques help in determining the main functions of the towns understudy on an objective base. A common feature of all the towns and cities is that they are trading and have business centres. However, most cities and towns perform additional functions also which give them distinctive characteristics. Towns are accordingly classified according to their dominant single function. This dominant single function of towns may be the trade, administration, defence or entertainment. So, it is evident that the towns have been studied from the origin, site, situation, morphological and functional points of view. The one aspect on which geographers are increasingly focusing their attention is the functional feature. In the functional classification of towns, efforts are being made to categorize towns and cities by their dominant economic functions. The central aspiration of functional classification of towns is to recognize their roles within urban systems and in process of urbanization. In reality, each town dominates some function and any change in the function may change the importance of specific location and its advantages also. In the functional approach of classification of towns, these are classified by their dominant function (Fig. 15.1). The functional classification of towns has been explained in the following paragraph.

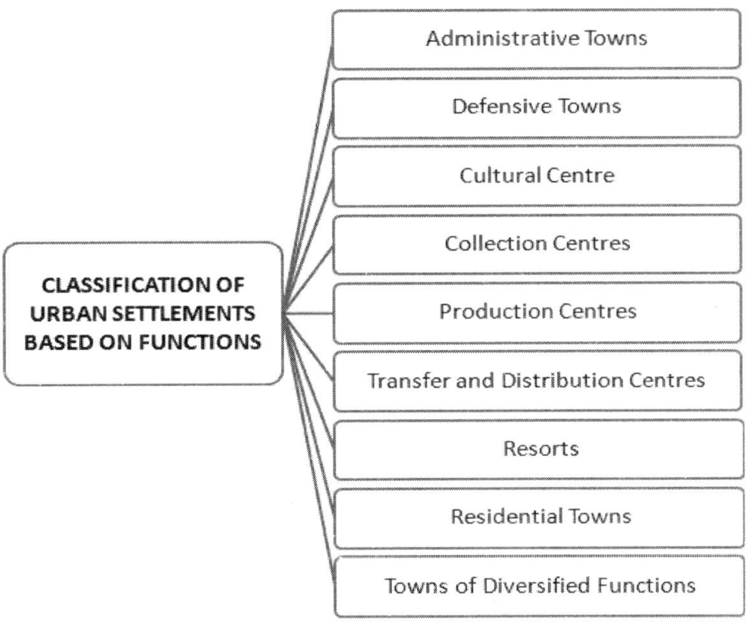

Fig. 15.1: Classification of Urban Settlements Based on Functions

Administrative Towns: This includes not only capital cities of countries but all centres of provinces, states, districts, and other administrative divisions of the country. Administrative towns are concerned mainly with public administration and contain many public buildings, ministries, and offices and usually head offices of state-run institutions. These are customarily the headquarters of state-run institutions such as banks, post offices, railways, trade and industries. The capitals being centres also house higher order specialized functions like universities, hospitals and headquarters of the political parties. The concentration of other significant enterprises such as public buildings, parks and sporting facilities tend to make capitals tourist centres, especially the royal palaces, mosques, cathedrals, churches, temples and other historical buildings of credit. There are considerably large administrative cities seen around the world, some of them are termed as mega cities such as Tokyo (2.7 million), Mexico City (16.6 million), Buenos Aires (11.8 million), Seoul (11.6 million), Beijing (11.3 million), Cairo (9.7 million), Jakarta (8.6 million), Paris (8.5 million), New Delhi (10.2 million) and London (7.4 million).

There are numerous province capitals also which have more than several millions of population. In India, Mumbai, Chennai, Hyderabad, Lucknow and Jaipur are some of the instances of the similar kind of administrative towns. The examples of small-sized administrative towns (capitals) are such as Male, capital of Maldives (40,000), Stanley, capital of Falkland with a population of only one thousand from the world. In India, Kohima, (60,650) and Itanagar (20,500) are the administrative towns with population less than one lakh each. Apart from ancient capitals and homes of the ruling families, there are many capitals which have recently formed for historical, political and strategic reasons. Mamabad in Pakistan, Ottawa in Canada, Brasilia in Brazil and Canberra in Australia is dying examples of such capitals. There are National capitals which house the administrative offices of central governments, such as New Delhi, Canberra, Beijing, Addis Ababa, Washington D.C., and London are designated administrative towns. Provincial (sub-national) towns can also have administrative functions, for example, Victoria (British Columbia), Albany (New York), Chennai (Tamil Nadu). Some towns which are winter capitals also come in the range of administrative towns, for example Jammu (India).

Defensive Towns: The days are passed when in most countries almost all towns had a defensive function, protecting its people and those of the surrounding countryside. In the medieval period, most of the towns and cities used to be formed on the defensive sites. Forts and garrisons used to be created at strategic places. The defensive towns have barracks, cantonments and training facilities for the armed forces, airfields, and harbours for warships. Visakhapatnam and Khadakwasla (India); Peshawar (Pakistan); Plymouth and Portsmouth (England); and Halifax and Nova Scotia (Canada) have been evolved as the defensive towns. In many garrison and defensive towns, naval dockyards and air bases, there is a clear-cut division of land use amid the civil and military authorities, so that the military installations are often at an interval from the town or are arranged in one part of the town. This is essential to maintain security, though usually many town people are contracted by the military. The city of Meerut and its cantonment, the city of Roorkee and its cantonment and similarly numerous other military and defensive towns have the civil and military components adjacent to each other. Army Headquarters have also evolved into traditional centres such as Aldershot in England and Butterworth in Germany.

Cultural Centre: There are various towns and cities around the world, almost in every country, which offer cultural functions predominantly. The Oxford and Cambridge cities in England are among the most suitable models of educational towns. In these towns, one may discover colleges, libraries, hostels, churches, playgrounds, parks and shopping centres. The environmental pollution in these towns is relatively insignificant. The cities of Harvard (USA), Heidelberg (Germany), Leiden (the Netherlands), and Aligarh, Varanasi, Pilani, Pantnagar and Roorkee (India) are also the good examples of the educational towns. There are many religious centres around the world. These religious towns may be the foundations of religious leaders (e.g. the Vatican City, Rome, the residence of Pope; or Lhasa, once the seat of the Dalai Lama of Tibet). These religious stations may be centres of pilgrimage, such as Jerusalem, Mecca, Medina, Karbala, Hardwar, Tripati, Balaji, Badrinath etc. In the towns where religion is an important function, many religious buildings, shops selling religious books, flowers and accommodation for pilgrims are witnessed. Such towns often perform subsidiary functions as tourist centres. The places of pilgrimage, such as Jerusalem, Mecca, Jagannath Puri, Varanasi etc. are respected as cultural towns. Many additional functions performed by the cities are health and recreation (Miami and Panaji), industrial (Pittsburgh and Jamshedpur), mining and quarrying (Broken Hill and Dhanbad) and transport (Singapore and Mughal Sarai). Furthermore, there are many towns which perform entertainment functions too such as Stratford-on-Avon, the birthplace of William Shakespeare (England), Hollywood (California) and Cannes (France).

Collection Centres: The mining towns, fishing ports and lumbering centres fall under the class of collection centres/towns where raw materials are obtained and may be refined to some extent. There are numerous metallic, non-metallic, precious stones and energy resources which are acquired from mines. The towns which assist these mines may be small settlements serving a distinct mine such as Zawar near Udaipur (Rajasthan), Bailadela (Madhya Pradesh) and Digboi (Assam). They may be large such as Raniganj, Hazaribagh (Bihar), Ipoh in the tin-rich Kinta valley of Malaysia, coal mining town of Kiruna in Swedan, Johannesburg in the midst of Witwatersrand gold fields of South Africa, Kuwait and Abadan in the oil-producing regions of Kuwait and Tehran, respectively. Such towns may have some industries related to the mineral mines, such as smelters, refineries and concentration plants. The shops in such towns sell mining equipment and special clothes needed for coal miners.

Fishing ports provide the ideal base for small boats which go to sea everyday or used by large vessels which stay at sea for days or weeks. Fishing ports are usually arranged around the harbour and have services and departments of landing, storing, cleaning, drying, packing and dispatching the fish, as well as canneries, fertilizer plants, fish meal plants or freezing plants too in some situations. In numerous fishing ports, other associated pursuits such as boat building, net making or repairing and fishing equipment are also found.

The foremost functions of lumbering towns are to collect and partly process the wood, and they often have saw mills. Some may also hold plants for making pulp and paper. The timber towns of Kathgodam (Uttrakhand), Kotdwar (Uttar Pradesh), Dimapur (Nagaland), Sabah (Malaysia), New Foundland and Grand Falls (Canada) are some examples of lumbering towns. Many forest-based towns recently are concerned not only with collecting the timber but also replacing it as conservation of forest become more and more important. Apart from the saw and paper mills, the lumbering towns have tree nurseries and research centres in addition to their previous function of log ponds and saw mills.

Production Centres: Urban places, town and cities in which some kind of manufacturing industry is a dominant function is identified as a production centre. The size and appearance of the town are influenced by the type of industry located there. For instance, Jamshedpur, Rourkela, Bhilai, Durgapur, Dhanbad and Bhadravati in India, Pittsburgh in the USA, Magnitogorsk in Russia and Birmingham in the UK are dominated by large steel plants. Such iron and steel producing towns are settled near the coal fields. In the manufacturing towns as the collection centres, transportation is very important for the transportion of raw materials and the finished goods. These days such towns are set up on channels of communication keeping mind accessibility factor. In Japan, there are such towns located between Tokyo and Osaka prefectures. In India, Rourkela, Bhilai, Dhanbad and Durgapur are also on the main routes of transportation and communication lines. In manufacturing towns, there is a segregation of houses and establishments; the officer quarters may be grouped at one place and that the labourers at the other. Birmingham (iron and steel) in England, Rochester and Detroit (iron and car manufacturing) in America and Ahmedabad and Surat (textile manufacturing) in India are some of the examples of manufacturing towns.

Transfer and Distribution Centres: The chief functions conducted at transfer centres are the trade, commerce and services. Towns which are concerned with the transfer and distribution of goods, however, have trade as their primary function. They include several types of towns such as market towns, sea ports and financial towns. Market towns are described by markets, a wide range of shops, stores, warehouses, godowns, cold storages and wholesale markets. Towns whose marketing functions are on a macro scale because they handle essential commodities in the world have the broad range of banks, insurance companies and other financial businesses. Kanpur, Ahmedabad, Vadodara, Indore, Bhopal, Patna, Lucknow, Ludhiana and Hapur in India, Norwich in England, Alexandria in Egypt, and Kumasi in Ghana from the world are the examples of such towns.

The most important trading and distribution centres are the ports. Moreover, most of the biggest cities in the world are seaports. Tokyo, Sao Paulo, New York, Shanghai, Mumbai, Los Angeles, Buenos Aires, Kolkata and Rio de Janeiro are all leading sea ports and have more than five million populations respectively. There are many popular inland ports on lakes and rivers including Kolkata on the Hooghly River, Hankow on Yangtze Kiang, St. Louis on the Mississippi, Baku on the bank of the Caspian Sea and Cleveland on Lake Erie. Apart from the infrastructure for trade, they have huge commercial sectors with shops, offices and financial institutions. The agricultural market towns such as Winnipeg and Kansas city; banking and financial centres like Frankfurt and Amsterdam; large inland centres like Manchester and St. Louis; and transport nodes such as Lahore, Baghdad and Agra are the examples of trading centres.

There is a high ratio of diversity in the functions performed by different ports. For example, there are general ports (Hamburg, Marseilles, Bandar Abbas, Karachi, Colombo, Malacca, Lobito etc.), passenger ports such as Kingston (Jamaica) and Jeddah (Saudi Arabia), outports (Hamburg Avon, London) and entrepot ports (Rotterdam, Aden, Singapore). The entrepot ports are characterized by large warehouse facilities and shipping and trading companies. In some of the towns, the predominant function is finance rather than trade or distribution of goods. Such towns comprise Frankfurt in Germany, Zurich in Switzerland, Amsterdam in the Netherlands, Beirut in Lebanon and Wall Street in New York. These towns and cities have stock markets, auction rooms, and numerous offices, financial houses, banks and commercial agencies.

Resorts: The urban places which serve to the recreation requirements of people are recognized as resorts or recreation towns. These urban places may be based on health-giving water (hot springs), seaside recreation, mountain climbing, cultural attractions, historical monuments, sport facilities, national parks and attractive scenery. Resorts and recreational towns have abundant hotels to accommodate visitors and also provide sporting facilities such as golf courses, swimming accessories, trekking and skiing. Moreover, they have numerous entertainment facilities, such as theatres, cinemas, nightclubs, magic shows and children parks. They also have a good assortment of buying facilities as most tourists like to purchase souvenirs, postcards, and clothing and stuff as an additional facility. Srinagar, Gulmarg, Pahalgam, Sonmarg (Kashmir), Shimla, Dalhousie, Manali (Himachal Pradesh), Mt. Abu (Rajasthan) and Darjeeling (West Bengal) are some of the examples of such towns in India. Moritz (Switzerland), Trieste. Padova (Italy), Gulu (Uganda), Wajir (Kenya), Murrie Mardan (Pakistan), Japanese (Wales), Aberdeen and Dundee (Scotland), and Samarkand, Bukhara and Khiva (Uzbekistan) are some of the examples of such towns around the world.

Residential Towns: In some towns, the chief function is clearly to house a concentration of population in sound way. In such areas, most of the land is devoted to houses, parks and hospitals. However large, increase in population is normally coordinated by some expansion of commercial activities. These towns are very well-connected with the major cities, which enables the commuters to get work each day. Shahdara, Sahibabad, Ghaziabad, Shakarpur, Ghazipur, Khichripur, Bahadurgarh, Sanpia, Gurgaon, Sohna and Badarpur are such towns situated around Delhi. In fact, the towns which come in this category are the suburbs and small towns and villages around the metropolitan cities. Kensington Palace in London, Avenue Montaigne in Paris, Fifth Avenue in New York, Ostozhenka in Moscow are some examples of residential location around the world.

Towns of Diversified Functions: As stated at the outset, towns are classified according to their major functions. The towns in which a large number of functions and activities are performed such as London, New York, Paris, Mumbai, Kolkata, Chennai etc. are difficult to put into the definite class and these towns are designated as diversified in functions. The town of Enschede was a famous textile centre of the Netherlands, close to the border of Germany. However, after the Second World War, textile industry declined and disappeared from this town. Now, the International Centre for Remote Sensing has been established, owing to which the city is developing again at a faster pace. Many towns have converted their sites in the past such as Delhi has shifted at several sites, i.e., Indraprastha, Surajkund, Mehrauli, Tughlakabad, Shahjahanabad, New Delhi etc. Sometimes great disasters like floods or earthquakes also lead to the shifting and rebuilding of towns such as San Francisco and California (USA), Tashkent (Uzbekistan), Aashikabad (Turkmenistan) and Agadir (Morocco) have been refurbished at new sites after the large earthquakes in recent history.

15.2.3 Classification Based on Population Size

It is an important criterion applied by the most of the nations to define urban areas. The lower and minimum limit of the population size for a settlement to be characterized as urban varies across the globe. It is 1,500 in Colombia, 2,000 in Argentina and Portugal, 2,500 in USA and Thailand, 5,000 in India and 30,000 in Japan. Besides this size of the population, the density of 400 persons per sq. km and share of non-agricultural workers are taken into consideration in India. Countries with the low density of population may choose a lower number as the cut-off compared to densely populated countries. In Denmark, Sweden and Finland, all places with a population size of 250 persons are proclaimed urban. The minimum population in the city of Iceland is 300 whereas, in Canada and Venezuela, it is 1,000 persons. The administrative structure is also a criterion for classifying a settlement as urban in some countries. In India, a settlement of any size is classed as urban, if it has a municipality, Cantonment Board or Notified Area Council. Likewise, in Latin American countries, such as Brazil and Bolivia, any administrative centre is considered urban irrespective of its population size. Thus, the definition of an urban centre is highly variable from one country to another country. To make the international data comparable, the United Nations (1958) recommended that the data on urban population should also be exhibited according to a standardized scale. Consequently, many of the countries have further classified their urban settlements into some categories by population size. By this recommendation of the United Nations, the Census of India also classifies the urban places into the six categories from class I to Class VI. By size, the towns can be arranged into urban market, town, city, metropolis and megalopolis etc. Settlements vary in size and functions from a small farmstead to a continuously built-up metropolis or conurbation performing complex socio-economic and administrative functions. Empirical studies have shown that settlements rarely grow up randomly, but there is a measurable degree of order in their sizes and spacing in the region. Contemporary cities continue to serve as market centres and in developed countries; geographers observe that market centres are designed in a regular pattern. The geographic concept of central place theory helps to describe the regular distribution of settlements and to explain why the regular distributions exist. Depending on the size and the services available and functions rendered, urban centres are designated as the town, city, million cities, conurbation, megalopolis are discussed below in detail (Fig. 15.2).

Town: The concept of 'town' can best be explained concerning 'village'. Population size is not the single criterion. Functional variations between towns and villages may not always be clear cut but specific functions such as manufacturing, retail and wholesale trade, and professional services exist in towns. A town consists of a place with a built-up area, defined boundaries, and local government that is larger than a village and generally smaller than a city.

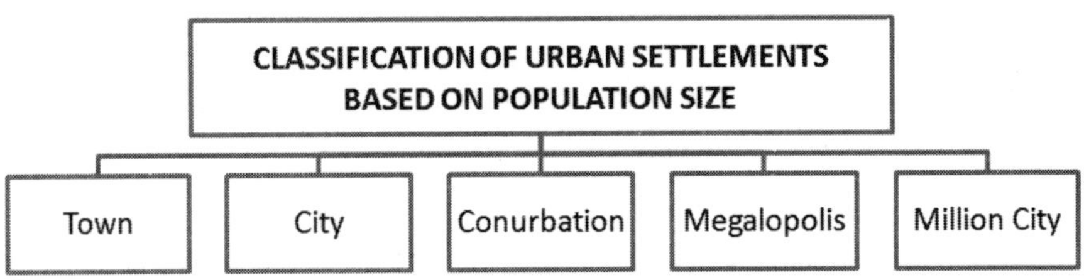

Fig. 15.2: Classification of Urban Settlements Based on Population Size

City: A city may be regarded as a leading town, which has surpassed its local or regional rivals. In the words of Lewis Mumford, "the city is, in fact, the physical form of the highest and most complex type of associative life." Cities are much larger than towns and have a larger number of economic functions. They tend to have transport terminals, major financial establishments and regional administrative offices. When the population crosses the one million mark, it is entitled as a million cities.

Conurbation: The term conurbation was invented by Patrick Geddes in 1915 in his book "Cities in evolution" and applied to a large area of urban development that resulted from the merging of originally separate towns or cities. The word conurbation originated from two words—continuous and urban area. It means continuous urban area and development. R.E. Dickinson has "Urban Tract" and Jean Gottman named it "Extended

City" or "Super Metropolitan Region" Greater London, Manchester, Chicago and Tokyo are examples of the conurbation. In real sense a conurbation is a region comprising a number of cities, large towns, and other urban areas that through population growth and physical expansion, have merged to form one continuous urban or industrially developed area. In most cases, a conurbation is a polycentric urbanized area, in which transportation has developed to link areas to create a single urban labour market or travel to work area.

Megalopolis: This Greek word meaning "great city", was popularised by Gottman (1957) and as the union of conurbations. Magalopolis is actually a large conurbation, where two or more large cities have sprawled outward to meet forming something larger than a metropolis and mega city. The urban landscape extending from Boston in the north to the south of Washington in USA is the best example of a megalopolis. A mega city or megalopolis is a general term for cities unitedly with their suburbs with a population of more than 10 million people. The New York was the first to attain the status of a mega city by 1950 with a total population of about 12.5 million. The number of mega cities is 25 now. The number of mega cities has progressed in the developing countries during the last 50 years vis-à-vis the developed countries.

Million City: These are the cities with at least a million habitants. These are different from megacities which are far larger and house at least 10 million people. The number of million cities in the world has been increasing as never before. As per the figures on population, London reached the million mark in 1800, followed by Paris in 1850, New York in 1860, and by 1950 there were around 80 such cities. The rate of increase in the number of million cities has been three-fold in every three decades around 160 in 1975 to around 438 in 2005. In India, according to Census of India (2011) there are 53 million cities.

15.2.4 Classification based on Location

The location for the development of urban settlement is highly significant. The location of urban centres with reference to function is also important criterion in urban geography. Earlier the locations of the urban settlements were based on the availability of water, building materials and fertile land. Today, while these considerations continue to be valid but modern technology performs a significant role in establishing urban settlements far beyond from the source of these materials (Fig. 15.3). For example, piped water can be provided to a distant settlement and building material can be transported from long distances. Apart from the site, the situation plays a significant role in the expansion of towns. The urban centres which are located close to an important trade route have experienced rapid development.

Cities on Trade Routes: The geographers, historians and economists are of the opinion that towns are the creation of the routes. As there is not even a single town in the world without roads leading to it. Some of the social scientists opine that towns are the exertion of traders. In their trades, they need to stay at night at a convenient point which leads to the development of small towns. Along with every route, there are numerous sites which have extraordinary advantages and infrastructure development. The stoppages along the main roads in the past were identified by inns and shops, around which sometimes developed the colony of artisans, carpenters and other servicemen. Such towns still may be found in the Sahara, South-West Asia, Central Asia, China, Mongolia, Rajasthan and Ladakh. Such towns, having inns, are placed at day-long journey intervals. Larger towns

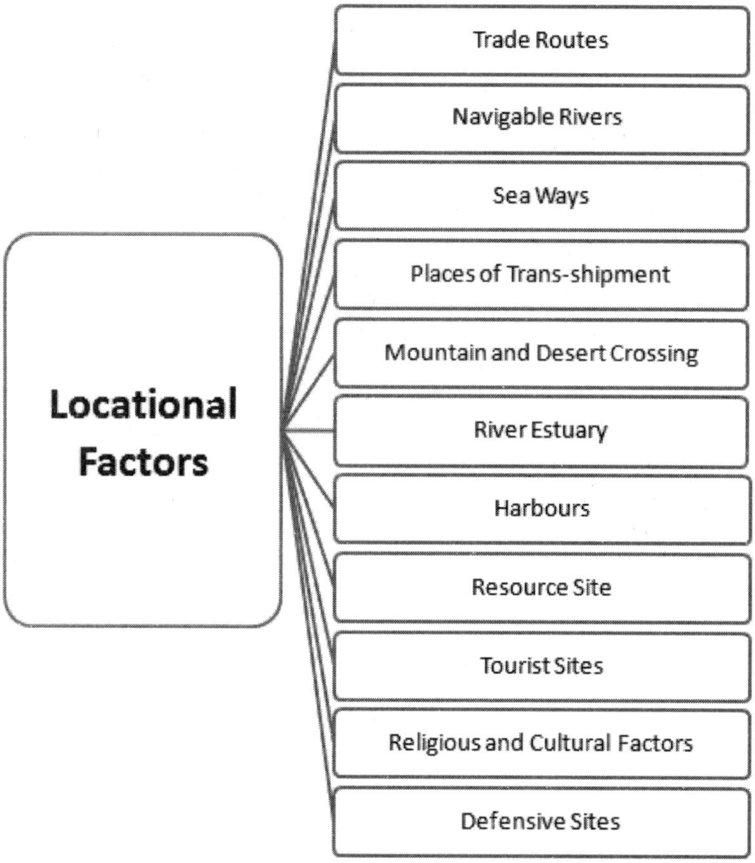

Fig. 15.3: Locational Factors Helping in the Development of Urban Settlements

such as Vienna, Milan, Damascus, Baghdad, Baku, Balkh, Bukhara, Samarkand, Jaipur, Jodhpur and Ajmer have developed at points where either mountain have come into contact with plains or where routes have converged in deserts near some source of water. The towns of Timbuktu (Mali, Africa Sokoto (Nigeria), Lanchow (China), Jarecho (Palestine), Jodhpur, Bikaner, Jaisalmer (India) are some of the examples which developed along the cross-roads in deserts.

Despite modern means of communications, the role of trade routes has become even more significant in the development of towns. Many modern towns have developed at huge railway junctions. The railway junctions of Mughalsarai (UP), Siliguri (West Bengal), Itarsi, Bina (Madhya Pradesh) and Tundla (UP) are the examples of such towns. The towns of Crewe, Stoke and Sweden in England; Memphis and Oklahoma in the USA; Orleans and Dijon in France; Oberhausen in Germany; Chelyabinsk and Omsk in Russia; and Wuhan and Karichow in China are the well-known examples of railway towns. Initially starting as a ideal location of tea-stalls, hotels and restaurants and houses of the railway employees, they acquired business and residential quarters and sometimes, industries and factories with workshops and workmen's lodging.

Cities on Navigable Rivers: The navigable rivers being known for their advatages also helped in the origin and development of towns. In the past, rivers had been the major routes of trade and many of them like Rhine, Volga, Danube etc., are still the busiest navigable rivers. Many towns have developed on the confluence of large rivers. In Europe, Mainz, Lyon, Ghent and Belgrade are the valid examples of such towns. In India, the cities of Allahabad, Patna, Monghyr and Bhagalpur are also the examples of towns which developed because of navigation and trade through the Ganga River. Some oasis towns in the deserts have the similar logic for germination because they are important steps on a desert journey. The traders and travellers must pass through them to obtain fresh supplies of water and food. The oasis of Samarkand, Bukhara, Medina, Kufra, Tumma, Hun (Libya), Beni Abbes, Al Saleb (Algeria), Mao (Chad) and Kidal (Mali) are some of the examples of such towns. The points where navigation ends also become as an ideal place for the origin of a town. At such points, cargoes are transferred from ship to train or trucks. In some areas, the occurrence of rapids and cataracts in the river course necessitate the portages and unloading. The cities of Buffalo and Cleveland in the USA, Lyon in France, and Hardwar, Sadiya, Dum Duma and Tezpur in India are the excellent examples of such towns.

Cities on Seaways: Seaways also afford sites favourable for the growth of towns. The ships converge at certain places along the sea coasts. The straits in this connection, offer ideal positions for the development of towns. It is interesting to note that all the straits have a large town, sometimes twin towns facing each other. Like the towns of Istanbul and Scutari (Turkey), Gibraltar (Spain) and Tangiers (Morocco) across the Strait of Gibraltar and Dover (England) and Calais (France) across the English Channel. The modern towns such as Ismailia and Suez on the Suez Canal and the Cristobal and Balboa on the Panama Canal are also the results of navigation and trade through the straits, rivers and canals. The town of Copenhagen at the entrance of Baltic Sea is another good example of a town situated along a strait. The cities of Aden, Singapore, Colombo and Hong Kong also developed because of their location on international trade routes.

Cities on Places of Transhipment: A town is likely to build along the points where goods have to be transferred from one type of vehicle to another. Along the sea coasts and river banks, towns develop where transhipment takes place. Many times the geographical conditions of a place impose a change in the means of transport. For a long time, break of the journey was necessary whenever a river had to be crossed, for bridges were not built in early times, especially over wide rivers. Crossing used to be made either by ferry or ford. Subsequently, the building of bridges began to facilitate the transhipment. The bridges provided a good opportunity for the traders of both the sides and towns started growing on both the ends of the bridges. Most big towns today are bridge towns. For example, London, Paris, Singapore, Vienna, Budapest, Orleans, Frankfurt, Narora, Srinagar, Hoshangabad, Surat and Howrah are some of the bridge towns. The towns of Cambridge and Bristol are also the examples of such towns.

Cities on Mountain and Desert Crossing: Mountain crossing by traders and travellers has also helped in the development of towns and cities in mountains. These mountain passes or gaps in ranges of hills channel lines of communication and are thus favourable situations for towns. At the foothills and near the mountain passes, the mode of transportation used to be changed. This is the point where wheeled vehicles can no longer penetrate, and further progress must be made on foot or by mule, donkey or horse. Peshawar, Karakoram, Kabul, Pathankot, Jammu, Kalka, Haldwani, Kotdwar, Siliguri, Dimapur in

India, Salt (Argentina), Santiago (Chile) and Coire or Chur (Switzerland) are few of the many examples of such towns. In some ways oasis towns in deserts have a similar reason for growth because they are necessary stages on a desert journey, traders and travellers must pass through them to obtain fresh supplies of food and water. This has resulted in a string of towns located on the desert fringe in many parts of the world. A similar transhipment from vehicle to camels sometimes occurs at the desert margins and is one reason for the existence of a line of towns along desert fringe in West Africa.

Cities on River Estuary: An estuary is a partially enclosed coastal body of brackish water with one or more rivers or streams flowing into it, and with a free connection to the open sea. Another site for commercial towns is ascertained where ocean shipping stops on an estuary and cargoes are shifted from the ship to an overland route. Aforementioned is a common type of town in Western Europe and in all countries in which river mouths are entered by the flood tide. London, Bordeaux, Hamburg, Baltimore and Philadelphia are some of the good examples of estuary towns.

Cities on Harbours: The position of harbours where seaways meet overland routes to the interior of the country favours the creation of towns. Aden, Gibralter, Hong Kong, Kolkata, Bombay, Madras, Alexandria, Rio de Janeiro, Melbourne, Sydney, Karachi and Tokyo are the examples of harbour towns. Apart from the trade routes, there are several favourable sites which help the development of towns.

Cities on Resource Site: The availability and utilization of resources also help in the development of towns. Many towns are established on the basis of exploitation of some specific resources. The most obvious examples of resource-based towns are the mining towns and fishing ports. There are sites having facilities of sports and the places having religious, administrative and cultural institutions. Some of the sites which have helped in the development of towns and cities have been illustrated in the next paragraphs. Mineral, precious metals and energy resources have helped in great deal in the development of towns. Many large towns had developed within a short period of time even in inhospitable regions, such as deserts, tundra, equatorial forests and undulating mountainous areas, when minerals such as gold, silver, copper and precious stones were found. The towns of Dawson City, Yellow Knife and Port Radium in Canada, Kalgoorlie and Koolgardie in Australian desert, and Norlisk on Yenisey river in Northern Siberia are some of the examples of such towns. Towns also grow up on sites where the more ordinary minerals such as iron ore, coal, asbestos, slate etc. are found. Minerals such as coal and iron ore are difficult to transport because of their weight and bulk, and thus coal fields, areas of iron ore deposits and that of other minerals become the urban and industrial regions. The towns of Raniganj, Jharia, and Daltonganj in India; Philadelphia and Baltimore in the USA; and Magnitogorsk, Donetz, Kuznet and Uralsk in Russia may be referred as examples of mineral towns. The hydro-electric power may not give rise to towns at the place of its generation. For example, the Bhakra Nangal Project is a huge source of hydel power, but not a single town has developed in its vicinity because from the centre of generation, the power that they produce is easily transported to more populous areas for use. The oil as resource too, is often transported by pipelines and tankers to distant refining centres.

Cities on Tourist Sites: Towns and cities also develop on attractive places where visitors, tourists and holiday-makers prefer to visit. These sites possess some advantages which act as pull factor and make it attractive to visitors and holiday makers. Hill stations in India (Shimla, Dalhousie, Manali, Darjeeling, Mussoorie, Nainital, Mt. Abu), Cameron in

Malaysia, and watering places having health-giving mineral springs, e.g. Bath in England, Baden in Germany, Sohna in Haryana and Pugga in Ladakh are some of the examples. Seaside resorts have also been considered as health-giving, and sea-bathing was taken as a cure from various skin diseases. Some of the best known seaside resorts are Nice and Cannes (South France), Miami in Florida (USA), Goa and Kollum beaches (India) and Bahamas beaches in West Indies islands. Moreover, mountain villages may grow into towns, or new towns may be built if the area is suitable for winter sports like ski and this has led to the development of many resorts in India, France, Switzerland, Japan, Italy and Australia. Klosters (Switzerland), Sapporo (Japan), Bariff (Canada), and Pahalgam, Gulmarg, Sonmarg, Leh and Manali (India) are some of the examples of such towns. Highlands also attract tourists who wish to climb and do trekking in the mountains. There are numerous people who prefer to enjoy the aesthetic beauty. Many tourists sincerely wish to view and enjoy the scenery in an area or visit places or buildings of historical or cultural interest. Such tourism rarely gives rise to new towns, but it does add new functions to the long-established towns. Most Asiatic, African and European capitals, such as New Delhi, Tehran, Ankara, Cairo, Baghdad, Beijing (Peking), Bangkok, Singapore, Kabul, Tashkent, London, Paris, Rome and Vienna are the places of great tourist interest, especially for those who are interested in the historical and cultural tourism.

Cities on Religious and Cultural Factors: Throughout the history, man has inner craving to satisfy his soul and attracted towards the holy and religious places and in doing so visit to the places of his cultural groups. For example, a shrine, a temple, a gurdwara or a church, built at the certain place which has religious significance, may become a centre of pilgrimage. A site may also be correlated with the life of a religious leader, e.g. Jerusalem, Vatican City (Italy), Mecca, Madina, Amritsar, Bodh-Gaya, Sarnath, Kedarnath, Badrinath, Hardwar, Dwarka, Pun, Tirupati and so on. The educational centres like universities and colleges may also lead to the development of towns and cities. The cities of Oxford and Cambridge in England, Harvard in the USA, Akademgorod (the science town) in Siberia, Trieste (Italy), and Aligarh, Pilani, Roorkee, Shantiniketan and Kharagpur (India) are some such examples. The choice of a site as the residence of a king, ruler or national leader may also cause town development because the administrative staff and traders will gather around the seat of power.

Cities on Defensive Sites: It is one of the most important factors responsible for the development of towns. The traders, businessmen and craftsmen need protection against the ravages of hostile armies and in times of trouble. Since defence was a major function of early towns, they were nearly always surrounded by strong walls, by water-filled moats or by other defensive works. Such defensive places led to the development of numerous towns. The defensive sites are of two main kinds. They are hill top sites and island sites. The Hill tops provide a convenient site to keep an eye on the enemies and are difficult to approach. There are numerous examples of such acropolis sites. Edinburgh, Athens, Ibadan (Nigeria), Chittorgarh, Amer (Jaipur), Gwalior and Jhansi (India) are the examples of hill top towns. Island is a piece of land surrounded by water on all sides. The sites surrounded by water are easy to defend because they are difficult to approach. There are many towns which developed either because of insular locations or swampy and marshy lands. The cities such as Hamburg, Paris, New York, Hong Kong, Singapore, Penang, Venice, Mumbai, Kolkata, Calicut, Cochin, Okha and Kandhla developed in the swampy lands of sea coasts, river banks etc. The towns may be built on promontories. There are some micro-geographical features which provide shelter from the tides and waves and help in the development of natural harbours, fishing towns and urban settlements. The fiord, lagoons, estuaries and straits between the main land and off-shore islands were often decided as the suitable places for the development of towns. The cities of Kolkata, Rangoon, Stockholm, Oslo, Riga and Rio de Janeiro are some of the examples of such towns.

15.3 Problems of Urban Settlements

People congregate to cities to avail the best of employment possibilities and civic amenities. Since most cities in developing countries are unplanned and creates severe congestion. The shortage of housing, vertical expansion and growth of slums are characteristic features of modern cities of developing countries. In many cities, an increasing proportion of the population lives in substandard housing, e.g. slums and squatter settlements. In most million-plus cities in India, one in four inhabitant's lives in illegal settlements and this is growing twice as fast as the rest of the cities. The settlements in developing countries suffer from various problems, such as an unsustainable concentration of population, congested housing and streets, lack of drinking water facilities. They also lack infrastructures such as electricity, sewage disposal, health and education facilities. Even in the Asia Pacific countries, around 60 per cent of the urban population lives in squatter settlements. The decreasing employment opportunities in the rural as well as smaller urban areas of the developing countries consistently push the population to the central places of urban areas. The enormous migrant population generates a pool of unskilled and semi-skilled labour force, which has already reached the saturation in urban areas. Cities in the developing countries suffer from several social ills like theft, crime etc. Insufficient financial resources fail to create adequate social infrastructure catering to the basic needs of the huge population. The available educational and health facilities remain beyond the reach of the urban poor. Health indices also present a gloomy picture in cities of developing countries. The lack of employment and education tends to aggravate the crime rates. Male selective migration to the urban areas distorts the sex ratio in these cities. The large urban population in developing countries not only uses but also disposes a huge quantity of water and all types of waste materials. Many cities of the developing countries even find it extremely difficult to provide the minimum required quantity of potable water and water for domestic and industrial uses. An improper sewerage system creates unhealthy conditions. Massive use of traditional fuel in the domestic as well as the industrial sector severely pollutes the air. The domestic and industrial wastes are either let into the general sewerages or dumped without proper treatment at unspecified locations. Both huge concrete structures erected to accommodates the population and industrial plants play a very conducive role in creating heat islands.

15.4 Summary

Cities, towns and rural settlements are linked through the movements of goods, resources, information and people. Urban and rural linkages and interdependence are of crucial importance for the sustainability of human settlements. As the growth of rural population has outpaced the generation of employment and economic opportunities and lead to increase in rural-to-urban migration particularly in the developing countries, which has put enormous pressure on urban infrastructure and services that are already under serious stress. It is urgent to eradicate rural poverty and to improve the quality of living conditions, as well as to create employment and educational opportunities in rural settlements. Full advantage must be taken off the complementary contributions and linkages of rural and urban areas by balancing their different economic, social and environmental requirements. The study of urban places has been central to several social sciences, including geography because of their importance in the distribution of population and the organization of production, distribution and exchange. The origin of urban places, their hierarchy, functions, morphology and demographic attributes have been summed up.

Review Questions

1. What do you mean by urban settlements? Classify the urban settlements on the basis of functions.
2. Describe the various types of urban settlements on the basis of location.
3. Give classification of urban settlements on the basis of size.

Analytical Questions

1. The changing transportation/communication technologies affected economic, social and cultural life of your city? Explain.
2. Name a city nearby your area. Characterize the city keeping in view the various stages of growth, its function, its population size, its site and situation.

Chapter 16
World Urbanization

16.1 Urbanization Process in World

Urbanization is no longer a phenomenon peculiar only to certain parts of the world rather it is a worldwide phenomenon. Urbanization is the process of becoming urban. At present, more than half of the world population lives in urban areas. In other words, it is the demographic process whereby a growing proportion of the population of a region or a country lives in urban areas. It is a feature of economically advancing nations, where it is transpiring at the much quicker rate than it did historically in the developed (Western) world. Urbanization is associated to industrialization. In general usage, urbanization is connected with the concentration of population in towns and cities. There are, however, three linked concepts which are correlated with urbanization. These include demographic phenomenon, structural change in society and urbanization as a behavioural process.

As a demographic phenomenon, urbanization is represented as a process involving the absolute and relative germination of towns and cities within defined areas (usually a country). This is usually represented as taking place in two stages. The first is an increasing proportion of the population is the resident of urban places and second is the proportion living in the particular places, increases. The end of the sequence is exhibited as an almost entirely urbanized society, with the large majority of its population living in a few large places. Combined with the demographic process is the structural change in the society, consequent upon the development of industrial capitalism. Cities are manifested in the foci of the exchange processes that are vital to the mode of production. With the latter, the search for productivity increases and led to the development of urban factories to reap the economies of scale, so that the benefits to be gained from the processes of concentration and centralization. The third concept linked with urbanization is that urbanization is the behavioural process. Urban areas, especially big cities, have been distinguished as hubs of social change, attitudes, values and behaviour patterns are transformed in the particular milieu of the urban place, characterized by its size, its density, and the heterogeneity of its occupants (urbanism) and then expanded to the rest of the population by manner of diffusion through the urban system.

In this expanded view of urbanization, the demographic component is shown as the dependent variable, the outcome of economic processes. It is the structural component that gives the driving force since it is the search for scale economies that leads to the need for cities in order of economic development to proceed. The secondary position in the model is the behavioural component with which social change introduced as a consequence of the creation of large cities. The three components interact, e.g. demographic growth stimulates structural change through multiplier effects, and behavioural changes attract immigrants, but the foundation of urbanization is economic change and, in circumstantial, the increase of large-scale production.

This model of urbanization has been questioned in contemporary times on some grounds, most of them relating to the primary role of the growth of factory production. First, it is denoted out that there were large cities in other parts of the world, notably Asia and Africa (Baghdad, Delhi, Lahore, Agra, Surat, Beijing, Shanghai, Damascus, Jakarta, Cairo, and Alexandria), long before the Industrial Revolution. Moreover, rapid demographic urbanization in the North-West Europe: city growth is not based on the factory alone (Taylor, 1986). Second, in many of the more advanced countries, demographic urbanization has halted, and the larger places are in decline. Late capitalism does not necessarily require the continued concentration of population. Third, in many of the less developed capitalist countries, the pace of demographic urbanization is far exceeding the pace of industrialization, and thus city growth is taking place without a central role for the factory. Demographic urbanization thus comes about for a variety of factors as part of the structuring of space within a social formation; there is no reason to assume that what is typical of one time and place is necessarily typical of others. This chapter deals with origin and growth of urbanization, trends and patters of at world and India level.

16.2 Origin and Growth of Urbanization

The process of urbanization in the world has the long history. Within the course of history, some periods have been favourable than others to the rise of urban centres. There are three aspects of urbanization. These are demographic, economic and psychological. The economic aspect is concerned with percentage of population engaged in tertiary activities. The psychological aspect can only be perceived and observed in the way of living of people. In the former aspects the data is difficult to obtain and for latter case it cannot be quantified and analyzed. Therefore, the growth pattern of the world urbanization is better studied here in terms of demographic aspect. The human population has lived a rural lifestyle through most part of the history. However, after urbanization started, the process of urbanization has undergone many dynamic changes. The industrial revolution has been the main factor in this change. The origin and growth of urbanization are described in the following paragraphs.

16.2.1 Ancient Period

The urban centres were founded during the pre-historic period when primitive man started domestication of plants and animals around 10 thousand years ago. In prehistoric and historic periods, numerous permanent settlements were instituted in Mesopotamia, Egypt, Greece, Indus Valley, China and Central America. The growth and origin of towns were made possible in the fertile valleys of river Nile, Tigris-Euphrates and Indus river valley. Along with it, the towns also developed and originated in Hwang Ho valley of East Asia, Aegean Island of South Europe, Greece Peninsula, Italy Peninsula, Coastal areas of Peru, countries of Isthmus and Mexico of Central America. In these areas, agrarian communities eventually gave rise to urban communities and urban centres. The excess production of food grains was perhaps, the main reason for the development of urbanization in prehistoric period. In these areas, the facilities of food, water and transport were available. All these facilities encouraged the man to live together at the suitable place and thus facilitated the evolution of towns. The prominent cities of the prehistoric period in the world are Ur and Babylon in Mesopotamia, Thebes and Alexandria in Egypt and Harappa and Mohenjo-Daro in India were prospered. In ancient times the increase in the number and size of urban centres occurred at the time of the two great colonizing periods of Greeks and Romans. As early as the seventh century BC there were several cities adjoining the Aegean Sea. The Greek movements derived its energy from the expansion of trade which promoted the growth of towns and cities. These towns were Cyrene, Neapolis, Alexandria, Salonica, Priene, Damascus etc. Various important Roman cities are Aosta, Turin, Autun, Mainz, Strasburg, Istanbul, Chester, Lincoln, Timgad etc. With the fall of Roman Empire, the organization and security were destroyed, and consequently, many cities were absconded throughout Western Europe.

16.2.2 Medieval Period

The medieval period in the world came into existence after the decline of Roman Empire and the end of this phase took place in the 15th century. The towns and cities in Europe re-emerged in the medieval period. During the medieval period, a whole swarm of little towns sprang up spontaneously which were normally placed under the protection of a feudal stronghold. Some medieval towns were also established during periods of colonization. After the eleventh century, the European countries gain the great increase in their overseas trade. Consequently, the West European countries were associated with trade and the merchants' travels which performed an important role in the revival of towns and cities. Thus, there was a sudden surge in urbanization. At the end of thirteenth century, Paris, London, Geneva, Milan, Venice, Amsterdam, Rotterdam, and Cologne were important cities of Europe. Some European cities kept their leading part as a Christian capital particularly in Italy, such as Venice, Geneva, Milan, Rome and Florence. The new towns grew up in the northern and southern America were emerged out due to administrative efforts are Tumbez, Vinague and Quito. Asia, Africa and European Russia also noted the emergence of new towns. Shanghai, Hwang Ho, Beijing also grew up this time. Moscow was the small settlement, but it became the capital of Russia. Baltimore and Novogrode towns also recorded a notable progress. Kyoto and Kamakuta towns in Japan came into existence at this time.

16.2.3 Modern Period

The modern period forms the third period in the history of urbanization. Since the age of discovery, the economic development of the world has steadily favoured the growth of urbanization and the strengthening of urban functions. Since the industrial revolution in the nineteenth century, the introduction of machine age with its large-scale industry has added to towns and cities in old countries an enormous flood of the population. "The swarming in all parts of the World of Europeans, imbued with urban civilization and natural founders of cities, has given birth to large numbers of new towns, first in North America, then throughout the southern hemisphere and more recently in Soviet Asia and the frozen regions of the north Canada and of Siberia (Perpillou, 1986).

In the Modern time, urban growth was provoked by the development of industry due to machinery and coal. Similarly, the improvement brought about by modern means of transport and communication and the appearance of various new trade routes have strengthened all trade centres and urban places. The modern trend of urbanization has profoundly transformed the structure of numerous countries of the world, though in varying degrees. In Europe and Anglo America, the districts in which there was an outburst of urbanization coincide with industrial areas. In the Twentieth century, some Asian countries and United Soviet States of Russia (USSR) have passed through an extraordinary spell of increase in the number and size of towns. Africa came latest in the field of urbanization but now undergoing an extraordinary development of new towns which are growing continually due to the regular influx of population. Before 1930, Africa had towns only on its coasts, but now it has some 50 towns with populations exceeding one lakh. Major cities in Africa are Cairo, Nairobi, Mombasa, Bulawayo, Duala, Abidian, Logos, Addis Ababa, Cape Town etc. Thus, in the modern age, the accelerating urbanization is resulting in a redistribution of population throughout the world. In general, every country of the world is experiencing an increasing proportion of urban to the total population after Second World War. The number of million cities is growing continually, and the oldest of them continue to become distended with new immigrants.

16.3 Trends of World Urbanization

The analysis of trends of urbanization in the world reflects not only demographic but also the economic and psychological aspects of change. The enormous increase in urban population is the incidence of post half of the twentieth century. The urbanization started with the beginning of the establishment of large industries and technological development. The urban population has recorded an increase of 252.5 million during 1800 and 1900 while the population recorded an addition of 2646.2 million during 1900 and 2000. The percentage of urban population in 19th century increase from 4.79 to 18.39 and in the 20th century the increase in urban population has shown an increase of 10 times from 18.39 to 47.00. After 1960, the tremendous increase in urban population was registered (Table 16.1). This high increase was made possible due to the great increase in the number of population of small and large size towns. The main reason behind this is the revolutionary change in the techniques and transport means and also the beginning of steel era. During the last

Table 16.1: Trend of Urban Population in the World

Year	*Total Population*	*Urban Population*	*Per cent*	*Growth Rate*
1800	906	43.40	4.79	-
1850	1171	100.80	8.60	26.45
1900	1608	295.80	18.39	39.00
1950	2510	716.70	28.55	28.46
1960	3027	961.40	31.76	34.14
1980	4415	1633.00	37.00	34.93
1990	5292	2382.00	45.01	45.87
2000	6260	2942.00	47.00	23.51

Source: UN Population Division, 2009-10.

four decades, developing countries have also noted an enormous increase in their urban population. This addition is more than the increase in urban population of developed countries. By this time Britain, Australia, USA and Canada have developed as the most urbanized nations of the world.

It is clear that the urban population in the world has shown the very high incidence of increase after 1960. This is basically due to the increasing attraction of people towards large size towns, the revolution in industrial and transport sector and unusual increase in urban population of developing countries. Because of all these factors, the urban population has progressed by more than two times during 1950 and 1980 in the world. In this period, an addition of 916 million populations is just equal to urban population in 1960. The growth rate of urban population has been diminished, and it is just half to that growth rate of 1990. It indicates that the rural population is also increasing with the urban population. The urban population has expanded at high pace after 1950 and at an exceptional pace after 1980. It will continue to progress further more with the time. It is very true that industrial and scientific revolution has left its influence on urbanization.

In 1991, about one-third of the Asia's and Africa's total population was urban, followed by Latin America (66 per cent) and Oceania (70 per cent) (Table 16.2). The urban population in Anglo-America (The USA and Canada) and Europe was 78 per cent and 75 per cent, respectively. In 2000, about 28 per cent of the Afro-Asian population was urban whereas in Latin America it was 68 per cent, in Europe 75 per cent and in North America over 80 per cent. It is expected and estimated that by 2025, about 57 per cent of the world population intend to be urban. By that time, about 50 per cent of the population in Asia and Africa shall be urban. The percentage of urban population in 2025 in Europe and Anglo-America would be about 90 per cent and 86 per cent respectively. This description, however, hides the fact that the Asian countries such as India, Indonesia, Philippines, South Korea, Pakistan, Bangladesh, Thailand and China have witnessed the growth of many mega cities in the meantime. The percentage of urban population in the developing countries is increasing at a much faster pace. Owing to this rapid growth of urban population, the world has witnessed to have over 50 per cent of the total world population as urban by 2010 A.D. The rapid urbanization in the recent past in developing countries and abundant migration from rural to urban areas will further enhance the proportion of urban population. No wonder, more people lived in urban areas of the less developed region of the world than in the urban areas of the more developed region. It is expected that by the year 2025 A.D., the urban dwellers of the present less developed realm would be more than double the urban dwellers of the present more developed realm.

Table 16.2: Continent-wise Urban Population

(In Per cent)

Continent	*1991*	*2000*	*2025**
1. World	43.0	50.0	57.0
2. Africa	34.0	38.5	49.6
3. Europe	75.2	75.0	90.0
4. Anglo-America	78.2	80.5	86.0
5. Latin-America	66.4	68.5	75.0
6. Asia	34.0	40.0	50.0
7. Oceania	70.4	72.5	75.3

*Projected Figures. *Source:* UN Population Division, 2009-10.

The world's urban population is currently growing at four times the rate of the rural population. Urbanization is rapid in the fast-growing economies of Asia-Pacific region, where the average annual urban growth rate is more than 4 per cent. The fastest urbanization rates are occurring in some of the least developed countries. Africa has the highest urban growth rate of all the world regions, i.e. 5 per cent per year. Nearly 50 per cent of the world population is living in urban places.

World population has grown exponentially in the 20th century from around 1.6 billion in 1900 to around 6.1 billion today, with each additional billion people being added more rapidly than the last century. The vast majority of this growth has occurred in the developing world. In 1950, just over one-half of the population of the developed world and just under one-third of the population of the entire world lived in urban areas (Table 16.3). At that time, there were only around 733 million people living in urban areas around the world and eighty-three cities in the world that could boast a million or more residents. Continued urbanization over the last 50 years has resulted in a situation whereby close to half of the world's population (47.1%) now live in urban areas. In absolute terms, the numbers of urban dwellers almost quadrupled between 1950 and 2000 going from 733 million to 2.857 billion. Especially over the last two decades, globalization driven by advances in transportation and telecommunications, and a positive political climate has created a global economy characterized by unprecedented levels of urbanization and more and bigger cities than ever before. Many cities, particularly those in East Asian countries that have enjoyed robust economic growth have grown spectacularly over the past 25 years, in some cases more than quadrupling in size. The more developed regions comprise Europe, North America, Australia/New Zealand, and Japan. The process of urbanization in developed countries has been very slow but steady and it has been accompanied by agricultural and industrial revolution. Developed nations have higher percentage of urban residents than less developed countries. However, urbanization is occurring rapidly in many less developed countries and it expected that most urban growth will occur in less developed countries during the times. The less developed regions comprise all regions of Africa, Asia (except Japan), Latin America and the Caribbean, plus Melanesia, Micronesia, and Polynesia.

Table 16.3: Urban Population Growth in Developed and Less Developed Regions

Region	*1950*	*1975*	*2000*	*2030*
World Total Population (millions)	2,519	4,068	6,071	8,130
More Developed Regions	813	1,047	1,194	1,242
Less Developed Regions	280	3,021	4,877	6,888
Percentage of Population Living in Urban Areas of World	29.1	37.3	47.1	60.8
More Developed Regions	52.5	67.2	73.9	81.7
Less Developed Regions	17.9	26.9	40.5	57.1
Distribution of the World's Urban Population				
More Developed Regions	58.3	46.4	30.9	20.5
Less Developed Regions	41.7	53.6	69.1	79.5

Source: World Urbanization Prospects, 2004.

Over the next 30 years (i.e. 2000-2030), the world's population is projected to grow at an annual rate of 1.8 per cent, or nearly double the rate expected for the total population of the world (almost one per cent per year). At this rate of growth, the world's urban population can be expected to double in 38 years. By 2030, demographers predict that around 61 per cent of the world's population will be living in urban areas, at which time the world's urban population will be approaching 5 billion. Compared against the rapid rise in the urban population, the growth of the world's rural population has been relatively slow (Fig. 16.1). While the world's urban population increased four-fold between 1950 and 2003, the world's rural population less than doubled going from 1.8 billion in 1950 to 3.2 billion in 2000. And while the world's urban population is expected to increase by almost 2 billion over the next 30 years, the world's rural population is actually expected to decline slightly falling from 3.3 billion in 2003 to 3.2 billion in 2030. Thus, all future population growth for the foreseeable future is expected to be absorbed in urban areas.

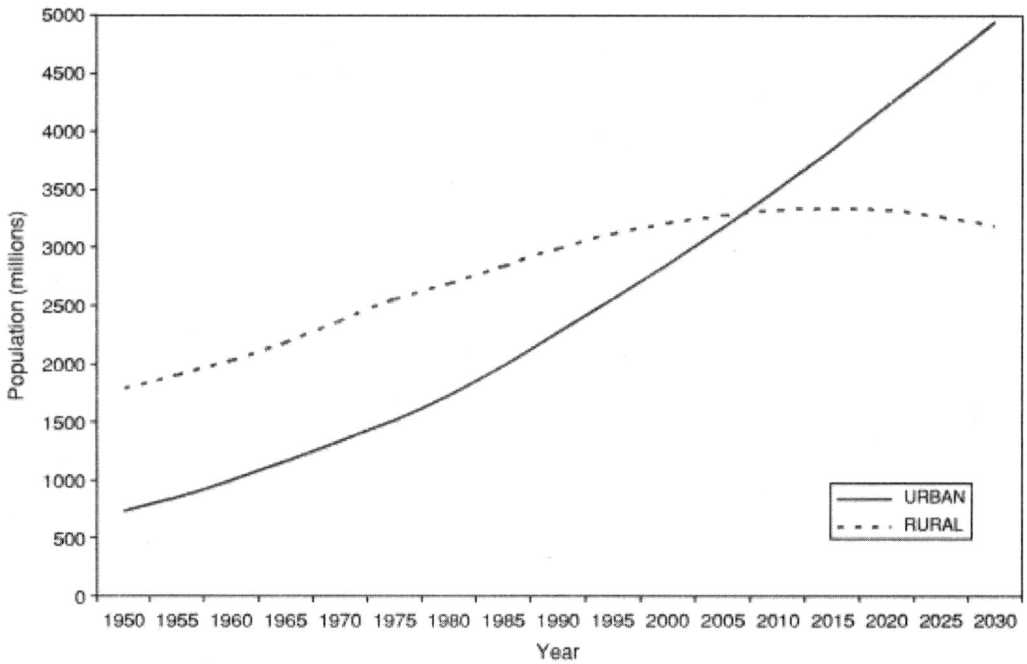

Fig. 16.1: Estimated and Projected Size of the World's Urban and Rural Populations, 1950-2030
Source: United Nations World Urbanization Prospects: The 2003 Revision.

Over the next 30 years, population growth in general and urban population growth in particular is expected to be particularly rapid in the developing world, averaging 2.3 per cent per year during 2000-30 (Fig. 16.1). Although much of the popular rhetoric on urbanization has left the impression that cities are currently growing too fast and that growth should be limited or somehow diverted, it is important not to lose sight of the fact that, for the most part, there is an economic logic to the pattern of urbanization (Hardoy *et al.*, 2001). In most cases, high growth rates are an indicator of success rather than failure and most of the world's largest cities are located in countries with the world's largest economies. Many cities in Pacific Asia, for example, have experienced dramatic economic growth, reflecting the fact that the region is completely integrated into the new global economy. Cities on the forefront of global restructuring such as Hong Kong, Singapore, Seoul, and Taipei have enjoyed unprecedented growth rates of more than 10 per cent per annum throughout the 1970s and early 1980s. All now rank among the top trading cities in the world and in fact, the level of gross national product (GNP) per capita in Hong Kong and Singapore exceeds that of many European countries. Urbanization and city growth are caused by a number of different factors including rural-urban migration, natural population increase, and annexation. Because rates of natural increase are generally slightly lower in urban than in rural areas, the principal reasons for rising levels of urbanization are rural-urban migration, the geographic expansion of urban areas through annexations, and the transformation and reclassification of rural villages into small urban settlements. The expansion of the metropolitan periphery can be caused both by the arrival of new migrants and by the sub-urbanization of the middle class out of the central city. The relative importance of each of these various causes of urbanization and suburbanization varies both within and between regions and countries.

16.4 Patterns of World Urbanization

There is an uneven distribution of the urban population in the world, and the disparities are increasing with the passage of time. This extremely general descriptive of urban trends and projections naturally masks considerable regional diversity. There are enormous differences in the pattern of urbanization between regions and even greater variation in the level and speed with which individual countries or indeed individual cities within regions are growing. Latin America, for example, is far more urbanized than Africa or Asia. The level of urbanization in Latin America—around 76 per cent—already matches that of North America as well as many European countries. Consequently, the rate of urbanization in Latin America is quite slow. Argentina, Brazil, Uruguay, Venezuela, and Chile, for example, are all well over 80 per cent urban while levels of urbanization are somewhat lower in most of Central America and the Caribbean. By variations in the degrees of urbanization, the world is categorized in four groups of low, medium, high and very high (Fig. 16.2). These categories are based on the percentage of urban population in the total population.

16.4.1 Less Urbanization

The countries in this group dominate agricultural activity. The agricultural practices are still unconventional and traditional with low industrial development. Poverty, unemployment is the main problems in these nations, which have led to the slow pace of urbanization. The nations these group has less than 25 per cent population living in urban areas. Mostly the countries are concentrated in Asia and Africa continents. In Asia, Afghanistan, Nepal, Bhutan, Bangladesh, Sri Lanka, Laos, Vietnam, Cambodia, Thailand etc. fall in this group. The low urbanized areas of Africa are Chad, Niger, west Sahara, Guinea Bissau, Ethiopia, Kenya, Uganda, Burundi, Rwanda, Malawi, Tanzania etc.

16.4.2 Medium Urbanization

These countries have the proportion of urban population between 25 to 50 per cent. They

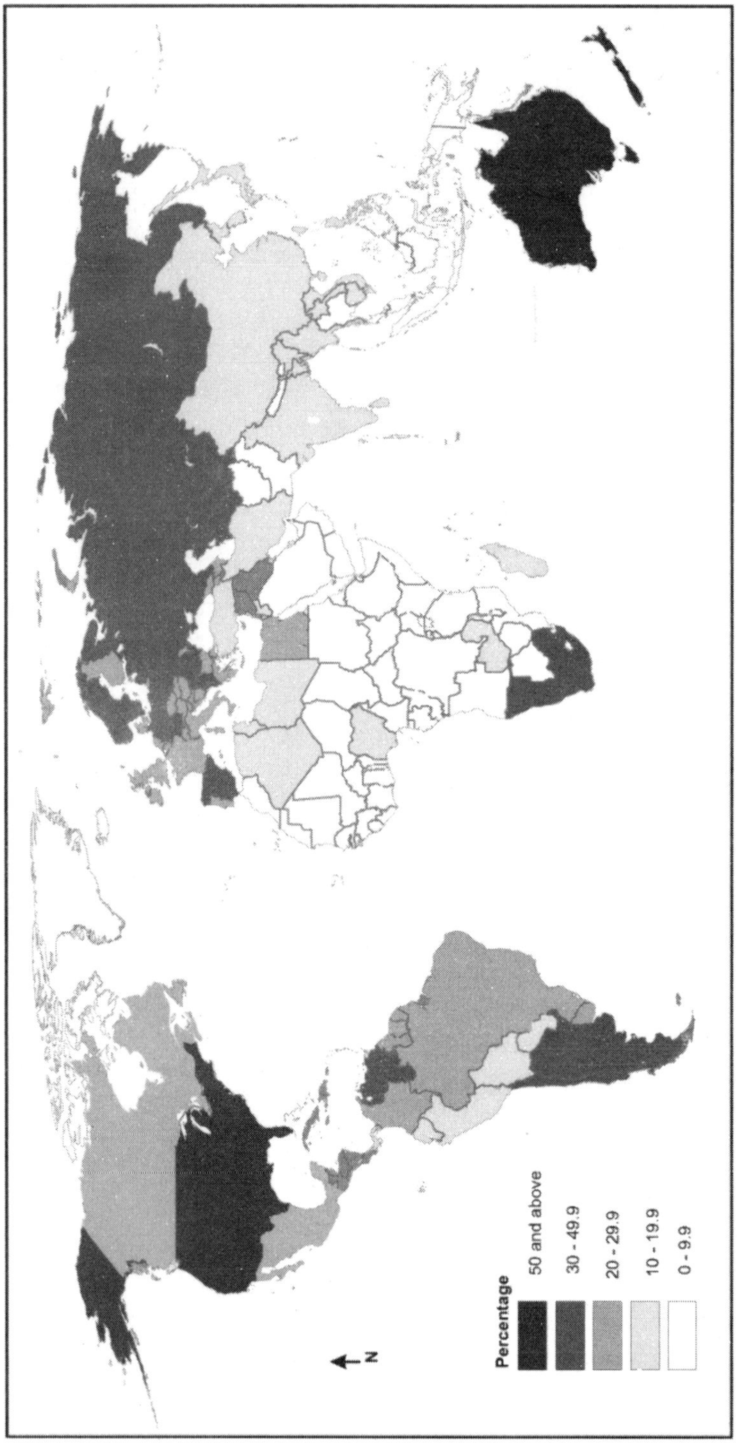

Fig. 16.2: Pattern of World Urbanization, 2009-10
Source: UN Population Division, 2009-10.

have touched the preliminary acceleration stage of urbanization. Though the economy of these nations is dominated by agriculture, here agriculture has attained the commercial status, along with the industrial economy. In this group, the nations of mineral-based industrial activities are also included where the economy is oil dominated. Many nations of Asia and Africa have medium urbanization because of desert climate and the production of mineral oil. Such nations are mainly distributed in South, East and South East Asia, Central and West Africa. Honduras, Costa Rica, Guatemala and El Salvador from Central America and Guyana, Surinam from South America have moderate urbanization. The countries from Africa falling in this group are Sudan, Mali, Ghana, Guinea, Togo, Benin, Somalia, Mozambique, Angola, Zaire, Namibia, Madagascar, Central Africa Republic etc. There are some areas like Egypt, Cameroon, Senegal, Liberia, Ivory Coast, Zambia etc. are about to jump up to from this category to high urbanization category due to the prosperity of minerals, plantation crops and coastal location. In Asian continent, the nations in this group are India, China, Indonesia, Pakistan, Maldives, Yemen etc. while Uzbekistan, Turkmenistan, Kirgizstan are rapidly proceeding towards high urbanization.

16.4.3 High Urbanization

Most of the nations are known for their industrial development in this category. In 1990, those developing countries, which made rapid industrial progress, are in this group. It includes areas which have the proportion of urban population between 50 to 75 per cent. These areas mainly belong to South America, North Africa and South Africa. In South America, Brazil, Peru, Bolivia, Venezuela, Chile, Argentina and Ecuador have the urban population of this proportion. These nations have experienced the high growth of large size towns, large size farms of agriculture and animal herding and their production is collected by distributers of nearby cities. There growth and activities have proliferated the urban development. These cities have emerged out as the hub of administrative, commercial and administrative functions. Mexico, Panama, Cuba, West Indies nations are also developed nations and have noted an increase in urban population. Paraguay, Peru, Bolivia, Ecuador, Columbia have developed high urbanized nations. In Central and South America, Sao Paulo, Mexico City, Buenos Aires and Rio de Janeiro have emerged out as the large urban agglomeration of the world. Libya, Tunisia, Algeria of Africa and Turkey, Kuwait, Iran, Mongolia, South Korea, North Korea of Asia is highly urbanized. The mineral-based industrial economy of these regions has encouraged urbanization. Most of the towns have their location along or near the sea coast. European nations have the domination of an urban population because of industrial development. France, Switzerland, Italy, Greece, Romania, Poland, Yugoslavia, Hungary, Bulgaria, Austria, Finland, Ireland, Czechoslovakia belong to this group.

16.4.4 Very High Urbanization

In this group, those nations are covered which have the urban population more than 75 per cent. The urbanization has reached the terminal stage in these nations. The proportion of urban population seems to be static or stagnant. USA, Canada, Britain, Spain, Germany, Holland, Belgium, Sweden, Norway, Denmark, Japan, Australia, New Zealand, and Israel are the nations falling in this regime. They have their economic, social, political, environmental development at the peak. Agriculture in these countries has fully mechanized and commercialized. Such system has reduced the population living in the villages and rural areas. The migration from rural to urban is not experienced in these areas. The urban population is scattered in decentralized manner. These nations have the concentration of urban population in some large size cities. New York, Tokyo, Los Angeles are urban agglomerations located in this group. In 2000, some nations joined this level of urbanization. They are Japan, Lebanon, Israel, Iraq, Saudi Arab, United Arab Emirates, Oman, Bahrain, Uruguay, Venezuela, Chili etc.

16.5 Urbanization in India

The history of urbanization in India is a story of spatial and temporal discontinuities. India is one of the nations in which signs of urbanization flourished as early as 3000 BC. The urban centres of Mohenjo-Daro and Harappa are the examples of prehistoric urbanization. During the ancient and medieval periods of Indian history, numerous towns and cities developed mainly because of social, economic, geo-political and cultural reasons. The earliest developments were restricted to western parts. In the early historical period, urbanization took place in Middle Ganga Plains and southern Indian Peninsula. The arrival of British and their occupancies of power through the East India Company led to the development of many cities and towns. Though some of the towns develop as industrial centres during the British period, they established trading centres to export the raw material from India to sell their finished products in the huge market of the sub-continent. The British also established many cantonments at the strategic points to administer the country. Although the process of urbanization recorded a steady growth after 1921, it got a quantum jump after independence. During the last 50 years, not only the old cities and towns expanded regarding size of the population, density and area, several hundred new towns have emerged and developed in the course. The urban population of India in 2001 far exceeded the total population of all the countries of world excepting China, Russia, USA and Indonesia. As discussed previously that there has been steady growth in the size and proportion of the urban population as well as the number of urban centres in India since independence. The number of urban centres and the level of urbanization and a rapid rise since 1951 are recorded.

16.5.1 Trend and Pattern of Urbanization in India

The urban growth and development in India has been through a prolonged and slow process of the progress of civilization and may be called cultural process. After a period of time when various dynasties and kingdoms were going through the process of establishments and downfall, the emergence of cities came into existence and called a political process. Lastly, in modern era the urbanization was mostly associated with industrialization and economic development and known as economic process. The Eleventh Five-Year Plan envisaged that urbanization should be seen as a positive factor in over-all development of nation as the urban sector contributes about 62 per cent of the GDP. There is also a growing realization that an ambitious goal of 9-10 per cent growth in GDP fundamentally depends upon a vibrant urban sector (Planning Commission, 2008). Urban population is considered to be an index of socio-economic development. The level of urbanization is measured regarding percentage of urban population to total population. The level of urbanization in India in 2001 was 28 per cent, which is quite low in comparison to developed countries. The total urban population has increased eleven-fold during the twentieth century. Enlargement of urban centres and emergence of new towns have played a significant role in the growth of urban population and urbanization in the country (Table 16.4). It is evident from the Table that the urban population is increasing steadily decade after decade. Still, the proportion of urban population in 2001 cannot be recognized as very high. The growth rate of urbanization has slowed down during last two decades, and by and large, India continues to be predominantly rural. It may also be remarked that the number of towns has been fluctuating from decade to decade. This is mainly due to the classification of towns of the previous census and addition of new towns. After 1961 Census, however, the number of towns has increased significantly. So far as the population of the country is concerned only 25.85 million lived in towns in 1901 and by 2001, it has increased by more than 285 million. At the time of the first census after independence in 1951, the population living in towns was 62.44 million. According to 1961 Census, however, the number has increased greatly. Despite a steady growth in the urban population in India, the annual rate of growth has declined from 3.83 per cent during 1971-1981 to 3.12 per cent during 1991-2001. In the decade of 1971-1981, the level of urbanization increased by 3.43 per cent. But in next decade, the increase in urban population has been only 3.12 per cent. This trend indicates urbanization in India has slowed down during the decade as compared to previous decades (Fig. 16.3).

Table 16.4: Trends of Urbanization in India, 1901-2011

Year	*Number of Towns and Urban Agglomerations*	*Urban Population (in Thousands)*
1901	1827	25,851.9
1911	1815	25,941.6
1921	1949	28,086.2
1931	2072	33,456.0
1941	2250	44,153.3
1951	2843	62,443.7
1961	2365	78,936.6
1971	2590	1,09,114
1981	3378	1,59,463
1991	4689	2,17,611
2001	5161	2,85,355
2011	7935	3,77,000

Source: Census of India, 2011.

According to the 2011 Census, the urban population had grown to 377 million showing a growth rate of 2.76 per cent per annum during 2001-2011. The level of urbanization in the country as a whole increased from 27.7 per cent in 2001 to 31.1 per cent in 2011—showing an increase of 3.3 percentage points during 2001-2011 compared to an increase of 2.1 percentage points during 1991-2001. It has been seen that the Indian economy has grown from about 6 per cent per annum during the 1990s to about 8 per cent during the first decade of the 2000s (Ahluwalia, 2011). This clearly reflects the power of economic growth in bringing about faster urbanization during 2001-2011 which constituted about 18 per cent of the total population. The average growth rate of the urban population was

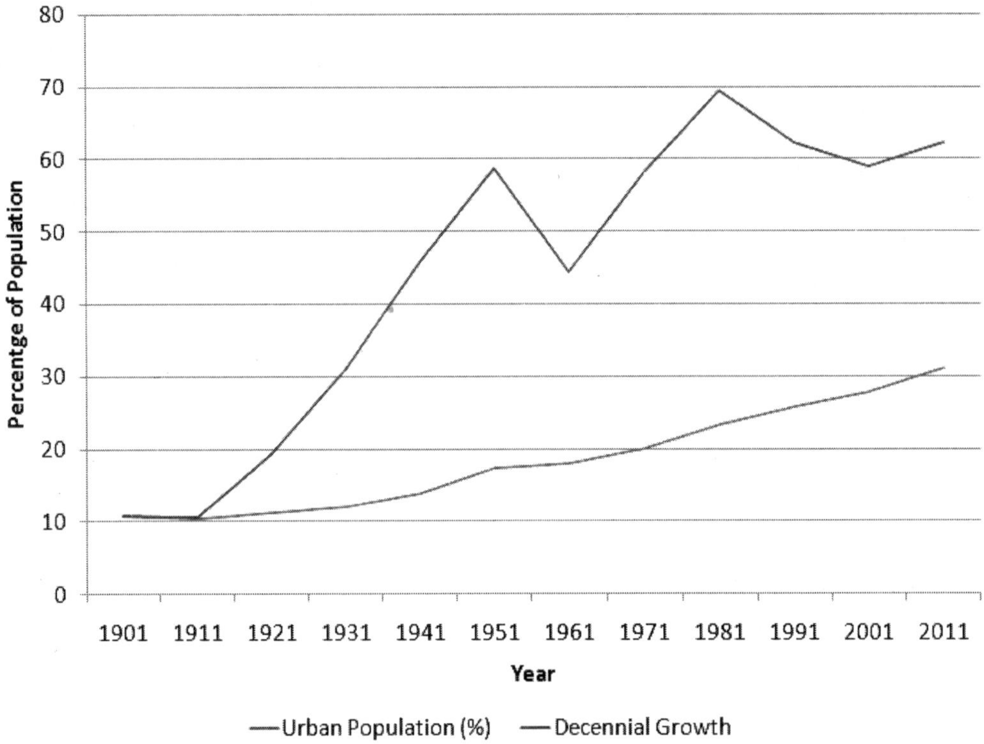

Fig. 16.3: Trends of Increase in Urban Population and its Decennial Growth in India, 1901-2011

2.32 per cent during 1951-61 which accelerated up to 3.79 per cent during 1971-1981. This was the highest urban growth since Independence. After 1981, the urban growth rate decelerated to 3.09 per cent during 1981-91 and further declined to 2.75 during 1991-2001. However, the declining growth rate was slightly reversed during 2001-2011.

It is worthwhile to note that urban population growth alone cannot speed up urbanization. More importantly, if urbanization has to occur, the urban population growth rate needs to be higher than the rural population growth rate. Thus, it is the urban-rural population growth differential that is critical to the process of urbanization. The natural increase, net rural-urban classification and rural-to-urban migration are components of urban population growth. An assessment of their relative contributions is very important to understand the dynamics of urban population growth. The available data from the 2011 Census at the moment does not allow for the separation of these two factors, but it does show the emergence of a large number of new towns in 2011. The number of towns at the national level increased from 5,161 to 7,935—a net addition of 2,774 towns (2,532 census towns and 242 statutory towns) in 2011 compared to the 2001 Census. As there has been no change in the definition of the urban between the 2001 and 2011 Censuses, this has contributed significantly to faster urbanization in spite of several metropolitan cities showing a huge decline in their growth rates (Kundu, 2011). On the other hand, the contribution of natural increases in urban population growth has declined from a peak of 62 per cent during 1981-91 to 44 per cent during 2001-2011. Yet the natural increase added a huge population of about 40 million in the urban areas during 2001-2011.

By level of urbanization, all the states and union territories are classified into three groups (Fig. 16.4). The pattern of urbanization is very diverse, but economically advanced states more or less show higher levels of urbanization. All the southern states, along with Punjab, Haryana, Gujarat, Maharashtra and West Bengal, have higher urbanization levels than the national average, but small states like Goa continue to top the list among states (62%), followed by Mizoram (51.5%). Among the major states, Tamil Nadu continues to be ahead of the others, with levels of urbanization at 48.4 per cent in 2011. States which lag behind are Himachal Pradesh at the bottom with a 10 per cent level of urbanization, followed

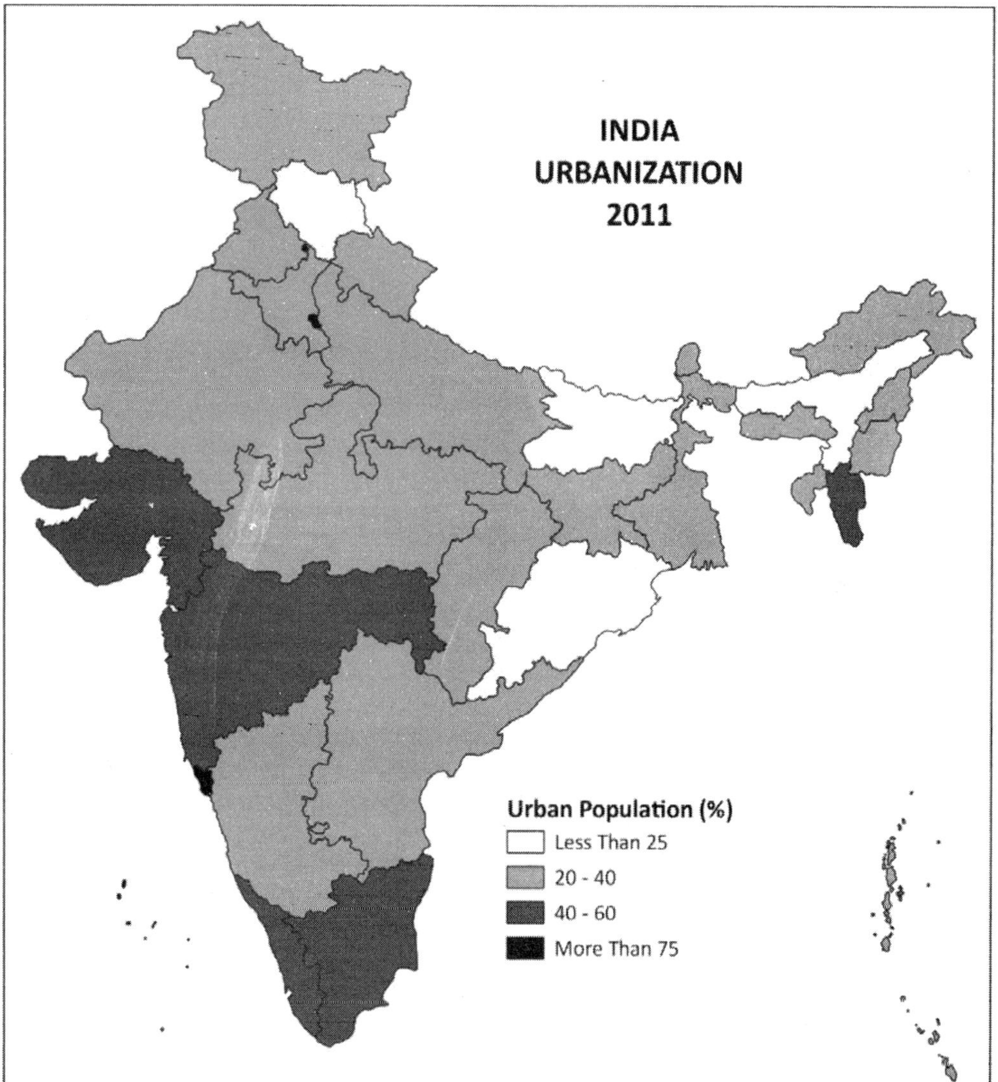

Fig. 16.4: Pattern of Urbanization in India
Source: Census of India, 2011.

by Bihar (11.3%), Assam (14%) and Odisha (16.6%). Other states like Uttar Pradesh, Rajasthan, Madhya Pradesh, Chhattisgarh and Jharkhand also continue to have lower levels of urbanization than the national average. Although the reversal in the declining trend in urban population growth rate at the national level is a major feature revealed by the 2011 Census, there are only 15 states and union territories which show an increased urban population growth rate during 2001-2011 compared to 1991-2001. Among them, Kerala, Andhra Pradesh, Karnataka, Gujarat, West Bengal, Bihar, Jharkhand, Chhattisgarh and Uttarakhand are the major states. A very high urban population growth has occurred in the states of Kerala and Andhra Pradesh; urban population growth rates have increased to 6.5 per cent per annum in Kerala and 3 per cent per annum in Andhra Pradesh during 2001-2011 compared to just about 1 per cent per annum during 1991-2001. In both Kerala and Andhra Pradesh, as well as in West Bengal and Gujarat, a large number of new towns have emerged as a result of rural-to-urban classification in 2011. The three categories are highly urbanized states, Medium urbanized states and less urbanized states. The highly urbanized regions are those regions which have more than 50 per cent of urban population. Three small political units of Delhi, Chandigarh and Puducherry are highly urbanized. Due to the small area and high concentration of urban population, the urban density in Delhi and Chandigarh is above 7,000 persons per square kilometre. Delhi is a national capital while Chandigarh is the Union Territory and capital of Punjab and Haryana. Lakshadweep, Daman and Diu, Goa and Mizoram are also small regions and are highly urbanized. The category of urbanization includes states and Union Territories of the country where urbanization ranges from 50 to 25 per cent is medium urbanized areas. The States and Union Territories of this group are Tamil Nadu, Kerala, Maharashtra, Gujarat, Karnataka, Punjab, Andaman and Nicobar Islands, Haryana, West Bengal, Andhra Pradesh, Manipur, Madhya Pradesh, Uttarakhand, Nagaland, Jammu and Kashmir and Tripura are falling in the moderate urbanization. The least or less urbanized regions of India are ones recording less than 25 per cent urban population. In this category, Sikkim, followed by Rajasthan and Jharkhand are stood high in urban population. The states like Uttar Pradesh, Arunachal Pradesh, Chhattisgarh and Meghalaya comes after the earlier ones in a concentration of urban population. Other states such as Odisha, Assam, Bihar and Himachal Pradesh record very low percentage of urban population.

The declining trend in the urban population growth rate observed during the 1980s and 1990s was reversed at the national level, and the level of urbanization increased faster during 2001-2011. The urban population grew from 286 million in 2001 to 377 million in 2011—an increment of 91 million, which is larger than the rural population increment of 90.5 million for the first time since Independence. A substantial increase in the urban population is due to a net rural-urban classification and rural-to-urban migration. A huge number of new towns emerged during the last decade, contributing significantly to the speeding up of urbanisation. On the other hand, although the contribution of the natural increase in urban growth has declined in terms of proportions, its share in absolute numbers (about 40 million) continues to be huge due to the large base of the urban population. This has implications not only for providing urban infrastructure and civic amenities, but also for reproductive and child health services in urban areas.

16.6 Problems of Urbanization

Urban centres throughout the world exhibit a far-fetched diversity of characteristics in terms of economic structures, levels of infrastructure, historic origins, patterns of growth, and degrees of formal planning. Yet, many of the tribulations that they face are strikingly familiar as cities grow, they become increasingly diverse. Every city has its relatively more wealthy and prosperous and relatively shoddier and poorer neighbourhoods. But in developing countries, shoddier neighbourhoods can have dramatically lower levels of basic services. Consequently, a large number of urban residents in developing countries suffer to a greater or lesser extent from severe environmental health challenges associated with insufficient access to clean drinking water, inadequate sewerage facilities, and insufficient solid waste disposal. A major recent United Nations report on the state of water and sanitation in the world's cities found that water distribution systems in many cities in the developing world are inadequate, typically serving the city's upper-and middle-class neighbourhoods but not rapidly expanding settlements on the urban fringe. Furthermore, the current data on the provision of water and sanitation in urban areas is very weak and the true situation is actually far worse than most international statistics suggest (UN-HABITAT, 2003). The large projected increase in the number of urban residents in the developing worldover in the next 20-30 years implies that municipal authorities responsible for these sectors face very serious challenges in the years ahead. In many cities, the scarcity of public water supplies forces many low-income urban residents to use other water sources such as private water vendors who charge many times more than the local public rate. Consequently, people in slums often must pay much more for lower quality water than other urban residents (Satterthwaite, 1997). The fundamental problems confronted by the developing countries are essentially due to demographic changes. The new migrants from rural areas are normally young males. The existing infrastructure of the city cannot usually cope with the influx of new migrants, and this leads to social problems. In most of the cities in these countries undergo from chronic housing shortages. This generates a proliferation of slums and squatter settlements. Central slums are usually in old, sub-standard buildings, which have been partitioned into tiny, cramped flats. Most newcomers originally move here in the search of work, but access to services is inadequate. There is a high prevalence of crime, suicide, drugs and alcohol. Rapid urbanization affects crime rates. Residents of different beliefs and behaviours are settled together abruptly do not have time to adjust or adapt to distinctive viewpoints, heading to violence. The government's incompetence to prevent comprehensive poverty induces an increase in burglary and other crimes. Frustration and alienation associated with a lower status, limited access to education, money and other resources push young people to join organized corruption and crime. These focal areas are usually nicknamed 'slums of despair.' Later, with more money and joined by the family, the early migrant may proceed to peripheral squatter settlements. Conditions here are fractionally better, but the huge informal settlements are a headache for the city authorities. It may take many years for the settlements to be provided with adequate water and electricity, education and healthcare. The self-built houses are often sub-standard with no regard for building codes and regulations. Cities in the developed world have social problems too, though they are more confined to inner city areas. Immigration is far less rapid, although still noticeable. Housing deficits are also less severe. Inner city areas are characterised by an increased incidence of single parents, elderly people and children in care. Death rates and infant mortality are higher, and life expectancy is lower while access to services is poorer than in outer suburbs. However, the scale of the problems is by no means as bad as in developing countries. The economic problems of developing countries include widespread under-employment and unemployment. The work in the informal sector is unregulated and poorly paid. The informal sector does not empower people to benefit from social security, making this support channel useless for the majority. The other significant problem facing by developed countries is decentralization. In recent years, companies have preferred sites away from the expensive city centres, in cheaper, more flexible out-of-town locations.

Improving public sanitation is another major urban environmental challenge that needs to be immediately addressed in virtually all cities in the developing world. Failure to collect garbage as well as inadequate waste management and recycling policies and practices mean that cities are being inundated in their own waste. In African cities, waste management has been described as "a monster that has aborted most efforts made by city authorities, state and federal governments and professionals alike" (Onibokun, 1999). As is the case of the water supply distribution network, sewerage systems are far better at meeting the needs of upper- and middle-class neighbourhoods than they are of servicing poorer neighbourhoods, particularly unregulated neighbourhoods on the urban periphery. A major environmental crisis is looming large as many developing countries as cities discharge ever increasing amounts of waste into the air or into freshwater bodies, threatening water quality and aquatic ecosystems. Biodiversity protects water and soil from contamination, stores and recycles nutrients, breaks down and absorbs pollutants and supports areas to recover faster from disasters. Biodiversity also provides people with medicine, food and air. Urbanization restricts our access to these resources. Water supplies are infected by bleaching of dangerous chemicals into the soil. In fact, water supply itself is a severe obstacle in numerous developing countries of the world. Water must be tapped from further at a much greater cost. The system of water delivery is also flawed. A quarter or more of water is lost as a consequence of leaking pipes and illegal 'tapping'. Illegal dumping of waste by the developed world has become a health hazard in most of the developing countries.

The extent that urban growth affects the local ecosystem can be controlled to some extent by high quality land management. Land is an essential ingredient in all urban growth, yet in most cities there have been virtually no effective measures to control land development. Although many cities have formulated master plans and guidelines too. These plans included guidelines on land development and the future direction of urban growth, rarely, if ever, have these plans been realized. Reasons for this include poor urban governance, poor critical assumptions, urban population projections underpinning these plans have often been extremely weak and the inability of plans to be adjusted and refined in the light of changing conditions, such as the invasion and settling of unused public space. Devising equitable land development policies remains one of the largest challenges facing planners and policy makers in many cities in the developing world.

Congestion in many large cities can also be extremely severe and air pollution is now a serious environmental concern in many cities of the world. Concentrations of carbon monoxide, lead, and suspended particulate matter in many large cities greatly exceed World Health Organization guidelines. Among the greatest environmental health concerns are exposure to fine particulate matter and to lead which contributes to learning disability in young children. A popular response to urban transportation congestion problems has been government investment in large-scale public transportation systems such as underground or overland metro systems. Less attention has been devoted to expanding and improving public bus networks, which tend to be overcrowded and poorly maintained. In many cities, private mini-bus companies have filled a hole in the market by providing low-cost urban transportation where standard bus routes have proved insufficient. Environmental problems are very much a hazard in the developing countries as in the developed world. Pollution is heavy—thick black—smog is universal in many countries as an outcome of too many cars, taxis and buses. The exhaust fumes from these vehicles blend into a toxic cocktail of gases. Suspended particulates in the air come from motor vehicle fuel combustion. Soot, dust, lead and smoke make up the particulates. They pose a severe threat to health. Lead alone can cause brain damage, learning disabilities and premature death in children. The World Health Organization asserted suspended particulate concentration should add up to less than 90 micrograms per cubic metre. The suspended particulate concentration soars over that estimation in cities with a population of 8 million or more. Respiratory problems particularly cardiovascular illness and lung cancer are becoming most common in people.

In some ways, the intricacies of the developing countries and the developed countries are very different. While governments in the developing world must try to increase the supply of services to satisfy the increasing population, those in the developed world must try to cope with economic slowdown due to decentralization and changing working patterns.

16.7 Summary

While urbanization levels and trends closely mirror global patterns of process of industrialization and economic development, this is still a remarkable transformation when compared with the situation at the beginning of the 20th Century, when only 13 per cent of the population lived in urban areas and there were just sixteen cities in the world that contained at least a million people. Presently, there are almost 400 cities around the world that contain more than a million residents and about seventy per cent of these are in less developed countries of the world. Rural and urban migration and the transformation of rural settlements into towns and cities have been important determinants of rapid urban growth but there has also been a general convergence in lifestyles in urban and rural areas as advances in transportation and telecommunication have caused distance and time to collapse. Urban functions are being spread over larger and larger geographic areas so that the traditional distinction between urban and rural areas is becoming increasingly redundant for many purposes. In a real sense, the contemporary urbanization is an outcome of last one hundred and fifty years. It has recorded rapid growth, and in some countries, it has reached a terminal state. It is clear that the urban population has a very high increase after 1950 and exceptional rise after 1980. It will continue to increase farther with the passage of time. It is very true that industrial and scientific revolution has left its influence on urbanization. Urbanization in India during ancient and medieval periods was associated with seats of administration, capitals and trading centres. After the advent of the Europeans in India, urbanization rate was expedited mainly because of the location and establishment of modern factories and industries. Southern India is more urbanized than Northern and Eastern India. This is because of the historical, socio-cultural and resource factors. The process of urbanization has gained momentum, and more people are migrating from rural to urban areas, but the quality of life in most of the urban places, especially in metropolitan and mega cities is declining. In case, adequate steps are not taken to prevent pollution and to improve quality of life by providing more social amenities, the life of the urban dwellers of India may become even more difficult which may be the cause of health hazards and catastrophes.

Review Questions

1. Describe the origin and growth of urbanization in the world.
2. Discuss the trends and patterns of urbanization in the world.
3. Elaborate the trends and patterns of urbanization in India.

Analytical Questions

1. Urbanization and rural-urban migration are two sides of a same coin. Explain taking examples of the city you are familiar with.
2. How does the vulnerability to climate change evolve with urbanization in the world?

PART 5

Population and Resources

Chapter 17
Concepts of Population-Resource Relationship

17.1 Introduction

Population is both a source of demand and pressure on resources. As the World Commission on Environment and Development (1987) noted, "the issue is not just numbers of people, but how those numbers relate to available resources. Thus, the population problem must be dealt with in part by efforts to eliminate poverty, in order to assure more equitable access to resources, and by education to improve human potential to manage these resources." Therefore, population and resources both are important for the development of a country. But, the ability of a country to absorb large increase in population depends upon a number of factors, including its size, endowment of resources, social structure and especially the stage reached in its economic development. Population growth and population density are always considered in relation to a nation's resources and economy. At the same time, we know that such resources are not easily measured or evaluated. Different societies and cultural groups have different needs, traditions, and aspirations. Different things in different regions can create different types of situation like under, over or ideal amount of population depending upon the availability of quality population, capacity to use resources and level of technology.

There are no simple indicator to measure the over, under and optimum population. Optimum population in one country may be overpopulation in another, depending on the level of economic development in the countries concerned. Similarly, changing social and economic conditions mean that optimum population today may be overpopulation tomorrow. Therefore, a single population size cannot be fixed to decide that this is optimum. The relationship keeps on changing according to time in a region. And also, the optimum population size varies in different countries according to the availability and the level of resource development. To understand the further relationship, it is important that the concept of under, over and optimum population are understood first. These are discussed below.

17.2 Carrying Capacity

17.2.1 Meaning and Definitions

The carrying capacity of land is defined as the number of people that a unit area of land can support in a given technological level and system of land use. Carrying Capacity is the number of people and the level of their activities which a region can sustain in perpetuity at an acceptable quality of life and without land deterioration. The concept of carrying capacity was developed in the agricultural and biological sciences to study and describe growth and dynamics of natural and domestic animal populations. Carrying capacity recognises that all habitats have a finite assimilative capacity. Theoretically, when this upper limit has been exceeded, a gradual environment decline will set in, ultimately producing adjustments to the population itself.

The carrying capacity is the population size that can live indefinitely using the resources available where that population lives. Take an example of an island on which a particular species of animals reside. As far as the food and water is available in sufficient quantity, the population of animals will grow and expand. But, when the population demand exceeds the limit of food and water supply, the decline in animal population starts. This limit is called the carrying capacity. Actually, carrying capacity is not fixed. It depends on several factors like demand, supply, growth rate etc. Further, in a drought year less food production would support fewer animals and in good years, it would support more animals. Therefore, it fluctuates in different situations also. It is also important to note that different geographic regions have a greater or smaller carrying capacity. Carrying capacity has often been the basis of policy formation in resource management. There are many attempts have been made to define carrying capacity; however, some definitions are given below.

According to Allan (1949), "the carrying capacity of an area is an estimate of the number of people that area will support in perpetuity, under a given system of land usage, without deterioration of land resources". Kaiser and Beadman (2002) defined carrying capacity as "the potential maximum production a species or population can maintain in relation to available resources." Clark (2003) in his *Dictionary of Geography* defined carrying capacity in several ways. According to him, carrying capacity is:

- The maximum biomass which an area can support for an indefinite period.
- The maximum number of species that an area can provide food for during the annual period of when conditions (e.g. of weather) are hostile.
- The maximum population of people of a given species for which an area can provide food.
- In agricultural scenario, the maximum number of grazing animals or the maximum amount of food crops that the land can support under a given level of management without suffering deterioration.

Blackie's *Dictionary of Geography* (2012) defines carrying capacity as the maximum number of 'users' that can be supported by a given resources or set of resources. For example, the greatest number of livestock that can be adequately fed on the output of a given area of pasture, the amount of plant life sustained in an ecosystem, the visitor capacity of a recreational area, or the number of vehicles that can move along a long without undue impedance.

Encyclopaedia Britannica defines carrying capacity as "the average population density or population size of a species below which its numbers tend to increase and above which its numbers tend to decrease because of shortages of resources. The carrying capacity is different for each species in a habitat because of that species' particular food, shelter, and social requirements."

UNEP (unknown) defines it as "the maximum number of individuals that, a given environment can support indefinitely, without detrimental effects to environmental state."

The above definitions, by and large, highlights that the carrying capacity is a kind of support which is provided by a region or area to its people, animals, or crops to a particular extent. If this extent is breached then the region experiences negative impacts like environmental degradation.

17.2.2 Types of Carrying Capacity

In recognition of the diverse nature of carrying capacity as a concept, a variety of types of carrying capacity have been identified. MacLeod and Cooper (2005) have specified four types of carrying capacity: physical, ecological, social, and economic. These are discussed below:

Physical Carrying Capacity: Physical carrying capacity is a measure of the spatial limit of an area. It is expressed as the number of units, an area can physically accommodate.

Ecological Carrying Capacity: At its simplest, this is a measure of the population that an ecosystem can sustain. In a recreational context, ecological carrying capacity can also be defined as the stress that an ecosystem can hold, in terms of changing visitor numbers or activities, before its ecological value is unacceptably affected.

Social Carrying Capacity: This is essentially a measure of crowding tolerance. It has been defined as the maximum visitor density at which recreationists still feel comfortable and uncrowded. In the absence of additional changes, beyond this density visitor numbers start to decline. The social carrying capacity can, however, be influenced by factors such as the recreational infrastructure, visitor attitudes, and socio-cultural norms.

Economic Carrying Capacity: This seeks to define the extent to which an area can be altered before the economic activities that occur in the area are affected adversely. Therefore, it attempts to measure changes in economic terms.

Assessment of carrying capacity is very difficult but it provides one of the most important tools for technical assessment of environmental, demographic, economic and social sustainability of a region. It is very much related with the ecological footprints (discussed in detail in Chapter 19). Figure 17.1 shows the number of Earths required to provide the resources used by humanity and to absorb their emissions for each year since 1960. This human demand is compared with the available supply: our one planet Earth. Human demand exceeds nature's supply from the 1980s onward, over-shooting it by some 20 per cent in 1999. To remain sustainable, the world in this scenario needs to lower its ecological footprint to a level below the carrying capacity of the global environment.

17.3 Under-Population

Under-population means that the size of the population is small when compared with the available resources of a country and given the level of existing technology. Also it is found in those regions where population is less than the availability of resources.

In other words, if the population of a country is below the optimum, i.e. below what it ought to be, then the country is said to be under-populated. Further, it can be stated that when the number of the people are insufficient to take the fullest possible advantage of the

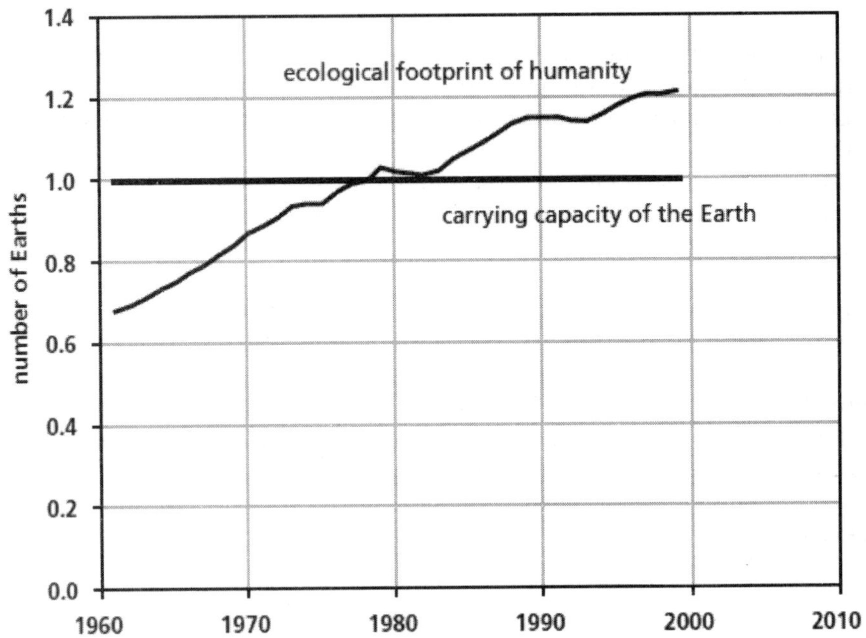

Fig. 17.1: Ecological Footprint *versus* Carrying Capacity
Source: Wackernagel and Rees, 1996.

natural and capital resources of the country, the region can be called as under-populated. Therefore, under population occurs when a population is too small to utilise its available resources, or where resources could support a larger population with no reduction in living standards. Examples of under-population are found in certain regions of low development, such as areas of subsistence agriculture and pastoral nomadism etc.

17.3.1 Characteristics of Under-Populated Areas

- In under-populated areas, resources are found in abundance as there is less population and technology which can make use of them.
- Due to the small size of population and abundance of resources, the employment opportunities are easily available.
- Low population also helps in reducing the pressure on social amenities in the region.
- Also, low population will create less or no pressure on services like housing, transport and other sectors.
- Small is always good, which leads to better planning of the region and decent standard of living of the citizens.

17.3.2 Negative Aspects Related to Under-Population

Besides many advantages, there are also many disadvantages of under-population. These are listed below:

- Due to less population, the available labour force is significantly inadequate to manage the abundant resources available in the region.
- Low population also results in low amount of production if it also lacks in required technology.
- Low production leads to less earning and consequently low saving and investments. Further, it leads to low standard of living of people.
- Low income per person and fewer numbers of people also affects the market size due to low demand.
- Finally, because of low output of goods and services, export of goods and services is also found to be low.

Therefore, under-population is both positive as well as negative for a country or region. It is good from social points of view but negative from economic point of view. Let's move towards the concept of over-population and see how it behaves in a area?

17.4 Overpopulation

Any area is overpopulated when the carrying capacity of that area is exceeded by its population. Simply, it means the area has more population than what it can support. Overpopulation exists where there is an excess of population over utilised or potential resources. It may result from an increase in population or a decline in resources. Therefore, it means, overpopulation occurs when resource development fails to keep pace with population growth. Advancement in technology over the years had led to increase in improved medical facilities for all. A direct impact of this has increased life expectancy which has contributed in increasing growth of population. In the past seven or eight decades or so, the growth of population has turned into overpopulation which was not the case in the past. Overpopulation is undesirable due to number of factors. For example, low mortality rate, better medical facilities, resource scarcity are few of the causes which result in overpopulation. As there is no measurement of overpopulation, it is simply characterised with low per capita income, high population density, low living standards, higher percentage of unemployment and outmigration. In extreme condition, the symptoms of overpopulation are famine, poverty, hunger, malnutrition etc. Some of the important factors are discussed below in detail.

17.4.1 Causes of Overpopulation

- Difference between birth rate and death rate is the root cause of overpopulation. The countries where there is a radical improvement in the medical facilities are experiencing rapid population growth. These countries have been able to control death rates of olds and new born childs due to which the population has increased rapidly. But the resources have not been developed in same proportion; consequently, the region has become overpopulated and unable to sustain the population.
- Better medical facilities and technological advancement were the biggest reasons

due to which balance between birth and death rates has permanently disturbed. Science was able to produce better means of producing food, which allowed families to feed more mouths. Medical science made many discoveries due to which they were able to control a range of diseases. Illnesses that had claimed thousands of lives till now were cured because of the invention of vaccines. Combining the increase in food supply with fewer means of mortality tipped the balance and became the starting point of overpopulation.

- Immigration is another cause of overpopulation in which many people prefer to move to developed areas where best facilities are available in terms of education, medical, security, employment etc. Thus, these people settle over the period and these places become overcrowded. It leads to more demand for food, clothes, energy and homes and gives rise to shortage of resources. Though the overall population remains the same, it just affects the density of population making that place simply overcrowded.
- Sometimes, psychology of people also contributes in making an area overpopulated. Lack of education and traditional mindset of people thinks that more hands, more money and less poverty. However, the reality is somewhat different. Families that have been through poverty, natural disasters or are simply in need of more hands to work, are also the major factors for overpopulation. As compared to earlier times, most of these extra children survive and consume resources that are not sufficient in nature.
- In most of the developing nations, large number of people who are illiterate, live below the poverty line and have little or no knowledge about family planning. Getting their children married at an early age increase the chances of producing more children. These people are also unable to understand the negative effects of overpopulation and this ignorance leads to severe economic and social crisis in their life.

17.4.2 Effects of Overpopulation

- The effects of overpopulation are quite severe. The most significant is the depletion of natural resources. As we know, that the Earth can only produce a limited amount of water and food, which is quite short of the current human needs. Most of the natural damage has been seen in the last 60-70 odd years just because of the growing population on the surface of the earth. Humans are cutting forests, degrading land, killing wildlife, causing pollution and creating a huge net of problems.
- Due to the overuse of natural resources, we are seeing some of the serious effects on our surrounding environment. Rise in the number of industries and transport network, both of them have badly affected the quality of air. Increase in CO_2 (Carbon dioxide) emissions leads to global warming. Melting of icecaps, changing climate, rise in sea level are some of the consequences that we have to face due to degradation of environment in near future.

17.5 Optimum Population

The optimum population can be defined as the size of population which the earth's carrying capacity can support and shall ensure the highest level of sustainable development in a region. The level of sustainable development here means that the relationship between man and nature is highly developed not at the cost of each other but in relation to each other. In other words, optimum population means the ideal number of the population that a country should have, considering its resources. The optimum means the best and the most desirable size of a country's population consistent with its resources. It is the right number. When a country's population is neither too big nor too small, but just that much which the country ought to have, it is called the optimum population.

At present many countries are experiencing manmade problems due to the disregard of environment. For example flood is no more a natural disaster, as it occures due to large scale deforestation to accomodate increasing population. Likewise, environment pollution is increasing day by day due to industrialization and urbanization. These problems are limiting the rapid economic development of a region. In tackling these anthropogenic problems, the pace of economic development gets hampered. Therefore, optimum population is one which makes a region more comfortable with respect to maximum resource development plus the suitable environment for the living conditions of the local.

Optimum population have been defined in several ways by different people. Cloud (1971) defined "optimum population as the one that lies within limits, large enough to realise the potentials of human creativity to achieve a life of high quality for all the inhabitants indefinitely, but not so large as to threaten dilution of quality or the potential to achieve it or the wise management of the ecosystem."

Knowles and Wareing (2011) have defined optimum population as "the size of population enabling maximum per capita output and the highest possible living standards under given economic and technological conditions."

Therefore, it is clear that given a certain amount of resources, technical knowledge and capital, there will be some definite size of the population at which real income of goods and services per capita will be the highest. This is the optimum size. The optimum number can, therefore, be defined as the one at which per capita income is the highest. Optimum population also refers to the size of a population that produces the best results according to chosen targets.

17.5.1 Features of Optimum Population

- In a country, having optimum size of population, the progress is very high. In a free society, more people mean more ideas. It also means more manpower to get work done.
- Better quality of life of the people is another important feature in the optimum size of population as it is capable of getting the maximum production as well as output. Better medical facilities, improved administration, social development are the positive sides in a optimum populated area.

17.6 Relationship Between Under, Over and Optimum Population

There are large number of resources by which much can be produced. But sometimes there are not enough people to carry out the work of production efficiently (known as state of under population). Under such conditions, population increase will add more people who can work and consequently there will be increase in the per capita output also. However, this increase cannot go on indefinitely. Further, when the shortage of man-power has been made up and the per capita income reaches to its maximum we can say that the optimum has been reached. If still population goes on increasing and the optimum is exceeded, then it is a state of overpopulation (Fig. 17.2). It means there are many people on the land. The resources will not be sufficient to provide gainful employment to all. They will be thinly spread over the teeming millions. Per capita income will diminish; the standard of living will fall; war, famine and diseases will be constant companions of such a people in the region.

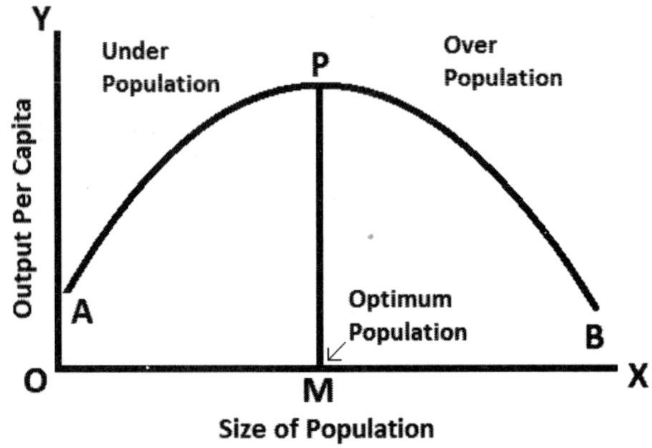

Fig. 17.2: Under, Optimum and Overpopulation

It is generally agreed that a small manageable increase in population is not objectionable in an expanding economy. However, it is clear that beyond a certain level, population increase may become excessive, so that the economy gets exhausted and problems associated with overpopulation such as poverty, malnutrition and starvation reach serious proportions. The problem lies in assessing when the optimum population for any given economy has been reached, or the point when population growth becomes excessive. Although, the determination of optimum population is difficult, it nevertheless seems clear that most of the developing countries have already passed this point. In a particular time, they were underpopulated, once the economic growth set in and medical facilities expanded, the balance (between resources and population) breached and the conflict between them has started. In this journey, what was the optimum population, they have not been able to understand and when they got understood, they were far ahead. Now, the challenge is to go back to that state which is optimum for them and sustainable for the future.

17.7 Population Pressure: Meaning and Definitions

Population issues in the present day world are considered vital because most of us believe that the development in an area was intimately related with its population growth. The problem of population pressure is quite visible in under-developed and developing countries. In simple words, it means that the region has excess population on its resource. This is due to the gap between population growth and means of economic production. It also means the gap in requirements and supply. As the gap widens, the existing means of production fails to support the ever increasing population. Ultimately, this leads to a stress on the sources of production. The stress is usually denoted by the term population pressure and means of production are resources.

Population pressure explains the relationships between the population and resources of an area particularly its capacity to produce food. Where the pressure of population on resources is great, then a situation of overpopulation may well exist. Population pressure has been defined in several ways. Some of the interpretations are given below.

Tauber (1970) defined population pressure as the slackening of the equilibrium between population and resources due to mounting strain of population. According to Clarke (1970) population pressure is caused by the imbalance between human numbers and their needs, and between physical and human resources of an area. Bernard (1977) defined population pressure as "it is a long-term process of deteriorating physical and human conditions occurring at many scales as a result of excess numbers of human and/or animals in relation to the ability of the land to support them." Mabogunge (1970) suggested that pressure of population should be conceived as a result of interaction between three variables—the land (resources), the people and the expectations. Based on above definitions, it is clear that population pressure creates long-term stress on a society's resources. It results in depletion of natural resources. The rapidly growing pressure requires equally rapid increase in food production. Since, the possibilities of extending the circumference of agricultural land any further are extremely limited, the only hope lies in increasing the yield per acre which will affect carrying capacity of land. The population pressure effects in several ways. Some of the impacts are explained below.

17.7.1 Consequences of Population Pressure

A large population has many effects which can be categorised in the socio-economic and environmental category.

Population Pressure and Environment: Growing population and the resultant human activity have started straining the environment (Fig. 17.3) to the extent that it can no longer recover quickly enough to be able to support the growing billions. It seems that in times to come, it is not the lack of food but the environmental degradation which is going to set the limits to growth. Certain natural resources may get depleted and the mankind may fail to develop the substitute for the same. For instance, take the case of petroleum oil, its reserves are too finite and there is no worthwhile substitute in sight as yet. The environmental issues are mainly the product of man's effort to feed and raise the standard of living of the rapidly growing population.

Population Pressure and Quality of Life: Economic development is generally measured in terms of growth in average per capita incomes and more appropriately in terms of rise in income levels, i.e., an increase in amounts of goods and services that one can actually buy. Thus, one of the important aspects of development is that improving quality of life. But increasing pressure of population will definitely taken affect this as the resources are continuously degraded and exhausted. Their benefits are now limited. For example, the people in urban area with better quality of life but are also facing lots of health issues due to air pollution.

Population Pressure and Use/Abuse of Resources: Growing population and quest for improvement in living standards together have necessitated continuous economic

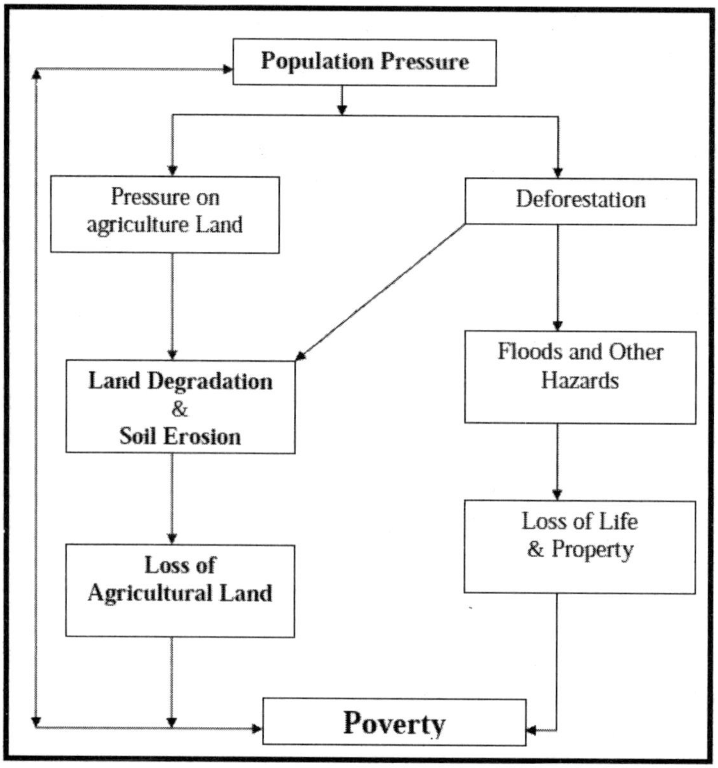

Fig. 17.3: Population Pressure, Environmental Problems and Poverty

development and hence greater and exploitative use of resources which at times could be called abuse of resources. Due to growing population pressure, the World has witnessed increasing abuse of resources specifically during last hundred years or so. For example, due to growing pressure of population since the beginning of 20th century, over 9 million hectares of forest land has been cleared for agriculture; the energy consumption in the world has increased 80 fold; the manufacturing activity has increased 100 fold; the withdrawal of groundwater has increased by more than 100 sq. km; the environmental pollution caused by industrial activity has increased significantly increasing the amount of methane in the atmosphere by 100 per cent, that of carbon dioxide by 25 per cent etc.

Thus, the population pressure increases, the human activities multiply, the amount of energy consumption increases, mountains of waste get generated, large amount of pollutants get emitted into the atmosphere and hydrosphere as by products of both manufacturing and agricultural activities. Thus, the increasing resource consumption and environmental degradation are the two basic issues of population-environment relationship which pose a great challenge for the development.

17.8 Summary

The relationship between all three (under, optimum, and overpopulation) is very sensitive. It is very difficult to remain in optimum size or in balance. All the three stages have their own positives and negatives. As said in the introduction, that in the changing social and economic conditions the optimum population of today may be overpopulation for tomorrow or under population of today might be optimum for future. Therefore, it is very difficult to predict the optimum size of population for any region or area. Further, I would say that the quantity of human resource (population) is not a problem but its quality is a major problem. If any country has less number of people, but they are well educated, highly skilled and equipped with modern technology can prove themselves a better population in terms of quantity as well as quality. However, if a country has huge human resource but of no quality, it is a problem while but if it has quality, then this size can also be termed as optimum. Therefore, the focus of the population policies should be at making the quality human resource instead of just human beings.

Review Questions

1. Define carrying capacity. Discuss its various types.
2. Differentiate between under-population and over-population and discuss their various impacts.
3. Define the concept of optimum population and analyze its benefits.
4. Critically evaluate the relationship between under, over and optimum population.
5. What do you mean by population pressure? Discuss the various impacts of population pressure.

Analytical Questions

1. Give an example why a country should be concerned about its national population being too small.
2. How you place your district/province/area under populated, over-populated or optimally populated? Discuss.

Chapter 18
Population Regions and Policies

18.1 Introduction

Geographers identify regions based on various physical, socio-cultural and economic characteristics. Physical regions, climatic regions, rainfall regions, soil regions, biotic regions are some of the examples of physical regions, while population regions, linguistic regions, industrial regions, agricultural regions, trade and commerce regions are the examples of socio-cultural and economic regions. Various attempts have been made to demarcate these types of regions (Whittlesey, 1936; Thorner, 1957; Spate, 1954; Karan and Jenkins, 1959; Sengupta and Sdasyuk, 1968; Singh, 1971; Sopher, 1980). In the same series, an attempt was also made by Ackerman (1967) to identify regions based on population, resources and level of technology in the world. These three indicators or components play significant role in any country's economic development. The natural and human resources are the base for the developmental process in which the technological advancement works as wheels of progress. A small description about these is given below and then details about the population-resource regions by Ackerman.

18.2 Natural Resources

Natural resources are the free gifts of nature and form one of the primary wealth to a country's economy. The natural resources play a very important role in the development of national and regional economy. These resources are not distributed equally and the different countries are cursed by the uneven distribution of natural resources and spatial variations in their development. But at present human community is facing many problems mainly due to lack of required amount of commodities and natural resources which are vital for the economic, social and cultural development. According to Hiremath (2007) at present, the scarcity of natural resources is felt more in the developing nations due to following reasons:

- First, mainly due to the exploitation by the colonial rulers in the past,
- Secondly, huge population, without proper knowledge of the natural resources, has also contributed to some extent.
- Thirdly, the enthusiasm of the government for a faster industrial and economic development has also caused great loss to the quality and quantity of natural resources.

- Fourthly, the ever growing population and its requirement of resources for survival have increased the pressure on natural resources.

The massive quantitative expansion in population size and concomitant pressure on natural resources along with lesser awareness of our natural wealth have resulted into loss of arable lands, disappearance of forests, land degradation, energy crisis, pollution hazards, regional water shortage and deterioration of water quality. Such consequential trends are blighting our natural resources and decreasing its productive potential for current and future generation.

18.3 Human Resource

Population is a major source of human development. But, again, its quantity and quality matters. Population growth affects environment primarily through the use of natural resources. With an increase in population there is more requirements of food and other facilities. Hence, more land is brought under cultivation. For which technological development becomes necessity. The technological development leads to several problems related to resource degradation, environmental change, disasters etc. As argued earlier, that it is very difficult to predict the optimum size of population for any region or area, therefore, the focus should be more on the quality aspects of the population.

The studies related to relationship between population and resources are of greater significance because of 'the realization that the continued explosive population growth was keeping the world in a state of unending crisis. The existing imbalance between population and resources is a question for the future development programmes. The developed world with 25 per cent of the world's population enjoys about 85 per cent share in the world resources, while the less developed world has only 15 per cent of the world resources but has to support as much as 75 per cent of the world's population. Therefore, the relationship tries to make us understand that level of technological development has played a significant role in increasing the resources for the developed world. Looking at the status of population, resources availability and technological advancement, Ackerman developed a scheme and divided the whole world into different population-resource regions. But, before discussing these regions, let's try to know him first.

18.4 Population-Resource Regions of the World

The work of Ackerman (1967) with respect to population-resource regions is quite significant. Three criteria were considered to get the picture of the world based on population-resource ratio by Ackerman. It includes factors related to population, resource and technology. Among these three variables, the quality of available technology is the most critical. According to him, the developed and developing countries of the world may be divided roughly into four types: technology-source areas with high population-resource ratios; technology-source regions with low population-resource ratios; technology-deficient areas with high population-resource ratios; technology-deficient areas with low population-resource ratios; and the arctic-desert type, technology-deficient and with few potential food-producing resources.

The most critical problem of production is that of increasing food supply at the same or a greater rate than the increase in population. Technology must play a key role in any plans to increase food production. There is doubt that improvement of food production can keep pace with population increase. Either a marked acceleration of the flow of technology or a marked reduction in population increase will be needed to avoid a world food crisis within this century. Over the longer run, limits exist for the number of people and the level of living that they can enjoy. The future adequacy of resources and technology will depend as much upon ethical choices and political decisions as on science and engineering. Based on this, a five-fold classification of the world has been done in the form of population-resource regions on the basis of population resource ratios and the availability of technology, discussed below.

18.4.1 United States Type

About one-sixth of the world's people live in technology-source areas with low population-resource ratios. Much of it lives in North America, Australia and New Zealand and in erstwhile Soviet Union. The population of these regions is not very large with respect to all the countries in the world. In terms of resources, they are well-stocked with known potential resources. The society is very much equipped with modern means of technology. With their extensive territories, these countries have access to vast natural resources. The countries included United States, Canada, Russia, Australia, New Zealand and Argentina (Fig. 18.1).

18.4.2 European Type

One-sixth live in resource and technology rich areas with high population-resource ratio. Here, industrialization and technology have permitted an expansion of resources through international trade. Most of the European countries and Japan fall in this category. These regions are elite regions as they are small in size and the resources are limited. The prosperity depends upon the degree of international exchange of skill, technology and goods etc. The countries included in this group belong to Europe like France, Germany, Britain, Switzerland, Austria, The Netherlands, Belgium etc. Japan and Israel are also in this category from Asia (Fig. 18.1).

18.4.3 Egyptian Type

Roughly one-half of the world population live in areas which are technology-deficient with high population/resource ratios, as in India, Pakistan and China. This type characterized with some of the most severe population problems. Therefore, these regions suffer from great imbalance of population and resources. The technology is yet to be advanced. The resource development is less. The living standard is poor. These countries are located in Africa (Egypt, Tunisia, Morocco etc.), Asia (India, China, Bangladesh, Pakistan, Nepal, Sri Lanka, Cyprus, Afghanistan etc.), and Europe (Albania, Greece, Yugoslavia etc.).

18.4.4 Brazilian Type

One sixth live in technology-deficient areas with low population/resource ratios, as in much of Latin America, Africa and South-East Asia. Here, resources, sometimes, remain unused

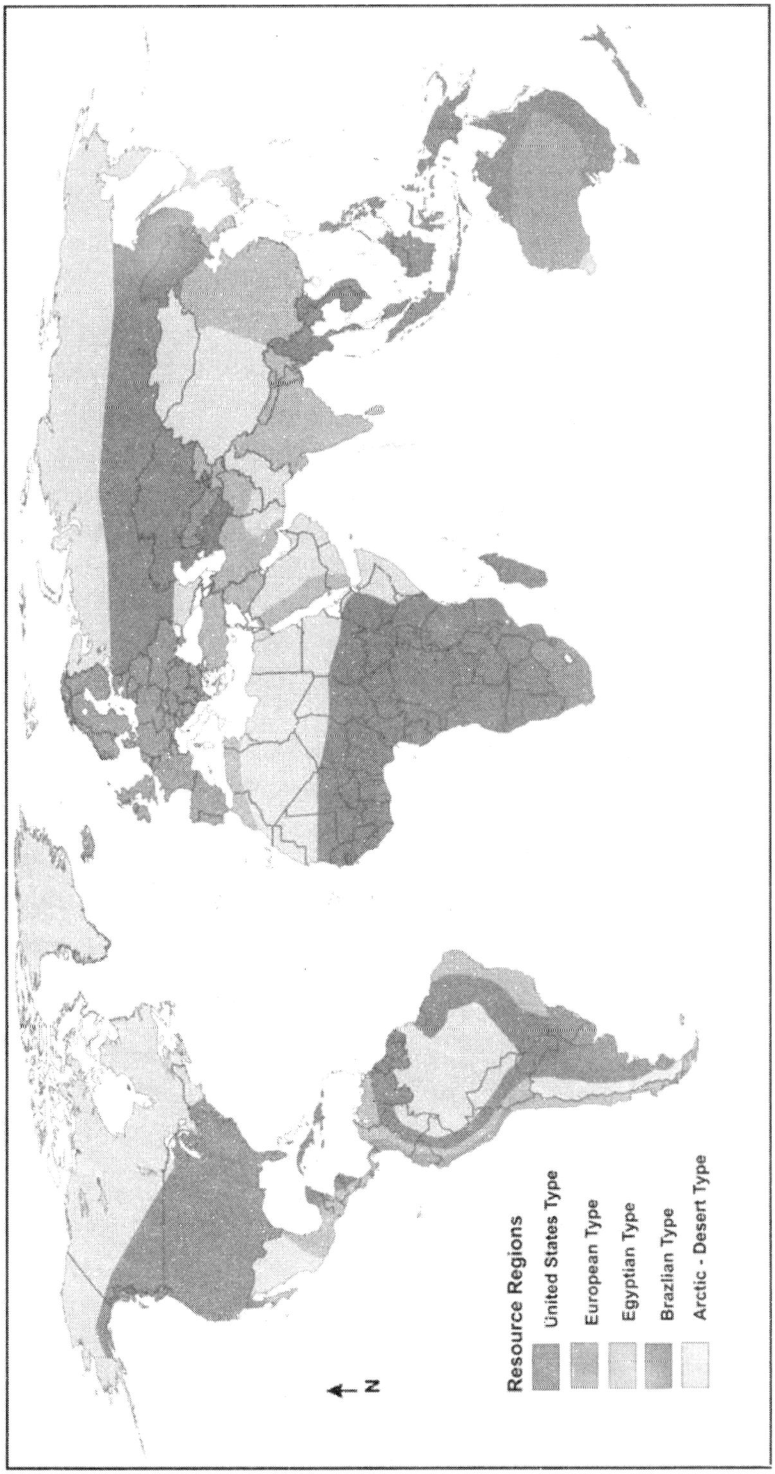

Fig. 18.1: Population-Resource Regions (According to Ackerman, 1967)

because of the problems of difficult environments. These are the technology deficient areas. The present day population size is well below the level that could comfortably be supported by known resources of the region. Most of the Brazilian type lands are found in Indo-China region, tropical Africa, and South America. In South America, Brazil, Venezuela, Paraguay are some of the examples.

18.4.5 Arctic-Desert Type

The largely uninhabited ice caps, tundra's and desert are mostly technology-deficient and offer little potential for development at the moment. These regions are fairly extensive, mostly uninhabited, and population is scattered. They have huge scope for the development of potential resources. Entire Antarctica, Greenland, northern parts of Russia and North America, Sahara desert, arid regions of Middle-East etc. are the regions included in this category.

This classification is a useful general guide and offers little help for more specific cases of pressure of population on resources. It is extremely difficult to define and measure in quantitative terms due to the dynamism of the variables involved: population, resource and technology, therefore, the efforts of Ackerman must be appreciated.

18.5 Population-Resource Regions of India

Like the classification of population-resource regions of world by Ackerman (1967), based on the potentiality of natural resources and level of development, the India can also be divided into three population-resource regions. These are Dynamic, Prospective, and Depressed or Problematic population-resource regions. These are discussed below:

18.5.1 Dynamic Population-Resource Regions

These regions are characterized with higher urbanization and industrialization. Further, these regions also have advance level of technology by which they can develop their natural resources. This category includes the areas surrounded by the large metropolitan centres of the country. They are found around the Delhi-NCR, Kolkata-Hugli, Mumbai-Ahmedabad, Chennai-Coimbatore and Bangaluru. All these centres attract a large amount population from surrounding area of and act as growth pole. Further, these regions also produce ripple effect for the development of infrastructural facilities like education, employment opportunities, transport, power, action and health has encouraged the grow tertiary and quaternary services in their hinterland.

18.5.2 Prospective Population-Resource Regions

In the Prospective population-resource region, in comparison to the Dynamic population resource region, the level of technological advance to use existed natural resource is low. These are characterised with moderate level of socio-economic development. Based on this, it can be stated that these regions have potential to increase the pace of development as their technology will advance due to which they are called prospective region. These regions are found in patches and are scattered throughout the country. These regions are found in Odisha, Jharkhand, Madhya Pradesh, Chhattisgarh and north-eastern states. These states are quite rich with respect to minerals, forest resources and huge potential for their future development.

18.5.3 Depressed or Problematic Population-Resource Regions

These regions represent unfavourable balance between population and resources. These regions are characterised with environmental constrains, poor infrastructural development, population burden, and poor development of natural resources. Overall, they show low potential for development and hence, called depressed or problematic regions. Poor resource use hinders the progress as well poor quality human resources. Mostly, represent rural backward areas of the country. These are mainly found in Uttar Pradesh, Western Ghats region, and tribal dominated areas of the country.

All the above discussed population-resource regions of India represent, indirectly, hints towards the development of natural resource based and their level of development by the human resource. This regionalization can be used for the planning purpose of the population-resource regions and their future development.

18.6 Population-Resource Relationship in India based on Land-Man Ratio

The work of Ackerman provides base to other scholars to understand the picture at macro level. As said, it is difficult to measure the relationship between population and resources. Ackerman has put India into the Egyptian type population resource region which is technology-deficient with high population/resource ratios. The technology is yet to be advanced. The resource development is less. The living standard is poor. As we know, that India is the 7th largest country of the world, therefore, it is possible that there will be large spatial variation in the country. Based on same criteria, it is difficult to get the regions within India. But, an attempt is made to understand it further the relationship between population and the available land resource. It is termed as land-man ratio, which depicts that how much land is available per capita in that region. The detailed description on this is given below.

18.6.1 Concept and Meaning

Land-man relationship answers the question that how much land is available to a man in a area, which is of paramount importance. It is required for various purposes like for food, shelter etc. The land-man ratio is the ratio between the land and the population of the area. The land-man ratio is calculated by dividing geographical area (land) from the population of the state or country. It gives us the ratio of land with respect to man at the unit of analysis. Since the size of the state and population varies, therefore, lot of spatial variations can be found in the land-man ratio in different areas. It is measured in terms of hectare per capita (ha/capita).

18.6.2 Trends and Spatial Patterns of Land-Man Ratio in India

A look on the Indian scenario after independence we will find that the land-man ratio is decreasing over the years. It is decreasing because the population has continuously increased. It was 0.91 hectare per capita in 1950-51, while in 2000-01 it was only 0.32 ha (Fig. 18.2). This rate was very high till 1980-81 because of high population growth rate. But now the pace is becoming slow. Therefore, it is clear that density of population (324 persons per sq. km, Census of India, 2001) found to be very high which is mainly concentrated in and around the urban areas, the land-man ratio is very low, while the states having low density of population found to be the surplus in land-man ratio. The per head availability of land resource in India leads to various environmental problem, especially land degradation. So for the management of various environmental problems, the land-man ratio presents to be a useful method to understand the population pressure in any area.

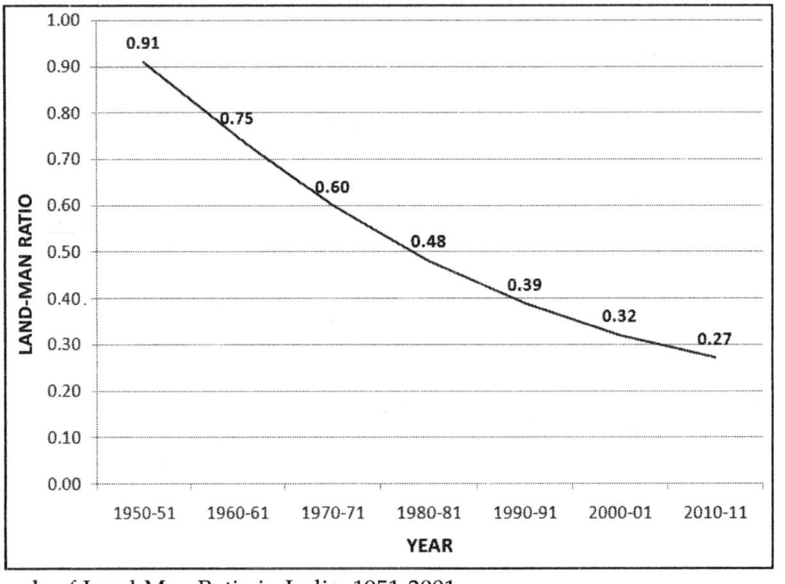

Fig. 18.2: Trends of Land-Man Ratio in India, 1951-2001

However, this situation is not favourable at all for India when we compare these figures with the large countries with less population like Australia, Canada, the USA, Argentina etc. But when we compare land-man ratio with Japan, the Netherlands, United Kingdom etc., the situation of India is found to be better. In India for obtaining a comprehensive picture of land-man ratio at state level, the states are grouped in five categories of land-man ratio. The ratio is categorized into five groups: Very High, High, Moderate, Low and Very Low.

Spatial patterns of land-man ratio in India at district level present a complex picture. Taking the 0.50 ha as the average land to support one person, the surplus and deficit nature of all states and districts is determined. The first three categories (very high, high and moderate) show surplus ratio and other two (low and very low) represent deficit status of land-man ratio. Very high land-man ratio (more than 1 ha/capita) is found in four states, namely, Arunachal Pradesh, Mizoram, Jammu & Kashmir and Sikkim. The second category has ratio between 0.75 ha/capita to 1 ha which is found in 5 states (Meghalaya, Manipur, Himachal Pradesh, Nagaland, Goa). All of these states are smaller states. Six states show moderate land-man ratio ranges between 0.50 ha to 0.75 ha/capita. It includes the state of Chhattisgarh, Rajasthan, Jharkhand, Uttarakhand, Madhya Pradesh and Tripura. The low land-man ratio (0.25 ha to 0.5 ha/capita). It includes some of the major and mainland states of the country. These are Odisha, Gujarat, Karnataka, Andhra Pradesh, Maharashtra and Assam. Very low land-man ratio is found in the most densely populated states of the country which ranges from 0.01 ha to 0.25 ha/capita. It includes the states of Haryana, Punjab, Delhi, Uttar Pradesh, Bihar, West Bengal, Kerala and Tamil Nadu.

At the macro level, it is found that the Indus-Ganga and Brahmaputra plains have very low land-man ratio including Kerala and some scattered districts in the eastern and western coastal plains. Very high land-man ratio is found in the western Rajasthan, the Laddakh region, north-west Gujarat, north-east India, Himachal Pradesh and Uttarakhand. The Deccan plateau region is characterized with moderate to very high land-man ratio. Therefore, the results show that population density is inversely proportionate to land-man ratio. Thus, in plains it is high while in hilly and plateau areas the land-man ratio is low. Thus, based on land-man ratio, it can be said that almost 15-20 per cent area of the country has high to very high land-man ratio. On the other hand, more than 50 per cent area is under low to very low land-man ratio. These areas can be taken as land-man regions which will also help for the planning also.

18.7 Population Problems in the World

Population of any country is not a problem. Actually, it is a resource, i.e. human resource. No doubt the quantity of it is a problem but, when it has quality, it becomes a huge resource. Various countries are facing scarcity of population, while some have huge numbers. Therefore, if a country has low population, it is a problem and also when it is more in number, it is also a problem. Both types of countries face different problems related to quantity and quality of population. But, when we talk about problems, we think about the negative consequences due to the population pressure. Some of the important problems related to population facing by different types of countries are listed below.

The problems related to population in the under-populated/developing countries are different from the developed countries. In the developed countries in Europe and North America, have the population problems related to the decline of birth rates and the increase in life expectancy. Both these problems have produced various important consequences. Like in European countries, the overall total population has been growing very slowly in the last decade or it has remained constant. Besides, the proportion of people who are old (age more than 65 years) is rapidly increasing. The population of younger population is continuously decreasing. It is clear that European countries have aged much faster than North American ones during the last 30 years (Fig. 18.3). In 2010, the percentage of population 65 and more was over 20 per cent in Germany and Italy and only 12 per cent in the United States. The ageing of the population in Europe, the low fertility and the increasing share of older people are biggest challenges and problems which are changing the local economies and societies of the country.

On the other hand, overpopulated countries try to control their population due to various problems. These problems are discussed in the section on Over-population in India and Associated Problems.

18.7.1 Over-Population in India and Associated Problems

We all know that India is the second largest country in the world after China. Therefore,

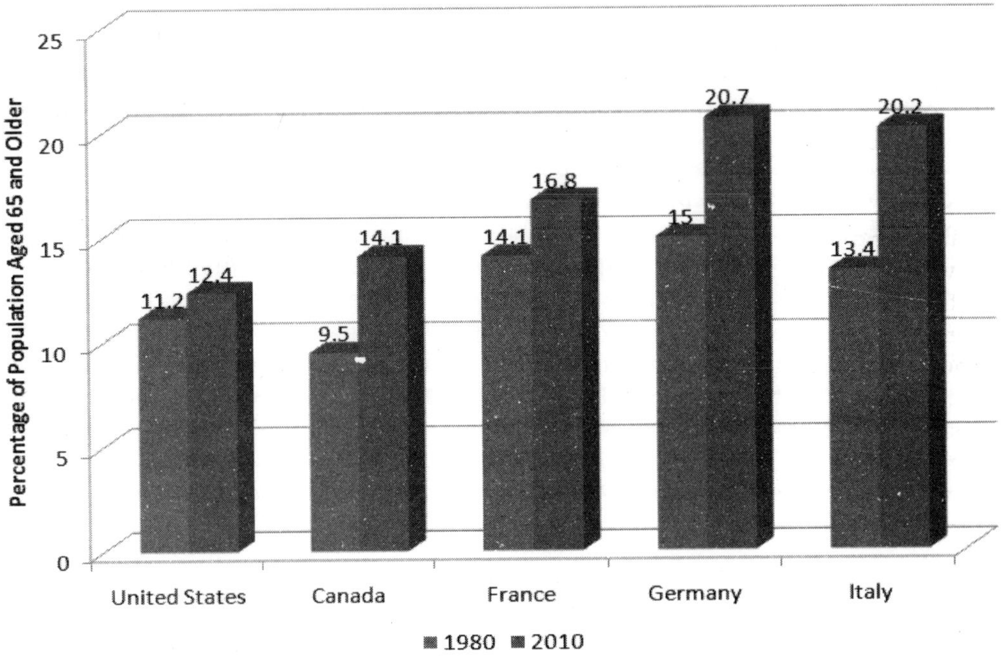

Fig. 18.3: Representative Countries of Europe and North America
Source: Peri (2011).

there are various problems related to population quite visible in the country. Increasing population in itself is a big challenge. Uncontrolled increase in population puts immense pressure on the natural resources and environment. The population demands that basic needs to be fulfilled. It puts immense pressure on land, particularly, agricultural land for producing maximum. The farmer tries to get maximum production by giving lots of inputs to land in the form of irrigation facilities, chemical fertilizers, insecticides and pesticides etc. These inputs force the land resource to give maximum which in result leads to land degradation. The productivity of land resource, over the years, declines. However, population kept on increasing.

Due to continuous increase in population, particularly, in urban areas, it puts immense pressure on the services and their maintenance provided by the government. Educational institutions need to be opened up and job opportunities needs to be created. If not, the quality of population cannot be ensured. For the development of the society, besides basic needs, education and employment are very important. Provision of standard of living becomes a major issue. In India, there is a great shortage of nourishment, especially that of balanced diet. The standard of living is poor and housing conditions are very poor which results into health problems. Economic and social disparity can widen over the time. The gap between rich and poor increases, unemployment and burden of aged population increases, Therefore, the country have more population tries to control it. China and India are the best examples in this regard.

18.8 Population Policies of China and India

18.8.1 Population Policies of China

The People's Republic of China was facing rapid increase in population since the starting of the second half of the 20th century. It was a serious challenge in front of the Communist Government when they came in the power in 1949. It was really difficult to provide better living condition when population was increasing with such a rapid rate. In response to this, government introduced various family planning related measures to overcome the population growth. In the 1970s, the government came up with population policy with the objective of reducing population growth. This policy aimed at 'later, longer, and fewer'. These three words emphasizes that later marriages and pregnancies, longer the intervals between two successive children and fewer children. In response to this, fertility rates were declined in a steeper trend in the next decade (from 5.81 in 1970 to 2.72 in 1978). This decline was almost half in a span of less than 10 years. However, population was still increasing. The large numbers of young people in the population were still producing large numbers of children. Therefore, in 1978 China introduced 'The One-Child Policy' which was comparatively harsh and debatable from policy-maker perspectives. The one-child policy of China experienced widespread criticism in the country itself, particularly, rural areas. As we all know, rural families considers children as working hands, particularly boys. Children are also seen as security in old stage. Due to these drawbacks, the policy was not implemented nationally, but was limited to urban areas. Almost, half of China's population lives in the countryside area which means a significant share of families were permitted to have a second child.

The policy also experienced wider criticism due to its future consequences. A major consequence of the one-child policy has been the changing patterns of sex ratio in the country. The one child policy forced the people to have only child. Among the families, birth of boys was preferred. The availability and use of ultrasound equipment allowed couples to selectively abort female foetuses due to which female babies were killed at birth. Therefore, one child policy lead to the higher mortality rates for female children. The data state that between 1954 to 1964, almost the same number of males and females were born. However, in 1982, the ratio of girls to boys born in China was 100:110. By the 1990s, it had risen to 100:111 at birth. Further, in addition to this more females were dying than males before celebrating their first birthday. Another reason was that female births were under-reported because couples whose first child is female were allowed to have a second child. However, couples whose first child is male are not allowed to have a second child. The government has prohibited the practice of identifying the sex of a foetus with the purpose of practising gender-specific abortions, but it was observed that there was no control over the operators of the machines.

Further, a society which have one child, no doubt, there will be too many aged people as the replacement is poor. The social security is less. The couples with single boy were comparatively less vulnerable than couples have girl because the girl child will move to her husband's house after marriage. Therefore, the another result of one-child policy was ageing of population as well increasing burden on the government from the social security point of view. Therefore, the policy has seen serious demographic changes since 1950s. At present, the country is moving with a rapid rate of economic development. The main reason behind the one-child policy was that China cannot keep pace of agricultural production with rapid population growth. The education, employment, services, facilities were some other major issues. Therefore, the policy has contributed significantly in changing the demographic characteristics of the country. Rapidly growing Chinese economy has the potential to contribute in narrowing the gaps between what people's of China and the Government thinks about the population growth which will help in the development of the country.

18.8.2 National Population Policy of India, 2000

Department of Welfare under the Ministry of Health and Family Welfare, Government of India formulated the India's National Population Policy in 2000 (NPP, 2002). The policy have immediate objectives and long term objectives. The immediate objective of the NPP 2000 is to address the unmet needs for contraception, health care infrastructure, and health personnel, and to provide integrated service delivery for basic reproductive and child health care. The medium-term objective is to bring the Total Fertility Rate to replacement levels by 2010, through vigorous implementation of inter-sectoral operational strategies. On the other side the long-term objective of the policy is to achieve a stable population by 2045, at a level consistent with the requirements of sustainable economic growth, social development, and environmental protection. The policy has also recommended 13 national socio-demographic goals, which are required to be achieved. These goals are:

- Address the unmet needs for basic reproductive and child health services, supplies and infrastructure.
- Make School education up to age 14 free and compulsory, dropouts are reduced at primary and secondary school levels to below 20 per cent for both boys and girls.
- Reduce Infant mortality rate below 30 per 1000 live births.
- Reduce maternal mortality ratio below 100 per 100,000 live births.
- Achieve universal immunization of children against all vaccine preventable diseases.
- Delayed marriage for girls, not earlier than age 18 and preferably boys after 20 years of age has been promoted.
- 80 per cent institutional deliveries and 100 per cent deliveries by trained persons are done.
- Universal access to information/counselling, and services for fertility regulation and contraception with a wide basket of choices are done.
- 100 per cent registration of births, deaths, marriage and pregnancy, yet to be achieved.
- Prevent and control communicable diseases.
- Integrate Indian Systems of Medicine (ISM) in the provision of reproductive and child health services, and in reaching out to households.
- The small family norm to achieve replacement levels of TFR is promoted.
- Bring about convergence in implementation of related social sector programmes so that family welfare becomes a people centred programme.

The policy has also suggested various promotional and motivational measures need to be undertaken to achieve the aforesaid goals. It has been stated that Panchayats and Zila Parishads will be rewarded and honoured for exemplary performance in universalizing the small family norm, achieving reductions in infant mortality and birth rates, and promoting literacy with completion of primary schooling. There is need to promote survival and care of the girl child and some cash incentives were also announced for the same. In the policy, a Family Welfare-linked Health Insurance Plan was also established. The policy states that crèches and child care centres will be opened in rural areas and urban slums which will facilitate and promote participation of women in paid employment. Further, various measures related to affordable choice of contraceptives with counselling services, facilities for safe abortion, ambulance arrangements for referral transportation etc. were taken and also promoted. Further, the policy concludes that the vast numbers of the people of India can be its greatest asset if they are provided with quality education, health and economically productive lives. The quality population of the country not only help in the speeding up the development process but also has the capacity to make the country healthy and wealthy.

18.9 Summary

The classification of world into various population-resource regions by Ackerman has provided a base for the further studies in understanding the relationship between population pressure and availability of resources. How the criteria adopted by Ackerman are very difficult to adopt and apply further as they are quite dynamic in their nature. But an attempt is made to take geographical area (land) and the population to identify land-man ratio based regions in India. Based on land-man ratio, the whole country is divided into two zones, surplus and deficit land-man ratio regions and at micro level into five zones. It is further suggested that more criteria can be used to identify the population-resource regions at various regional scales.

Review Questions

1. Highlight the major characteristics of the Population-Resource regions of the World.
2. Critically evaluate and analyze the One-child Policy of China.
3. Evaluate the major characteristics of National Population Policy of India.
4. Discuss the trends and patterns of land-man ratio in India.
5. Analyze the population problems in the developed and developing countries.
6. Write a brief note on the population-resource regions of India.

Analytical Questions

1. Prepare map of population density and land-man ratio of your district/area/region. Compare and analyze them.
2. Is Ackerman's criterion of classification of population-resource region applicable in your country? Justify your answer.

Chapter 19
Ecological Footprint and Resource Curse

19.1 Introduction

In the present time, the relationship between population and resources has reached in very complex situation. Population pressure is a harmful situation for any region from its development point of view. The population pressure is exceeding the carrying capacity of the earth surface. This relationship has been analyzed by various scholars from different points of view. Important among them are Ecological Footprints (EFs) and the resource curse. The relationship between population and resources is also analyzed through the ecological footprints. It is a fundamental concept to measure sustainability and the unequal use of land resources on the planet.

19.2 Ecological Footprints

The ecological footprint is one of the most important methods for ecological resource accounting. The ecological footprint is an estimate of human pressure or load on global ecosystem. It can also be said that the footprint takes into account the total impact of people on the environment. The ecological footprint is a kind of 'load' measurement put on by a given population on nature. It explains that how much land we need to fulfil the requirements of the present population in terms of resource. Therefore, an ecological footprint represents an area of productive land and aquatic systems to produce the resources used, and to absorb the wastes generated by population of a defined area.

19.2.1 Origin and Concept

The concept of EFs was developed by Mathis Wackernagel and William Rees in the early 1990s. EFs were defined as "the area of productive land and water ecosystems required to produce the resources that the population consumes and assimilates the wastes that the population produces, wherever on Earth the land and water is located" (Wackernagel and Rees, 1996).

According to Ecological Footprint Atlas (2010), "the ecological footprint is a measure of the demand human activity puts on the biosphere."

EF asks, "How large an area of productive land is needed to sustain a population indefinitely at current levels of technology and consumption, wherever that land may be located?" (Rees, 1996).

The EFs measures human demand on the biosphere in terms of the land and sea area required to provide the resources we use and to absorb the waste we generate. This includes all the cropland, grazing land, forest and fishing grounds used to produce food, fibre and timber, to absorb the carbon emitted in burning fossil fuels, and to provide space for infrastructure (Anonymous, 2008).

Simply, it is an estimate of human pressure on global ecosystem, expressed in global hectare/capita which means a kind of ecological burden on the planet under prevailing technological levels. Further, it can be said that EFs (i) measures the amount of land, and (ii) aquatic resources that must be used to continuously sustain a population, based on its consumption levels at a given point.

Therefore, the size of a footprint depends on the volume and types of natural resources used by the population of the area. Further, it depends on lifestyles choices, income levels and technological factors. Therefore, a footprint provides compelling evidence of the impacts of consumption. It can also be equated with the concept of carrying capacity.

19.2.2 Characteristics

Ecological footprint is the measurement of humanities dependence on natural resources. Some of the important characteristics are given below:

- EFs is an estimate of human pressure on global ecosystems.
- The size of an EF is not static; it keeps on changing through time, depending on population, their consumption levels, resource use and level of technology.
- EFs are measured in global acres (or global hectares) which help in comparing the existing biologically productive capacity at any level.
- Various uses, mostly mutually exclusive uses, compete for biologically productive land and water. This includes human; flora; fauna; and conservation uses.
- The majority of the human activities related to consumption and the wastes they generate can be tracked.

19.2.3 Scales of Measurement

Ecological footprint can be measured or evaluated at various levels like individual level or cities, state, regional, countries or the entire planet level. It is measured in global hectare per capita. The ecological footprint calculated for a country includes the resources contained within the goods and services that are consumed by people living in that country, as well as the associated waste.

19.2.4 Basic Concepts related to Ecological Footprints

Biocapacity: It is the amount of productive area which is available to produce resources and to absorb the waste produced by human beings. It is usually expressed in global hectares.

Ecological Overshoot: It occurs when humanity's demand on nature exceeds the global biocapacity (Fig. 19.1). Because trees can be harvested faster than they regrow, fisheries can be depleted more than they restock, CO_2 can be emitted into the atmosphere more than ecosystem can sequester it. Overshoot causes carbon accumulation in the atmosphere, fisheries collapse, deforestation spreads, biodiversity is lost, freshwater becomes scarce. Therefore, such overshoot leads to depletion of Earth's life-supporting natural capital and a build-up of waste. At present, the ecological overshoot is no more a local phenomena. Human demands on nature has riser steadily to a level where the human economy is now in global overshoot.

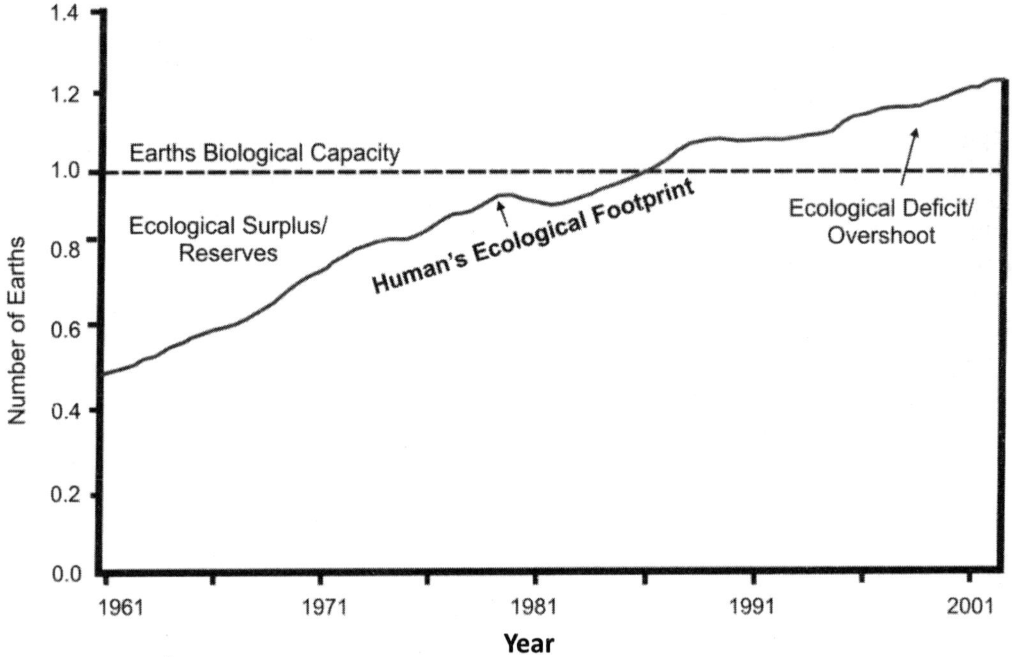

Fig. 19.1: Basic Concepts in Ecological Footprints

Ecological Deficit or Reserve: An ecological deficit occurs when the footprint of an area's population exceeds the biocapacity of the area. In other ways, an ecological reserve exists when the biocapacity of an area exceeds the footprint of its population (Fig. 19.1).

Biological Productive Areas: Wackernagel *et al.* (1997) defined biologically productive areas as (a) arable land, (b) pasture, (c) forest, (d) sea space (used by marine life), (e) built up land, and (f) fossil energy land (land reserved for carbon dioxide absorption). The current global biologically productive area is 10.8 billion hectares, of which, 21 per cent is productive ocean and 79 per cent is productive land. The total biologically productive area on land and water in 2007 was approximately 11.9 billion hectares.

19.3 Spatial Patterns of Ecological Footprints

19.3.1 Global Scenario

In 2007, total ecological footprint worldwide was 18.0 billion global hectares (gha); with world population at 6.7 billion people, the average person's footprint was 2.7 gha. But there were only 11.9 billion gha of biocapacity available in that year (or 1.8 gha per person).

This overshoot of 50 per cent means that in 2007, humanity used the equivalent of 1.5 Earths to support various consumptions. Further, it also explains that it took the Earth approximately a year and six months to regenerate the resources used by humanity in that year. In 1961, humanity's Footprint was about half in comparison to what the Earth could support. Humanity was living off the planet's annual ecological interest and not drawing down its principal. Therefore, human demand first exceeded the planet's ability to meet this demand around the 1975s.

19.3.2 Regional Scenario

The footprint of humanity (average 2.7 ha/person) is not evenly distributed throughout the globe. When one looks at the ecological footprint on a region-by-region basis, severe disparity is visible. Based on the level of ecological footprints the world can be divided into three categories: high, moderate, and low ecological footprint regions. High ecological footprint regions include those areas where the human load is more than 6 ha/capita. It includes the regions likes North America, European countries and Oceania (Australia and New Zealand). The footprint level in North America is close to 12 ha while in European countries above 6. This region mainly comprises the developed countries of the world. Moderate ecological footprint values ranges from 2 to 4 ha/capita. It includes mainly Latin America. Asian and African countries have lowest ecological footprints in the world (Less than 2 ha/capita). The discussion clearly demonstrates that the level of development and industrialization have a positive relationship with magnitude of ecological footprints. Based on this, the whole earth can be divided into continents having high, moderate and low ecological footprints. This simple comparison immediately gives an idea of the level of resources consumed by citizens of different countries, with a wide range of lifestyles.

19.3.3 Country Level Scenario

Figure 19.2 explains that there the countries with largest population have small footprints than the world's major industrial and developed countries. The countries of rest of the world are far behind the USA in their ecological footprints. However, it has only 294 million population which is much less than the China and India where EF is less than 2 ha/per capita. It shows that how much pressure the US economy puts on the earth. Countries like Germany, Japan and Brazil also have moderate size of population and small geographical area but puts huge pressure on the earth.

The Ecological Footprint model is most useful as a tool for management and used to highlight gap between two or more individuals or groups, and further suggests areas for movement and change.

19.4 Ways to Reduce Ecological Deficits

Some of the measures to reduce ecological deficits are suggested below:

- Use resource efficient technology to reduce demand on natural resources.
- Reduce human consumption while preserving quality of life. For example, reduce the need for fossil fuel by making cities, pedestrian friendly.

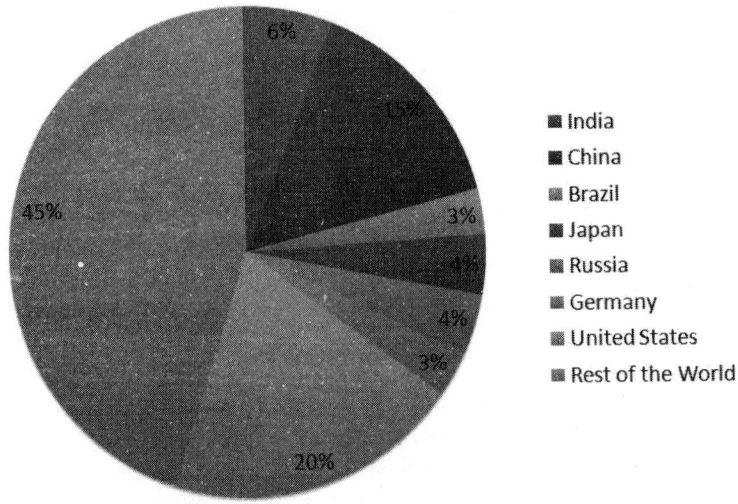

Fig. 19.2: Ecological Footprints of Selected Countries (Per Person, By Country, 2003)
Source: India's Ecological Footprints: A Business Perspective (2008).

- Lower the size of human family: so the total consumption decreases even if per capita demand remains unchanged.
- Invest in natural capital, e.g. implement resource extraction method that increase rather than compromise the land's biological productivity, thereby, increasing supply.

19.5 Concept of Resource Curse

It has been observed for some decades, that, the possession of vast natural resources like oil, natural gas, or other valuable mineral deposits or natural resources does not necessarily bestow economic success. Many African countries such as Angola, Nigeria, Sudan, and the Congo are rich in oil, diamonds, or other minerals. But yet their peoples continue to experience low per capita income and low quality of life. However, the East Asian economies like Japan, Taiwan, Korea, Hong Kong and Singapore have achieved the standards of living like Western countries despite many constraints of being rocky islands or peninsulas with virtually no exportable natural resources. Auty (1993 and 2001) coined the phrase "natural resource curse" to describe this baffling scenario. The use of the word spread rapidly.

The curse of natural resources—the observation that countries rich in natural resources tend to perform badly—has been shown empirically and analyzed in a number of recent studies. These studies include Auty (1993), Sachs and Warner (1999, 2001), and Gylfason *et al.* (1999) and many others, particularly emerged late in the 20th century. The study by Behera and Mishra (2012) proves that in the Indian states the hypothesis of the resource curse is valid. It is argued that it is possibly due to weak institutions polices made by instaurations. The phenomenon of resource curse in Indian states revolves around the various issues like the quality of policy-making institutions and their implementation methods.

19.6 Conclusions

The chapter analyzed the relationship between population and resources. It has been seen the ecological footprint of human beings is on increasing side which not only affects human itself but it also puts the immense pressure on the sustainability of mankind on this earth surface. Therefore, it is recognised that human perspective in geography is very important which should have a positive approach towards the development process. It must believe in economic efficiency, social inclusiveness and environmentally sustainability based developmental process.

Review Questions

1. Discuss the concept of ecological footprints in details.
2. Analyze the conceptual origin and characteristics of ecological concepts.
3. Differentiate between ecological overshoot and ecological deficit.
4. Analyze the spatial patterns of ecological footprints in world.
5. Write a short note on the concept of resource curse.

Analytical Questions

1. Differentiate the difference between carrying capacity and ecological footprint.
2. The concept of natural resource represents the irony between more resource availability and least development. How?

Bibliography

Ackerman, E.A. (1967). "Population, natural resources, and technology", *The Annals of the American Academy of Political and Social Science,* 369(1): 84-97.

Ackerman, E.A. (1970). "Geography and demography", In G.J. Demko, H.M. Rose and G.A. Schnell (eds.) *Population Geography: A Reader*, New York: McGraw Hill Book Company.

Ahluwalia, M. (2011). "Prospects and policy challenges in the 12th plan", *Economic and Political Weekly*, 46(21): 88-105.

Ahmad, A. (2012). *Social Geography of India,* New Delhi: Concept Publishing Company Pvt. Ltd.

Ahmad, E. (1952). "Rural settlement types in Uttar Pradesh: United Province of Agra and Ondh", *Annals of Association of American Geographers,* 42: 223-246.

Ahmad, K.S. (1941). "Environment and the distribution of population in India", *Indian Geographical Journal,* 16: 117-134.

Alcott, B. (2016). "Population matters", In H. Kopnina and E. Shoreman-Quimet (eds.). *Sustainability: Key Issues,* London & New York: Routledge.

Allan, W.A. (1949). "Studies in African land usage in northern Rhodesia", *Rhodes-Livingstone Papers,* No. 15, London: Oxford.

Andaya, B.W. and Andaya, L.Y. (2015). *A History of Early Modern Southeast Asia, 1400-1830,* Cambridge: Cambridge University Press.

Anonymous (2008). *India's Ecological Footprints: A Business Perspective,* Hyderabad: Confederation of Indian Industry (CII).

Anonymous (2012). *Blackie's Dictionary of Geography,* Mumbai: Blackie & Sons.

Auty, R. (1993). *Sustaining Development in Mineral Economies: The Resource Curse, Thesis,* New York: Oxford University Press.

Auty, R. (2001). *Resource Abundance and Economic Development,* World Institute for Development Economics Research, New York: Oxford University Press.

Baviskar, A. (1995). *In the Belly of the River: Tribal conflicts over Development in the Narmada Valley,* New Delhi: Oxford University Press.

Beaujeu-Garnier, J. (1966). *Geography of Population,* London and New York: Longmans.

Behera, B. and Mishra, P. (2012). "Natural resource abundance in the Indian states: Curse or boon", *Review of Development and Change,* 17: 53-73.

Bernard, F.E. (1977). "Population pressure: A preliminary assessment with special reference to Kenya", *East African Geographical Review,* 15: 43-68.

Bhende, A.A. and Kanitkar, T. (2000). *Principal of Population Studies,* 13th Revised Edition, Mumbai: Himalaya Publishing House.

Blache, P. Vidal de La (1965). *Principles of Human Geography,* London: Constable Publishers.

Buttimer, A. (1976). "Quantitative Revolution and Theoretical Geography," In W.K.D. Davis (ed.) *The Conceptual Revolution in Geography,* New Jersey: Rowman and Littlefield, 140-56.

Carter, G.F. (1974). *Man and Land: A Cultural Geography*, New York: Holt and Rinehart.

Catro, A.P. and Nielson, E. (2003). *Natural Resource Conflict Management Case Studies: An Analysis of Power, Participation and Protected Areas, Rome*, Food and Agriculture Organisation (FAO).

Census of India (2001 and 2011). *Final Population Totals*, Office of Registrar General and Census Commissioner, New Delhi: Government of India.

Census of India (2001). *Population Distribution and Density in India*, Government of India.

Census of India (2011). *Scheduled Tribes of India*, Registrar General of India, New Delhi.

Centre for Social Studies (CSS) (1997). "Surat: Resettlement and Rehabilitation in Gujarat", In J. Dreze, M. Samson, and S. Singh (eds.) *The Dam and the Nation: Displacement and Resettlement in the Narmada Valley*, New Delhi: Oxford University Press, 169-182.

Chandana, R.C., (2006). *Geography of Population*, Jaipur: Kalyani Publishers.

Chandana, R.C. (2008). *Population Geography*, Jaipur: Kalyani Publishers.

Chandna, R.C. (2014). *Geography of Population*, Kalyani Publishers, Jaipur.

Chandna, R.C. (2008). *Geography of Population: Concepts, Determinants and Patterns*, 7th Edition, New Delhi: Kalyani Publishers.

Chatterjee, S.P. (1961). "Physical features and population distribution of population in West Bengal", *Calcutta Geographical Review*, 23: 1-19.

Chorley, R.J. and P. Haggett (1967). *Integrated Models in Geography*, Part IV, London: Methuen Co. Ltd.

Clark, A.N. (2003). *Dictionary of Geography*, London: Penguin Books.

Clarke, J.I. (1971). *Population Geography and Developing Countries*, Oxford: Pergamon Press.

Cole, V. and Sinclair, A.J. (2002). "Measuring the ecological footprint of a Himalayan tourist centre", *Mountain Research and Development*, 22(2): 132-141.

Compton, P. (1969). "Internal migration and population change in Hungary between 1959 and 1965", *Transaction of the Institute of British Geographers*, 47: 111-130.

Cox, K.R. (1972). *Man, Location and Behaviour: An Introduction to Human Geography*, Toronto: John Wiley and Sons.

Davis, K. (1951). *The Population of India and Pakistan*, Princeton: Princeton University.

Demangeon, A. (1933). *Les Problems de Geographic Humaine*, Paris: Librairie Armand Colin.

Demko, G.J., Rose, H.M. and Schnell, G.A. (1970). *Population Geography: A Reader*, New York: McGraw Hill.

Durand, J.D. (1974). *Historical Estimates of World Population: An Evaluation, Analytical and Technical Reports*, No. 10, Philadelphia: University of Pennsylvania, Population Studies Centre.

Eberhard, D.M., Simons, G.F. and Fennig C.D. (eds.) (2019). *Ethnologue: Languages of the World*, 22nd Edition, Dallas, Texas: SIL International.

Eyre, S.R. (1964). "Determinism and ecological approach to geography", *Geography*, 1(49): 369-76.

Fellmann, J.D., Getis, A., Getis, J. and Malinowski, J.C. (2005). *Human Geography: Landscape of Human Activities*, 8th Edition, New York: McGraw-Hill.

Finch, V.C. and Trewartha, G.T. (1957). *Element of Geography: Physical and Cultural*, New York: McGraw-Hill Boom Company.

Foot, D.K. and Milne, W.J. (1984). "Net migration estimation in an extended multiregional gravity model", *Journal of Regional Science*, 119-134.

Fouberg, E.H., Murphy, A.B. and de Blij, H.J. (2009), *Human Geography: People, Place, and Culture*, 9th Edition, New Jersey: John Wiley & Sons, Inc.

Franklin, S.H. (1956). "The pattern of sex ratios in New Zealand", *Economic Geography*, 32(2): 162-176.

Gale, S. (1973). "Explanation theory and models of migration", *Economic Geography*, 49: 257-274.

Galle, O.R. and Taeuber, K.E. (1966). "Metropolitan migration and intervening opportunities", *American Sociological Review*, 31(1): 5-13.

Geddes, A. (1942). "The population of India: Variability of change as a regional demographic index", *Geographical Review*, 32: 563-573.

Geddes, P. (1949). *Cities in Evolution*, London: Williams & Norgate.

Ghosh, S. (1970). "Physical and economic factors in the population distribution of Bihar", *The National Geographical Journal of India*, 16: 16-70.

Gosal, G.S. (1961). "Internal migration in India: A regional analysis", *The Indian Geographical Journal*, 36(3): 106-121.

Gottman, J. (1957). "Megalopolis or the urbanization of the north-eastern seaboard", *Economic Geography*, 33(3): 189-200.

Gould, W.T. and Prothero, R.M. (1975). "Space and time in African population mobility", In L.A. Kosinski and R.M. Prothero (eds.) *People on the Move: Studies on Internal Migration*, London: Methuen and Co. Ltd., 39-49.

Gregory, D. (1981). "Human agency and human geography", *Transactions*, Institute of British Geographers, 6: 1-6.

Groeschl, S. and Doherty, L. (2000). "Conceptualizing culture", *Cross Culture Management—An International Journal*, 7(4): 12-17.

Guelke, L.C. (1971). "Problems of scientific explanations in geography", *Canadian Geographer*, 15:38-53.

Gylfason, T., Herbertsson, T.T. and Zoega, G. (1999). "A mixed blessing: Natural resources and economic growth", *Macroeconomic Dynamics*, 3: 204-225.

Haggerstrand, T. (1967). *Innovation, Diffusion as Special Process*, translated by A. Pred, Chicago: Chicago University Press.

Haggett, P. (1983). *Geography: A Modern Synthesis*, New York: Harper & Row Publishers.

Hardoy, J.E., Mitlan, D., Satterthwaite, D. (2001). *Environmental Problems in an Urbanizing World*, London: Earthscan.

Harris, R.C. (1971). "Theory and synthesis in historical geography", *The Canadian Geographer*, 15: 157-72.

Heatwole, C.A. (2006). "Culture: A Geographical Perspective" in *World Communities: What is a Culture?*, Online Resource Guide, New York State Education Department.

Hiremath, S.S. (2007). "Pressure of population on natural resources in India", In B. Thakur, B. (ed.) *Perspectives in Resource Management in Developing Countries*, Volume 2 (Part-I): *Population, Resources and Development*, New Delhi: Concept Publishing Company Pvt. Ltd., 419-436.

Hoebel, E.A. (1972). *Anthropology: The Study of Man*, 4th Edition, New York: McGraw-Hill.

Human Development Report (2010). The Real Wealth of Nations: Pathways to Human Development, New York: UNDP.

Husain, M. (1999). *Human Geography*, 2nd Edition, Jaipur: Rawat Publication.

Husain, M. (2011). *Human Geography*, Jaipur and New Delhi: Rawat Publications.

James, P.E. (1972). *All Possible World*, Indianapolis: The Odyssey Press.

Jansen, C. (1969). "Some sociologist aspects of migration", In J.A. Jackson (ed.), *Migration*, Cambridge: Cambridge University Press, 11-59.

Johnston, R.J. *et al.* (1986). *The Dictionary of Human Geography*, Oxford: Blackwell Reference.

Jones, H.R. (1981). *Geography of Population*, London: Harper and Row.

Joseph, G. (1975). "A markovian analysis of age/sex differences in inter-regional migration in Great Britain", *Regional Studies*, 9: 69-78.

Kaiser, M.J. and Beadman, H.A. (2002). "Scoping study of the carrying capacity for bivalve cultivation in the coastal waters of Great Britain," The Crown Estate, Interim Report.

Kellog, C.E. (1950). *Food, Soil and People,* New York: The Manhattan Publishing Company.

King, H. (1927). "The geography of settlements in southwest Lancashire", *Geography,* XIV: 193-200.

Kirk, W.K. (1951). "Historical geography and concept of behavioural environment", *Indian Geographical Journal,* 25: 125-60.

Knowles, R. and J. Wareing (1976). *Economic and Social Geography: Made Simple,* Germany: Heinemann.

Knowles, R. and Wareing, J. (2011). *Economic and Social Geography,* 25th Impression, New Delhi: Rupa Publications India Pvt. Ltd.

Knox, P.L. and Marston, S.A. (2016). *Human Geography: Places and Regions in Global Context,* Essex, UK: Pearson Education.

Kundu, A. (2007). "Migration and exclusionary urban growth in India", 6th Dr. C. Chandrasekaran Memorial Lecture, International Institute for Population Sciences, Mumbai.

Kundu, A. (2011). "Politics and economics of urban growth", *Economic and Political Weekly,* 46(20): 10-12.

Lee, E.S. (1966). "A theory of migration", *Demography,* 3: 47-57.

Lenartowicz, T. and Kendall R. (1999). "A framework for culture assessment", *Journal of International Business Studies,* 30(4): 781-798.

MacLeod, M. and Cooper, J.A.G. (2005). "Carrying capacity in coastal areas", In M. Schwartz (ed.) *Encyclopaedia of Coastal Science,* The Netherlands: Springer.

Malthus, T.R. (1798). *An Essay on the Principal of Population as It Affects the Future Improvement of Society, with Remarks on the Speculations of Mr. Godwin, M. Condorcet and Other Writers,* London: J. Johnson.

Massey, D.S. and Nancy A.D. (1988). "The dimensions of residential segregation", *Social Forces,* 67: 281-315.

Maurya, S.D. (1989). *Urbanization and Environmental Problems,* Allahabad: Chugh Publications.

Meitzen, A. (1895). *Siedlung and Agrarwesen der Westgermane and Ostgermanen,* 3 Volumes and Atlas, Berlin: W. Hertzder, Keltan, Romer Finner and Slawen.

Morse, B.F. (1992). *Sardar Sarovar: The Report of the Independent Review,* Ottawa: Resources Future International.

Mumford, L. (1938). *The Culture of Cities,* New York: Harcourt Brace.

Munier, N. (ed.) (2007). *Handbook on Urban Sustainability,* Dordrecht, The Netherlands Springer.

National Population Policy (2002). Department of Welfare, Ministry of Health and Family Welfare, Government of India, New Delhi.

NCERT (2018). *Fundamentals of Human Geography,* Textbook for Class XII, National Council of Educational Research and Training, New Delhi.

Norton, W. (2007). *Human Geography,* New York: Oxford University Press.

Notestein, F.W. (1945). *Population: The Long View,* Chicago: Chicago University Press.

Onibokun, A.G. (1999). *Managing the Monsters: Urban Waste and Governance in Africa,* International Development Research Centre, Ottawa.

Overbreek, J. (1974). *History of Population Theories,* Rotterdam University Press, Netherland.

Padel, F. (1992). "The Position of Tribal People in India", Submission to the Independent Review, January 29.

Panelli, R. (2004). *Social Geographies: From Difference to Action,* London: Sage Publications.

Peri, G. (2011). *Migration: Challenges and Policies,* CESifo DICE Report 4/2011.

Perpillou, A.V. (1986). *Human Geography,* London: Longman.

Peterson, W. (1958). "A general typology of migration", *American Sociologist Review,* 4: 256-266.

Population Reference Bureau (PRB) (2010). *World Population Data Sheet,* Washington DC.

Population Reference Bureau (PRB) (2012). *World Population Data Sheet*, Washington DC.

Pryor, R.J. (1969). "Laws of Migration? The Experience of Malaysia and Other Countries", *Geographica*, University of Malaya, 5: 65-76.

Pryor, R.J. (1971). *Internal Migration and Urbanization*, Monograph Series, Geography Department. James Cook University.

Rana, L. (2008), *Geographical Thought: A Systematic Record of Evolution*, New Delhi: Concept Publishing Company Pvt. Ltd.

Rao, M. (1994). "An imagined reality: Malthusianism, neo-Malthusianism and population myth", *Economic and Political Weekly*, January 29: 40-52.

Ravenstein, E.G. (1885). "The laws of migration", *Journal of the Statistical Society of London*, 48(2): 167-235.

Ravenstein, E.G. (1889). "The law of migration", *Journal Royal Statistical Society*, 49: 241-303.

Rees, W. (1996). "Revisiting carrying capacity: Area-based indicators of sustainability", *Population and Environment: A Journal of Interdisciplinary Studies*, 17: 195-215.

Reilly, W.J. (1929). *Method for the Study of Retail Relationship*, University of Texas Press, Austin.

Rogers, A. (1966). "A Markovian policy model of inter-regional migration", *Paper of Regional Science Association*, 17: 205-224.

Rossi, P. (1955). *Why Families Move*, Glencoe: The Free Press.

Rubenstein, J.M. (2010). *Contemporary Human Geography*, New Delhi: PHI Learning Private Limited.

Rubenstein, J.M. (2010). *The Cultural Landscape: An Introduction to Human Geography*, 11th Edition Miami, University of Ohio: Pearson.

Sachs, J.D. and Warner, A.M. (1999). "The big push, natural resource booms and growth", *Journal of Development Economics*, 59: 43-76.

Sachs, J.D. and Warner, A.M. (2001). "Natural Resources and economic development: The curse of natural resources", *European Economic Review*, 45: 827-838.

Satterthwaite, D. (1997). "Urban Poverty: Reconsidering its Scale and Nature", *IDS Bull*, 28: 9-23.

Sauer, C.O. (1925). "The Morphology of Landscape", University of California Publications in Geography, 2, Reprinted in J. Leighly (ed.) (1974). *Land and Life*, Berkeley, CA: University of California Press, 315-350.

Schwartz, D. and Singh, A. (1999). *Environmental Conditions, Resources, and Conflicts: An Introductory Overview and Data Collection*, UNEP.

Shyrock, H.S. *et al.* (1976). *The Methods and Materials of Demography*, New York: Academic Press.

Singh, L.R. (2012). *Fundamentals of Human Geography*, Allahabad: Sharda Pustak Bhawan.

Singh, L.R. (2009). *Fundamentals of Human Geography*, 2nd Edition, Allahabad: Sharda Pustak Bhawan.

Singh, R.L. (1997). *Environmental Geography*, Allahabad: Prayag Pustak Bhawan.

Sinha, V.N.P. (1976). *Chhotanagpur Plateau: A Study in Settlement Geography*, New Delhi: B.K. Publications.

Smith, D.M. (1977). *Human Geography: A Welfare Approach*, London: Edward Arnold.

Smith, T.L. *et al.* (1960). *Fundamental of Population Study*, New York: Lippincott Company.

Sorre, M. (1952). "Les fondements de la géographie humaine", *Annales de Géographie*, 61: 128-130.

Soundaram, S.V. (2007). "Population pressure in Tamil Nadu: A Temporal Study", In B. Thakur (ed.) *Perspectives in Resource Management in Developing Countries*, Volume 2 (Part-I): *Population, Resources and Development*, New Delhi: Concept Publishing Company Pvt. Ltd., 462-469.

Spate, O.H.K. (1952). "Toyanbee and Huntington: A Study in Determinism, *Geographical Review*, 68: 406-28.

Spate, O.H.K and Learmonth, A.T.A. (1954). *India and Pakistan*, London: Methuen & Co. Ltd.

Staszewski, J. (1957). "Vertical distribution of world population", Polish Academy of Sciences, *Geographical Studies, No. 14*. Warsaw.

Stern, R.W. (2003). Changing India, Cambridge: Cambridge University Press.

Stewart, J.R. and Warntz, W. (1959). "Some pattern of the geographical distribution of population", *The Geographical Review*, 49 (2): 270-272.

Stoddart, D.R. (1972a). "Darwin's Impact on Geography", In W.K.D. Davies (eds.) *The Conceptual Revolution in Geography,* New Jersey: Rowman and Littlefield, 52-68.

Stoddart, D.R. (1972b) Geography and Ecological Approach, In W.K.D. Davies, *The Conceptual Revolution in Geography,* New Jersey: Rowman and Littlefield, 301-11.

Stoddard, R.H. and Prorak, C.V. (2004). "Geography of religion and belief systems", In G.L. Gaile and C.J. Willmott (eds.) *Geography in America at the Dawn of the 21st Century,* New York: Oxford University Press.

Stoddard, R.H., Blouet, B.W. and Wishart, D.J. (1986). Human *Geography: People, Places and Culture,* New Jersey: Prentice Hall, Englewood Cliffs.

Stouffer, S.A. (1940). "Intervening Opportunities: A Theory Relating Mobility and Distance", *American Sociologically Review*, 5: 845-97.

Stouffer, S.A. (1960). "Intervening opportunities and competing migrants", *Indian Journal of Regional Science*, 2(1): 1-26.

Sudhira, H.S., Ramachandra, T.V. and Bala Subrahmanya, M.H. (2007). "City profile: Bangalore", *Cities*, 24(5): 379-390.

Tansley, A.G. (1946). *Introduction to Plant Ecology,* London: Allen and Unwin.

Taylor, G. (1921). "The evolution and distribution of race, culture, and language", *Geographical Review*, 11(1): 54-119.

Taylor, G. (1951). *Geography in Twentieth Century: A Study of Growth, Fields, Techniques, Aims and Trends,* New York: Philosophical Library.

Taylor, P.J. (1986). "The world-system project", In R.J. Johnston and P.J. Taylor (eds.) *A World in Crisis? Geographical Perspective,* Blackwell: Oxford and New York, 333-354.

Thakur, B. (ed.) (2007). *Perspectives in Resource Management in Developing Countries,* Volume 2 (Part-I): *Population, Resources and Development,* New Delhi: Concept Publishing Company Pvt. Ltd.

Thomlinson, R. (1965). *Population Dynamics: Causes and Consequences of World Demographic Change,* New York: Random House.

Thompson, W.S. and Lewis, D.T. (1965). *Population Problems,* New Delhi: Tata Mc-Graw Hills Publishing Co. Ltd.

Trewartha, G.T. (1969). *A Geography of Population: World Patterns,* New York: John Willey and Sons.

United Nations (1973). "The Determinants and Consequences of Population Trends: New Summary of Findings on Interaction of Demographic", *Economic and Social Factors,* Volume 1, Department of Economic and Social Affairs, New York.

United Nations (1990), *World Population Prospects,* New York.

United Nations (1998), *World Population Prospects,* New York.

United Nations (2004). *World Urbanization Prospects: The 2003 Revision,* Department of Economic and Social Affairs, Population Division, United Nations Publications.

United Nations Demographic Yearbook, (UNDY, 2015). Demographic Yearbook, 66th Issue, New York.

United Nations Demographic Yearbook, (UNDY, 2017). Demographic Yearbook, 67th Issue, New York.

Valenty, D.I. (1978). *The Theory of Population,* Progress Publisher: Moscow.

Wackernagel, M. and Rees, W. (1996). *Our Ecological Footprint: Reducing Human Impact on the Earth*, Gabriola Island, BC: New Society Publishers.

Wackernagel, M., Onisto, L., Bello, P., Callejas Linares, A., López Falfán, I.S., Méndeze: García, J., Suárez Guerrero, A.I., Suarez Guerrero, G.S (1999). "National natural capital accounting with the ecological footprint concept", *Ecological Economics*, 29: 375-390.

Wallace, R. (1753). *A Dissertation on the Numbers of Mankind, In Ancient and Modern Times*, Edinburgh.

Warf, B. (2006). *Encyclopaedia of Human Geography*, California: Sage Publication.

Weeks, J.R. (2002). *Population: An Introduction to Concepts and Issues*, Belmont, CA: Wadsworth Publishing Company.

White, C.L. and Renner, G.T. (1948). *Human Geography: An Ecological Study of Society*, New York: Appleton-Century-Crofts.

Whitehead, J. (2010). *Development and Dispossession in the Narmada Valley*, New Delhi: Pearson.

Wolpert, J. (1975). "Behavioural aspect of the decision to migrate", In E. Jones (ed.) *Readings in Social Geography*, Oxford: Oxford University Press, 191-199.

Woods, R. (1979). *Population Analysis in Geography*. London: Longman.

World Bank (1982). *Operational Manual Statement, No. 2.34*, Washington D.C.: World Bank.

World Commission on Environment and Development (1987). *Our Common Future*, Oxford and New York: Cambridge University Press.

Wright, J.K. (1947). "Terrae Incognitae: The Place of Imagination in Geography", *Annals of the Association of American Geographers*, 37: 1-15.

Wunsch, G.J. (1978). *Introduction to Demographic Analysis: Principles and Methods*, New York: Springer.

Yasmi, Y., Schanz, H. and Salim, A. (2006). "Manifestation of conflict escalation in natural resource management", *Environmental Science and Policy*, 9: 538-554.

Zelinsky, W. (1966). *A Prologue to Population Geography*, New Jersey: Prentice Hall.

Zelinsky, W. (1971). "The hypothesis of the mobility transition", *Geographical Review*, 61: 219-249.

Zipf, G.K. (1949). *Human Behaviour and the Principle of Least Effort: An Introduction to Human Ecology*, Cambridge: Addison-Wesley.

Index